STANDARD COSTING

STANDARD COSTING

by

J. BATTY

D.Comm. (S.A.), M.Com. (Dunelm), A.C.W.A.,
M.I.O.M., M.B.I.M.

THIRD EDITION

MACDONALD AND EVANS LTD.
8 JOHN STREET, LONDON, W.C.1
1970

First Published March 1960
Reprinted September 1962
Second Edition February 1966
Reprinted December 1966
Third Edition July 1970

©

MACDONALD & EVANS LTD

1970

S.B.N. 7121 1921 3

By the same Author

MANAGEMENT ACCOUNTANCY
INDUSTRIAL ADMINISTRATION AND MANAGEMENT
CORPORATE PLANNING AND BUDGETARY CONTROL

Printed in Great Britain by Richard Clay (The Chaucer Press), Ltd.,
Bungay, Suffolk

PREFACE TO FIRST EDITION

Although this volume was written primarily for Accountancy students—especially those studying for Part II of the Intermediate and Parts A and B of the Final Examinations of the Institute of Cost and Works Accountants—the needs of practising Cost and Works Accountants and Management students have been kept in mind and have been covered.

The reader is taken, stage by stage, through the entire field of Standard Costing. In addition to showing *how* the techniques are applied, it is also shown *why* they are applied. For the student both aspects are essential. If he is to give maximum service to business and to the community, the practising accountant must have a sound knowledge of theory *and* practice.

The terminology closely follows that recommended by the Institute of Cost and Works Accountants. Every attempt has been made to explain the variances in a logical manner, and where there is no generally accepted definition of a variance or its mode of calculation I have put forward my own interpretation. The coining of the term "sub-variance" has, as its main purpose, the making of a clear distinction between the principal variances and their subdivisions.

Past examination questions are included at the end of the book. These were selected from papers set by the Institute of Cost and Works Accountants, and I am very grateful to the Council and Secretary of the Institute for their permission to use them.

My thanks are offered to a number of people, including students, who were kind enough to give assistance in the preparation of the book. N. R. C. Mackenzie, Esq., B.Sc.(Econ.), A.A.C.C.A., A.C.W.A., and E. D. Wade, Esq., B.Sc.(Econ.), obligingly read the proofs. I am indebted to Mrs N. Laxton, B.Sc., of the South-East Essex Technical College for her advice on the application of the method of Least Squares to the problem of the separation of fixed and variable costs. R. Forman, Esq., B.A., an Industrial Economist, and F. E. V. Nolan, Esq., M.A., A.C.A., Lecturer in Accounting at King's College in the University of Durham, were kind enough to read the manuscript and to give me the benefit of their knowledge. Mr. Nolan gave me my first introduction to Standard Costing, and so to him I must be doubly grateful. I especially wish to acknowledge the part played by my wife, who sacrificed much leisure in order to type the entire manuscript.

Needless to say, any opinions expressed on controversial matters are my own.

J. BATTY

March, 1960.

PREFACE TO THIRD EDITION

SINCE the last edition, a number of changes have taken place in the principles and terminology adopted in the book. Accordingly, the text has been amended to include the latest developments.

Because of the interest shown in Standard Costing by Work Study Engineers, more material has been added on Budgetary Control and costing systems, so that the syllabus of the Institute of Work Study Practitioners has been covered. For ease of reference the examination questions are included at the end of each chapter.

February, 1970.   J. BATTY

CONTENTS

FORMS AND DIAGRAMS

CHAPTER 1

HISTORICAL COSTING: INTRODUCTION

THE need for cost accountancy is now universally accepted. Commencing in the engineering industry with crude attempts to ascertain costs, so as to be able to fix prices, the term "cost accountancy" now embraces a multitude of functions, all directly connected with improving business efficiency. Assisting management in the formulation of policy; predetermination of costs; measurement of efficiency; prompt presentation of information to management, thus enabling them to take necessary action to maintain efficiency; advice on price fixing and the designing of routines and procedures: these are all examples of the matters dealt with by the cost accountant.

Historical costing, the ascertaining and recording of Actual Costs when, or after, they have been incurred, was one of the first stages in the growth of the cost accountant's work. "Cost" is divided into its elements: direct labour, direct materials, and overheads. An attempt is then made to show how much of each element, in terms of money, has been expended on each job or product. Depending upon the reliability of the system adopted for collecting and dealing with the detailed costs, the final "cost" of a product may emerge somewhere between a very rough guide and a reasonable estimate.

To be able to say that a tool of management is being employed usefully it is necessary to consider what that tool is supposed to do. With cost accountancy there is clearly a duty to show the true cost of producing a product or performing a service and to provide management with information on all aspects of the functioning of the business. This must be done in such a manner and with such speed that decisions may be made which, when acted upon, obtain and maintain maximum efficiency.

MANAGEMENT ACCOUNTANCY

Cost accountancy is part of "management accountancy." The latter is a generic term which embraces all branches of accountancy used to assist managers in reaching rational decisions and controlling business operations.* Subjects which would come within its scope are as follows:

* For a fuller discussion see J. BATTY, *Management Accountancy*. Macdonald and Evans.

1

1. HISTORICAL COSTING

There are two *basic* costing systems: job costing and process costing. These have to be adapted to suit specific circumstances and may be pre-fixed "contract," "unit," "operations" or some other suitable name. In essence, they all attempt to record the *actual* costs of a job, product, process, operation or other suitable cost unit.

In their first stage of development these systems content themselves with dealing with costs after they have been incurred. When they become more sophisticated they are used along with predetermined costs—standard or budgeted. With job costing, estimated costs may be employed for showing the likely costs to be incurred. These differ from true standard costs because they attempt to show what expenditure will be incurred rather than *should* be incurred. This aspect is considered further in Chapter 2.

2. BUDGETARY CONTROL

This technique involves corporate planning and the establishment of budgets which reflect the consequences of the plans in financial terms.* A modern development has been the concept of *participative management* as applied to budgeting, whereby line managers are encouraged to take an active part in the establishment of budgets. A framework for budgetary control is given in Chapter 3.

3. MARGINAL COSTING

Marginal costing recognises that cost behaviour is of prime importance in decision making. In the short period it may be necessary to sell products at prices which do not cover *total* costs. For this reason, it is argued, by distinguishing between marginal costs and fixed costs a more realistic pricing policy can be pursued. In turn, the calculation of profit and valuation of stocks are affected.

The greatest value of marginal costing is possibly in *responsibility accounting* when areas of responsibility are defined in terms of cost. The distinction between fixed and marginal (variable) costs enables managers and supervisors to see which costs can be controlled within their own cost centres. This aspect is considered more fully in subsequent chapters.

4. FINANCIAL ACCOUNTING

Financial accounting is concerned with the keeping of financial records to show the consequences of external transactions. It includes the preparation of interim and annual profit and loss accounts and is influenced by the requirements of the Companies Acts.

Management accountancy stresses the *integration* of all accounting

* See J. BATTY, *Corporate Planning and Budgetary Control*. Macdonald and Evans.

systems within the framework of a comprehensive Management Information System. Unfortunately, in many companies this integration has not been achieved. Indeed, financial accounting has tended to be the main influence in the design of accounting systems. The fact that the interests of shareholders and managers should coincide has not been appreciated by many accountants.

5. REVALUATION ACCOUNTING

Changes in the value of money—prices rising and, therefore, each £ being worth less than before—has created financial problems. If a business charges *current* prices—and this is normal practice—then it should attempt to recognise *current* costs. Plant, machinery and other fixed assets purchased years ago may now cost appreciably more to replace. This may also apply to some current assets such as raw materials, especially when prices are rising very rapidly.

Revaluation accounting recognises that the changes in the value of money affect the earning of profit. If depreciation is based on original costs there is a real danger that profit will be overstated and, if distributed as dividends, the capital employed will not be maintained intact. If fixed assets are revalued, the costs can be matched with revenue in an acceptable fashion. Differences of opinion exist on how best revaluation accounting can be carried out.

These are the main areas which are generally included in management accountancy. There are other variations which could be mentioned, such as control accounting, decision accounting and management by objectives, but these are all versions of forward-planning and control. In the modern approach to management accountancy there is considerable importance attached to the *predetermination* of plans which are then expressed in financial terms. The philosophy of standard costing is based upon the need to look into the future and calculate what costs should be within the conditions expected. Above all, there should be a positive attempt made to reach a high level of efficiency before the standard costs are determined.

EMPLOYING ACTUAL COSTS

Actual Costs are expenditures incurred on direct labour, direct materials, and overheads—they represent money spent; an historical fact which volumes of records cannot alter. That the use of Actual Costs *alone* has many disadvantages is now generally acknowledged. These will be discussed under the headings given below:

(1) Accuracy of costs.
(2) Interpretation of costs.
(3) Action on costs.

ACCURACY OF COSTS

Absolute accuracy cannot be obtained, for all costs of single products are estimates. A high standard has to be the aim, such as may be achieved by having a system that uses well-established routines which record all important facts and allow costs to be ascertained without undue difficulty. Unfortunately, not all systems achieve the desired end: some of the common failings are discussed below.

Labour costs

There are many possible methods which may be used to record the times spent on operations or processes. Time sheets, and similar records, completed by hand, tend to give approximate times only. Mechanical time recorders, with clear instructions and constant checks on their proper use, are the only certain means of obtaining accurate times.

The treatment of certain costs, associated with labour, often leaves much to be desired. The time taken in setting-up a machine is sometimes regarded as a cost of direct labour and sometimes as an overhead cost. The disposal of overtime premiums is another procedure which has not been standardised—in a badly run system they may even be "lost" in any way which most suits the particular circumstances.

If costs are to be of value there must be standardisation of methods for producing, and the appropriate grade of labour for each type of work has to be clearly defined. Any variation in times or rates will then be of some significance; otherwise, increases or reductions—a longer or shorter time or higher or lower rate—*may* mean that the costs are becoming less (or more) accurate, but there can be no check on this fact. Only when the expected accuracy has been *predetermined* will it be possible to say what progress is being made.

Material costs

Every issue of materials from the Stores should be covered by a Material Requisition. Moreover, the actual, physical issue, if there is to be accurate costing, must agree with the quantity shown on the requisition. All too often requisitions are insisted upon, but they become meaningless because the exact quantities called for are not issued. "Systems" which allow issues or receipts to be made without duly authorised forms cannot hope to achieve any accuracy in costing.

The pricing of issues, so that materials may be charged to production, obviously affects the ultimate cost of a product or job. The prices used may be "average" or "first-in, first-out" or some other form. If the first-in, first-out method is used, one issue may be priced much lower than the next one, even though they are made within one hour of each other. In such circumstances, which is the accurate or true cost? One guess is as good as another.

Overhead costs

With overhead costs the charge to each unit of production is based on an estimate. There can be no charging of a definite quantity of material or booking of a definite number of minutes. It is in this field of costing, therefore, that inaccuracy may be the greatest. An attempt has to be made to allocate and apportion costs to departments and products according to the relative benefit received, or responsibility incurred, by each. Some methods achieve a high degree of accuracy, whereas others are hopeful guesses which are hopelessly inaccurate. Those used for determining the overhead rate, and coming in the former category, are discussed in a later chapter.

Conclusion.—From what has been said the student will appreciate that absolute accuracy is impossible to achieve. Yet a high standard of accuracy is essential; otherwise, the costs ascertained will be of very limited value.

INTERPRETATION OF COSTS

Accuracy, on which observations have just been made, will affect the interpretation of the costs. Inaccurate costs will usually result in a wrong interpretation of the degree of efficiency being achieved. There is, in addition, the psychological impact on the management: if unable to rely on the accuracy of information given, some managers—the optimists—will possibly deduct a percentage from the Actual Cost before making a decision; others may add an allowance to cover contingencies. In both cases there is an attempt to arrive at an accurate cost—something which should have been supplied in the first place.

Even when a costing system is based on well-conceived ideas and sound procedures, Actual Costs may be misleading. If present efficiency is thought to be different from that achieved in the past, or that expected, how is this fact to be checked? Previous Actual Costs are no true guide to present or future efficiency, for they too may be inflated with the inclusion of preventable inefficiencies. Take, for example, the direct labour times for a particular operation. The operational times, on different dates, may read as follows:

Date of performance	Component 300-2. Operation "X" Time per Unit (minutes)
January 2nd	14
January 4th	20
January 5th	17
January 6th	25
January 7th	16

Confronted with these times and required to suppy a direct labour cost the accountant has to determine which time he will take. Is he to take:

(a) the lowest; or

(b) the highest; or

(c) the average of the five items; or

(d) the average of a selected number of items (excluding, say, the 14 or the 25 minutes), thus obtaining a "fairer" average.

Even the lowest time may include some inefficiency or, if a sound method of timing is not in operation, may not even be the actual time taken.

The matter does not end there. To ascertain a cost for a complete product, assembled from dozens of components, involves taking a large number of times. Accordingly, the final cost, when all the guesswork has finished, may be far from accurate. If the overhead costs are to be absorbed by use of the same times the final total cost will be even less reliable as a measure of changes in efficiency.

In addition to different quantities and prices for materials, labour, and services, there is also the possibility of costs varying because of different volumes of output being produced. The fixed overhead cost per unit of output will vary with the total number of units produced, or hours worked, in a period. A reduction in volume should mean an increase in unit cost, whereas a larger volume should result in a lower unit cost. Often management is confronted with very different costs, from one period to another, for exactly the same product. For pricing, or other purposes, is the lowest, the highest, or the average cost to be taken?

A distinction has to be made between "normal" and "abnormal" costs, for only the former may be regarded as the true costs of the products. A clear understanding of why abnormal costs arise is obviously essential. That they have, in the long run, to be recovered in the price is not denied, but for sound interpretation their separation from the normal costs of producing and selling is essential. The cost of idle facilities is particularly important. As already emphasised, changes in volume result in varying charges being made for fixed costs *per unit* of output; with idle facilities, brought about by, say, a trade depression, the volume of production is likely to be abnormally reduced, so, clearly, unless there is a clear segregation of the abnormal cost, the unit costs will be shown as being abnormally high. Yet because conditions are unfavourable, prices which cover normal costs only may have to be accepted. For sound decisions, a realistic approach to cost finding is essential.

ACTION ON COSTS

Prompt action, before it is too late to correct adverse tendencies or before too much damage has been done, should be stimulated by any sound costing system. With Actual Costs, even if a reasonably correct interpretation of costs is managed, the delay which usually takes place before all the information on which the action is taken is available, tends to make such action very much a formality, which does little to further cost control and improve efficiency.

The costs relating to direct labour and materials, unless there is an efficient system of collection and routing of information, may be delayed for quite a time. With Actual Overhead Costs there *will*, inevitably, be a considerable time-lag before the cost sheets can be completed. The overhead rates cannot be calculated until the total costs and units produced (or hours worked) in a period are known. Since these totals will not be known until the end of a period, the cost accountant and his staff are confronted with the calculation of the overhead rates at a time when they should be presenting, and interpreting, cost reports to management. The delay is thus further aggravated.

The use of predetermined rates, which anticipate what Actual Costs and activity will be, can do much to expedite the availability of cost figures, but these rates, like the costs on which they are based, will include inefficiencies. Furthermore, there is introduced an added complication—under- or over-absorption of overhead costs.

To maintain efficiency it is first necessary to define and understand the term. For a business to be efficient all functions which enter into production have to be examined and made to operate in the best and cheapest manner, therefore obtaining maximum returns for minimum cost. Costs may then be predetermined and used as yardsticks against which future performance can be measured. For any system to achieve these objectives there is, impliedly, a degree of management planning and control which rarely exists in any historical costing system. If it does exist, then the state of purely historical costing has been passed.

With Actual Costs, because of their historical nature and possible inclusion of inefficiencies, no useful comparisons, in order to check efficiency, are possible. Furthermore, the lack of planning and control does not allow these checks to be made as the work proceeds—so essential if effective measures are to be taken.

OVERCOMING THE DISADVANTAGES OF HISTORICAL COSTING

The principal disadvantages of using Actual Costs may be summarised as follows:

1. Accuracy of the costs is often open to doubt, so little reliance can be placed on them.*

* An argument may be put forward that, since little reliance can be placed on Actual Costs, the same applies to the variances because they are the differences between Actual and Standard Costs. However, it must be remembered that the methods used for accumulating Actual Costs when Standard Costing is employed will be the best available and will be those assumed when the Standard Costs were set.

2. Sound interpretation of costs, because of all the "unknowns," is virtually impossible.

3. There is no yardstick against which efficiency can be measured. For this purpose Actual Costs are of little value.

4. Delays in taking action are inevitable, so inefficiencies are not kept to a minimum.

The use of carefully predetermined costs for specific conditions and a stated volume of output, overcomes these difficulties. Personal judgments, which may be biased, are replaced by scientific methods, which are used to determine what costs should be in any set of circumstances. Actual Costs are then regarded as a measure of the efficiency actually achieved; the predetermined (Standard) costs are the true costs. Explanations and, where necessary, detailed examples of how Standard Costing achieves the desired objectives are covered in subsequent chapters.

EXAMINATION QUESTIONS

1. Indicate the main characteristics, advantages and/or disadvantages of:

   (a) Historical Costing
   (b) Standard Costing
   (c) Marginal Costing
   (d) Uniform Costing

   (I.C.W.A.)

2. One pioneer of standard costing has described cost analysis with historical consting as being equivalent to "unscrambling an omelette."
   Discuss this view and explain the disadvantages associated with historical costing.

3. Outline the main objectives of a cost accounting system. How would you ensure that these were achieved.

CHAPTER 2

STANDARD COSTING: INTRODUCTION

DEFINITION OF STANDARD COSTING

STANDARD COSTING is a system of cost accounting which makes use of predetermined Standard Costs relating to each element of cost—labour, material and overhead—for each line of product manufactured or service supplied. Actual Costs incurred are compared with the Standard Costs, as the work proceeds, the differences between the two being known as "variances"; these are analysed by "reasons" so that inefficiencies may be quickly brought to the notice of the persons responsible for them, and appropriate action may be taken.

The above definition of Standard Costing as a "system of cost accounting" implies that there is a planned and co-ordinated arrangement of all matters relating to costing. A body of procedures built on haphazard lines, not being chosen as the most suitable for the business concerned, cannot be regarded as a standard costing system, even though it purports to use Standard Costs. In all cases, the needs of the particular business have to be assessed, before the Standard Costs are set, and the principles which are to form the basis of the system are put into a specific written form. Unless due care is taken, a business may be burdened with a system which is both inappropriate and too costly.

If proper control over functions through the efficient use of costing information cannot be exercised it will usually follow that, strictly speaking, there are no Standard Costs. The latter represent anticipated costs under given conditions and for an expected volume of output. To be able to perform the necessary functions at the anticipated cost there is, necessarily, a need for efficient control of performances, otherwise any predetermined costs may be regarded as estimated costs only and not true Standard Costs. In the absence of essential, corrective forces these estimated costs are unlikely to be realised. On the other hand, if a system provides for comparison of Actual and Standard Costs and for remedial action, as indicated by variances, then there is a good chance that carefully predetermined costs will not be exceeded; in fact, they may even be bettered. Needless to say, since the concern is with what costs *should be,* the use of a Standard Cost should indicate that the best way of producing the particular product has been determined, and is being adopted.

Actual Costs are costs incurred on producing, selling, and distributing

9

a product or service. They reflect, therefore, value received; the wages and salaries paid out, the prices given for materials, the expenses incurred, and the degree of efficiency achieved in producing and selling, will all be indicated in the Actual Cost of the product.

If Actual Costs exceed Standard Costs, or vice versa, the differences are known as variances. The importance of the correct interpretation of these cannot be over-emphasised, for it is the action taken on the strength of the variances which makes or mars a standard costing system. Correctly analysed, variances show how adverse tendencies can be corrected. Careless or incorrect usage, such as criticism at the wrong time or in the wrong place, may undermine all trust in the system operated. Antagonism and suspicion on the part of executives, clerks, foremen, supervisors, and workers can bring about its failure. For maximum efficiency there must be complete confidence from all concerned.

The precise form the system will take will not be the same for all businesses. However, with most systems a number of definite principles can be followed and certain features should be present. These principles will be explained in later chapters. The features normally found in a standard costing system are:

1. Once Standard Costs have been set, full details are entered on a Standard Cost Card. One such card is normally kept to cover each major component, or product, made. It shows the breakdown of total unit cost into direct material, direct labour, and factory overhead. In addition are shown expected achievements in terms of physical units to be produced and hours to be worked. Great care should be taken to ensure that all Standard Cost Cards are accurately compiled, for the information given by them is used as a basis for calculating the appropriate standard data needed to make comparisons with Actual Cost and also for compiling direct labour and direct material budgets.

   Theoretically there is no logical reason why unit costs relating to administration and selling and distribution should not appear on the Standard Cost Card. In practice, since the anticipated costs for these functions are recorded in budgets, these budgets serve the same purpose as the Standard Cost Card. Actual Costs are compared with Standard Costs shown on the appropriate budget.

2. Forms and documents, designed to cover standard procedures, standard quantities, and/or Standard Costs, are used.

   If possible, performances which are "exceptions to the rule" are automatically singled out by the use of forms which are distinctive in shape, colour, or some other aspect.

   Thus, for example, the issue of direct materials from Stores will be authorised by a Standard Material Requisition. The appropriate department, say Production Control, will issue this form. On it will be shown the standard quantities of material required to manufacture a specified number of components or products. If additional material is found necessary an Excess Material Requisition, printed on a distinctive coloured paper, is used. Material returned to Stores for any reason is covered by another form, a Material Return Note, once more in a distinctive, though this time different, colour.

3. Statistical records are maintained. These are in addition to the books of account described in (6). Their extent will vary according to the system being used. The collation and analysis of costs is essential for all systems; only the amount of detail and mode in which the detail is kept will differ to meet the needs of the particular business.

4. Variances are isolated and evaluated in terms of sterling.

5. Statements and variance reports are prepared for all levels of management. These have to be appropriate to the particular level of management being informed. Examples are given in Chapters 25 and 26.

6. Books of account are kept to record all transactions. The normal double-entry accounting principles are followed, these being adapted to record Standard Costs. A Journal will usually be essential for any accounting system. However, it is in the use of the Ledger, the principal book of account, that the accounting for costing shows two main differences in approach. The recording may be done in a Cost Ledger or in an Integrated (Cost and Financial) Ledger. In the former case all internal transactions relating to material, labour, and overhead costs appear in a ledger used only for that purpose. The external transactions, covering purchases and sales and related matters, are entered in the Financial Ledger. With the Integrated System both costing and financial transactions are entered in the one ledger.

The principal object of a system is to enable management, when necessary, to take the appropriate action and thus correct any adverse tendencies while maintaining, as far as possible, anticipated efficiency. If records kept lose touch with this purpose, then they should be amended or discontinued. This applies equally to any part of the system: with changing conditions—inevitable in all businesses—there must be a keen watchfulness on all aspects and, when warranted, revisions should be made. Constant amending for every minor change should not, of course, be practised, for if this were done the system would very soon tend to become unmanageable and the records would lose much of their usefulness, especially for comparison purposes.

ADVANTAGES OF STANDARD COSTS

By adopting carefully compiled Standard Costs the weaknesses of an historical costing system, which records only Actual Costs when the transactions have been finalised, are overcome. The following are the advantages to be gained from the use of Standard Costs:

1. Standard Costs are a yardstick against which Actual Costs can be compared. The alternative is to compare Actual Costs for one period with Actual Costs of another period. To be able to assume that Actual Costs can be used as a basis of comparison the following questions would have to be answered:

    (a) Which accounting period can be taken as the base period?
    (b) Assuming the first question can be answered satisfactorily, how many previous Actual Costs should be compared with the cost being investigated?
    (c) If a number of Actual Costs is necessary, should they be averaged and, if so, which is the most suitable average to adopt—the arithmetic mean, median, mode, or other average?
    (d) If there is no great difference between the previous Actual Cost and the present Actual Cost, can it be assumed that the latter is as low as it could have been, and that there are no inefficiencies?

    These, and similar questions, should be answered before comparing Actual Costs with Actual Costs. Unfortunately no satisfactory answer is possible to the majority of such queries; it is for this reason that Standard Costs are essential.

2. The analysis of variances as part of the ordinary accounting routine ensures that regular checks are made upon expenditure incurred. Deviations from the pre-determined standards of performance can quickly be localised and, taking advantage of the "principle of exception," management can concentrate upon matters which are not proceeding according to plan.

3. The clerical work associated with costing is usually reduced and yet much more useful information is made available to management. Under the older types of costing systems voluminous records, many of which were of little value, were kept. Often information would be recorded just in case it was needed. The reduction in time and effort needed for costing arises, chiefly, from the following:

    (a) Reduction in the cost of report preparation. Less time is required, which in turn allows more prompt presentation, thus enhancing the value of the reports.

(b) Some records can be kept in terms of quantities only, sterling values being omitted. This is of special importance for Stores or Stock Ledgers; pricing of requisitions is simplified, and the balancing is in quantities only. The total Standard Cost can be obtained by multiplying the quantity of each type of material or component by the appropriate standard price per unit. The ratio between Actual and Standard Cost can be used for converting total Standard Cost to total average Actual Cost.

Preliminary work may, of course, be very great, but once the Standards have been developed, they can be used until amendment becomes necessary.

4. Interpretation of management reports is made easier and there is a reduction in the time taken to study these reports. All matters requiring attention are readily apparent, for superfluous details are not shown; management thus need not be troubled with unimportant matters.

5. Provided the Standards are constantly being studied with a view to improvement, control over costs is greatly facilitated. Moreover, if prompt action is taken on the lines indicated by the study it should be possible to reduce costs. Cost control and cost reduction are probably the most important aims of any costing system, and Standard Costing gives due recognition to this fact.

6. Setting Standards requires a detailed study of all manufacturing, administrative, selling, and distribution functions so that they may be made efficient. This fact alone usually results in improved methods being adopted, with resultant lower costs. Cost centres are established, lines of authority are defined, and responsibilities for costs are clearly assigned to supervisors and workers. In carrying out this preliminary work it is possible to eliminate inefficiencies and generally improve all aspects of making the product and reaching the consumer. Thus, for example, the setting of Standards for labour may require the use of work study, with consequent benefits.

7. Production and pricing policies can be formulated with certainty before production takes place. Standards set along objective lines are to be preferred for this purpose, for Actual Costs may include excessive usage of material, abnormal labour times, or an inequitable charge for overhead. In competitive industries there can be no provision, in price, for the costs of inefficiency.

8. Once the Standard Costs have been compiled they can be used as a basis for other gains, such as the provision of an incentive scheme of payment for employees.

9. Full recognition is given to the fact that true costs should not include waste and other abnormal losses.

10. Development of a fully comprehensive control system is greatly facilitated when standard costing is already in existence.

Further details of these advantages are given in later chapters.

THE EFFICIENT USE OF STANDARD COSTING

Standard Costing may be regarded as a technique which is complementary to the ordinary costing system, which will be some form of process or job costing. Although the Standard Costs are of prime importance, they are of limited value by themselves; to ignore Actual Costs means that the localisation of inefficiencies cannot be achieved.

Though Standard Costs can be of value in all types of commercial and industrial undertakings the highest degree of efficiency in their use is to be obtained where a product or its components can be standardised. This implies that they are of maximum value used in conjunction with a process costing system. In the special-order type of business, using job costing, there is such a wide variety of products of a non-standard nature that the cost of setting Standards becomes prohibitive and out of proportion to the value received from their use. The full use of Standard Costs may not, therefore, be practicable. However, the adoption of Standard Costs for many of the components which go into non-standard products may be possible. Parts which are common to a number of heterogeneous finished products can be standardised and Standard Costs developed. In this way the advantages outlined can accrue, to some extent, even to enterprises using job costing.

JOB COSTING

Job costing is mentioned in the previous paragraph. It is the system of costing used when non-standard jobs are made to customers' specifications. Contractors, general engineering factories, shipbuilders, and furniture manufacturers are just a few of the many businesses which employ job costing. Because each order is different, all costs incurred on an individual job are booked to a cost sheet reserved for that job (Fig. 1).

Very briefly, the procedures involved in job costing may be as follows:

1. An enquiry is received from a customer.
2. The costs expected to be involved for the job in question are estimated. These form the basis of the price quoted.
3. If a firm order is received for the job, a production order is completed.
4. Once a job has been commenced the tracing of the following costs is essential—

JOB COST SHEET					
Description			**Job No.**		
....					
Date Commenced.................			**Date Completed**		
Date	Ref.	Details	Material £	Labour £	Overhead £

Summary   £   **Customer** ....
   Material   ...   ...
   Labour   ...   ...
   Overhead   ...   ...

   Total Factory Cost   ...   **Price Obtained**   ... £
   Add Selling and
         Distribution ...   **Profit/Loss**   ...   ... £
   Add Administration ...

           £

FIG. 1.—*Job Cost Sheet*

(*a*) Direct material costs—authorised and traced by Material Requisitions.

(*b*) Direct labour costs—controlled and traced by the use of Job Clock Cards.

(*c*) Factory overhead costs—absorbed by the use of pre-determined, normal overhead rates.*

(*d*) Selling, distribution, and administration costs are added to total factory costs, possibly on the basis of a standard percentage.

* These are not to be confused with Standard Overhead Costs. Predetermined overhead costs for job costs are based on an estimate of what *actual* costs *will be.* Standard Costing attempts to show what they *should be* for clearly defined conditions and circumstances.

5. A Cost Ledger or Integrated Ledger is maintained.

6. As each job is completed, the total cost and price obtained are compared and the profit earned or loss incurred is ascertained.

Various summaries or abstracts are employed to classify and analyse the costs for posting to Cost Sheets, Stores Ledger and the Cost or Integrated Ledger. Reference is made to using predetermined overhead rates. These allow Job Cost Sheets to be completed as early as possible, thereby allowing management to see what has happened in terms of profitability as early as possible. In addition, they tend to eliminate wide fluctuations in the overhead rate. Unfortunately, these benefits are offset to some extent by the inevitable emergence of under- or over-absorption of overhead costs. These have to be disposed of via the Profit and Loss Account or by adjustment of Work-in-progress, Cost of Sales and Finished Goods Accounts. Sometimes supplementary overhead rates are employed as a means of adjusting a large under- or over-absorption of overhead costs.

Because of the nature of special-order industries, it will be essential to employ special-order (job) costing. However, if elements of jobs are repetitive and capable of being standardised the predetermination of Standard Costs for such elements becomes possible and advisable. This allows a higher standard of efficiency to be achieved, and cost control is greatly facilitated. When each job is entirely different, cost control *in detail* is difficult to carry out, and therefore the fullest use should be made of the wider form of control afforded by a budgetary control system.

Job costing in its pure form can be expensive to operate in terms of accounting and clerical costs. If it has to be employed the fullest use should be made in the production control system of the labour and machine times accumulated. Moreover, in the large concern there will be a necessity to introduce a suitable form of machine accounting, which should be linked with appropriate control systems for material, labour and overhead costs. Obviously, in the absence of predetermined standard costs there will be no suitable measures against which to compare the actual performances, and this fact has to be appreciated from the start. There will be no previous actual costs, because each job is quite different; there should be the estimated costs obtained to calculate a price for the quotation and, while these will tend to contain inefficiencies, provided they have been carefully compiled they are clearly better than nothing. Although comparison of actual and estimated costs does not permit adequate control, it should allow a form of profit control for each individual job. Management can see what gain or loss results from each order obtained. The control may be facilitated by incorporating marginal costing into the job costing system.

PROCESS COST SHEET

Accounting Period ....

Date	Ref.	Mat.	Labour	O/head	Cost Centre No. 1			Cost Centre No. 2		
					Mat.	Lab.	O/head	Mat.	Lab.	O/head

Summary			Production	
Dept. No. 1	£	£	No. of Units	
Materials	xxx			
Labour	xxx		Cost per Unit	£
Overhead	xxx	xxx		
Dept. No. 2				
Materials	xxx			
Labour	xxx			
Overhead	xxx	xxx		
		£xxx		

FIG. 2.—*Process Cost Sheet*

PROCESS COSTING

Process costing is the second principal method of cost accounting. It is generally employed when a standard product is being made which involves a number of distinct processes performed in a definite sequence. In oil refining, chemical manufacture, paper making, flour milling and cement manufacturing, as well as many other industries, this method is used. The object is to trace and record costs for each distinct stage. Here the concern is not with finding the costs for individual units as in job costing, but with obtaining the average cost per unit for each accounting period. Often by-products or joint products are produced, and these have to be considered when calculating the average cost per unit.

The total time spent and materials used on each process, as well as services such as power, light and heating, are all charged. For this purpose a Process Cost Sheet may be employed (Fig. 2).

The Process Cost Sheet is a summary of all operations for the month. The current operating charges are entered on the sheet showing:

1. The transfer cost from the previous operation.
2. The costs incurred by each operation showing material, labour and overhead in separate columns.

This separation of transfer costs and conversion cost is extremely important, for the charges incurred by a department are its measure of efficiency. These are the responsibility of the head of the department, so it is readily apparent what has been incurred within that department, and the cost is not distorted by changing costs in previous processes. The sheet can be used as a basis for:

(a) Closing entries at the end of each month.
(b) Operating statements, without need to look up the ledger accounts.

Within the Cost Ledger an account is kept for each process. The direct material, direct labour and factory overhead costs are transferred from the Process Cost Sheet. These are debited to the process account, and then any completed units are credited to cover the transfer to the next process. The balance on the account represents the work-in-progress at the end of the period, which, of course, becomes the opening balance for the *next* period. An example of a process account is as follows:

Process Account I

	£		£
To Direct material	400	By Transfer to	
„ Direct labour	300	Process II	1100
„ Factory overhead	600	„ Balance c/d	200
	£1300		£1300
To Balance b/d	£200		

The units involved in each process may also be shown.

Because of the repetitive, standardised nature of the processes, units produced and conditions, it is possible to employ standard costing to its fullest extent. Calculation and analysis of cost variances allows costs to be controlled, and the yield variances show the efficiency obtained in converting the raw materials to the finished product.

HYBRID COSTING SYSTEMS

Many costing systems do not fall neatly into the category of either job costing or process costing. Often systems use some features of both main costing systems. Many engineering companies use *batch costing*, which treats each batch of components as a job and then finds the average cost of a single unit. Another variation is *multiple costing*, used when many different finished products are made. Many components are made which are subsequently assembled into the completed article, which may be cycles, cars or other products of a complex nature. Costs have to be ascertained for operations, processes, units and jobs, building together until the total cost is found. Different names may be used to describe either process costing or job costing. Thus, for example, *unit costing* is the name given to the system where there is a natural unit, such as a sack of flour, a hundredweight of cement or a barrel of beer. *Operation costing* is a variation of unit costing, and is used when production is carried out on a large scale, popularly known as mass production. *Operating costing* is the term applied to describe the system used to find the cost of performing a service such as transport, gas or electricity. These are all variations of process costing. *Contract* or *terminal costing* is the name given to job costing employed by builders and constructional engineers.

All these methods ascertain the actual cost. In addition, as indicated earlier, there may be superimposed on a particular system standard costing and/or marginal costing, both of which are special techniques.

These differences in costing techniques or methods do not affect the observations made regarding the conditions necessary for the efficient use of Standard Costs. Provided the operations involved, whether for a product or service, are repeated time and time again, so that standardisation of product and methods becomes possible, Standard Costs can effectively be adopted.

TWO "SYSTEMS" FOR MODERN MANAGEMENT

At this stage it should be apparent that, under modern conditions, management should think in terms of *two* costing "systems" only, standard costing and job costing. One or the other, or both, determined by circumstances, can be used.

The haphazard "after-the-event" approach to managerial problems —taking action when the maximum damage has been done—should not be tolerated. Efficient production has to be pre-planned and, at each stage in the operation of the plan actual and expected achievements must be compared, taking any necessary remedial action to correct "off-the-course" tendencies. Standard costing is consistent with and, indeed, part of this forward-looking approach. Wherever possible, therefore, Standard Costs should be used. Only when the nature of the product is non-repetitive, and non-standard, will job costing alone be adopted.

Small, as well as large, business units can successfully adopt modern costing principles. A large complex organisation will normally require a complicated system. A small or medium concern with fairly simple operational problems should find that a relatively simple system will meet its needs. The basic principles remain the same; the structures in which they operate will vary according to the requirements of the particular business. Remember the object is to serve management; accordingly, the system should fit into and be appropriate to the individual business concerned. Complexities or refinements should not be introduced unless they serve a useful purpose.

In all cases the natural choice of method for determining Actual Cost will tend to be the choice of method for calculating Standard Cost. That is to say, if the nature of the product is such that batch costs should be adopted, then the Standard Cost will reflect the ideal or expected* average cost of a component, in a typical batch, and under stated conditions. Just as under a batch costing system the Standard Cost will be built up, operation by operation, until a total unit cost is obtained. Similarly, when production takes the form of a continuous flow of raw materials through a number of distinct processes, each unit of product being identical with the next—such as in chemical processing, cement manufacturing and flour milling—then the Standard Costs will be compiled having full regard to the fact that process costing is the appropriate system to adopt.

EXAMINATION QUESTIONS

1. List briefly the advantages of Standard Cost methods for all purposes, including those not directly related to costing.

(I.C.W.A.)

2. In order to introduce Standard Costing into an organisation where historical costing is used at present, what steps would you take, and what modifications are likely to be necessary to the following:

(a) the basic cost records;
(b) the cost statements to be rendered to the management.

Present your answer in the form of brief notes.

(I.C.W.A.)

3. Do you consider that a system of Standard Costs could be useful to a concern specialising in the manufacture of non-standard components to customers' individual specifications? Owing to the special nature of the components, repeat orders very rarely occur.

Give your views, with reasons.

(I.C.W.A.)

4. Discuss "Standard Costs," their advantages and disadvantages, and the conditions under which you consider their adoption to be of greatest use. Indicate the circumstances under which the use of Standard Costs could be misleading.

(I.C.W.A.)

5. What is meant by Standard Costs; in what circumstances may they be safely employed; what advantages do they offer?

(I.C.W.A.)

* Ideal and expected standards are defined in Chapter 4.

6. If cost information is limited to an analysis of Actual Costs, state how this would affect cost control.

(*I.C.W.A.*)

7. On the assumption that the investigation and correction of unsatisfactory conditions revealed by variances are essential to the effective use of standard costing, briefly outline the assistance which the cost accountant should give to management to promote success.

(*I.C.W.A.*)

CHAPTER 3

BUDGETARY CONTROL

STANDARD COSTING AND BUDGETARY CONTROL

To be able to set, and use, Standard Costs, some form of budgeting will be essential. There is the need to forecast the level of output, and the conditions which will operate in the periods the Standard Costs are to be used. Both have to be determined before the Standard Costs are set, for changes in output or conditions will, inevitably, tend to increase or reduce Standard Costs.

Budgetary Control in its complete form involves a predetermined plan in financial terms, to cover all phases of business activities, and the operation of that plan in such a way that anticipated profit is, as near as possible, achieved.

Many alternative plans are considered before the final one, showing desired profitability, is adopted. Thus, if the plan chosen fulfils expectations it may be assumed that the best use has been made of the available resources.

Executives and other responsible officials assist in preparing the budgets. Data, relating to all functions, are collected and then translated into monetary terms. Budgets, covering both expected revenues and related costs, corresponding to functional responsibilities and broken down to departmental responsibilities, are prepared. Each specialist thus, in effect, says, "I expect to do this." In this way he knows what is expected of him and if, when the plan is operated, he does not achieve his set target, this fact will be pointed out to him by the use of suitably drafted statements which show clearly any variations between budgeted and actual revenues or costs. Management is thus able effectively to control all functions. This operates for each individual and for the business as a whole. The correct "balance" and co-ordination between all budgets can be maintained—most essential for efficient operation. If sales are falling off it may be necessary, in order to conserve adequate cash resources and to avoid building up excessive stocks, to reduce the rate of production. A major step of this nature will clearly require consideration of all budgets. These will cover:

1. Production.
2. Sales.
3. Direct materials.
4. Direct labour.
5. Manufacturing overhead costs.

6. Selling and distribution.
7. Administration.
8. Working capital.
9. Capital expenditure (*i.e.* assets).
10. Long-term plans.

A complete system of Budgetary Control can be adopted along with standard costing or job costing; in fact, this procedure is to be recommended. Standard Costs anticipated for a period represent, in the case of prime costs and when aggregated, the totals shown in the individual budgets for the appropriate level of activity. Thus, for direct materials, the standard material cost for each product will form the basis for the preparation of the Direct Material Budget. Because of the lack of direct correlation between (*a*) the manufacture and sale of products, and (*b*) the incurring of indirect costs, there is not the same relationship between the appropriate budgets and overhead costs as there is between prime costs and their related budgets. For overhead costs there is, in effect, a reversal of the procedure adopted with prime costs. Instead of building up budgets from individual Standard Costs, anticipated totals for the various classes of expense are used. For the purpose of control there is usually an analysis, followed by apportionment of the overhead costs to cost centres or to sales territories and, finally, to products. Not unnaturally, there is thus a great similarity between Standard Costs and Budgetary Control for overhead costs. This fact will be shown in the chapters relating to standard overhead costs, whether these relate to selling and distribution, administration, or research and development.

Budgetary Control adopts a more "general" approach to giving service to management than does standard costing. A comparison of financial accounting with cost accounting will serve to illustrate the difference between a "general" and "detailed" approach. Financial accounting is concerned with measuring the effectiveness of business as a whole; it shows whether a profit is made or a loss sustained. Cost accounting, on the other hand, deals with individual products, ascertaining and controlling their costs and measuring the profitability of each one. In practice, as indicated above, the two systems will conjoin so that it will be difficult to separate one from the other completely; to do so would serve no useful purpose.

MAIN OBJECTIVES OF BUDGETARY CONTROL

Budgetary Control should aim at achieving three main objectives and these are as follows:

1. Forecasting and Planning.
2. Co-ordinating all functions so that they work in harmony.
3. Control of performances and costs.

Policy-making is the prerogative of the board of directors. Top management then takes over and makes the forecasts and budgets. The former represent *probabilities* relating to sales, production, and costs, whereas the budgets are the finalised forecasts, now part of the co-ordinated plan. Before the master plan is settled a number of alternatives are considered and the best one is selected bearing in mind:

(a) profitability;
(b) stability;
(c) continued existence.

There is now recognition that maximum profit is not necessarily the ideal criterion. Violent fluctuations in trade are very undesirable: the social obligation to employees requires a fair employment policy. Continued existence and steady growth are more important than the maximisation of profit in a particular period.

Management theory recognises a law known as the *Harmony of Objectives.* This means that the aims of employers are utilised to the achievement of a company's objectives. Through co-ordination of all budgets Budgetary Control can help in this task. Employees of all levels are induced to work together towards a common goal.

Control comes through variance analysis and reporting as described for Standard Costing.

EFFECTIVENESS OF BUDGETARY CONTROL

Whether Budgetary Control can be as effective as Standard Costing is open to doubt. There are two reasons for this fact: the lack of detailed knowledge regarding the costs of each product and the reliability of the budgeted costs. The first requires no comment, except that in certain jobbing industries the work is so heterogeneous that detailed standards cannot be prepared and, therefore, budgeted costs are the only alternative.

As regards the second point, it is as well to notice that there are a number of ways which may be employed in establishing budgeted costs. Basically, though, these may be classified as follows:

1. Budgeted costs which are based on predetermined costs which represent efficient operations at replacement prices expected to be ruling in the future budget periods.

    These are the true Standard Costs as advocated throughout this book.

2. Budgeted costs which are based on past experience, or the average of a number of past years or some other equally arbitrary method.

    These costs do not represent efficient performances or replacement prices, and therefore cannot be regarded as a foundation for planning, co-ordination, and control. In short, this method is not to be recommended. It is likely to give a false sense of security: a scientific title (Budgetary Control) is being employed and yet all that is being done is to say: "We have done this in the past, and we hope to continue in the future." The fact that historical costs, possibly representing a very low level of efficiency, are being employed, is hidden in the guise of something which is called Budgetary Control. Unfortunately, too, managers may be misled into thinking that they are employing an up-to-date technique.

ADVANTAGES OF BUDGETARY CONTROL

The principal advantages which may accrue from the employment of Budgetary Control are summarised below. Whether these benefits are realised, and to what extent, depends very much on the system and the attitude of management. Some systems are much more efficient than others; a costly and elaborate system is not necessarily the best, because there is such a thing as "over control." If unnecessary refinements do not add to the usefulness of a management accountancy technique, then they should not be employed.

Briefly, the possible advantages are as follows:

1. Policy, plans, and action taken are all reflected in the Budgetary Control system. There is formal recognition of the targets which the business hopes to achieve.
2. Everyone working in the business should know what is expected of him. One of the first essentials of sound management is to let each man know his responsibilities.
3. Deviations from the plans made are brought to light through variance analysis, and corrective action is stimulated by reports, statements, and personal contact.
4. Delegation of responsibilities is given positive recognition by the preparation of budgets for each budget centre.
5. Co-ordination is achieved by the interlocking of all the budgets: (a) through a master budget, and (b) by the necessary organisation which is watched over by the budget controller.

PREPARATION OF BUDGETS

The principal forecasts and budgets are listed earlier in the chapter. Here the concern is with the preparation of these budgets.

THE SALES FORECAST/BUDGET

A specimen Sales Forecast is given in Fig. 3. This has been simplified; in practice, much more detail would be found. There are two problems: (a) determination of quantities, and (b) calculation of standard prices. In some cases, when jobbing production is involved, forecasts must be made in terms of expected sales values only.

ANNUAL SALES FORECAST

Year ending.....................

	Last Year	Total Year	First Quarter	Second Quarter	Third Quarter	Fourth Quarter
Southern Area						
UNITS of:						
Product A	10,000	11,000	3,000	5,000	1,000	2,000
Product B	12,000	13,200	4,000	4,000	3,000	2,200
Product C	6,000	6,600	1,000	2,000	2,000	1,600
Northern Area						
UNITS OF:						
Product A	4,000	4,400	1,000	1,000	1,000	1,400
Product B	16,000	17,600	5,000	4,000	4,000	4,600
Product C	10,000	11,000	3,000	4,000	2,000	2,000
Southern Area						
VALUE of:	£	£	£	£	£	£
Std. Price						
Product A £0·5	5,000	5,500	1,500	2,500	500	1,000
Product B £1·0	12,000	13,200	4,000	4,000	3,000	2,200
Product C £0·1	600	660	100	200	200	160
	17,600	19,360	5,600	6,700	3,700	3,360
Northern Area						
VALUE of:	£	£	£	£	£	£
Std. Price						
Product A £0·5	2,000	2,200	500	500	500	700
Product B £1·0	16,000	17,600	5,000	4,000	4,000	4,600
Product C £0·1	1,000	1,100	300	400	200	200
	19,000	20,900	5,800	4,900	4,700	5,500
Grand Totals £	36,600	40,260	11,400	11,600	8,400	8,860

FIG. 3.—*Specimen Annual Sales Forecast*

NOTE

An annual sales forecast is illustrated. In order to show responsibilities the forecast is divided into sales areas. Quarterly figures are illustrated: a further subdivision to show four-weekly details may be included on the forecast; alternatively, the breakdown may be carried out on separate work sheets. A further analysis into sales quotas, showing the responsibilities of individual salesmen, can also be covered on work sheets.

The methods used for obtaining the data required are summarised below:

1. Opinions of Salesmen and Sales Managers.
2. Statistical forecasting techniques after the details have been collected by the use of Market Research or from the company's order book.

In some businesses the sales forecast is the commencement of planning. For others, the Production Forecast is the first step.

PRODUCTION FORECAST

The Production Forecast is a statement of the output expected in a future budget period—usually the following year. It may be expressed in one of the following:

(a) Units;
(b) tons;
(c) Standard Hours.

As indicated earlier, a number of forecasts will probably be necessary before the appropriate one is selected. Where necessary, adjustments must be made for any stocks to be carried.

The form the forecast would take depends upon circumstances. Usually the quantities would be shown for each department (known as a "budget centre"). Information would be taken from Machine Loading Charts, Material Specifications, Time Schedules, and other records. There should be close co-operation and collaboration between accountants, production engineers, work study engineers, and other key personnel.

PRODUCTION COSTS FORECASTS

The forecasts for production costs should follow the conventional break-down of costs, which is as follows:

1. Direct Material.
2. Direct Labour.
3. Direct Expense.
4. Factory Overhead Costs.

The preparation of the Direct Material Forecast involves the conversion of material specifications into the requirements of the production forecast. Fixing of the standard prices should be the joint responsibility of the Purchasing Agent and Accountant.

Work study should be employed to establish the standard times. These can then be employed for converting into direct labour requirements. Finally, the standard rates are used to arrive at the direct labour cost for each department. An example of a forecast is given opposite (Fig. 4).

DEPARTMENTAL LABOUR FORECAST

Budget Centre X **Period:** from ....

to.........................

Output: 4000 units 'A'
9000 units 'B' } 34,000 standard hours.
4000 units 'C'

Employees	Number	Hours	Standard Rate	Direct Labour Cost	Total
			£	£	£
Male Skilled Semi-skilled Unskilled					
Female Skilled Semi-skilled Unskilled					
Juniors Male Female					
					£

FIG. 4.—*Specimen Departmental Labour Forecast*

NOTES

1. The headings and rulings given may be varied to suit particular requirements.
2. Each department's requirements are covered in the same way—one departmental forecast for each. All these forecasts are summarised on a direct labour forecast summary.
3. Once the preliminary classification of labour into its principal grades has been carried out, the labour requirements needed for each product can be estimated. The operations involved are listed, and then standard times are set.
4. The standard times are preferably established by use of work study. Alternatively, they may be set by reference to past performance records.

Preparation of the Factory Overhead Cost Budget follows the lines shown in Chapter 16. A flexible budget should be employed because this is the only effective method of controlling costs.

SELLING AND DISTRIBUTION COSTS

Chapter 18 covers the requirements for the budgets for selling and distribution. Here further details are given for advertising. The

ADVERTISING BUDGET (advertising media)

For Year Ending................

Expense	Total £	National Newspaper £	Local Newspaper £	Magazines and Journals £	Outdoor £	Television £	Cinema £	Catalogues £	Exhibitions £	Samples and Gifts £	Miscellaneous £
Salaries											
Rent—Advertising Office											
Rates—Advertising Office											
Travelling Expenses—Advertising											
Lighting and Heating											
Payments to Agencies, Newspapers or other "suppliers"	£										

FIG. 5.—Specimen Advertising Budget: Advertising Media

ADVERTISING BUDGET (Products)

For Year Ending................

Expense	Total £	Product "R" £	Product "S" £	Product "T" £	Product "U" £	Product "V" £	Product "W" £
National Newspapers							
Local Newspapers							
Magazines and Journals							
Outdoor (hoardings, bills)							
Television							
Cinema							
Catalogues							
Exhibitions							
Samples and Gifts							
Miscellaneous	£						

FIG. 6.—Specimen Advertising Budget: Products

Advertising Budgets for *media* and *products* may be taken as illustrations of typical budgets (Figs. 5 and 6).

Methods used for fixing the advertising appropriation to be spent each year are listed below:

1. Percentage of total sales value of the budget period.
2. Percentage of total profit as shown by the Master Budget.
3. Amount being spent by competitors.
4. Amount that the company believes it can afford.
5. The estimated sum required to sell the forecasted sales.

The most appropriate method for the business concerned should be selected.

ADMINISTRATION COSTS BUDGET

The details given in Chapter 21 show how the Administration Costs Budget is compiled.

CO-ORDINATION OF THE SYSTEM

Any system of Budgetary Control must be co-ordinated through a Master Budget. The planning of volume and profit are essential, and the most important figures are summarised in the Budgeted Profit and Loss Account (Fig. 7) and Master Budget (Fig. 8).

In looking at the problem of defining the Profit Target the directors may consider the following:

1. *Minimum rate of profit*

This is the rate which is just worthwhile; if a lower rate is expected, alternative investments should be considered. The rate paid on the *market price* of gilt-edged securities may be a guide to what is a minimum rate.

2. *Normal rate of profit*

To the minimum rate of profit it is usual to add a percentage to cover the risk involved, bearing in mind the nature of the product or service being produced and sold. The rate would vary from, say, 2% in industries with stable demand to, say, 20% for ventures which are highly speculative.

3. *Target Profit*

This is the profit which will appear on the Master Budget, and it is around this that all other budgets will be built. All the factors affecting profit will have to be taken into account. The burden of taxation, future conditions, and the policy being followed will have a considerable influence on the final figure.

What is a reasonable rate of return on capital employed (total assets used) is often difficult to determine. Nevertheless, the problem has to be faced and resolved before budgetary control is installed. This measure provides general management with a yardstick against which they can assess their own performances.

	This Year		Last Year	
BUDGETED PROFIT AND LOSS ACCOUNT **For the Year Ending....................**	Product A	Product B	Product A	Product B
	£	£	£	£
1. SALES				
Manufacturing Costs:				
Direct Labour				
Direct Material				
Factory Overhead				
Add Opening Stock				
Less Closing Stock				
2. COST OF GOODS SOLD	£	£	£	£
3. Gross Profit (1 less item 2)				
4. Selling and Distribution Costs				
5. Administration Costs				
6. NET PROFIT (3 less items 4 and 5)	£	£	£	£

FIG. 7.—*Typical Budgeted Profit and Loss Account*

NOTES

1. There are differences of opinion on what is meant by a "master budget." It is generally regarded as a summary budget which incorporates all other principal budgets. Disagreement exists on the *form* the summary should take.

2. Some accountants regard the budgeted Profit and Loss Account and Balance Sheet as the Master Budget. The Profit and Loss Account shows the expected profit or loss for the budget period, whereas the Balance Sheet or Position Statement summarises capital, liabilities, and assets.

MASTER BUDGET

For the Year Ending....................

Normal Capacity .... standard hours (100%)

Capacity Budgeted .... standard hours

	Budgeted Figures		
	Product A £	Product B £	Total £
I. SALES			
Manufacturing Costs:			
Direct Labour			
Direct Material			
Factory Overhead			
Add Opening Stock			
Less Closing Stock			
2. COST OF GOODS SOLD	£	£	£
3. Gross Profit (1 less item 2)			
4. Selling and Distribution Costs			
5. Administration Costs			
6. NET PROFIT (3 less items 4 and 5)	£	£	£
7. Fixed Assets			
8. Current Assets			
9. CAPITAL EMPLOYED	£	£	£
10. Ratio of Profit to Capital Employed			
11. Ratios of Sales to Capital Employed			
12. Current Ratio			
13. Quick Ratio			
	£	£	£
14. PROFIT APPROPRIATIONS			
15. Net Profit (6 above)			
Less Dividends			
Transfer to General Reserve			
Transfer to Asset Replace-ment Reserve			
Taxation			
16. TOTAL APPROPRIATIONS	£	£	£
17. PROFIT AND LOSS BALANCE (15 less item 16)	£	£	£

FIG. 8.—*Specimen Master Budget*

EXAMINATION QUESTIONS

1. In drawing up a scheme of Budgetary Control, what considerations should be taken into account, and how should they be provided for?

(*I.C.W.A.*)

2. What is meant by the expression "pre-determined costs"? For what purposes are they used and how are they prepared?

(*I.C.W.A.*)

3. "Standard costing is always accompanied by a system of budgeting, but budgetary control may be operated in businesses where standard costing would be impracticable."

Discuss this statement, and indicate the method and use of budgetary control systems in the type of business mentioned in the latter part of the quotation.

(*I.C.W.A.*)

4. Production costs of a factory for a year are as follows:

Direct wages	£80,000
Direct materials	£120,000
Production overheads, fixed	£40,000
Production overheads, variable	£60,000

During the forthcoming year it is anticipated that:

(*a*) the average rate for direct labour remuneration will fall from £0·34 per hour to £0·32 per hour;
(*b*) production efficiency will be unchanged;
(*c*) direct labour hours will increase by 33⅓%;
(*d*) the purchase price per unit of direct materials, and of the other materials and services which comprise overheads will remain unchanged.

Draw up a budget and compute a factory overhead rate, the overheads being absorbed on a direct wages basis.

(*I.C.W.A.*)

5. Under any scheme of Budgetary Control how would you provide for fluctuations in proportions of overheads? Explain your answer fully.

(*I.C.W.A.*)

6. A manufacturer produces standard lines, but also takes in work of a non-standard character. In preparing a system of standard costs, show how you would deal with the special work, bearing in mind that the cost and financial accounts are agreed.

(*I.C.W.A.*)

7. As cost accountant you are asked to advise a company on the best method of absorbing overheads and to compute the rate or rates to be applied. No cost accounts have been kept, but estimates have been prepared for jobs undertaken on the following basis:

Estimated materials and direct wages, plus 150% on direct wages for factory overheads, plus 15% on factory cost for all other overheads. To this figure a further 15% is added for profit.

The accounts for the year show the following figures:

Direct material	£21,000
Factory overheads	£27,500
Selling overheads	£3,000
Sales	£75,000
Direct wages	£18,500
Administration overheads	£5,000
Distribution overheads	£1,500
Net loss	£1,500

There are two production departments and the overhead rates for the departments vary considerably.

    (a) Summarise your computation and observations.
    (b) State what advice you would give to the management.
    (c) Suggest lines on which further investigation should proceed.
(I.C.W.A.)

8. Explain the different uses of:

    (a) standard costs,   (b) flexible budgets,
    (c) fixed expense budgets.

with particular reference to the control of costs.
(I.C.W.A.)

9. The classification of all overhead expenditure in a manufacturing business of medium size has formerly been by nature of expense only. This has been for cost finding purposes, where an overall rate of overhead absorption, based upon direct wages, has been used. You are about to introduce (a) more precise product costing, and (b) budgetary control procedures.

Explain how you would approach the problems of overhead classification, allocation, apportionment and absorption, bearing in mind that the cost centres for overhead absorption are not necessarily the same as the centres of budget responsibility.
(I.C.W.A.)

10. Draw up a budget of service department costs, using your own figures.
(I.C.W.A.)

11. The accounts for a manufacturing company for a year are as follows:

Direct materials	£175,000
Direct wages	£100,000
Variable factory overheads	£100,000
Fixed factory overheads	£100,000
Other variable costs	£80,000
Other fixed costs	£80,000
Profit	£115,000
Sales	£750,000

Two products, A and B, are manufactured, and during the year output and costs were as follows:

	A	B
Output (units)	200,000	100,000
Selling price (each)	£2	£3·50
Direct materials (each)	£0·50	£0·75
Direct wages (each)	£0·25	£0·50

Factory overheads are absorbed as a percentage on direct wages; other overheads, half fixed, half variable, have been computed to amount to £0·5 per unit for product A and £0·6 per unit for product B.

During the coming year it is expected that demand for product A will fall by 25%, and for product B by 50%; it is decided to manufacture a further product C, the costs, etc., for which are estimated as follows:

Output (units)	200,000
Selling price (each)	£1·75
Direct materials (each)	£0·375
Direct wages (each)	£0·25

It is anticipated that the other variable costs per unit will be the same as for product A.

Compile a budget to present to management, showing the current position, and the anticipated results for the coming year.

(I.C.W.A.)

12. Outline the steps necessary for the preparation of a detailed man-power estimate which would be of value in preparing a labour budget.

Compile a man-power estimate for a production department showing the break-down to cost centres of the various grades of labour required.

(I.C.W.A.)

13. What difficulties would you expect to find in the compilation of a flexible budget?

Give sufficient detail to justify any assumptions you make. How would such a budget be used?

(I.C.W.A.)

Chapter 4

THE DEVELOPMENT OF STANDARD COSTS FOR MANUFACTURING

As a preliminary to the development of Standard Costs it will be necessary to consider, *inter alia*, the following matters:

1. A preliminary survey, before setting Standard Costs, to ensure that all functions are being carried out as efficiently as possible.
2. The location and size of cost centres and the assignment of responsibilities.
3. The type of Standard Cost and, as a corollary, the type of standard costing system to adopt.
4. Material, labour, and overhead requirements must be ascertained for each product and as a whole (the setting of Standard Costs).
5. Choice of an accounts classification which will clearly throw to light any variances, clearly distinguishing controllable and uncontrollable variances.

The items which require enlargement and explanation will be discussed below, either in this or in later chapters.

THE LOCATION AND SIZE OF COST CENTRES

A business should be divided into sections representing functional responsibilities; only in this way can effective cost control be exercised. The orthodox division by functions is as follows:

1. Manufacturing, divided into:

   (a) producing departments, which are responsible for the actual manufacture of the products and, accordingly, where direct costs are incurred;

   (b) service departments, which generally "serve" the producing departments and in which no direct costs are incurred.

2. Administration.
3. Selling and Distribution.
4. Research and Development.

To be able to locate responsibility, and thus control costs, the cost accountant, in collaboration with the production engineer, must further subdivide the manufacturing division into "cost centres." A cost centre is a department or part of a department, or item of equipment or machinery, or a person or group of persons, in respect of which costs are accumulated and over which cost control can be exercised.

The physical lay-out of the factory and the cost centres very often coincide, but such correlation is not essential; there may be one department which covers a particular function, but this may be divided into a number of cost centres. A single operation being performed by men and machines could be a cost centre.

If management feel that the allocation and apportionment of costs, to a section or operation, are justifiable by results—closer cost control —then a cost centre should be created. Each supervisor should clearly understand the full extent of his responsibilities and, also, which costs are capable of being controlled by him. To achieve these aims a cost centre should be defined so as to cover only those matters which clearly come within the jurisdiction of its supervisor.

TYPES OF STANDARD COST

A Standard is a predetermined measure relating to material, labour or overhead: it is a reflection of what, under stated conditions, is expected of plant and personnel. A Standard is primarily an expression of quantity and a Standard Cost is its monetary expression: quantity multiplied by price. It shows what the cost should be; therefore, a Standard Cost may be regarded as the true or real cost of the product concerned.

There is some discord among accountants as to which conditions or circumstances should be taken as a basis for setting Standard Costs, and for this reason there emerges a number of different types, the principal of which are as follows:

Standard Costs based on:

1. Ideal conditions.
2. Expected (attainable) conditions. } Current Standards.
3. Basic conditions.　　　　　　　　Basic Standards.

In addition there is a Standard Cost based on normal conditions; that is, those conditions which prevail over the entire life of a trade cycle. This Standard Cost attempts to cover variations in production from one period to another and one year to another: accordingly, it is an average which takes in both boom and slump conditions. The concept of a Normal Standard Cost is thus, in many cases, purely theoretical, and in practice would be very difficult to apply, or, if applied, would bear little relation to reality at any particular time. However, as will be shown in the next chapter, when setting Standard Costs for overheads, the long-period absorption of all overhead costs, including the cost of idle facilities, is of great importance.

COSTS BASED ON IDEAL CONDITIONS (IDEAL STANDARD COSTS)

A target is set which, if achieved, would represent a high level of efficiency. The assumption made is that the most favourable production conditions will be attained; the plant will operate at maximum possible efficiency, and the management will be such as to be capable of the highest performance.

To produce a particular product an absolute minimum of direct materials, at prices which are at the lowest possible level, is assumed. Similarly, with direct labour, the times and rates allow no deviation, however slight, from the very high standard of efficiency attainable with perfect conditions. Overhead costs are also set with maximum efficiency in mind. Extremely careful use of all services—lighting, heating, internal transport, and maintenance—is anticipated.

Clearly, assumptions of this kind presuppose a state of knowledge of external market conditions, and internal efficiency, that rarely exists. Even if machines are 100% efficient—which is a rare occurrence—the human element, consisting of executives, clerks, supervisors, and workers, will usually ensure that maximum efficiency is not attained. Moreover, any deviations from ideal performances may not always be the fault of a person employed within the particular business concerned. In the case of, say, material prices, the buyer is subjected to both internal and external influences. A fault in production, resulting in excessive spoilage, so that the buyer has immediately to obtain a further supply of an essential material, irrespective of cost, is certainly outside his field of responsibility. An unexpected shortage, due to the cornering of the market by a few large buyers, is another example of a situation in which a price increase would lead to uncontrollable material cost increases.

Stock valuation and the disposition of variances are affected by the choice of Standard: with Ideal Standards there is a tendency to undervalue stocks and to overstate variances. These, in turn, affect the figure of profit. The attitude of management and men and the interpretation of results may not be those desired. Thus the psychological impact of never reaching the targets set may result in a deterioration of morale which, in turn, reduces efficiency still further, thus commencing a chain-reaction of ill effects.

In practice, unfortunately, ideal conditions rarely operate, so for this reason, if Ideal Standard Costs are used, large unfavourable variances inevitably emerge. Even when advocated, the ideal conditions usually refer to a specific plant and not to an industry. That is to say, for an individual factory ideal conditions are presumed within the local environment. In this case it will be apparent that an Ideal Standard and an Expected Standard will, though not exactly the same, be somewhat similar.

From what has been said it should not be assumed that Ideal

Standards have no place in a standard costing system. There may be instances, particularly for a specific plant, where they can be successfully adopted. In an automated factory, having an efficient system of production control, including preventive maintenance, and also enjoying the trust and confidence of all personnel, Ideal Standards may be feasible. Even if uncontrollable factors, such as prices paid for material, do not come up to ideal expectations, there will, obviously, be much to gain from achieving the desired state for the controllable factors, such as labour times and material quantities. Since the plant conditions are approaching "perfection," there is a good chance that maximum efficiency will be obtained, so, accordingly, many of the disadvantages already outlined will disappear.

COSTS BASED ON EXPECTED (ATTAINABLE) CONDITIONS (EXPECTED STANDARD COSTS)

In this case the target set represents what should be achieved under *actual* conditions, when plant and other facilities have been made, by positive action, as efficient as possible. All functions entering into manufacture are examined with this view in mind, and only when the necessary action to bring about improvements has been made will the Standard Cost be set.

The expected efficiency may not be what is desired, but rather what can be obtained with the existing plant, facilities, and personnel. In each element of cost to be incurred an allowance for contingencies is included. The extent or size of the additional allowances will be largely determined by the plant and facilities to be actually used. Thus, for example, an efficient machine of a particular type will be capable of a definite performance. If, however, that machine is now nearing the end of its useful life, or it is operated by trainee operators, then maximum efficiency cannot be expected. Accordingly, the standard times will be set having full regard to these shortcomings.

A major failing of the Expected Standard Cost is the necessity for constant revision. As conditions change so should the Standards. Unless great care is taken, the Standard Costs may become meaningless and comparisons, between periods, of little or no value. This point is developed in connection with Current Standards.

Provided Standard Costs are set in anticipation of obtaining the best results out of available facilities, Expected Standards can be used to great advantage. The variances will show divergencies from attainable targets, and this fact, in itself, constitutes a recommendation. Departmental managers and supervisors will understand the targets set, and variances will therefore represent a falling off in efficiency, not, as is often the case when Ideal Standards are used, failure to reach the "impossible."

On the related matters of stock valuation and disposition of variances the Expected Standard may be better than the Ideal Standard. The values placed on materials, work-in-progress, and finished goods will tend to be more acceptable than when ideal conditions—which do not actually exist—are assumed. Material quantities and prices, and labour times and rates will be as near as possible to actual quantities, prices, or rates. Accordingly, stock values will tend to be more realistic, not being understated as when Ideal Standards are used. Whether or not an extremely conservative approach to stock valuation is justified, in times of rising prices, is a debatable point—possibly there is a case for it. However, from a long-term viewpoint it will usually be recognised that the adoption of Expected Standards will result in satisfactory valuation of stock, disposition of variances, and calculation of profit. These matters are discussed further in the chapter devoted to Stock Valuation and Disposition of Variances.

Current Standards.—Ideal or Expected Standards, because they relate to present-day conditions, are normally known as Current Standards.

COSTS BASED ON BASIC CONDITIONS (BASIC STANDARD COSTS)

A Basic Standard Cost is one which may be fixed having regard, in the base year, to either ideal or expected conditions. It differs from the "Ideal" or "Expected" in that it is not generally revised with changed conditions, but remains in force for a long period of time.

The Basic Standard Cost is rather like an index figure against which subsequent price changes can be measured. If, in 1965 (the base year), the Standard Cost of a particular raw material entering into a product is £5, and in 1970 is £6, then it is evident that there has been an increase of 20%. The principle is thus similar to that used in the well-known cost-of-living price index.

CURRENT AND BASIC STANDARD COSTS COMPARED

GENERAL COMPARISONS

Need for Revision

Current Standards relate to current conditions and, therefore, require revising when conditions change. They may thus operate only for a short period before revision.

This is not to say that Standards must for ever be in the process of being revised—minor changes in conditions will not warrant revision of Standards. However, if changes take place which cast a serious doubt upon the accuracy of the variances to such an extent that management is likely to take, through misinterpretation, the wrong action, then the Standards should be revised.

By adopting Basic Standard Costs the accountant can avoid constantly revising the Standards. This fact allows the value of being able to compare the costs of different periods to be retained and, moreover, the variances are regarded, by the staff concerned, as being of value and not something which, within a short period, are likely to be reduced by amendment of the Standards. On the other hand, it can be argued that Standards should be capable of being attained and, therefore, to obtain the best results, when significant changes take place, the Standards should be revised.

Stock valuation

Another argument in favour of Basic Standards is that connected with stock valuation; both Actual and Standard Costs are recorded, so stocks can be valued at Actual Cost. Under one method of accounting for Current Standard Costs it is possible to arrive at the value of raw materials in terms of actual cost (*see below* Accounting Method I).

Provision of incentive to greater effort

Under both Current and Basic Standards there are targets which management hope to achieve. With Basic Standards these targets are shown in the form of ratios which show increased, or reduced, efficiency.

Methods of recording

Basic Standard Costing normally requires dual records—debits and credits are kept at *both* Actual and Standard Cost. This fact, linked with the need to calculate ratios, adversely weighs against the use of Basic Standards.

Basis of comparison

With Basic Standards only, comparisons will relate to, say, why increases in prices or rates between one period and another have occurred, *e.g.* why the labour rate for a particular grade has risen from £0·60 per hour in 1966 to £0·65 in 1970. On the other hand, with Current Standards, the enquiry would revolve around why, say, a particular price had exceeded the Standard Cost. The Basic Standard's comparisons, therefore, tend to cover a longer period than the Current Standard's comparisons and, accordingly, when studying trends, the former should be of greater value than the latter.

Undoubtedly, there is much in favour of adopting Basic Standard Costs. The very fact that a revision may be unnecessary for a number of years is a major advantage—with Current Standard Costs an annual revision will usually be essential. It should be noticed, however, that even Basic Standards cannot remain, without revision, for an indefinite period. If the Standard is allowed to remain in force for a very long period it loses its value for comparative purposes. Unusual or exceptional circumstances occurring at different times over a long period will inevitably, in the end, call for revision of the Basic Standards. Eventually, the basic conditions become so remote in time that present conditions are entirely different, and valid comparisons cannot be made.

The much wider use of Current Standard Costs no doubt arises from the ease of installation and operation of a system using these and, also, the provision of a measure, closely related to current conditions, which allows, to the practically minded accountant, a realistic guide to the degree of efficiency actually achieved.

To obtain the maximum benefits some accountants go so far as to advocate the use, together, of both Basic and Current Standard Costs. Certainly, in appropriate circumstances, there is merit in this suggestion. Thus, for example, efficiency in production may be measured by the use of Current Standard Costs, and the long-term trend of costs, used to assess product prices, may be obtained from Basic Standard Costs.

COMPARISON OF ACCOUNTING SYSTEMS

The accounting systems used for recording Standard Costs and variances can be divided into two types according to whether Current Standards or Basic Standards are being adopted:

1. Current Standard accounting systems

These may be divided into two principal forms, the main differences between them being in the way the variances are recorded and the time when they are calculated, so that they may be recorded. The Work-in-Progress Account * may be regarded as the central point, where the differences in recording are revealed: accordingly, the two forms may be distinguished by reference to the Work-in-progress Account as follows:

(a) *Method I.*—Debit Work-in-progress Account with Actual Cost and credit it with Standard Cost.

(b) *Method II.*—Both debit and credit entries in the Work-in-progress Account are made at Standard Cost.

Under Method I the variances are calculated at the end of each accounting period and are then analysed by reasons. In the Cost Ledger the control accounts for materials, labour, and overheads are kept at Actual Cost. The Work-in-progress Account is the only account affected by the Standard Costs and variances. The variance for material prices will relate to usage only, whereas, with Method II, the variance is calculated when the materials are actually purchased. This delay, generally, in isolation of variances is a weakness of Method I.

Method II overcomes the principal weakness of Method I in that it

* Also known as Work-in-*Process* Account.

brings forth the variances when, or before, the accounting entries are made. Usually provision is made for isolation of daily or weekly variances, thus enabling management to take action in good time.

2. Basic Standard accounting systems

There are two outstanding features of accounting for Basic Standard Costs and these are:

(a) The recording, side by side, of Standard and Actual Costs, both for debits and credits.

(b) The use of ratios, often stated as percentages, to show the relation between standard performance and actual performance (may be Basic Standard Costs compared with Actual Costs and/or with Current Standard Costs).

Some systems may use three columns, one for Actual Costs, one for Standard Costs, and one for variances. Alternatively, instead of the column for variances, the ratios could be shown.

Chapters 9, 10, and 11 give a detailed explanation of these accounting systems for Basic and Current Standards.

EXAMINATION QUESTIONS

1. Define "cost variance". In practice "total cost variance" would be divided into material cost variance, wages variance, expense variance etc.

These variances may again be divided. Into what divisions would you separate these variances?

Some variances may either directly or indirectly cause other variances. Give examples, and show how you would bring these facts to the attention of management.

(I.C.W.A.)

2. (a) Write brief notes on the steps necessary and objects aimed at in sales forecasting and profit planning.

(b) Design a simple form suitable for a summarised profit plan for a company with three products. Figures are not required, but the information provided for should be appropriate for higher management.

(I.C.W.A.)

CHAPTER 5

THE SETTING OF STANDARD COSTS FOR MANUFACTURING

THE setting of Standard Costs requires consideration of the following:

1. Quantities
2. Price or rates
3. Qualities or grades
} for each element of cost entering into a product, *i.e.* Material, Labour, Overhead.

The production engineer and cost accountant will have to collaborate in setting Standards. As already indicated, a detailed study of the functions necessary for the manufacture of the product will be an essential preliminary: it is for this reason that the cost accountant must have the assistance of production officials. The recording of Standard Costs and variances and the interpretation and presentation of results to management are the cost accountant's primary responsibilities.

STANDARD COSTS FOR DIRECT MATERIALS

If the benefit resulting from incurring a cost can be traced directly to a product, then such cost is a direct cost. Thus, if material is used to make a saleable product, the cost incurred for that material can be traced to a specific product or batch of products by means of a Material (Stores) Requisition. The leather which enters into a pair of shoes can be traced to that pair, or the batch in which that pair appears, so, accordingly, the leather is direct material. On the other hand, the material which is used on maintaining the machinery which produces the shoes will be indirect material, for the benefits from the cost incurred cannot, in this case, be traced directly to any particular product or batch of products.

MATERIAL QUANTITIES (MATERIAL UTILISATION)

Standardisation of the materials, both as to qualities and sizes, should precede the determination of quantities of materials. The aim should be to achieve maximum economies in material usage. Fixing of the precise quality or grade ensures that the customer gets what he expects and the business can be certain of consistently producing the desired grade of product at minimum material cost.

An analysis of a product's material requirements is necessary. This will lead to the preparation of a list which shows, precisely, the types or specifications, and the quantities, of materials which enter into the product for which the Standard Cost is being compiled. The list prepared is known as a Standard Material Specification.

Where the material quantities are directly related to the weight of the product the standard quantities are easy to ascertain. This is so for nuts, bolts, nails, and similar products. In other cases reference to past performances, making due allowance for any changed conditions, will be a guide to the quantities required. A more objective method is probably provided by test runs. If a number of tests are taken on different days and where necessary, under different conditions, and an average of these is calculated the standard quantity resulting should be quite satisfactory.

Of extreme importance, when setting standard quantities, are the following:

(a) Due allowance must be made for cutting and other normal waste.

(b) Where the waste from one product can be used on another product it will be necessary, if of significant value, to credit the product causing waste with the value of such waste.

The setting of a standard allowance for waste may be far from easy: the type of Standard being adopted will obviously affect the calculation. If the allowance is too high many inefficiencies in material usage will not appear in the Material Usage Variance; if too low, unfavourable variances may not represent inefficiencies. In most cases it should be possible to calculate the unavoidable waste, and this could be used as the standard allowance for waste for Ideal Standards. For an Expected Standard to be realistic, it is advisable to allow a *small* percentage for avoidable waste. No precise figures can be stated, for this will depend, to a large extent, upon the nature of the material.

MATERIAL PRICE

Any Material Price Variances are normally referred to the Purchasing Department for explanation, so, before setting Standards for material prices, it is advisable to ensure that the purchasing and storekeeping functions are efficient. In particular, a study of the following should be made:

1. Procedures for receiving, recording, inspecting, and, where necessary, returning to supplier the materials purchased.
2. Minimum and maximum and re-order levels for each type of material.
3. Discount policy—whether it is the practice to take discounts for prompt payment.
4. Lay-out of bins, and types of bins used, and location of the different types of materials in the stores.
5. Means of transporting materials to the producing departments.

The aim should be to increase efficiency in purchasing and store-keeping and thus keep down, directly or indirectly, the material prices. Where the practice of including purchasing and store-keeping costs in the price of materials is followed, an increase in efficiency will result in a direct reduction in that price. If the purchasing and store-keeping costs are included in manufacturing overheads, then these will be reduced.

The type of Standard Cost to be used—whether Ideal or Expected—will affect the choice of standard prices. If an Ideal Standard is adopted the prices anticipated for ideal conditions will be taken: the most efficient purchasing and storekeeping, the possibility of bulk purchasing, and the taking of all discounts, and other "ideals" will all be assumed.

Where Expected Standards are to be adopted, anticipated efficiency will not, normally, be as great as for Ideal Standards. The particular method used for pricing issues will determine the standard price: if the "first in, first out" or the "average price" method is used, then if a large balance of material is being carried in stock the standard price could be the "first in, first out" price or the "average" price, as the case may be.* If fresh purchases within the future period are anticipated, then due regard should be given to any possible increase or reduction in prices: an analysis of trends should indicate which way prices are likely to move. Even with Expected Standards there should be an aim to achieve a high degree of efficiency, but, in this case, due allowance should be made for any existing practical difficulties.

If Ideal Standards are to be adopted, because of the expectation of a high degree of efficiency, the standard prices will tend to be below the prices at which the actual purchases are made; accordingly, stocks, at Standard Cost, will be undervalued on the Balance Sheet. This disadvantage can, of course, be overcome by adopting Basic Standard Costs, thus recording Actual Costs. Even with Basic Standard Costs, the choice of standard prices is important. To allow useful comparisons with future actual prices the use of a basic price which does not deviate too widely from expected price is to be recommended. Obviously though, when the Basic Standards have been operating for a long period this aim will be difficult to obtain.

STANDARD COSTS FOR DIRECT LABOUR

The workers directly engaged upon the manufacture of a product are known as direct labour. The benefit derived from the labour costs incurred (direct wages) can be traced to a particular product or batch of products. In the example given above, for direct material, leather which goes to make a shoe was stated to be direct material. Using the same illustration, it can be stated that the machine operator who, say, cuts out the leather uppers from hides, will be direct labour.

* This assumes that the prices paid were not abnormally high or low.

A thorough analysis of the labour operations involved in the manufacture of a product will be an essential preliminary. Close attention must be paid to the grading of labour, for the time taken for an operation by a particular grade of worker may not be the same if a different grade is used. The possibility, and desirability, of substituting machines for hand labour and of improving the plant lay-out should be considered before the Standards are set.

LABOUR "QUANTITIES"

The labour "quantity" to be embodied into a product is usually indicated by the number of minutes or hours that the appropriate grade of worker will take to perform the total number of operations necessary to manufacture that product. Different methods may be used to arrive at the standard times, and the detailed procedures may differ, depending on the type of industry involved. Nevertheless, it is possible to generalise and state two principal methods which may be used to determine standard times. These are as follows:

1. Use of past performance records.
   Obviously because of the aim to achieve maximum efficiency, the use of past records, without due adjustment, will represent a retrograde step. Any necessary adjustments may involve more trouble than a complete setting of the standard times by scientific means.
2. Test runs, setting the times of the essential, basic operations, by the use of work study.
   The times taken by different workers for each operation will be obtained and, to set the Standard, an average time calculated. As for material quantities, due allowance must be made for unavoidable and possibly—depending on the type of Standard—some avoidable losses. Recognition of the need to allow for fatigue is important.

The importance of method (2), where it can be adopted, is very great. Management can obtain results which are independent of previous performances, an independence which is so essential if objective standards are to be developed. Moreover, since standardisation of methods and conditions will have to be achieved, a lower labour cost, per unit of product, should result.

LABOUR RATE STANDARD AND GRADES OF LABOUR

Labour rates paid in the past—last month or last year—are very often a poor guide to what rates will be paid in the future. The supply and demand conditions relating to labour are far from static, so accordingly labour rates may change quite often. A very careful analysis of all factors likely to affect wage-rates is the safest approach. The object is to foretell, as far as possible, the actual rate which should be paid during, say, the next year. Only by making due allowance for the future trend of wages can a useful Standard Cost be calculated.

Obviously, when an agreement between union and employer covers a number of future months, then the rate stated may be adopted as the standard rate for those months.

If a bonus or premium scheme of payment is in operation the cost accountant will have to decide whether to include the anticipated extra payments in the standard rates or in the manufacturing overhead. In the former case the amount to be added to the basic rate to arrive at the Standard may be obtained by reference to past records. A similar estimate, if the alternative method is adopted, could be used to augment manufacturing overheads.

When a piece-rate method of payment is in operation the Standard Cost will be the fixed rate per piece. Moreover, in normal circumstances, there will be no difficulty as regards the guaranteed minimum wage—normally paid in this country—for all operatives should be able to earn more than such minimum.

The extra amount paid for overtime—the difference between the normal basic hourly rate and hourly rate paid when overtime is worked —which is usually called the "overtime premium," requires special consideration. The general rule is that overtime premiums should be debited to a manufacturing overhead account. If this rule is followed, then, for practical capacity working, no difficulty is presented as regards fixing the standard labour rate. On the other hand, if the level of operations needed makes overtime working inevitable there is a case for including an overtime premium allowance in the standard rate. The overtime premium becomes a part of a recognised practice—something expected—therefore it can rightly form part of the standard rate.

When both male and female workers are employed and these are of various grades and ages the number of possible rates may become very great and, as a consequence, the operation of the Standard Costing system may become complex and costly. The adoption of a few rates only, provided the rates to be grouped together for averaging are carefully selected, can give very good results. Average rates may be calculated for each department. Thus there may be one rate for, say, the Preparation Department and another for the Mixing Department. In addition, or alternatively, average rates, which consider the different grades of labour, may be considered necessary. There may be average rates for:

(a) Males over 18 (or 21) years of age.
(b) Males under 18 (or 21) years of age.
(c) Females over 18 (or 21) years of age.
(d) Females under 18 (or 21) years of age.

The rates for apprentices may require special consideration.

Calculation of the Standard Labour Cost once times, grades, and rates have been determined, is quite simple. The standard hours for the product are multiplied by the standard rate.

STANDARD COSTS FOR OVERHEADS

A preliminary survey of overheads will be necessary: the aim should be to examine each item of expense with a view to reducing the amounts spent under each heading; e.g. Heating, Lighting, General Labour, etc. Every function which involves an indirect cost should be surveyed: the number of indirect workers in relation to direct workers, the clerical procedures, the use made of services—all these should be given attention. The correct use of internal transport, lights, motors, and other essential services should be stressed, maximum efficiency in utilisation being the aim.

Having due regard to any possible improvements which may take place when a survey has been made, the problem of fixing Standards can be attempted. The procedure to follow is shown below.

PROCEDURE FOR FIXING STANDARD OVERHEAD RATES

The procedure may be summarised as follows:

1. Determine—

   (a) Units of products to be made by producing cost centres.

   (b) Work to be performed by service cost centres.

   These will be fixed having regard to existing production and selling capacity which have been amended by reference to future policy.

2. Divide the overhead costs into—

   (a) Fixed—those which tend to remain constant, in total, irrespective of output.

   (b) Variable—those which tend to vary directly, in total, with output. Usually it is assumed, for convenience, that each unit produced bears the same amount of variable overhead, e.g. 10s. per unit. This may not always be correct but is, for convenience, usually a reasonable assumption to make and there is normally no significant loss in accuracy.

   (c) Semi-variable (or Fixed-variable)—those which have a fixed element and a variable element. In effect, a semi-variable overhead cost, for this classification, is a hybrid cost falling neither into (a) nor (b) completely, but is made up of a part from each. There is a certain degree of variability, but this is irregular.

3. Calculate the fixed, variable, and semi-variable overhead costs expected to be incurred for each producing cost centre and each service cost centre.

The amounts will be set for the level of activity fixed under (1) above.

4. Calculate the standard overhead rate for each service cost centre.
5. Apply the service cost centres' rates to each producing cost centre.
6. Calculate a standard overhead rate for each producing cost centre.

The matters coming under these six headings can now be considered more fully.

STAGE 1: QUANTITIES TO BE PRODUCED

This section will be divided into two to cover an explanation of:

(a) Capacity for *producing cost centres.*
(b) Capacity for *service cost centres.*

(a) CAPACITY FOR PRODUCING COST CENTRES

The activity expected from plant, in terms of production hours or units of production, must be estimated before fixing the standard overhead rate. Obviously, for given conditions, the greater the activity, the larger the total overhead cost: 30,000 units of a certain product will cost more to produce than 10,000 units. The extent of the extra overhead cost will, of course, depend upon the size of the variable and semi-variable elements contained in total overhead.

There are many meanings given to the term "production capacity," the chief of which are as follows:

I. Maximum theoretical capacity

The maximum—100%—is expected of plant. There are no breakdowns, no waiting time, and no delays. If the various machines can operate a total of 2000 hours per month, provided they are operating fully at all times, then the maximum theoretical capacity is 2000 hours or, if a unit of production takes up one hour, 2000 units of production.

Maximum capacity will very rarely be achieved, so its use as a basis for calculating overhead cost cannot be recommended. However, it does provide a basis for understanding the other methods now to be described.

II. Normal capacity

This is usually taken to mean one of two things, either:

(a) Normal Capacity to Manufacture (also known as Practical Capacity); or
(b) Normal Capacity to Manufacture and Sell.

These two meanings require further explanation.

(a) *Normal capacity to manufacture.*—Maximum theoretical capacity is calculated, and from this is deducted an allowance to cover all *normal* time losses due to breakdowns, setting up machines, material shortages, labour absenteeism, and holidays. An efficient level of operations is assumed.

The size of the allowance will largely depend upon the types of product being manufactured and the efficiency of plant. The attitude of management to the type of Standard Cost to adopt will also influence the amount to be allowed. With Expected Standard Costs *all* estimated losses, due to normal causes, will be taken into account: a smaller figure will be used if Ideal Standard Costs are to be adopted. Obviously, a modern plant should have fewer stoppages than an old, outdated plant. Having regard to all relevant circumstances and the aim of management, a figure which represents 20% of maximum capacity will often be a quite reasonable allowance and, in some cases, a much higher figure would not be exorbitant.

Usually a yearly, estimated capacity figure is taken, for this has the advantage of smoothing out seasonal or monthly variations in production.

(b) *Normal capacity to manufacture and sell.*—Practical plant-capacity potentialities and sales may not coincide: in fact, in some industries, they never do. Some accountants argue that failure to achieve necessary sales to keep plant operating at practical capacity will, at times, be inevitable, and this will bring about abnormal idleness. The number of hours representing the Capacity to Manufacture can be reduced by the expected abnormal idleness, and the overhead rate thus be increased to cover the cost of idle facilities. The variable cost per unit of production will, of course, be the same under either method; it is the fixed cost per unit which will differ, for the treatment of that part of the fixed cost which represents idle facilities is where there is a difference in approach.

A comparison of (a) and (b) and Maximum Theoretical Capacity is possible as shown in Fig. 9.

The period upon which estimates are based for the Normal Capacity to Manufacture and Sell is sometimes taken to cover the estimated serviceable life of the plant and equipment. Alternatively, the length of the business cycle can be used, say, seven years. The latter period is an approximate guide only: reference to post-war experience will show that this is so.

The theoretical concept of Normal Capacity to Manufacture and Sell has much to recommend it, for the principle is an extension of the idea of eliminating seasonal production variations, adopted with the "Capacity to Manufacture." The fluctuations estimated to take place over the life of the plant, or over the trade cycle, are averaged in the same way as the monthly fluctuations, when a yearly overhead rate is adopted. The costs of idle facilities are, of course, included in the overhead rate.

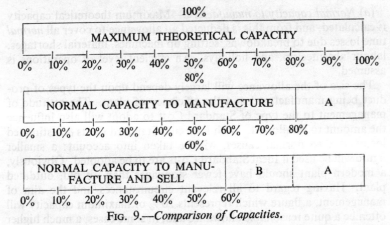

FIG. 9.—*Comparison of Capacities.*

NOTES

1. A = Normal time losses due to normal idleness, breakdowns, lack of materials, holidays, and other, similar, causes.

2. B = Idle facilities due to the inability of the sales force to obtain sufficient orders to cover available plant capacity. (There will be a price below which selling price will not be allowed to fall. This will tend to limit the volume of sales. On pricing see Chapter 26.)

3. Maximum Theoretical Capacity is reduced by 20% to give Normal Capacity to Manufacture. A further reduction, again of 20%, is taken so as to give the Normal Capacity to Manufacture and Sell. These percentages would, of course, vary from industry to industry and even between different business enterprises in the same industry.

From a practical point of view the method tends to be weak; this is due to the uncertainty and, accordingly, difficulty of accurately estimating long-term sales. When adopted, large variances are inevitable. Moreover, because the overhead rate is inflated to cover the cost of idle facilities there is a danger, when prices are based on costs, that orders will be lost.* There are many arguments in favour of rates based on the Normal Capacity to Manufacture. The unit costs are more reliable and, from a practical viewpoint, more useful to management. Recent costs are being considered, not the expected average costs over the next few years. Decisions on whether to make components or purchase them from outside contractors are greatly facilitated.* The costs of idle facilities are not covered up, but instead can be brought to the notice of the management through variance analysis. Another factor is that the accounting rule for valuation—cost or market value, whichever is lower—is easier to apply. Unused capacity, it is argued, is not a true cost, and therefore should not be included in the values attached to the stocks of finished goods or work-in-progress. Normal Capacity to

* These matters are discussed in Chapter 28.

Manufacture has, thus, much to offer. Unfortunately, it has a major disadvantage. In times of depression there may be a large under-absorbed capacity, and yet the product costs being accumulated, and acted upon by management, will ignore this fact. Accordingly, even if Normal Capacity to Manufacture is adopted as the basis for calculation of the overhead rate, there is a case—when full capacity is not being used—for additional measures being taken. Any expected falling off in sales should, if possible, be anticipated, and any resulting reduction in capacity estimated. In some cases it may be possible to use a supplementary overhead rate to cover the cost of idle facilities. Management will then be aware of the true cost of producing and, at the same time, know that the extra overhead, calculated per unit of product, has, if possible, to be covered. The next meaning given to production capacity provides a means of covering the cost of idle facilities.

III. The short-period capacity to sell

This is similar to the Normal Capacity to Manufacture in that an estimate is taken to cover, say, a year only. It differs in that total sales expected for the period, instead of total, possible, production for the period, forms the basis for the calculation of the overhead rate. Because a short period is taken instead of a number of years, this approach is likely to be more useful than where the Normal Capacity to Manufacture and Sell is used: the shorter the period being reviewed, the greater the accuracy is likely to be—the sales for one year can be estimated with reasonable accuracy, but it becomes a different story when a number of years' sales have to be estimated. The costs of idle facilities are, in this case, covered by the overhead rate. For many accountants this fact constitutes a weakness of the "Capacity to Sell": management, they argue, should be fully aware of the cost of such facilities, when they are present.

Conclusion on capacity to adopt

The choice of the appropriate capacity to use, when calculating the standard overhead rate, is a matter for the individual business concerned.

Generally speaking, if sales tend to fluctuate from one year to another the Short Period Capacity to Sell would appear appropriate. When the volume of sales remains reasonably constant the Capacity to Manufacture may be used. The presence of abnormal idle facilities may be covered by the use of a standard overhead rate, which is supplementary to the ordinary, standard overhead rate. Usually it will be unwise to ignore one factor—sales or production—relying solely on the other as the basis of the calculation. Sales and production are very much related and, moreover, are dependent upon each other.

(b) CAPACITY FOR SERVICE COST CENTRES

A "service cost centre" is one which incurs indirect costs only. To be able to set Standard Costs for a service cost centre it will be necessary to estimate the producing departments', service departments', and administrative departments' requirements of Heating, Power, Maintenance, and other Services. These Services can be converted into terms of cost by consideration of indirect materials, indirect labour, and "outside" services needed to provide them. In the case of, say, Power, there will be a direct link between production and power usage. With other Services, such as Maintenance, there will not be the obvious correlation between production and usage. Even so, it should be possible, without undue difficulty, to estimate the service requirements. The calculation of the overhead rate is discussed below.

STAGE 2: DIVISION OF OVERHEAD COSTS INTO FIXED, VARIABLE, AND SEMI-VARIABLE ELEMENTS

Fixed overhead costs

Within a stated range of output, total fixed overhead costs tend to remain constant. Accordingly, there is normally no great difficulty in setting these.

The fact that these costs are not rigidly "fixed" should, however, be remembered. If management decides on a change of policy there may be an increase, or reduction, in fixed overhead costs.

Variable overhead costs

Those costs which vary directly with physical production are known as variable overhead costs. The variable *rate* is normally assumed to be the same for all levels of output; if 1000 units are produced and the variable overhead is £1000, then if, later, 2000 units are to be produced the total is assumed to be £2000. Obviously, some items may not vary directly with the volume of production: in one period there may be a large number of rejected parts, in another, very few rejections; breakdowns, and other cost-incurring functions, may similarly vary. Nevertheless, this assumption is usually justified, and results based on it are reasonably accurate.

Semi-variable overhead costs

An estimate of the fixed element in the semi-variable overhead costs should be obtained and then, for the particular output involved, an estimate of the variable overhead cost can be ascertained.

Division of overhead costs into those which remain constant so long as policy remains unchanged, and those which tend to vary directly with increases or decreases in volume of output, serves many useful purposes. Since each cost is being classified according to characteristic behaviour, the task of predetermining what it should be, under stated conditions and for a given output, is greatly facilitated.

Another, equally important, advantage is that which may accrue to management. Policy-making and the solving of managerial problems are made easier. Knowledge of marginal costs is often essential to arrive at reasonable conclusions—essential if profit is to be maximised. Moreover, intelligent understanding and disposition of overhead variances will often be greatly assisted by this separation into fixed and variable elements.

Not to be forgotten is the importance of clearly distinguishing controllable and uncontrollable variances. Many fixed costs are outside the control of departmental managers, foremen, and supervisors, whereas variable costs are often controllable.

The principal methods adopted to separate fixed and variable costs are explained in Chapter 16. Summarised, they are as follows:

(a) Use of a regression chart (or scattergraph).

(b) Application of the method of least squares.

(c) Preparation of a flexible budget which shows expected costs for a number of volumes of production, costs for "intermediate" volumes being found by straight-line interpolation.

Methods (a) and (b) are statistical techniques applied to this particular problem. The flexible budget, for Standard Costing, may be regarded as being the most important of the three, both for its usefulness in assisting to predetermine costs and for its important role in aiding cost control. Strictly speaking, (c) may not be a separate method but, as will be shown in Chapter 16, may be a practical application of (a) and (b).

Unless there is a limit set on spending for the volume of output actually achieved, foremen and supervisors are unlikely to be fully aware of the importance of cost control. "Cost consciousness" is taught by bringing excessive spending to the notice of those concerned. For the current output for each cost there is a stated allowance which, if exceeded, requires to be explained. The requisitioning of exorbitant quantities of materials or supplies or the growth in the number of indirect labour hours will be questioned. In this way control over costs is achieved, for no efficient supervisor will wish to be the subject of constant criticism.

STAGES 3, 4, 5, AND 6. CALCULATE THE STANDARD OVERHEAD COST AND OVERHEAD RATE FOR EACH COST CENTRE

A budget is prepared to show, in broad detail, the anticipated overhead costs. The period covered by the budget is very often one year, though six months, for some businesses, may prove more useful. The budget is broken down into four-weekly control periods. With direct costs, daily control is possible, but with many overhead costs, comparisons, with budgeted and actual, may usefully be made only on a four-weekly basis.

There are two types of budget. First, there is the fixed budget which shows *one* volume of output and related costs. Secondly, there is the flexible budget, designed to cover a number of possible outputs and the cost structures for each one. The fixed budget will have limited usefulness except for the most stable type of business, because it is almost impossible to forecast the volume of output accurately. On the other hand, provided the budget is carefully compiled, the activity achieved should fall within the range of activities covered by the flexible budget.

The summary of the procedure, shown above, assumes that a factory will have producing *and* service cost centres and that a standard overhead rate is required for each. In a manufacturing organisation these assumptions will usually be justified.

With job costing, the use of predetermined overhead rates is quite common. The principles involved in ascertaining future costs are similar under the two methods of cost accounting. There is an important difference, however, which arises when considering the nature of the costs. For job costs the aim will be to predetermine costs so as to show anticipated Actual Costs. Standard Costing assumes that production is carried out efficiently so the predetermined overhead costs, naturally, must reflect this fact. There is no question of calculating the costs so that they will agree with future Actual Costs: to do so would be to anticipate inefficiencies and, in effect, be a party to them. As observed earlier, all functions which result in overhead costs being incurred should be examined, and necessary improvements made, before the standard overhead costs are determined.

The observations, already made, on the capacity to adopt and the choice of the type of Standard Cost, are at this stage most relevant. A decision on these two vital questions should, of course, have already been made.

Past experience, and present and future trends, are likely to provide the foundation for standard overhead costs. An analysis of the overhead costs incurred for a number of past years, in particular noting trends and outputs, is the usual way. Alternatively, when new departments have been introduced, past records may provide the means of projecting intelligent estimates of what overhead costs are likely to be. On the other hand, some costs may be predetermined more scientifically by test runs or by the use of time-and-motion studies. There will, of course, be a limit to the costs which can be set by one of these means: only when the functions which incur the costs follow a definite pattern will, say, work study be useful. The number of boilermen required to maintain a certain number of boilers, or the number of labourers required to sweep a factory floor a desired number of times per day, can be ascertained by study of the work involved and the determination of a time per work unit. If the boilers are manually fed, calculation of coal usage per hour and a boilerman's "tonnage" per hour will indicate man-power requirements. Similarly, a standard time for a square yard of floor should allow an estimate to be made for the number of sweepers. Remembering the effect of trends, in prices and production, and the fact that the object is to set standard overhead costs which reflect efficient performance, one or more of the above methods may be adopted.

The variable costs will tend to be more difficult to estimate than the fixed costs. In the case of the latter, provided the factors which cause them—often the policy followed—remain unchanged, there should be little variation from year to year.* Variable costs, on the other hand, vary with changes in volume of output, and in efficiency (or inefficiency!). Each type of variable cost is examined and then, having regard to all relevant facts, a figure is fixed. The stage-by-stage build-up of a budget is discussed in Chapter 16.

Some overhead costs will be incurred by one cost centre alone, and a direct charge to that centre will then be necessary. When a cost is to be incurred on behalf of a number of cost centres it will be necessary to carry out an apportionment. The object should be to trace responsibility to be incurred, or benefit to be taken by each cost centre, and apportion the cost on the basis of the findings. Possible methods consider for each cost centre, floor space, cubic capacity, capital values, direct wages, number of employees, and kilowatt hours. The principle involved is to find a factor which is related to the cost being considered and then apportion on a pro-rata basis. Thus, for example, heating costs may be regarded as being related to space occupied by a cost centre and apportioned on that basis. The same basis could be adopted for rent and rates and depreciation of buildings. When considering supervision costs, either direct wages or the number of employees may be the appropriate factor.

Once all costs have been taken to cost centres it may be necessary to adjust the totals shown for each service cost centre. Inspection and Stores will probably use a certain amount of Power and, most likely, Stores will give some service to Power. To arrive at cost figures which are reasonably accurate, thus enabling Standard Costs to be set for service cost centres, any significant degree of interrelationship should be estimated, and any necessary apportionments made.

The next step is the transfer of service-cost-centre costs to producing cost centres. This may be done by the adoption of one of the methods shown below:

(a) Calculate a standard overhead rate for each service cost centre and then charge to producing cost centres according to anticipated usage.

(b) Apportion, on a predetermined basis, the total costs for service cost centres to each producing cost centre.

(c) Use a combination of (a) and (b).

* Assumes stable prices or rates.

The first method, which is listed as Stage (4) above, is likely to give maximum control over costs. A standard rate per hour or other unit is calculated and then, in the budget, each producing cost centre is charged with the appropriate cost, found by multiplying standard hours, or standard units, by the standard rate. Typical standard service units are pounds for steam, gallons for water, cubic feet for gas, and kilowatt hours, or units of electricity, for power.

A formula to arrive at the standard rate for *each* service cost centre is:

$$\frac{\text{Total Standard Cost for service cost centre}}{\text{Total standard service units (or hours) for centre}}$$

The rates for all service cost centres, as indicated, are then used to apply the total service costs to producing cost centres. If the *actual* usage of each service is charged to the producing cost centres at the standard rate, irrespective of Actual Costs incurred, a variance can be calculated for each service cost centre, thus enabling, where necessary, an investigation into spending.

Method (*b*) is similar to (*a*) but, instead of using a *rate*, each service cost centre's total is apportioned, on an equitable basis, to the producing cost centres. Suggested bases for apportionment are as follows:

Name of service	Basis of apportionment to producing cost centres (in each case for standard output)
Inspection	Anticipated usage by each producing cost centre. (May be on a time basis or on the number of products inspected for each.)
Stores	Materials to be used. (May be on values, quantities, or the number of Standard Material Requisitions.)
Building services	Space occupied (square or cubic footage).

Other services can be apportioned in a similar manner.

A combination of the two methods can often be used to advantage. Even if the adoption of a standard rate per hour, or unit of service, is felt to give the best results for most services, there may be some costs which require an alternative approach, such as an apportionment of Building Service and Fixed Costs, on the basis of floor space occupied by each producing cost centre.

Having transferred all service centre costs to producing cost centres, a standard overhead absorption rate can be calculated. Generally speaking, any one of the methods normally used to absorb overhead costs could be adopted for Standard Costing. However, to obtain satisfactory results, the choice of method should be limited to one of three—the machine hour rate, the direct-labour hour rate, or the direct-wages

percentage rate. Many costs are incurred on a time basis, so the merits
of the first two methods are obvious: both recognise the importance
of time in relation to incurring costs—whether machinery *or* hand
labour is predominant will determine the precise choice of one or the
other.

With *historical costing*, if the direct-wages percentage rate is to be
satisfactory it has to be adopted where all workers carrying out similar
operations are paid the same rate of pay and, furthermore, if machines
are used where these are of a type which incur approximately the same
amount of overhead cost. A standard costing system rigidly defines the
grade of labour and the rate to be paid for each operation, therefore
the normal criticism, regarding different rates of pay, will not apply. In
addition, provided each cost centre consists of similar machines, or uses
different absorption rates for machines which are dissimilar, since the
worker's time and the machine time will coincide, application of the
direct-wages percentage will tend to give the same result as the machine
hour rate. The fact that procedures and times are standardised will also
tend to improve the accuracy of the amount of overhead recovered by
this method. Because of its simplicity, support of the direct-wages percentage rate, in place of the direct-labour hour rate, appears to be inevitable. When machine hours and direct labour hours do not coincide,
such as, for example, when a number of automatic machines are operated by one man, the use of the machine hour rate is to be preferred.

The formulae for the three methods of calculating standard rates are
as follows:

(*a*) Direct labour hour rate:

$$\frac{\text{Total standard overhead cost for producing cost centre}}{\text{Standard direct labour hours for producing cost centre}}$$

(*b*) Machine hour rate:

$$\frac{\text{Total standard overhead cost for machine *}}{\text{Standard machine hours}}$$

(*c*) Direct wages percentage rate:

$$\frac{\text{Total standard overhead cost for producing cost centre}}{\text{Standard direct wages for producing cost centre}} \times \frac{100}{1}$$

Both (*a*) and (*b*) give a rate per hour. If a particular operation takes
one hour, then the overhead applied will be equivalent to the appropriate hourly rate. Method (*c*) gives a percentage which shows the
relation between overhead cost and direct wages cost. When the
percentage is 100 and direct wages for an operation amount to £1,

---

* Or group of similar machines.

then overhead cost is £1: when the percentage is 50 the overhead cost is £0·50.

As indicated, the choice of method of absorption will depend upon the circumstances. When conditions between producing cost centres are far from similar, say when one centre is highly mechanised with few direct workers, whereas another has no machinery the work being performed manually, then the machine hour rate and the direct-wages percentage rate, respectively, may be adopted.

EXAMINATION QUESTIONS

1. You are required to prepare labour cost standards in a large firm producing a diversity of products. Describe *three* ways in which these Standards could be prepared, tabulate the advantages of each and state your preference.

(*I.C.W.A.*)

2. Describe the preparation of the direct wages element of a production cost budget both with and without the advantage of a standard costing system. In establishing standard direct wages rates what information is required from the planning department and how would it obtain this information?

(*I.C.W.A.*)

3. Under present-day conditions it is often found to be extremely difficult to maintain standards of cost without frequent adjustments. State the main causes and give your views as to the remedies which could be applied.

(*I.C.W.A.*)

4. A company's products pass through different operating centres. Cost centres are established for each operating centre, collecting all wages costs and other items of expense except direct materials. A cost-unit rate is pre-determined for each cost centre detailing each class of expense. Product costs are compiled from these standard costs.

Give a schedule of the items that would be shown in such a cost-centre account, explaining the origin of its charges and the method by which the standard cost unit rates would be calculated and controlled.

(*I.C.W.A.*)

5. What factors would you consider when preparing a budget of plant and machinery maintenance? Describe how the expenses included in this budget would be controlled by management and absorbed in the costs.

(*I.C.W.A.*)

6. By what methods should Standard Costs be prepared, and what use would be made of budgets for this purpose?

(*I.C.W.A.*)

7. Would you treat overtime pay as part of Wages or as an Overhead? Give your reasons.

(*I.C.W.A.*)

8. Describe how a method of Standard Costs is operated, showing what additional internal arrangements are necessary for its working successfully. To which classes of manufacture is it best suited?

(*I.C.W.A.*)

9. Describe fully the basis upon which Standard Costs are obtained and state their uses to the management. Illustrate your answer with an example.

(*I.C.W.A.*)

10. How would you treat the following as to their effect on Standard Costs:

(*a*) Exceptional expenditure, *e.g.* abnormally large and expensive repairs due to explosion or flood and not covered by insurance.

(*b*) Prolonged periods of overtime.

(*I.C.W.A.*)

CHAPTER 6

ANALYSIS OF MANUFACTURING VARIANCES

STANDARD COSTING aims at revealing the difference between pre-determined Standard Costs and Actual Costs in respect of the following:

1. *PRICE*, which may be analysed into—

    (a) Material price.
    (b) Labour rate.
    (c) Factory overhead as per the budget.

2. *QUANTITY*, which may be analysed into—

    (a) Material quantity.
    (b) Labour hours.
    (c) Overhead hours for the production achieved.
    (d) Overhead hours for the period irrespective of volume of production.

In each case there is a comparison made between anticipated, efficient performance, measured in monetary terms (the Standard Cost), and what has actually been achieved, also measured in monetary terms (the Actual Cost). Any difference is known as a Variance.

So as to follow the conventional division of cost into its elements a study of variances is normally made under each of the headings: "material," "labour," and "overhead." There are some variances, however, which may be regarded as being of a "general" type; that is, they can apply to all elements of cost. These will be considered before going on to a discussion of material, labour, and overhead variances.

"GENERAL" VARIANCES

Many of the following are not different variances from those which are calculated for material, labour, and overhead. Rather they are descriptions of the variances appearing under the elements of cost; they indicate particular characteristics of the other variances. Thus, for example, it is possible to have a Controllable Variance in respect of materials; this is nothing more than a Material Variance which is the responsibility of a particular person; it is not a different variance. These remarks also apply to uncontrollable variances, favourable variances and unfavourable variances: they describe the principal variances.

The chief of these "general" variances are explained below.

TOTAL COST VARIANCE

As the name implies, the Total Cost Variance is the difference between the Total Standard Cost and the Total Actual Cost. It is a net variance and, accordingly, can also be obtained by setting off *all* variances, favourable and unfavourable, against each other.

CONTROLLABLE AND UNCONTROLLABLE COST VARIANCES

Controllable Variance

If a variance can be regarded as the responsibility of a particular person, with the result that his degree of efficiency will be reflected in its size, then this is said to be a Controllable Variance. Thus, generally speaking, an excess usage of material by a particular department is known as a Controllable Variance, being the responsibility of the foreman in charge of the department. It should not be forgotten, however, that the excess usage may be outside the control of the department using the material. If there is some defect in the material the responsibility may rest with the Inspection Department for non-detection and, further back along the line of responsibility, the supplier.

Uncontrollable Variance

If a variance is due to extraneous causes, such as a national increase in the labour rates of workers belonging to a particular trade, then it is said to be "uncontrollable." Any responsibility for the variance cannot be assigned to a particular department or person, but must be regarded as being due to circumstances outside the control of individuals employed by the business concerned.

Importance of distinction between Controllable and Uncontrollable Variances

This division into Controllable and Uncontrollable Variances is extremely important. The fact that a variance may be controllable in some circumstances but uncontrollable in others has already been noticed; this observation is important and should be kept in mind when analysing variances. The *reason* for the variance is the factor which determines the category into which it, or part of it, falls. In some cases, as will be obvious, a variance may be caused by a multitude of reasons; if so, where possible, each reason should be determined and its financial cost determined.

From the point of view of disclosure of variances to responsible officials it is a good plan to emphasise the Controllable Variances. Where the responsibilities of managers and foremen are quite heavy, the information should be kept to a bare minimum: a selection only of Controllable Variances should be presented, the emphasis being on those which require investigation and possibly corrective action. This follows the well-known "principle of exception," whereby those matters which are going right are disregarded, and any deviations from efficient performances are investigated.

FAVOURABLE AND UNFAVOURABLE VARIANCES

When a variance is a reflection of efficiency—Actual Cost lower than Standard Cost—it is said to be a "favourable" one. On the other hand, when Actual Cost exceeds Standard Cost, the difference is an "unfavourable" variance.

Other names for unfavourable variances are "debit" variances and "adverse" variances. Favourable variances are also known as "credit" variances. The "debit" and "credit" prefixes arise from the way the variances are recorded in the books of accounts—unfavourable variances are debited, whereas favourable variances are credited. The term adverse variance speaks for itself.

The assumption that a Favourable Variance is a sign of efficiency, whereas an Unfavourable Variance denotes inefficiency, can be justified only if Standard Costs have been correctly set. If Standards are wrong, variances become meaningless.

All variances should be stated in monetary terms: quantities without costs are of limited use and value. This is not to say that physical quantities should never be used: as will be shown later, reports at foreman level may usefully show hours lost or quantities of materials wasted; however, these are not true variances.

METHODS VARIANCE

When Standards are set, the normal practice is to have regard to the correct production methods to adopt: these methods, in effect, become incorporated into the Standard Costs. If for some reason, a different method is adopted, then a variance will result and, since the best possible methods should be used for setting the Standards, this will tend to be an unfavourable variance. In practice, this variance is likely to have limitations. If a non-standard method is used there will tend to be some difficulty in proving that a variance results from the change of method only, and from no other reason. The variance should only arise irregularly, for if it is to be the *practice* to use a different production method, then the Standard Cost will require revision.

REVISION VARIANCE

To avoid the considerable amount of work involved in amending Standard Costs, and also to clearly segregate controllable and uncontrollable costs, it may be decided to make use of a "Revision Variance

Account." The effects of a particular change, say a price increase or wages-rate increase, can be isolated and will not then require analysing by causes. Where the price or rate increase is uncontrollable there is, obviously, little to be gained by revising the Standard Costs, so a Revision Variance is a recommended expedient. In effect, it is an interim adjustment device, allowing the Standard Costing system to operate usefully even though there have been significant "price" or "quantity" changes. Needless to say, if the system is to be efficient there is a limit to the number of revision variances which can be used.

The precise method adopted to segregate the extra cost (the Revision Variance) will vary according to the particular accounting system adopted. Essentially the problem is to separate, from the principal variance, the effect of an uncontrollable change. If, for example, there is a national wage award in an industry the additional cost can be credited to a "Labour Control Account" and debited to a "Wages Revision Variance Account."

SUB-VARIANCES

The principal variances are those which relate, in total, to quantity or price deviations from Standard. Taken together, the two variances equal the appropriate cost variance. Thus, for example, the Material Price Variance and Material Usage Variance may be regarded as principal variances which, jointly, form the Material Cost Variance. Beyond the initial division into "quantity" and "price" there is no further breakdown of the cost involved.

If a principal variance is analysed into its constituent parts, a cost being calculated for each part, then, to indicate that this subdivision has taken place there is much to gain by coining a new word. Rather than refer to each part as a variance, when, in actual fact, it is only part of a variance, the term "sub-variance" can be used. Immediately this description is seen, there will be a clear understanding that only part of a variance is being dealt with.

The so-called Mixture Variance, Yield Variance, and Calendar Variance may, to follow the suggestion on terminology, be regarded as sub-variances. In each case the cost involved may be calculated with certainty, and it forms part of a principal variance.

Both the Yield Sub-variance and the Mixture Sub-variance are described below. The most usual application is in connection with materials, although labour sub-variances can be calculated. As will be apparent, from the examples given to illustrate the calculation of sub-variances the Material Yield Sub-variance and the Material Mixture Sub-variance, in total, equal the Material Usage Variance.

For convenience, a discussion of the Calendar Variance is deferred until the overhead variances are dealt with.

Yield Sub-variance

From a given standard input of materials there will be expected a
certain yield: this is known as the "standard yield." If the actual yield
differs from the standard yield it is possible to calculate a Yield Sub-
variance, this being the difference between actual and standard yields
evaluated by reference to standard output price. An example is given
in Chapter 8.

In process industries it is often essential to be able to control the input
and consequent yield of each operation. The finished product of the
first operation becomes the raw material of the second operation; the
finished product of the latter the raw material of the third operation, and
so on. To obtain maximum efficiency each stage should be systemati-
cally "watched": the input and yield will have to be weighed or
measured, and recorded.

If the production process is continuous, as, for example, where a conveyor is used to transfer materials from one operation to another, then
the yield for the connected group of operations taken as a whole can
be calculated. However, to achieve maximum control the checking
and recording of input and yield and the calculation of yield variances
should be done for each operation. Obviously, therefore, this alternative procedure will be followed only when single operation control is
impracticable.

An unfavourable Yield Sub-variance shows that, in total, more than
the standard quantity of materials has been used. A favourable sub-
variance indicates that less than the total standard quantity was required.

Often yields are expressed as percentages. If from a standard input
of 110 lb there should be a yield of 100 lb, then the percentage is:

$$\frac{\text{Yield}}{\text{Input}} \times \frac{100}{1} = \frac{100}{110} \times \frac{100}{1} = 90 \cdot 9\%$$

Without calculating the sub-variance it should be apparent, from the
percentage, whether or not the process being carried out is efficient. A
sudden percentage increase, or decrease, will usually indicate that an
investigation is required. In effect, the percentage will represent an
index of efficiency in operating.

The precise way in which information on yields will prove useful depends upon the type of business concerned. In the steel industry any
appreciable change in yield, from an input of metal, may indicate that
the practice followed for pouring the molten metal is not complying
with that laid down as being the most efficient and which has been assumed in the calculation of the standard yield. When the normal pouring losses, due to splashing and similar reasons, are estimated the most

efficient method of producing will be kept in mind. Any deviation there-from will often be shown as a lower yield. In the manufacture of biscuits the yield of good biscuits will be affected by efficiency in shaping and baking. In the canning of vegetables or meat, the yield obtained will vary with such factors as the quality of the "ingredients" purchased and the care with which they are handled.

By daily analysis of the Yield Sub-variance greater control over costs can be exercised; this, in itself, is important. Not to be forgotten, how-ever, is the fact that a larger yield will, generally speaking, mean that customers can receive their requirements earlier. There will tend to be a reduction in the time needed to complete an order, a fact which should, as does adherence to a standard material mixture, increase the goodwill of the manufacturer concerned.

Mixture Sub-variance

The Mixture Sub-variance considers the proportions of materials or labour for a specified output. If, for example, the mixture is varied so that a larger than standard proportion of more expensive materials is used, then there will be an unfavourable sub-variance. When a larger proportion of cheaper materials is included in the mixture, then a favourable Mixture Sub-variance will result.

Failure to use the standard mixture may be due to one or more of a number of reasons. There may be a shortage of one of the specified materials, an alternative having to be used. Often the sub-variance, in such a case, will be uncontrollable; this will be so when fire, flood, labour strike, or similar occurrence cuts off the main supply of a material, thus resulting in a grave shortage. On the other hand, failure to re-order material in good time may be the fault of the official in charge of initia-tion of Purchase Requisitions, or of the Purchasing Department for not placing the Purchase Order quickly enough after receiving a Requisition, or for not placing it with a reliable supplier. Another reason may be that the Stores have issued a substitute material due to, say, the correct material not being unpacked, or because the material, being in an in-accessible rack because of inefficient storekeeping, cannot be issued ex-cept with great difficulty. These, and other reasons, will be brought to light by analysis and investigation of the sub-variances. Many can be eliminated by the issue of instructions regarding procedures. Obviously, for example, inefficient storekeeping should not be tolerated, so, ac-cordingly, everyone concerned should fully understand the correct procedures.

In foundries a standard material mixture will often be essential. Castings, to be suitable for a specified purpose, cannot be made in a haphazard fashion: for the best results the standard proportions have to be clearly defined. Similarly, steel and other metals must comply with clearly defined specifications to be suitable for machining or other operations. In chemical processing, flour milling, biscuit making, meat processing and sausage manufacturing, sweet manufacturing, and in the production of many foodstuffs it may be possible to employ the Material Mixture Sub-variance usefully as a means of quality and cost control.

The reputation of the manufacturer can be jeopardised by deviations from the standard mixture. This is especially so when a product is described, to a customer, according to its material specifications. Also, if a commodity is "branded," a trade name being adopted, a guarantee of quality is implied. Moreover, this quality must be consistently achieved, or the trade name will become meaningless, and the goodwill of the business will suffer.

MANUFACTURING VARIANCES FOR EACH ELEMENT OF COST

The variances for each element of cost are explained below. They are covered in the following order:

1. Material Variances.
2. Labour Variances.
3. Overhead Variances.

MATERIAL VARIANCES

The *Material Cost Variance* may be regarded as a "total" variance subdivided into:

(a) *Material Price Variance*, which is the difference between Actual and Standard prices of the material used, multiplied by Actual quantity.

(b) *Material Usage Variance*, which is the difference between the Actual and Standard quantities of the material used, valued at Standard price.

These are the principal material variances, but, in addition, there are others which may be regarded as "sub-variances" and which are contained in the Material Usage Variance. An example of a sub-variance is the Material Mixture Variance (or Material Mixture Sub-variance). An explanation of these sub-variances was given in the previous section.

Reasons for Material Price Variance

The most usual reasons for a Material Price Variance can be summarised as follows:

(a) Changes in the basic prices of materials.

(b) Failure to purchase the quantities anticipated when Standards were set, resulting in higher prices directly, or indirectly, through not obtaining quantity discounts.

(c) Not taking cash discounts when Standards were set in anticipation of receiving all such discounts.

(d) Changes in the charges incurred for transport inwards, purchasing and storekeeping, when these are debited to the material cost, thus increasing the issue price per unit of material.

(e) Failure to purchase the standard quality of material, this resulting in a different price being paid.

Normally the Purchasing Agent will be asked to explain the Material Price Variance. He may be required to prepare a statement which analyses the reasons for the variance. The Purchasing Department may not, of course, always be responsible for paying more or less than the standard price: a general price increase would obviously be outside its jurisdiction. The purchase of smaller quantities may be due to lack of capital, which is a financial matter.

Reasons for Material Usage Variance

The Material Usage Variance may be caused by some, or all, of the following:

(a) Sub-standard or defective material.

(b) Carelessness in the use of materials.

(c) An abnormal number of components or products failing to pass inspection, further materials being necessary for rectification.

(d) Pilferage.

(e) Wastage due to inefficient production methods or unskilled employees.

(f) A quality of material being used other than that specified as standard.

(g) A non-standard material mixture being used.

The analysis of causes of the usage variance may be greatly facilitated by adopting a Standard Material Requisition. Any extra materials will thus have to be authorised on a special form called an Excess Material Requisition. The Standard Form will be the authority for standard quantities only. For the additional materials a distinctive form—say, of a particular colour—can be used. All such forms can readily be sorted into the principal reasons for the variances.

A summary statement can be compiled and submitted to the departments concerned. In particular, the aim should be to show the types of materials, the operators and foremen involved, and the causes of the deviations from efficient performances.

The Material Usage Variance is of the utmost importance. Accordingly, much benefit can be obtained by the prompt presentation of a statement of the reasons for, and details of, the variances. Incipient troubles and inefficiencies can be traced and corrected before large losses have occurred.

LABOUR VARIANCES

The *Labour Cost Variance* may be regarded as a "total" variance subdivided into:

(a) *Labour Rate Variance*, or *Wages Rate Variance*, which is the difference between the Actual and Standard rates of the workers employed, multiplied by the Actual hours.

(b) *Labour Efficiency Variance*, which is the difference between the Actual and Standard labour hours, valued at the Standard rate.

As already shown, in connection with the Material Usage Variance, it is possible to divide variances into what may be regarded as "sub-variances." This is not to say that management will benefit from being given a multitude of sub-variances; indeed, care should be taken to ensure that unnecessary sub-variances are *not* calculated. Strictly speaking, for a difference between Actual and Standard Costs to be called a variance or sub-variance, such difference should be capable of being stated, with reasonable accuracy, in terms of sterling. *Causes* of variances should not be regarded as sub-variances unless they can be so valued; minute analyses can serve no useful purpose, for management will have time for serious or significant matters but not for minor details. If sub-variances are to be calculated the aim must be to keep the number to a minimum, where possible having a sub-variance to cover all related causes. Thus, for example, a sub-variance may cover "labour quality," including such matters as lack of training, low-grade workers, or dissatisfaction due to an existing grievance. Needless to say, the calculation of such a sub-variance may present some difficulty, the maintenance of detailed records being unavoidable. The cost accountant must resist the temptation to expand his "empire" by employing additional clerks to keep more and more records. Costing is not an end in itself; it is a "tool" which loses some of its usefulness if it becomes too costly and unwieldy.

Reasons for Labour Rate Variance

Causes of the Labour Rate Variance are shown below:

(a) Changes in basic wage-rates.

(b) Employing a man of a grade different from the one laid down as the standard grade for the job. Thus a chargehand may carry out the work normally done by an ordinary operator or, alternatively, an apprentice or trainee may be called upon to do the work. In either case, a wage-rate which is different from the standard wage-rate will be paid.

(c) Where an overtime allowance is included in the standard rate, but an excessive amount of overtime is worked.

The Labour Rate Variance may be the responsibility of the producing cost centre, as, for example, when a foreman carelessly employs the wrong grade of labour on a job. Sometimes, the variance may be brought about by indiscriminate awards, when the responsibility must be laid at the door of the department which authorises changes in wage-rates. Often it will be an uncontrollable variance, for rates are usually determined by the supply and demand conditions of the labour market, backed by the negotiating strength of the particular trade union. Needless to say, if a foreman is responsible for the variance he should be informed of the details so that any necessary corrective action can be taken.

Reasons for Labour Efficiency Variance

The reasons for the Labour Efficiency Variance may be outlined as follows:

(*a*) Use of sub-standard employees due to—

(*i*) Insufficient training.
(*ii*) Incorrect instructions.
(*iii*) Workers' dissatisfaction.

(*b*) Failure to obtain the best results from employees due to—

(*i*) Poor working conditions—inadequate, or excessive, heating, lighting, and ventilation.
(*ii*) Inefficient organisation—delays in routing work, materials, tools, and instructions.
(*iii*) Use of machinery and equipment which is defective, or the wrong type for the operations being performed.
(*iv*) Incompetent supervision.

The actual causes of the variance when it arises should be carefully listed and, where practicable, sub-variances calculated. It is normally the best guide to labour efficiency, so prompt action can result in large savings.

Provided the standard time for a job or operation is accurately calculated, there is much to be gained from letting the operator know what is expected of him. The standard time can be shown on the Route Sheet which goes with the job, thus showing the target at which the operator should aim. If the standard time has been carefully set the pace indicated will allow the worker to continue his normal working day without excessive fatigue. If additional time—above Standard—is needed, a system of special authorisations, similar to the one suggested for materials, may be adopted: excess time can be covered by special time tickets.

OVERHEAD VARIANCES

For factory (manufacturing) overhead costs, the variances are calculated for the factory, as a whole, or separately, for each producing cost centre and service cost centre.*

There are many different ways of classifying manufacturing overhead variances; in addition, there is no standardised terminology for describing the main variances. This state of affairs is not confined to published works because a great many variations also exist in practice.

In this and subsequent chapters an attempt has been made to produce a classification which is both logical and flexible. If too many variances are calculated the analysis may become excessively costly. On the other hand, if only two variances are calculated, the value obtained may be very negligible. Usually the minimum information requirements are data on spending, efficiency and capacity utilisation. When presenting this information it is advisable to consider the variances in terms of fixed costs and variable costs, thus showing the full effects of changes in the volume of output.

Examples of classifications which have been adopted are as follows:

1. *Two-way overhead variance analysis*

As implied, only two variances are computed—a volume variance and a total budget variance (including both the budget and efficiency variances as defined below).

2. *Three-way overhead variance analysis*

In this case the variance analysis is composed of three variances—budget, efficiency and volume. Many accountants would regard this as a satisfactory *primary* analysis giving vital information on the key areas for efficient management.

3. *Multiple overhead variance analysis*

There are many different forms which come under this heading. One of special interest is the analysis suggested by the Institute of Cost and Works Accountants.† This takes the overhead variance and divides it into "volume" and "expenditure." A further division takes place under each of these main categories:

    (*a*) *Overhead Volume Variance:*

        (*i*) Seasonal Variance.

        (*ii*) Calendar Variance.

        (*iii*) Capacity Usage Variance.

        (*iv*) Volume Efficiency Variance.

---

* Clearly, for effective control separate variances for each cost centre will normally be essential.

† *Terminology of Cost Accountancy*, 1966.

(b) *Expenditure Variance:*

    (i) Overhead Price Variance.
    (ii) Overhead Efficiency Variance.
    (iii) Overhead Utilisation Variance.

Since the Overhead Volume Variance is regarded as the over- or under-absorption of *fixed* overhead costs it follows that all variances coming under the heading (a) should also be concerned with fixed costs.

On the definitions followed in this book the variances (a) (i) and (a) (ii) would be regarded as sub-variances. The variance (b) (iii), according to the *Terminology*, arises from using more or less than the standard quantity of a *service*. Strictly, this again is a sub-variance. The concern is with a particular service such as heat, power or maintenance. Because a specific service is usually only part of the overhead cost incurred by each cost centre, it follows that the Utilisation Variance may not be easily segregated. Indeed, there may be considerable difficulty in making the calculation "balance" with the remaining variances. The integrated approach to variance calculations as described in this book is to be preferred—each constituent variance can be added together to arrive at the main variance.

The brief definitions given below cover the main manufacturing overhead cost variances. Further details are given in later chapters.

The *Overhead Cost Variance*, which is a "total" variance—difference between total, Standard, and total, Actual overhead for the output achieved—can be subdivided into:

(a) *Overhead Budget* (*Expenditure*) *Variance*, which is the difference between the budgeted overhead (total per budget) and actual overhead (total spent for period). This variance is a measure of efficiency in spending. With the *two-* and *three-way* variance analysis this is an adequate definition of the Budget Variance. If the *multiple* variance analysis is employed the term Overhead *Expenditure* Variance may be preferred, this being made up of price, efficiency and utilisation. This alternative approach is given in Chapter 16.

(b) *Overhead Efficiency Variance*, which attempts to measure efficiency for the output actually achieved. The standard efficiency (in terms of hours) is compared with actual efficiency (in terms of hours), each multiplied by the standard overhead rate for the actual production, any difference being the Efficiency Variance.

(c) *Overhead Volume Variance,** which shows any idle hours, or overtime hours, evaluated by reference to the standard overhead rate.
The variance is thus the difference between the actual level of
activity, irrespective of actual output, valued at standard overhead rate, and the standard level of activity, valued at that rate.

(d) *Overhead Calendar Variance (or Sub-variance),* which may be regarded as an "adjustment variance." When the Standard Costs
are set, for each accounting period, a fixed number of working
days will be anticipated. If, for example, a business has an accounting period which covers 22 working days (4 weeks × 5½
days) and the Standard Costs are fixed with this number of days
in mind, then, obviously, if this number is not worked, or is exceeded, the overhead charges will not be as expected. Moreover,
because the length of the accounting period is different, the Overhead Volume Variance will be affected and will require adjustment.
A *Seasonal Variance* is of a similar nature—it arises because
there are fluctuations in the output.

The exact nature of all the above variances will be more apparent
when the methods of calculation are understood.

Reasons for Overhead Budget Variance

As already noticed, the Budget Variance is a measure of efficiency in
spending. If actual overhead exceeds standard overhead there has been
excess spending in respect of one or a number of the elements which go
to make up total overhead cost.

The causes of the variance can be obtained by comparing Actual and
Standard for each overhead account, *e.g.* Rent A/c, Heating A/c, Lighting A/c and Insurance A/c. A statement, shown in terms of spending—
Standard and Actual—for each cost centre, can be prepared. The
analysis may show that some items of overhead exceeded Standard,
whereas others were less than Standard. The reasons, in *both* cases,
should be ascertained. Under-spending may not always be a mark of
efficiency, and should be investigated with the same thoroughness as
used for analysing overspending.

Reasons for Overhead Efficiency Variance

There is great similarity between the Overhead Efficiency Variance
and the Labour Efficiency Variance. Both arise from consideration of

---

* This definition assumes a fixed budget for overhead costs. The volume variance
as defined here is also known as the Overhead Capacity Variance: in fact, the
terms are interchangeable. An alternative definition is possible. Some accountants take the efficiency and capacity variances together and call the product the
Overhead Volume Variance. A further alternative is the term Activity Variance
used as a synonym for the Volume Variance.

the actual and standard times for a given output. Not unnaturally, therefore, the reasons for the Labour Efficiency Variance, already outlined above, may be the same as for the Overhead Efficiency Variance.

Reasons for Overhead Volume Variance

An analysis of the reasons for the Overhead Volume Variance involves consideration of the factors which bring about either idle time or overtime of plant and facilities.

In the case of idle time the principal causes may be as follows:

(*a*) Failure of the Sales Department to obtain sufficient orders.
(*b*) Machine breakdowns.
(*c*) Non-delivery of essential materials.
(*d*) Defective materials.
(*e*) Labour troubles.
(*f*) Inefficient planning—routing of work or faulty instructions.
(*g*) Power failures.

These should be regarded as possible causes—they may not be the only ones, nor will they necesssarily all be present together.

Reasons for Overhead Calendar Variance (*or Sub-variance*)

The Overhead Calendar Variance is really a cause in itself—more or fewer days worked than the number anticipated in the budget. Moreover, as already shown, it is nothing more than an adjustment of the Volume Variance. Accordingly, by the definition already suggested, this variance may, strictly speaking, be regarded as a sub-variance. Why the actual number of days is different from the standard number of days, for the particular period, is a matter not to be overlooked. Not to be forgotten, however, is the fact that, over a year, the budgeted number of days may actually be worked. Holidays will fall in some months but not in others; provided these are anticipated, the variances should cancel each other out. When a flexible budget is used the costs, relating to the particular activity achieved, can be ascertained without recourse to the Calendar Variance. For this reason some accountants do not favour the use of the Calendar Variance.

GENERAL NOTE ON REASONS FOR VARIANCES

The reasons given, to explain the different variances, are those commonly encountered in variance analysis. There will, no doubt, be others, some arising in particular industries only. Even those mentioned, it should be appreciated, will not apply in all circumstances: a variance may arise from a single cause or from a number—the variance analyst should, of course, be aware of all possibilities. In practice, these will not normally present any difficulty, for the enlightened business will maintain records which clearly indicate the common causes of its variances.

THE INTERDEPENDENCE OF VARIANCES

Because variances are classified, in the manner already indicated, this does not mean that each one is a separate and distinct problem, to be dealt with in isolation. Indeed, nothing could be further from the truth, for all variances are, in some way, related and interdependent. This statement applies equally to the variances arising for each element of cost—material, labour and overhead—as to each subdivision—price and quantity—of such variances.

A Labour Rate Variance may be favourable, and its "twin," the Labour Efficiency Variance, unfavourable. The reason may be simply that a lower grade of labour has been employed, at a rate below standard and, because of their lack of skill, the employees have failed to achieve standard efficiency. A similar occurrence could take place for material; a cheaper grade may be used with a reduction in efficiency in usage.

The employment of lower-paid workers may affect the Material and Overhead Variances. Lack of skill may lead to a high rate of spoilage and therefore an unfavourable Material Usage Variance. Both the Overhead Efficiency Variance and the Overhead Volume Variance could be brought about by the same sub-standard workmanship. Longer hours taken, for a specified output, would result in an unfavourable Efficiency Variance. Breakdowns or stoppages may be abnormally high, leading to an unfavourable Volume Variance.

These are but a few of the many instances which illustrate the interdependence of variances. If the variance analyst is to guide management along the paths to greatest efficiency he should be well aware of this close relationship.

EXAMINATION QUESTIONS

1. "The investigation and correction of variances is a function of management."

Set out as a tabulation two variances which may be met in dealing with *each* of the following—wages, material and overhead. Give a brief explanation of each, and outline possible managerial action.

(*I.C.W.A.*)

2. Where Standard Costing is used, what cost variances may be attributed to labour? Differentiate between the variances due to the efficiency of the actual labour force, and those due to the faulty use of labour management.

(*I.C.W.A.*)

3. Define the following:

  (a) Expense Variance;
  (b) Expense Utilisation Variance;
  (c) Overhead Variance;
  (d) Overhead Efficiency Variance;
  (e) Volume Variance.

(I.C.W.A.)

4. In the operation of a Standard Costing system cost results have differed from the Standards. Specify five different variances and against each give a definition which would assist management to understand the meaning of each variance.

(I.C.W.A.)

5. In order to reduce cost it is necessary to instil a "cost consciousness" into the minds of foremen and charge-hands. In what ways can this be done?

(I.C.W.A.)

6. When a variance analysis is presented to management it is possible that a gain over one Standard may help to cause a loss over another Standard, *e.g.* an excessive cost of wages may have been caused by the use of a material purchased at less than Standard price.

Using two examples other than the one given, explain how you would present and interpret the analysis of variances in such cases.

(I.C.W.A.)

7. Define:

  (a) direct wages;
  (b) indirect wages;
  (c) efficiency ratio;
  (d) activity ratio;
  (e) wages variance;
  (f) wages rate variance;
  (g) wages analysis sheet.

(I.C.W.A.)

8. A business expanding rapidly uses historical costing methods. Towards the end of a year the reconciliation of cost and financial accounts reveals considerable differences between overheads incurred and overheads in production. It is suggested that the differences would not have occurred if a Standard Costing system had been used.

Give your views on this suggestion, indicate the type of difference likely to have arisen, and show how the differences would have been avoided and/or indicated in Standard Costing.

(I.C.W.A.)

9. How can cost data be utilised to aid the management in detecting losses, and aid them in effective economies? Illustrate by forms and concrete examples.

(I.C.W.A.)

CHAPTER 7

CALCULATION OF PRINCIPAL MANUFACTURING VARIANCES

ONE of the most important things to remember in connection with the calculation of variances is that the total variance for each element of cost is divided into other variances and therefore, when the variances have been calculated, the accuracy of the calculations can be checked by "balancing" the total variance with the *net* total of the other variances. Thus the Material Cost Variance can be calculated and then the result checked against the net total of the Material Price Variance and the Material Usage Variance.* It is essential to "net" the price and quantity variances, for one may be favourable and the other unfavourable. For the purpose of emphasis the rule may be restated as:

Cost Variance = Price Variance ± Quantity Variance

The basic calculations necessary to arrive at the variances are shown below. A "fixed" budget for overheads—one relating to a specific output—is assumed throughout the calculations. However, when actual activity and standard activity vary considerably the fixed budget will be of limited value; the adoption of a flexible budget, showing different overhead costs for different levels of output, is normally essential to obtain accurate overhead variances. The calculations necessary for obtaining variances, when using a flexible budget, will be illustrated in Chapter 16.

CALCULATION OF MATERIAL VARIANCES

MATERIAL COST VARIANCE

This is concerned with material total cost—Actual and Standard: the difference is the variance. In summary form the calculation may be stated as:

$$\left(\begin{matrix} \text{Actual} \\ \text{quantity} \end{matrix} \times \begin{matrix} \text{Actual} \\ \text{price} \end{matrix} \right) - \left(\begin{matrix} \text{Standard} \\ \text{quantity} \end{matrix} \times \begin{matrix} \text{Standard} \\ \text{price} \end{matrix} \right)$$

The standard quantity must relate to the production actually achieved, *e.g.* units or tons of output.

* This will not always apply for Accounting Method II, covered later. The Material Price Variance is calculated on purchases and *not* usage, so reconciliation with the Cost Variance may not be possible.

MATERIAL PRICE VARIANCE

As implied by the name, the concern is with price; the question to be answered is whether Actual price is more or less than Standard price. The calculation involved is:

$$\left(\begin{array}{c}\text{Actual} \\ \text{price}\end{array} - \begin{array}{c}\text{Standard} \\ \text{price}\end{array}\right) \times \begin{array}{c}\text{Actual quantity of} \\ \text{material used}\end{array}$$

which, abbreviated, can be expressed as $(AP - SP)AQ$.

MATERIAL USAGE VARIANCE

This variance shows whether the Standard quantity of material, for the Actual output, has been bettered, or exceeded. The only acceptable measure of the difference is, of course, at Standard price.

The variance may be obtained as follows:

$$\left(\begin{array}{c}\text{Actual quantity} \\ \text{of material}\end{array} - \begin{array}{c}\text{Standard quantity of material} \\ \text{for production achieved}\end{array}\right) \times \begin{array}{c}\text{Standard} \\ \text{price}\end{array}$$

or

$$(AQ - SQ)SP$$

EXAMPLE OF MATERIAL VARIANCES CALCULATION

QUESTION

Standard production data

The Standard Cost Card shows the following details relating to the materials required to produce Component No. 124-8:

Standards per Component:

Price of material "A" £0·05 per unit
Quantity of material "A" 4 units

Actual production data

The Actual production and related material data are as follows:

Produced in period 1000 units of Component No. 124-8
Price of material actually used = £0·06 per unit
Number of units of material "A" actually used = 4100

Calculate: (a) Material Cost Variance.
(b) Material Price Variance.
(c) Material Usage Variance.

ANSWER

(a) Material Cost Variance

Referring back to the Question it will be seen that the relevant details are as follows:

Standard price = £0·05 per unit

Standard quantity of materials for Actual output = 4000 units (*i.e.* 1000 components × 4 units of material)

The Standard Cost is, therefore, 4000 × £0·05 = £200;

The Actual Cost is 4100 × £0·06 = £246·00

Accordingly the Material Cost Variance is:

Total Actual Cost   = £246·00
Less Total Standard Cost =   200·00
                          ————
                        £ 46·00

The Actual Cost exceeds the Standard Cost, so the variance is unfavourable.

(*b*) *Material Price Variance*

The formula is used as follows:

$$(AP - SP)AQ = (£0·06 - £0·05) \times 4100$$
$$= £0·01 \times 4100$$
$$= £41·00 \text{ (unfavourable)}.$$

(*c*) *Material Usage Variance*

$$(AQ - SQ)SP = (4100 - 4000) \times £0·05$$
$$= 100 \times £0·05$$
$$= £5·00 \text{ (unfavourable)}.$$

SUMMARY FOR (a), (b), AND (c)

Material Cost Variance   = £46·00 (unfavourable).

Material Price Variance = £41·00
Material Usage Variance =   5·00   £46·00 (unfavourable).

CALCULATION OF LABOUR VARIANCES

LABOUR COST VARIANCE

The calculation for the Labour Cost Variance is given by:

(Actual hours × Actual rate) − (Standard hours × Standard rate)

Standard hours are calculated by reference to the production actually achieved.

LABOUR RATE VARIANCE

The remarks made in connection with the Material Price Variance also apply to the Labour Rate Variance. The difference is, of course, that the Labour Rate Variance is concerned with labour hours and wage-rates instead of material quantities and material prices. The formula is:

(Actual rate — Standard rate) × Actual number of hours

or

(AR — SR)AH

LABOUR EFFICIENCY VARIANCE

This is obtained as follows:

$$\left(\begin{array}{c}\text{Actual} \\ \text{hours}\end{array} - \begin{array}{c}\text{Standard hours for} \\ \text{Actual output}\end{array}\right) \times \text{Standard rate}$$

or

(AH — SH)SR

EXAMPLE OF LABOUR VARIANCES CALCULATION

QUESTION

Standard production data

From the Standard Cost Card, relating to Component No. 124-8, the following data are obtained:

Standards per Component:

Labour rate = £0·20 per hour
Hours   = 2 per component

Actual production data

1000 units of Component No. 124-8 produced
Labour rate   = £0·21 per hour
Hours worked = 1950

Calculate: (*a*) Labour Cost Variance.
(*b*) Labour Rate Variance.
(*c*) Labour Efficiency Variance.

ANSWER

(*a*) *Labour Cost Variance*

Standard labour rate = £0·20 per hour
Standard number of hours for Actual production = 2000 (1000 units × 2 hours per unit)
Standard Cost = 2000 × £0·20 = £400·00
Actual Cost   = 1950 × £0·21 = £409·50

The Labour Cost Variance is, therefore, as follows:

Total Actual Cost   = £409·50
Less Total Standard Cost =   400·00

£9·50 (unfavourable).

(b) Labour Rate Variance

$$(AR - SR)AH = (£0·21 - £0·20) \times 1950$$
$$= £0·01 \times 1950$$
$$= £19·50 \text{ (unfavourable)}.$$

(c) Labour Efficiency Variance

$$(SH - AH)SR = (2000 - 1950) \times £0·20$$
$$= 50 \times £0·20$$
$$= £10·00 \text{ (favourable)}.$$

NOTE.—Actual hours are less than Standard hours so there is a favourable variance and the formula is slightly different so that the larger number of hours appears first.

SUMMARY FOR (a), (b), AND (c)

	£
Labour Cost Variance	= 9·50 (unfavourable)

Labour Rate Variance	= 19·50 (unfavourable)
Less Labour Efficiency Variance	= 10·00 (favourable)
	£9·50 (unfavourable).

The Rate and Efficiency Variances, it should be noticed, are "netted" to arrive at the figure shown for the Labour Cost Variance. Calculation of both is essential, for a price variance is normally uncontrollable, whereas a quantity variance is controllable.

CALCULATION OF OVERHEAD VARIANCES

OVERHEAD COST VARIANCE

This is obtained by deducting Standard overhead cost from Actual overhead cost, for an unfavourable variance, or Actual from Standard for a favourable variance.

An extremely important point—often overlooked—is that the Standard Cost should relate to the production actually achieved; this is observed by taking the standard hours for the actual production and multiplying by the standard overhead rate.*

OVERHEAD BUDGET VARIANCE

The Budget Variance is obtained by comparing the total overhead cost, shown in the budget, with total overhead cost actually incurred; the difference between the two represents either excessive spending (an unfavourable variance) or reduced spending (a favourable variance).

* When a flexible budget is employed two separate rates—fixed and variable— will be essential. See page 233 *et seq.*

If actual hours worked are below, or above, the standard hours anticipated in the budget the Budget Variance may not mean very much. Thus, for example, if budget expenditure and activity are £1000 and 2000 hours respectively, but actual expenditure and activity are £950 and 1500 hours respectively, then there is a favourable variance of £50. Can this be said to represent efficiency? If the £1000 in the budget is reasonably accurate, the answer must be in the negative; in fact, the true variance should be an unfavourable one. The reason for this anomaly is the lack of co-ordination between Budget Activity and Actual Activity: the use of a flexible budget overcomes this difficulty.

OVERHEAD EFFICIENCY VARIANCE

The calculation involved is as follows:

$$\left(\begin{array}{l} \text{Actual} \\ \text{hours} \end{array} - \begin{array}{l} \text{Standard hours for} \\ \text{Actual production} \end{array} \right) \times \begin{array}{l} \text{Standard} \\ \text{overhead rate} \end{array}$$

or

$$(AH - SH)SOR$$

Note carefully that the standard hours relate to actual production. The object is to test the efficiency achieved for the actual production: the variance is thus analogous in nature to the Labour Efficiency Variance.

OVERHEAD VOLUME VARIANCE *

The Overhead Volume Variance shows the "loss" or "saving" on available hours; that is, whether less than standard hours have been worked or whether unexpected overtime has occurred. The formula is shown below:

$$\left(\begin{array}{l} \text{Actual hours} \\ \text{for period} \end{array} - \begin{array}{l} \text{Standard hours} \\ \text{for period} \end{array} \right) \times \begin{array}{l} \text{Standard} \\ \text{overhead rate} \end{array}$$

or

$$(AH_P - SH_P)SOR$$

The principal object is to measure idleness or overtime *irrespective* of the actual production. If the plant should operate, in each period, for 5000 hours, but in a period only 4700 hours are worked, then the 300 lost hours form the basis of the variance calculation.

OVERHEAD CALENDAR VARIANCE (OR SUB-VARIANCE)

Only when the Actual number of working days differs from the Standard number of working days will this variance be calculated. Probably the simplest approach is to calculate the Standard daily rate and then multiply the *Actual* number of days less than, or greater than,

* Also known as Overhead Capacity Variance (see page 74).

the *Standard* number of days, by such rate. This may be simplified as shown below:

$$\left(\begin{matrix}\text{Actual no. of} \\ \text{working days}\end{matrix} - \begin{matrix}\text{Standard no. of} \\ \text{working days}\end{matrix}\right) \times \left(\frac{\text{Total o'head per budget}}{\text{Standard no. of days}}\right)$$

or

$$(AD - SD)\left(\frac{TO}{SD}\right)$$

The three variances—Budget, Efficiency, and Volume—will, taken together, be equal to the Overhead Cost Variance. To include the Calendar Variance in the "balancing," it will be necessary to adjust the number of standard hours relating to the "Overhead Volume." Obviously, if more working days are involved the plant capacity will be greater: the number of hours (volume) is thus increased, or reduced, in direct proportion to the increase, or reduction, in working days. This may be shown as follows:

$$\left(\frac{\text{Standard hours for adopted capacity}}{\text{Standard number of working days}}\right) \times \begin{matrix}\text{Number of Actual} \\ \text{working days}\end{matrix}$$

When this is done the Calendar Variance represents nothing more than an "adjustment" of the Volume Variance.

EXAMPLE OF OVERHEAD VARIANCES CALCULATIONS

QUESTION

Standard production data

The Standard Cost Card shows the following information, in respect of Component No. 124-8:

$$
\begin{aligned}
\text{Standard hours for period} &= 2200 \\
\text{Standard number of days} &= 24 \\
\text{Standard overhead cost} &= \pounds1100 \\
\text{Standard production} &= 1100 \text{ units}
\end{aligned}
$$

Actual production data

$$
\begin{aligned}
\text{Hours worked} &= 1950 \\
\text{Days worked} &= 22 \\
\text{Overhead cost} &= \pounds1200 \\
\text{Actual production} &= 1000 \text{ units}
\end{aligned}
$$

Calculate: (*a*) Overhead Cost Variance.
         (*b*) Overhead Budget Variance.
         (*c*) Overhead Efficiency Variance.
         (*d*) Overhead Volume Variance.

"Balance" these variances ((*b*), (*c*), and (*d*) should equal (*a*)) and then calculate:
         (*e*) Overhead Volume Variance (amended to allow for Calendar Variance).
         (*f*) Overhead Calendar Variance (or Sub-variance).

ANSWER

(a) Overhead Cost Variance

Standard overhead rate $= \dfrac{\pounds1100}{2200 \text{ hours}} = \pounds0\cdot50$ per hour.

Standard hours per unit of production $= \dfrac{2200}{1100}$ hours $= 2$ hours per Unit.

Standard Cost is, therefore, 2000 hours $\times$ £0·50, which is £1000.

The 2000 hours are the Standard hours for the *Actual* production. Actual Cost is £1200.

The Overhead Cost Variance is therefore:
Actual Cost £1200 — Standard Cost £1000, *i.e.* £200.
Since Actual exceeds Standard, the variance is unfavourable.

(b) Overhead Budget Variance

Actual expenditure	$= \pounds1200$
Less Standard expenditure per budget	$= \pounds1100$
	£ 100 (unfavourable).

(c) Overhead Efficiency Variance

$$(\text{SH} - \text{AH})\text{SOR} = (2000 - 1950) \times \pounds0\cdot50$$
$$= 50 \times \pounds0\cdot50$$
$$= \pounds25 \text{ (favourable)}.$$

(d) Overhead Volume Variance

Ignoring the Calendar Variance, the calculation is:
$$(\text{SH}_P - \text{AH}_P)\text{SOR} = (2200 - 1950) \times \pounds0\cdot50$$
$$= 250 \times \pounds0\cdot50$$
$$= \pounds125 \text{ (unfavourable)}.$$

The student should observe that, in this case, because the Actual number of hours is *less* than the Standard number of hours an unfavourable variance emerges! This is not so with the Efficiency Variance, for, when calculating that variance, the interest is with hours—Actual and Standard—for the production actually achieved. The Volume Variance is concerned with the hours worked irrespective of output achieved.

SUMMARY FOR (a), (b), (c), AND (d)

Overhead Cost Variance $= \pounds200$ (unfavourable)

		Unfavourable	Favourable
Overhead Budget Variance	$=$	£100	
Overhead Efficiency Variance	$=$		£25
Overhead Volume Variance	$=$	125	
		£225	£25

Net Unfavourable Variance $= \pounds225 - \pounds25$
$$= \pounds200$$

(e) Overhead Volume Variance (with Calendar Variance)

A smaller number of days have been worked, so, to be logical, the number of hours representing plant capacity should be reduced. This may be done as already indicated on page 74, viz.:

$$\frac{2200 \times 22}{24} = \frac{6050}{3} = 2016 \cdot 66.$$

The amended Overhead Volume Variance is therefore $(2016 \cdot 66 - 1950) \times £0 \cdot 50$, which, simplified, is $66 \cdot 66 \times £0 \cdot 50$, making £33·333 (unfavourable).

(f) Overhead Calendar Variance

Using the appropriate formula, shown above, the following applies:

$$(24 - 22) \times \left(\frac{£1100}{24}\right) = 2 \times £45 \cdot 833$$
$$= £91 \cdot 666$$
$$= £91 \cdot 667 \text{ (unfavourable).}$$

SUMMARY OF (a), (b), (c), (e), AND (f)

Overhead Cost Variance = £200·00 (unfavourable).

	Unfavourable £	Favourable £
Overhead Budget Variance =	100·000	
Overhead Efficiency Variance =		25·000
Overhead Volume Variance =	33·333	
Overhead Calendar Variance =	91·667	
	£225·000	£25·000
Net Unfavourable Variance =	£200·000	

The calculation of the Calendar Variance thus has the effect, in this case, of reducing the Overhead Volume Variance.

EXAMINATION QUESTIONS

1. Using suitable figures, show clearly how:

(a) Yield Variance

(b) Calendar Variance

are computed in a Standard Costing system.

Mention three other types of variances and explain what each represents.

(I.C.W.A.)

2. A company produces a certain chemical, the standard materials cost being:

40% material X at £20 per ton.
60% material Y at £30 per ton.

A Standard loss of 10% is expected in production. During one month 171 tons of the chemical were produced from the use of 90 tons of material X at £18 per ton and 110 tons of material Y at £34 per ton.

Calculate the following variances for the month:

(*a*) material price;
(*b*) material mixture;
(*c*) material yield.

(*I.C.W.A.*)

3. From the following basic data calculate:

(*a*) Efficiency Variance;
(*b*) Volume Variance;
(*c*) Calendar Variance.

Item	Budget	Actual
Number of working days	20	22
Standard man-hours per day	8000	8400
Output per man-hour in units	1·0	1·2
Total unit output	160,000	221,760
Standard overhead rate per man-hour	£0·10	

(*I.C.W.A.*)

4. The Standard Cost Sheet for producing a job consisting of 100 articles for the Harem Manufacturing Co. showed:

Materials—

60 lb of material A at £0·50 per lb.
50 lb of material B at £0·60 per lb.

Direct wages—

20 hours operation 1 at £0·450 per hour.
30 hours operation 2 at £0·600 per hour.
40 hours operation 3 at £0·800 per hour.

Overheads—

Based on direct wages at £0·700 per hour.

Actual costs of this job were:

Materials—

70 lb of material A at £0·525 per lb.
48 lb of material B at £0·650 per lb.

Direct wages—

25 hours operation 1 at £0·400 per hour.
28 hours operation 2 at £0·600 per hour.
40 hours operation 3 at £0·825 per hour.

Prepare a table to show:

(*a*) the Standard and Actual costs of the job;
(*b*) the variances analysed as between quantity and price.

(*I.C.W.A.*)

5. Define: (a) wages variance; (b) wages rate variance; (c) labour efficiency variance.

Illustrate your answer with an example of each calculated from the following figures:

Actual hours worked	5600
Standard rate per hour	£0·25
Actual wages paid	£1260
Standard hours produced	4000

(I.C.W.A.)

CHAPTER 8

CALCULATION OF MANUFACTURING SUB-VARIANCES

A PRICE or quantity variance may be divided into a number of sub-variances. Theoretically, there could be as many sub-variances as there are reasons for a price or quantity variance. In practice, evaluation in terms of sterling may be extremely difficult and in some cases impossible. Moreover, the provision of minute detail would not very often justify the cost of calculation and preparation. For these reasons, therefore, the number of sub-variances should be kept to a minimum. Calculation and presentation to management of the principal variances relating to price and quantity, provided the major causes of the variances are made known, will often be quite sufficient.

Many of the sub-variances will be accumulated by keeping detailed records. Thus if a careful check is to be kept on the quantity of material scrapped it is possible to have a Material Scrap Sub-variance. Materials should be purchased in a form suitable for the purpose to which they are to be put. If sheet steel is to be cut into certain sizes or shapes, then the "ideal" size of steel sheet should be ascertained. A standard allowance for scrap can be fixed and, if the actual scrap exceeds the standard, due to say the wrong size of sheet being purchased, then a Material Scrap Sub-variance can be obtained. The actual scrap figure can be accumulated from Material Requisitions: each requisition can be analysed into, say, "Standard quantity for work done," "Standard scrap allowance," "Actual scrap incurred." The records kept would then show the total excessive scrap for the period.

When a number of definite processes form the manufacturing cycle, then it may be possible to set a standard allowance, for normal material loss, in each process. Similarly, spoilage of units in each process may be pre-estimated. As shown earlier, the allowance for any loss is greatly influenced by the type of Standard adopted. The definition of "normal loss" will, accordingly, vary according to the Standard being used. An Ideal Standard will require a lower normal loss allowance than an Expected Standard. Irrespective of the precise definition adopted, however, the normal loss will usually be regarded as a true cost of the product. If to produce 1000 good units it is necessary, due to inherent difficulties in the process, whether from failure of the human element or the machine, to put into the process the equivalent (in terms of cost) of 1100 units, then the unit cost of the good products will be the total cost of 1100 units divided by 1000. Any excessive spoilage should be calculated as a Sub-variance. The Yield Sub-variance will show the *overall* loss or gain. This can then be analysed to show the reasons for an excessive loss of material or for extra time taken.

Some sub-variances are capable of calculation from totals. The principal of these are the Mixture Sub-variance and Yield Sub-variance. Examples, with necessary explanations, will be shown below.

EXAMPLES OF MATERIAL VARIANCE CALCULATIONS INCLUDING MATERIAL MIXTURE SUB-VARIANCE

QUESTION

Standard Cost Card (materials only)

Standard mixture for 100 lb of "AY" Chemical:

		£
40 lb material "A" at £0·10 lb =		4·00
50 lb „ "B" at £0·05 lb =		2·50
20 lb „ "C" at £0·07 lb =		1·40
110 lb		7·90

	lb	Percentage
Standard output for above mixture =	100	90·9
Standard Loss =	10	9·1

Actual production data

2000 lb of "AY" chemical produced.

Actual material usage:

820 lb material "A" at £0·11 lb
980 lb „ "B" at £0·08 lb
410 lb „ "C" at £0·06 lb
2210 lb

	lb	Percentage
Actual Output =	2000	90·5
Loss =	210	9·5.

Calculate: (a) Material Cost Variance.
(b) Material Price Variance.
(c) Material Usage Variance
(d) Material Mixture Sub-variance.

The first three variances to be calculated and summarised before proceeding to (d).

ANSWER

(*a*) *Material Cost Variance*

Standard Cost for Actual production (2000 lb):

	£
800 lb of "A" at £0·10 lb =	80·00
1000 lb of "B" at £0·05 lb =	50·00
400 lb of "C" at £0·07 lb =	28·00
	£158·00

Actual Cost for 2000 lb:

	£
820 lb of "A" at £0·11 lb =	90·20
980 lb of "B" at £0·08 lb =	78·40
410 lb of "C" at £0·06 lb =	24·60
	£193·20

The Material Cost Variance is £35·20 (unfavourable).

(Actual Cost £193·20 − Standard Cost £158·00)

(*b*) *Material Price Variance*

The formula, already stated, is (AP − SP)AQ. Taken for each type of material the variance is, therefore, as follows:

Material "A" (£0·11 − £0·10) × 820
  = £0·01 × 820
  = £8·20 (unfavourable)

Material "B" (£0·08 − £0·05) × 980
  = £0·03 × 980
  = £29·40 (unfavourable)

Material "C" (£0·07 − £0·06) × 410
  = £0·01 × 410
  = £4·10 (favourable)

Note for material "C" the Actual price is less than the Standard price!

SUMMARY

	Unfavourable	Favourable
	£	£
Material "A"	8·20	
Material "B"	29·40	
Material "C"		4·10
	£37·60	£4·10

The net unfavourable variance is £33·50.

(c) *Material Usage Variance*

For each type of material the formula may be applied as follows:

Material "A"   £
$\qquad$ (820 − 800) × £0·10 = 20 × £0·10 = 2·00 (unfavourable)

Material "B"
$\qquad$ (1000 − 980) × £0·05 = 20 × £0·05 = 1·00 (favourable)

Material "C"
$\qquad$ (410 − 400) × £0·07 = 10 × £0·07 = 0·70 (unfavourable)

$\qquad\qquad\qquad$ Net unfavourable variance   £1·70

SUMMARY OF (a), (b), AND (c)

Material Cost Variance	£35·20 (unfavourable)
Material Price Variance	£33·50 (unfavourable)
Material Usage Variance	£ 1·70 (unfavourable)
	£35·20

(d) *Material Mixture Sub-variance*

Part of the Material Usage Variance is due to using a mixture which does not comply with the predetermined standard mixture. For the question being answered, the Material Mixture Sub-variance may be obtained by using for *each type* of material the following formula:

$$\left(\begin{array}{c}\text{Actual proportion} \\ \text{of material}\end{array} - \begin{array}{c}\text{Standard proportion} \\ \text{of material}\end{array}\right) \times \text{Standard price}$$

The Standard proportion has to relate to the Actual usage of 2210 lb (not the Standard usage of 2200 lb). This proportion has to be calculated in respect of *each type* of material; a summary of what is involved is:

$$\frac{\begin{array}{c}\text{Standard} \\ \text{Total for each} \\ \text{type of material}\end{array} \times \begin{array}{c}\text{Total} \\ \text{Materials} \\ \text{used}\end{array}}{\text{Standard total materials}}$$ which shows: Standard proportion of each type of material to total of materials used

CALCULATIONS

Material "A"

Standard proportion for Actual usage $\quad \dfrac{800 \times 2210}{2200} = \dfrac{8840}{11} = \underline{\underline{803·64}}$

Material "B"

Standard proportion for Actual usage $\quad \dfrac{1000 \times 2210}{2200} = \dfrac{11{,}050}{11} = \underline{\underline{1004·54}}$

Material "C"

Standard proportion for Actual usage $\quad \dfrac{400 \times 2210}{2200} = \dfrac{4420}{11} = \underline{\underline{401·82}}$

Material Mixture Sub-variance

   Material "A"

$$\left(\begin{array}{c} \text{Actual} \\ \text{proportion} \\ 820 \end{array} - \begin{array}{c} \text{Standard} \\ \text{proportion} \\ 803\cdot64 \end{array} \right) \times \text{Standard price £0·10}$$

$$= 16\cdot36 \times £0\cdot10$$
$$= £1\cdot636 \text{ (unfavourable).}$$

   Material "B"

$$\left(\begin{array}{c} \text{Standard} \\ \text{proportion} \\ 1004\cdot54 \end{array} - \begin{array}{c} \text{Actual} \\ \text{proportion} \\ 980 \end{array} \right) \times \text{Standard price £0·05}$$

$$= 24\cdot54 \times £0\cdot05$$
$$= £1\cdot227 \text{ (favourable).}$$

   Material "C"

$$\left(\begin{array}{c} \text{Actual} \\ \text{proportion} \\ 410 \end{array} - \begin{array}{c} \text{Standard} \\ \text{proportion} \\ 401\cdot82 \end{array} \right) \times \text{Standard price £0·07}$$

$$= 8\cdot18 \times £0\cdot07$$
$$= £0\cdot573 \text{ (unfavourable).}$$

Summary Material Mixture Sub-variance

Material	Unfavourable £	Favourable £
"A"	1·636	
"B"		1·227
"C"	0·573	
	£2·209	£1·227

Net unfavourable variance = £0·982.

NOTE.—The Material Usage Variance is £1·700 (unfavourable). Taking away the Material Mixture Sub-variance, there is a balance of £0·718 to be explained. Obviously, this figure represents excess usage: it may be checked, for each type of material, as shown below:

$$\left(\begin{array}{c} \text{Standard quantity for} \\ \text{total materials } used \end{array} - \begin{array}{c} \text{Standard quantity for} \\ \text{Standard total materials} \end{array} \right) \times \text{Standard price.}$$

   Material "A"

$$\left(\begin{array}{c} \text{Standard quantity} \\ \text{for Actual} \\ 803\cdot64 \end{array} - \begin{array}{c} \text{Standard quantity} \\ \text{for Standard} \\ 800 \end{array} \right) \times £0\cdot10$$

$$= 3\cdot64 \times £0\cdot10$$
$$= £0\cdot364 \text{ (unfavourable).}$$

Material "B"

$$(1004\cdot54 - 1000) \times £0\cdot05$$
$$= 4\cdot54 \times £0\cdot05$$
$$= £0\cdot227 \text{ (unfavourable)}$$

Material "C"

$$(401\cdot82 - 400) \times £0\cdot07$$
$$= 1\cdot82 \times £0\cdot07$$
$$= £0\cdot127 \text{ (unfavourable)}$$

Total (unfavourable variance) $= £0\cdot718$

EXAMPLE OF MATERIAL YIELD SUB-VARIANCE

There is no generally accepted method for the calculation of the Material Yield Sub-variance. The word "yield" denotes "output," but this fact is not always directly recognised in the calculations used to ascertain the sub-variance. Often *inputs* of material for a specific output are considered. To be logical, however, there appears to be a strong case for using a formula which considers Standard and Actual *outputs*. The generally accepted definition of this sub-variance—difference between Standard and Actual Yield—gives support to this view.

A summary of three possible approaches to the calculation of the Yield Sub-variance is as follows:

1. (Standard yield − Actual yield) × Standard yield price
2. (Actual input − Standard input) × average Standard input price
3. (Actual loss − Standard loss) × average Standard input price

Using the Question shown immediately above for the Material Mixture Sub-variance it is possible to illustrate the principles involved.

METHOD (1)

The relevant details are that the actual input is 2210 lb and output 2000 lb. The standard loss is 10 lb from 110 lb. For an input of 2210 lb the standard loss should be $\frac{2210}{1} \times \frac{10}{110} = 200\cdot91$ lb, which makes the yield 2009·09 lb.

The Yield Sub-variance is, therefore, (2009·09 − 2000) × yield price per lb.

The yield price per pound is found by dividing £7·90 by 100 lb, which gives £0·79

Multiplying 9·09 × £0·79 gives a Yield Sub-variance as follows:

£0·718 (unfavourable).

METHOD (2)

Using the same figures, but by considering input only, it is possible to arrive at the £0·718 figure already calculated.

The average standard input price is $\frac{£7·90}{110}$, i.e. £0·0718 per lb. From the formula, already stated, the Material Yield Sub-variance may be calculated:

$$(2210 - 2200) \times £0·0718 = 10 \times £0·0718$$
$$= £0·718 \text{ (unfavourable)}.$$

METHOD (3)

This is simply a variation of Method (2). Actual and standard losses are compared, and any difference is multiplied by the average Standard input price. Thus:

$$\left(\frac{\text{Actual loss}}{210} - \frac{\text{Standard loss}}{200}\right) \times £0·0718$$
$$= £0·718 \text{ (unfavourable)}.$$

NOTE.—Standard loss is based on an *output* of 2000 lb. In Method (1) the standard loss was calculated on an *input* of 2210 lb.

EXAMINATION QUESTIONS

1. A manufacturing company operates a Standard Costing system and showed the following data in respect of the month of November 1957:

Actual number of working days	22
Actual man-hours worked during the month	4300
Number of products produced	425
Actual overhead incurred	£1800

Relevant information from the company's budget and Standard cost data is as follows:

Budgeted number of working days per month	20
Budgeted man-hours per month	4000
Standard man-hours per product	10
Standard overhead rate per man-hour	£0·50

You are required to calculate for the month of November 1957:

(a) the Overhead Variance;
(b) the Calendar Variance;
(c) the Volume Variance.

Show your workings.

(I.C.W.A.)

2. A company manufacturing a special type of facing tile, 12 in. × 8 in. × ½ in., uses a system of Standard Costing. The standard mix of the compound used for making the tiles is:

1200 lb material A at £0·070 per lb.
500 lb material B at £0·150 per lb.
800 lb material C at £0·175 per lb.

This compound should produce 12,000 sq. ft of tiles of $\frac{1}{2}$ in. thickness.

During a period in which 100,000 tiles of the standard size were produced, the material usage was:

7000 lb material A at £0·075 per lb.
3000 lb material B at £0·160 per lb.
5000 lb material C at £0·180 per lb.

Present the cost figures for the period showing:

(a) Material Price Variance;
(b) Material Mixture Variance;
(c) Yield Variance.

(I.C.W.A.)

3. Common brass is an alloy consisting of 70% copper and 30% zinc. In melting and pouring it is expected that a 4% loss of metal will occur. Standard prices are £400 per ton for copper and £90 per ton for zinc. Using suitable figures for the purpose of illustration, show clearly how you would reveal:

(a) Material Price Variance;
(b) Material Mixture Variance;
(c) Yield Variance.

(I.C.W.A.)

4. A company manufacturing two products operates a Standard Costing system. The Standard overhead content of each product in cost centre 101 is:

Product A £4·80 (8 direct labour hours at £0·60 per hour).
Product B £3·60 (6 direct labour hours at £0·60 per hour).

The rate of £0·60 per hour is arrived at as follows:

Budgeted overhead   £1,140
Budgeted direct labour hours   3,800

For the month of October 19... the following data was recorded for cost centre 101:

Output of product A   200
Output of product B   400
No opening or closing stocks.
Actual direct labour hours worked   4,640
Actual overhead incurred   £1,280

You are required to:

(a) calculate the total overhead variance for the month of October 19...;
(b) show its division into:

(i) Overhead Expenditure Variance;
(ii) Volume Variance;
(iii) Overhead Efficiency Variance.

Show your workings.

(I.C.W.A. adapted)

CHAPTER 9

ACCOUNTING FOR STANDARD COSTS: CURRENT STANDARD COSTS (1)

THE methods of accounting for Standard Costs have already been discussed. Summarised they are as follows:

1. For Current Standard Costs—

   (a) *Method I.* Debit Work-in-progress with Actual Costs and credit with Standard Costs.
   (b) *Method II.* Debit and Credit Work-in-progress Accounts with Standard Costs.

2. For Basic Standard Costs.

Both Actual and Standard Costs appear on the debit and credit sides of the Ledger, *i.e.* a dual record is kept.

The principles involved will be shown by working through an example, given in question-and-answer form, and using in this chapter Current Standard Costs: Method I. For simplicity, the fact that a factory would be divided into cost centres has been ignored. Refinements will be introduced in a later chapter.

QUESTION ON CURRENT STANDARD COSTS: METHOD

The O.M. Co. Ltd. manufactures a Component, Part No. 108-9, which is known as a "Rectifier." The following information relates to this component.

Standard Cost Card

"Rectifier" Part No. 108-9

Materials

	£	£
2 pieces "A" at £0·05 each	0·100	
10 lengths "M" at £0·10 each	1·000	
		1·10

Labour

| 4 hours at £0·50 per hour | 2·00 |

Factory Overhead

| 4 hours at £0·25 per hour | 1·00 |

| Standard Cost per unit | £4·10 |

NOTES.—Budgeted Monthly figures:

Production Hours	2000
Components	500 units
Factory Overhead	£500

Factory Overhead Rate £0·25 per hour.

Data for January, 19...

D.1 Opening Stock of Raw Materials (i.e. at January 1st)

	£
1000 pieces "A" at £0·05 each	50·00
4000 lengths "M" at £0·10 each	400·00
	£450·00

D.2 Purchases made in January

	£
800 pieces "A" at £0·05 each	40·00
400 " " £0·06 each	24·00
5000 lengths "M" at £0·09 each	450·00
	£514·00

D.3 Raw Materials used in January

	£
1100 pieces "A" at £0·05	55·00
5200 lengths "M":	
4000 at £0·10 each	400·00
1200 „ £0·09 each	108·00
	£563·00

D.4 Direct Labour in January

	£
1000 hours at £0·50 per hour	500·00
840 „ „ £0·51 per hour	428·40
	£928·40

D.5 Actual Factory Overhead for January = £600·00

D.6 Actual Production

    460 units completed
    40 fully complete as to materials, but only half-complete
      for labour and overhead

D.7 Sales for January

    400 units at £7 each.

NOTE.—Selling and Distribution Overheads and Administration Overheads are to be ignored.

Required: (*a*) Control Accounts in Cost Ledger.

          (*b*) Calculation of variances.

          (*c*) Posting of variances to appropriate accounts.

          (*d*) Trial Balance at January 28th.

Journal entries are not to be shown.

ANSWER: ACCOUNTING METHOD I

Below is shown, stage by stage, a suggested solution to the problem. Explanatory notes, cross-referenced, where necessary, to the Question, commence in the next paragraph. Each entry can be followed by reference to the Notes, *e.g.* N.1 in the folio column relates to Note 1, which will explain the entry. At the top of each account, (A) denotes that an account is debited (or credited) at Actual; (S) that it is debited (or credited) at Standard. (*See also* Fig. 10.)

NOTE 1

The first step, in any accounting problem, is to enter, in the appropriate accounts, the opening balances.

In this question there is only the opening stock of raw materials (D.1 in question). The entries are:

        Debit: Stores Control A/c.

        Credit: Cost Ledger Control A/c.

SPECIAL NOTES.—From the question it is obvious that both a Financial Ledger and a Cost Ledger are kept. It will be necessary, therefore, in order to have a double-entry system, to open a Cost Ledger Control Account which is debited or credited with any transactions *which originate in the financial books*.

The principles shown will apply even to Integrated Accounts, *i.e.* where *one* set of books is kept and the cost accounting is chiefly collation and analysis ("third entries"). In such case, however, instead of a Cost Ledger Control Account, there will be Control Accounts for Debtors and Creditors and a Cash Account, and these will be part of the double-entry system.* Under some systems of integrated accounts a Cost Control Account is used, but this is usually nothing more than a "suspense" or "clearing" account, and does not serve the same purpose as a Cost Ledger Control Account.

* Describes a *Factory* Integrated Accounts system. A *complete* system will include all Asset and Liability Accounts.

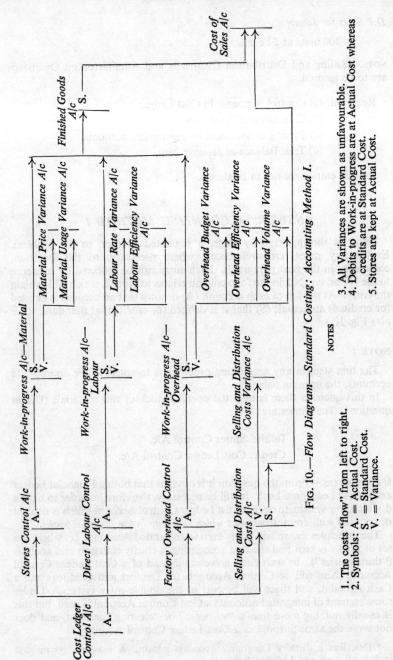

Fig. 10.—Flow Diagram—Standard Costing: Accounting Method I.

NOTES

1. The costs "flow" from left to right.
2. Symbols: A. = Actual Cost.
             S. = Standard Cost.
             V. = Variance.
3. All Variances are shown as unfavourable.
4. Debits to Work-in-progress are at Actual Cost whereas credits are at Standard Cost.
5. Stores are kept at Actual Cost.

NOTE 2.—TOTAL PURCHASE OF RAW MATERIALS (D.2 IN QUESTION)

The entries are, at January 28th:

> Debit: Stores Control A/c.
> Credit: Cost Ledger Control A/c.

SPECIAL NOTE.—The Material Price Variance is *not* calculated until the materials are actually used. This does not apply with Accounting Method II.

NOTE 3.—RAW MATERIAL USED (D.3 IN QUESTION)

At January 28th:

> Debit: Work-in-progress A/c.—Material.
> Credit: Stores Control A/c.

SPECIAL NOTES.—A Work-in-progress Account represents the accumulated cost, to date, of components, or products in the course of manufacture. In Standard Costing it may be shown as follows:

(*a*) one account with no distinction made between the elements of cost: *or*

(*b*) one account, in columnar form, to show clearly each element of cost:

Dr.				*Work-in-progress Account*				Cr.
	Details	Material £	Labour £	Overhead £	Details	Material	Labour	Overhead
Jan. 1	To Balances b/d	20·00	25·00	30·00				

or,

(*c*) three separate accounts—one for Material, one for Labour and one for Overhead.

Either (*b*) or (*c*) should be used: the calculation and recording of variances is then greatly facilitated. In the solution, method (*c*) is adopted.

It will be apparent that the "first-in, first-out" method of issuing materials has been followed.

Because the transaction concerns only the Cost Ledger (the Financial Ledger is not affected) no entry is made in the Cost Ledger Control Account. The double-entry is possible without using the latter account.

NOTE 4.—DIRECT LABOUR (D.4 IN QUESTION)

At January 28th:

> Debit: Direct Labour Control A/c.
> Credit: Cost Ledger Control A/c.

then:

> Debit: Work-in-progress A/c.—Direct Labour
> Credit: Direct Labour Control A/c.

SPECIAL NOTE.—The Direct Labour Control Account could have been omitted altogether. In a more difficult problem, however, a Labour Control Account may be essential. The example attempts to show the principles involved so that any problem may be solved.

NOTE 5.—FACTORY OVERHEAD (D.5 IN QUESTION)

At January 28th:

> Debit: Factory Overhead Control A/c.
> Credit: Cost Ledger Control A/c.

then,

> Debit: Work-in-progress A/c—Overhead.
> Credit: Factory Overhead Control A/c.

NOTE 6.—VALUATIONS OF FINISHED COMPONENTS AND WORK-IN-PRO-GRESS AT JANUARY 28TH (OBTAINED FROM D.6)

Finished components: 460 units completed.

Partly-finished components (Work-in-progress) } 40 { All materials issued: half-complete labour and overhead.

In terms of finished units, therefore, production may be regarded as:

500 complete—materials.
480 „ —labour (460 + (40 ÷ 2))
480 „ —overhead (460 + (40 ÷ 2))

These figures are generally termed "equivalent production." The time spent on the unfinished units is normally estimated by production officials.

The unit cost is found by dividing units of equivalent production into total cost for each element of cost. Thus the *actual unit costs* * are:

$$Material \quad \frac{£563 \cdot 00}{500} = £1 \cdot 126 \text{ per unit}$$

$$Labour \quad \frac{£928 \cdot 40}{480} = £1 \cdot 934 \text{ per unit}$$

$$Overhead \quad \frac{£600 \cdot 00}{480} = £1 \cdot 250 \text{ per unit}$$

Finished units cost

Material	460 × £1·126	= £517·96
Labour	460 × £1·934	= £889·70
Overhead	460 × £1·250	= £575·00

Work-in-progress cost

Material	40 × £1·126	= £45·04
Labour	20 × £1·934	= £38·70
Overhead	20 × £1·250	= £25·00

* Calculation of *actual* unit costs is not essential for the completion of the answer. Where necessary the figures have been rounded off.

Standard Costs for Actual production are:

Actual production × Standard price/rate = Standard costs

	(*Units*)	Cost (*per Std Cost card*)	(*Totals*)
		£	£
Material	500	1·10	550·00
Labour	480	2·00	960·00
Overhead	480	1·00	480·00

These are divided between Finished Goods and Work-in-progress as follows:

	Goods	Progress
	£	£
Material	506·00	44·00
Labour	920·00	40·00
Overhead	460·00	20·00

Entries:

Debit: Finished Goods Account ⎱ Cost of Finished Goods transferred
Credit: Work-in-progress Accounts⎰   *at Standard Cost*

then,

(*a*) Credit: Balances of work-in-progress in Work-in-progress Accounts and carry down to the next period (*at Standard Cost*).

(*b*) Calculate the Variances and post to the Variance Accounts.

The balances on each Work-in-progress Account will, of course, add up to the *net* total variance.

CALCULATIONS OF VARIANCES

Material Cost Variance

Actual Cost − Standard Cost
= £563 − £550
= £13·00 (unfavourable)

Material Price Variance

The concern is only with those items which deviate from Standard: accordingly, when standard and actual prices or quantities coincide, no calculation is necessary, *e.g.* Material "A". Actual Price = £0·05, which is the same as Standard Price, so there is no variance.

Material "M" Variance:

Using the formula, already explained:

$$(SP - AP)AQ = (£0·10 - £0·09) \times 1200$$
$$= £0·01 \times 1200$$
$$= £12·00 \text{ (favourable)}$$

Material Usage Variance

    Material "A":

$$(AQ - SQ)SP = (1100 - 1000) \times £0·05$$
$$= 100 \times £0·05$$
$$= £5·00 \text{ (unfavourable)}$$

    Material "M"

$$(AQ - SQ)SP = (5200 - 5000) \times £0·10$$
$$= 200 \times £0·10$$
$$= £20·00 \text{ (unfavourable)}$$

Summary—Material Variances

            Material Cost Variance = £13·00 (unfavourable)

	Unfavourable	*Favourable*
	£	£
Material Price Variance		12·00
Material Usage Variance	25·00	
	£25·00	£12·00

Net Unfavourable Variance = £13·00

NOTE.—The Material Variances are calculated on usage, *not* on purchases, and not until the end of the period.

Labour Cost Variance

        Standard Cost — Actual Cost (for 480 units)
        = £960·00 — £928·40
        = £31·60 (favourable)

Labour Rate Variance

$$(AR - SR)AH = (£0·51 - £0·50) \times 840$$
$$= £0·01 \times 840$$
$$= £8·40 \text{ (unfavourable)}$$

Labour Efficiency Variance

$$(SH - AH)SR = (1920 - 1840) \times £0·50$$
$$= 80 \times £0·50$$
$$= £40·00 \text{ (favourable)}$$

(The standard hours are computed — 480 units × 4 hours.)

Summary—Labour Variances

    Labour Cost Variance £31·60 (favourable)

	Unfavourable	Favourable
	£	£
Labour Rate Variance	8·40	
Labour Efficiency Variance		40·00
	£8·40	£40·00

Net Favourable Variance = £31·60 (favourable).

Overhead Cost Variance

    Actual overhead − Standard overhead for 480 units
    = £600 − £480
    = £120 (unfavourable)

Overhead Budget Variance

    Actual overhead − Budgeted overhead
    = £600 − £500
    = £100 (unfavourable)

Overhead Efficiency Variance

    $(SH - AH)SOR = (1920 - 1840) \times £0·25$
    = 80 × £0·25
    = £20 (favourable)

The concern is with the standard hours for the actual production (*i.e.* 480 units).

Overhead Volume Variance

    (Budgeted hours − Actual hours) × Standard overhead rate
    = (2000 − 1840) × £0·25
    = 160 × £0·25
    = £40 (unfavourable)

Summary—Factory Overhead Variances

    Overhead Cost Variance = £120·00 (unfavourable)

	Unfavourable	Favourable
	£	£
Overhead Budget Variance	100·00	
Overhead Efficiency Variance		20·00
Overhead Volume Variance	40·00	
	£140·00	£20·00

Net Unfavourable Variance = £120·00

Balancing Work-in-progress Accounts

The Work-in-progress Accounts can now be "balanced." This is done by posting the variances to the appropriate Work-in-progress Accounts, and completing the double-entry in the price and quantity variance accounts.

The procedure is as follows:

> *Favourable Variance:*   Debit: Work-in-progress A/c.
>
> Credit: Variance A/c.
>
> *Unfavourable Variance:* Debit: Variance A/c
>
> Credit: Work-in-progress A/c.

For example, the Material Price Variance (favourable) of £12 will be debited to the Work-in-progress Account and credited to the Material Price Variance Account. The other variances are similarly dealt with.

If the calculations are accurate, once the variances are posted, the Work-in-progress Accounts will "balance." Since the price and quantity variances go to make the total variance—*e.g.* Material Cost Variance—this is not, of course, posted.

NOTE 7.—SALES FOR JANUARY (D.7 IN QUESTION)

SPECIAL NOTE.—Sales amount to 400 units at £7 each. Until a Profit and Loss Account is compiled, the £7 need not enter into the Cost Ledger. A record will, of course, be kept in the Financial Ledger.

For the purpose of recording the details in the Cost Ledger, a Cost of Sales Account is opened. In this account, where appropriate, any selling costs are debited.

At the end of each month or quarter the total Sales (units sold × selling price) are debited in the Cost Ledger Control Account and credited in the Cost of Sales Account. A credit balance on the Cost of Sales Account will represent a profit which can be transferred to Costing Profit and Loss Account. At the end of the same period the manufacturing variances are usually transferred to the Profit and Loss Account; this then shows the *Actual* profit or loss. These entries are *not* required in the answer to this problem.

The important figure is the Standard Cost of £4·10. From this, by multiplying it by the units sold, can be obtained the Standard Cost of Sales.

The entries necessary are:

> Debit: Cost of Sales A/c.
>
> Credit: Finished Goods A/c.

A Trial Balance is then compiled.

The student is advised to work carefully through the Accounts shown overleaf before going on to the next chapter.

ANSWER

Cost Ledger of the O.M. Co. Ltd.

Dr.   Cr.

(A)   *Stores Control Account*   **(A)**

		£			£
Jan. 1 To Cost Ledger Control A/C	N.1	450·00	Jan. 28 By Work-in-progress —Material	N.3	563·00
„ 28 „ Cost Ledger Control A/c	N.2	514·00	„ 28 „ Balance	c/d	401·00
		£964·00			£964·00
Jan. 29 To Balance	b/d	£401·00			

(A)   *Work-in-progress Account—Materials*   **(S)**

		£			£
Jan. 28 To Stores Control	N.3	563·00	Jan. 28 By Finished Goods	N.6	506·00
„ 28 „ Material Price Variance	N.6	12·00	„ 28 „ Balance	c/d	44·00
			„ 28 „ Material Usage Variance	N.6	25·00
		£575·00			£575·00
Jan. 29 To Balance	b/d	£44·00			

(A)   *Work-in-progress Account—Direct Labour*   **(S)**

		£			£
Jan. 28 To Direct Labour Control	N.4	928·00	Jan. 28 By Finished Goods	N.6	920·00
„ 28 „ Labour Efficiency Variance	N.6	40·00	„ 28 „ Balance	c/d	40·00
			„ 28 „ Labour Rate Variance	N.6	8·40
		£968·40			£968·40
Jan. 29 To Balance	b/d	£40·00			

(A)   *Work-in-progress Account—Overhead*   **(S)**

		£			£
Jan. 28 To Factory Overhead Control	N.5	600·00	Jan. 28 By Finished Goods	N.6	460·00
„ 28 „ Overhead Efficiency Variance	N.6	20·00	„ 28 „ Balance	c/d	20·00
			„ 28 „ Overhead Budget Variance	N.6	100·00
			„ 28 „ Overhead Volume Variance	N.6	40·00
		£620·00			£620·00
Jan. 29 To Balance	b/d	£20·00			

(A)   *Direct Labour Control Account*   **(A)**

Jan. 28 To Cost Ledger Control	N.4	£928·40	Jan. 28 By Work-in-progress —Labour	N.4	£928·40

(A)   *Factory Overhead Control Account*   **(A)**

Jan. 28 To Cost Ledger Control	N.5	£600·00	Jan. 28 By Work-in-progress —Overhead	N.5	£600·00

Dr.   (S)   *Finished Goods Account*   (S)   Cr.

		£			£
Jan. 28 To Work-in-progress A/c:	N.6		Jan. 28 By Cost of Sales	N.7	1640·00
Material		506·00	,, 28 ,, Balance	c/d	246·00
Labour		920·00			
Overhead		460·00			
		£1886·00			£1886·00
Jan. 29 To Balance	b/d	£246·00			

(S)   *Cost of Sales Account*

Jan. 28 To Finished Goods	N.7	£640·00

Cost Ledger Control Account   (A)

				£
Jan. 1 By Stores Control		N.1		450·00
,, 28 ,, Stores Control		N.2		514·00
,, 28 ,, Direct Labour Control		N.4		928·40
,, 28 ,, Factory Overhead Control		N.5		600·00
				£2492·40

Material Price Variance Account

Jan. 28 By Work-in-progress —Material		N.6	£12·00

Material Usage Variance Account

Jan. 28 To Work-in-progress —Material	N.6	£25·00

Labour Rate Variance Account

Jan. 28 To Work-in-progress —Direct Labour	N.6	£8·40

Labour Efficiency Variance Account

Jan. 28 By Work-in-progress —Direct Labour		N.6	£40·00

Overhead Budget Variance Account

Jan. 28 To Work-in-progress —Overhead	N.6	£100·00

Overhead Efficiency Variance Account

Jan. 28 By Work-in-progress —Overhead		N.6	£20·00

Overhead Volume Variance Account

Jan. 28 To Work-in-progress —Overhead	N.6	£40·00

Trial Balance of the O.M. Co. Ltd.
January, 28th 19...

		Dr. £	Cr. £
Stores Control Account		401·00	
Work-in-Progress Accounts	£		
Material	44		
Labour	40		
Overhead	20		
	—	104·00	
Finished Goods		246·00	
Cost of Sales		1640·00	
Cost Ledger Control			2492·40
Material Price Variance			12·00
Material Usage Variance		25·00	
Labour Rate Variance		8·40	
Labour Efficiency Variance			40·00
Overhead Budget Variance		100·00	
Overhead Efficiency Variance			20·00
Overhead Volume Variance		40·00	
		£2564·40	£2564·40

EXAMINATION QUESTIONS

1. Design a simple flow diagram to illustrate Standard Costing procedure when production department accounts are debited at Actual, and credited at Standard, cost. Show two service, and two production, departments. Costs should be confined to material, wages, and overhead without additional detail. The main variances for direct costs, and for indirect, should be shown.

(*I.C.W.A.*)

2. Explain the use and purpose of Control Accounts. Give two examples with specimen entries for three months.

(*I.C.W.A.*)

3. You wish to institute Control Accounts in respect of materials purchased and used in your factory. What purposes do Control Accounts serve? What accounts would you institute and from what sources would the entries be derived?

(*I.C.W.A.*)

4. Draw a simple diagram, showing clearly the flow of accounting information from the wages analysis through the main accounting groups, variances, and stock accounts to the final cost statement.

(*I.C.W.A.*)

5. A factory manufactures two joint products, A and B. The standard ratio of production is Product A, 60% and product B, 40%. Standard costs of manufacturing 60 A units and 40 B units are as under:

		£
Materials	2000 yd	200·00
Labour	1020 hrs	127·50
Overheads	62¾% of Labour	85·00
		£412·50

Standard cost per unit of Product A is £4·37 and of Product B is £3·75.

During a particular period, production was 55 units of A and 45 units of B and actual costs for the period were:

		£
Materials	2050 yd at £0·11	225·50
Labour	1040 hrs at £0·14	145·60
Overheads		100·00
		£471·10

Show the Cost Ledger accounts for the period, bringing out the variances.

(*I.C.W.A.*)

6. A foundry producing castings of a standard alloy uses standard costs. The standard mixture is as follows:

40% material A at £300 per ton
30% material B at £100 per ton
10% material C at £420 per ton
20% scrap metal of this alloy

It is expected that from each charge there will be a 5% loss in melt, 35% will be returned to scrap stock (runners, heads etc.) and 60% will be good castings. Scrap is credited and charged at the standard average cost of the metal mixture.

In a certain period the following materials are purchased and used:

380 tons material A at £310 per ton
330 tons material B at £110 per ton
90 tons material C at £420 per ton
200 tons scrap metal at standard price

From this material, 608 tons of good castings are produced, and 340 tons of scrap metal are returned to scrap metal stock.

Present information to management, showing standard metal costs, and variances from standard in respect of this period.

(*I.C.W.A.*)

CHAPTER 10

ACCOUNTING FOR STANDARD COSTS: CURRENT STANDARD COSTS (2)

ACCOUNTING METHOD II records *raw material*, work-in-progress, and finished goods *at Standard Costs*. This objective is achieved by *debiting* and *crediting* the "central account," Work-in-progress Account, with *Standard Costs*.

Under Accounting Method I, the Work-in-progress Account is *debited* with *Actual Costs* and *credited* with *Standard Costs*. As a result, work-in-progress and finished goods are kept at Standard, *but the raw materials are at Actual*.

ACCOUNTING FOR MATERIALS METHOD II

Immediately materials are purchased the price variances are calculated: there is no waiting, as under Method I, for the materials to be used.

Upon receipt of invoices for materials purchased, it will be necessary to convert the actual prices to standard prices. This is done by referring to the Standard Cost Card; the concern is with actual quantity at standard price. The usual practice is to convert each invoice and then enter it into a Purchases Book (Fig. 11).

PURCHASES BOOK

Date	Ref.	Supplier	Description of materials	Actual quantity Standard price	Total Standard cost	Actual quantity Actual price	Actual cost	Variance (U or F)	Reasons
					£		£	£	
Jan. 2	110	X.Y.	"A"	200 at £0·05	10·00	200 at £0·05	10·00	Nil	
Jan. 28	150	A.P.	"A"	100 at £0·05	5·00	100 at £0·06	6·00	1·00 (U)	New Supplier (emergency)

U = unfavourable; F = favourable.

FIG. 11.—*Purchases Book* (Specimen Page)

The variances are isolated when the invoices are entered so no time is lost in focusing attention on inefficiencies. At the end of each period the columns are added up and then the following entries, with an un-favourable variance, are necessary:

Stores Control A/c (Std.)	Dr.	xxx
Materials Price Variance	Dr.	xx
To Cost Ledger Control A/c		xxx

A Standard Material Requisition is used for issuing materials from the Stores. Any additional materials are then authorised by special requisitions. Materials not used, when returned to the Stores, can be covered by a Material Return Note. These excess usages and returns are then recorded and, obviously, variances are revealed. Properly planned, a system will show daily variances which, if significant, will call for prompt action.

ACCOUNTING FOR DIRECT WAGES: METHOD II

By the provision of appropriate columns on wages sheets or by use of special variance analysis sheets it is possible to isolate wage rate variances, at frequent intervals, e.g. once a week. The standard rate is obtained from the Standard Cost Card and the actual rate from the wage records.

The use of supplementary time tickets to authorise any time above standard time will greatly facilitate the accumulation of totals for extra hours taken on particular operations. A system can also embrace cases where less than the standard time has been taken. Once an operation has been completed the Standard Time Tickets, which may also be the Route Card or Instruction Card (explaining the operation), can be returned to the Costing Office and any unused time treated as a reduction of the accumulated, unfavourable hours, or as an increase of the total, favourable hours. Any necessary action to correct an unfavourable Labour Efficiency Variance can take place promptly—there is no waiting until the end of the accounting period, when any variance analysis will have become, by that time, largely a matter of history. Daily analysis of efficiency variances is often accompanied by tremendous savings.

ACCOUNTING FOR OVERHEAD: METHOD II

Day-to-day control of material prices and quantities and labour hours is often possible. For overhead, the same aim, though very desirable, is not easily achieved. In overhead charges there is not the same degree of standardisation to be found. Certainly, both indirect material prices and indirect labour rates enter into the calculation of the total overhead cost. There is, however, a lack of uniformity in the way the costs are incurred. One month some charges may be very high, another month quite low. Moreover, many overhead costs do not vary directly with output.

For indirect labour it is possible to envisage some form of control. The rates—Standard and Actual—can be compared and, in addition, the number of indirect workers in relation to direct workers can be kept within well-defined limits. In some cases a possible way of controlling overheads is to make an analysis of the principal types of cost. The Standards for such costs can be shown on an overhead analysis sheet and, as Actual Costs are incurred, each can be entered at the side of the appropriate Standard Cost. If an Analysis Sheet is designed to cover a number of months, a trend should become apparent: any deviation from this trend may call for investigation.

ANSWER: ACCOUNTING METHOD II

Answering the same question as covered for Method I in Chapter 9, the necessary entries are illustrated below:

Cost Ledger of the O.M. Co. Ltd.

Dr. (S)		£	(S)		Cr. £
			Stores Control Account		
Jan. 1 To Cost Ledger Control	N.1*	450·00	Jan. 28 By Work-in-progress —Material and Usage Variance	N.3	575·00
,, 28 ,, Cost Ledger Control and Material Price Variance	N.2	560·00	,, 28 ,, Balance	c/d	435·00
		£1010·00			£1010·00
Jan. 29 To Balance	b/d	£435·00			

(S)		£	(S)		£
			Work-in-progress Account—Materials		
Jan. 28 To Stores Control	N.3	550·00	Jan. 28 By Finished Goods	N.6	506·00
			,, 28 ,, Balance	c/d	44·00
		£550·00			£550·00
Jan. 29 To Balance	b/d	£44·00			

(S)		£	(S)		£
			Work-in-progress Account—Direct Labour		
Jan. 28 To Direct Labour Control and Variances	N.4	960·00	Jan. 28 By Finished Goods	N.6	920·00
			,, 28 ,, Balance	c/d	40·00
		£960·00			£960·00
Jan. 29 To Balance	b/d	£40·00			

* Explanatory notes follow the ledger accounts. N.1 = Note 1.

Dr. (S)   *Work-in-progress Account—Overhead*   (S) Cr.

		£				£
Jan. 28 To Factory Overhead Control A/c and Variances	N.5	480·00	Jan. 28 By Finished Goods	N.6		460·00
			„ 28 „ Balance	c/d		20·00
		£480·00				£480·00
Jan. 29 To Balance	b/d	£20·00				

(A)   *Direct Labour Control Account*   (A)

Jan. 28 To Cost Ledger Control	N.4	£928·40	Jan. 28 By Work-in-progress —Labour and Variance A/c	N.4		£928·40

(A)   *Factory Overhead Control Account*   (A)

Jan. 28 To Cost Ledger Control	N.5	£600·00	Jan. 28 By Work-in-progress —Overhead and Variance A/c	N.5		£600·00

(S)   *Finished Goods Account*   (S)

		£				£
Jan. 28 To Work-in-progress A/cs:	N.6		Jan. 28 By Cost of Sales	N.6		1640·00
Material		506·00	„ 28 „ Balance	c/d		246·00
Labour		920·00				
Overhead		460·00				
		£1886·00				£1886·00
Jan. 29 To Balance	b/d	£246·00				

(S)   *Cost of Sales Account*

Jan. 28 To Finished Goods A/c	N.6	£1640·00	

Cost Ledger Control Account   (A)

					£
			Jan. 1 By Stores Control	N.1	450·00
			„ 28 „ Stores Control	N.2	514·00
			„ 28 „ Direct Labour Control	N.4	928·40
			„ 28 „ Factory Overhead Control	N.5	600·00
					£2492·40

Material Price Variance Account

					£
			Jan. 28 By Stores Control	N.2	£46·00

Material Usage Variance Account

Jan. 28 To Stores Control	N.3	£25·00	

Dr.   *Cr.*

Labour Rate Variance Account

Jan. 28 To Direct Labour Control	N.4	£8·40			

Labour Efficiency Variance Account

			Jan. 28 By Work-in-progress —Labour	N.4	£40·00

Overhead Budget Variance Account

Jan. 28 To Factory Overhead Control	N.5	£100·00			

Overhead Efficiency Variance Account

			Jan. 28 Work-in-progress —Overhead	N.5	£20·00

Overhead Volume Variance Account

Jan. 28 To Factory Overhead Control	N.5	£40·00			

Trial Balance of the O.M. Co. Ltd.
January 28th, 19...

		Dr. £	Cr. £
Stores Control Account		435·00	
Work-in-progress Accounts	£		
Material	44		
Labour	40		
Overhead	20		
	—	104·00	
Finished Goods		246·00	
Cost of Sales		1640·00	
Cost Ledger Control			2492·40
Material Price Variance			46·00
Material Usage Variance		25·00	
Labour Rate Variance		8·40	
Labour Efficiency Variance			40·00
Overhead Budget Variance		100·00	
Overhead Efficiency Variance			20·00
Overhead Volume Variance		40·00	
		£2598·40	£2598·40

NOTES ON SOLUTION (CROSS REFERENCED TO FOLIO COLUMNS IN ACCOUNTS)

It is assumed that the student has worked through the answer given for Method I. Accordingly, the principal differences between Method I and Method II will be emphasised, the procedures where they are in agreement having already been covered. (*See also* Fig. 12.)

NOTE 1

The opening stock of raw materials is at Standard Cost. Therefore it is a simple matter to debit Stores Control and credit Cost Ledger Control Account.

NOTE 2

Purchases for January are:

> 1200 pieces of Material "A"
> 5000 lengths of Material "M"

At standard prices, these are as follows:

	£
Material "A"	60·00
Material "M"	500·00
Standard Cost =	£560·00

The Actual Cost is £514·00. Taking Standard Cost and deducting Actual Cost, there is a Price Variance of £46·00 (favourable).

Using the now familiar formula (AP − SP)AQ, it is possible to check the variance figure:

Material "A."   (£0·06 − £0·05) × 400
  = £0·01 × 400
  = £4·00 (unfavourable)

Material "M."   (£0·10 − £0·09) × 5000
  = £0·01 × 5000
  = £50·00 (favourable)

Net Variance   = £46·00 (favourable)

The entries are thus:

		Dr.	Cr.
Stores Control A/c	Dr. (Std.)	£560·00	
To Cost Ledger Control (Actual)			£514·00
To Material Price Variance			£46·00

This principle is followed for *all* variances. The double entry is completed *without posting the variances to the Work-in-progress A/c.*

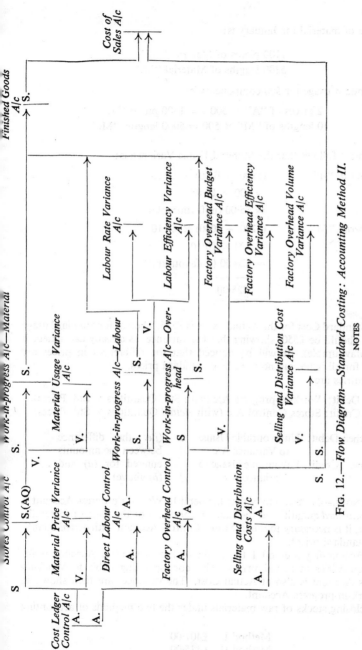

FIG. 12.—Flow Diagram—Standard Costing: Accounting Method II.

NOTES

1. The costs "flow" from left to right.
2. Symbols: A.   = Actual Cost.
             S.   = Standard Cost.
             S. (AQ) = Standard Cost for Actual Quantity.
             V.   = Variance.

3. All Variances are shown as unfavourable.
4. Debits and credits to Work-in-progress are at Standard Cost.
5. Stores are kept at Standard Cost.

NOTE 3

Usage of material for January is:

> 1100 pieces of Material "A."
> 5200 lengths of Material "M."

The standard usage for 500 components is:

> 2 pieces of "A" × 500   = 1000 pieces "A."
> 10 lengths of "M" × 500 = 5000 lengths "M."

From this it follows that the Material Usage Variance is:

Material "A"	$(1100 - 1000) \times £0.05$
	$= 100 \times £0.05$
	$= £5.00$ (unfavourable)
Material "M"	$(5200 - 5000) \times £0.10$
	$= 200 \times £0.10$
	$= £20.00$ (unfavourable)
	$£25.00$

The Standard Cost for the Actual usage is £575, whereas for Standard usage the cost should be £550, showing that the variance, as already calculated, is £25 (unfavourable). It will be noticed that the differences in prices are ignored for all issues are now made at standard prices.

The entries are:

(*a*) Debit: Work-in-progress A/c (with Std. Quantities × Std. Prices).
(*b*) Credit: Stores Control A/c (with *Actual* Quantities × Std. Prices).

> then Debit: Unfavourable Usage to Variance A/c ⎫
> *or*,   Credit: Favourable Usage to Variance A/c ⎬ (*i.e.* the difference between the amounts entered for (*a*) and (*b*) above)

SPECIAL NOTE.—Note carefully that the debit to Work-in-progress Account is for the *standard* quantities at the standard prices. For the issue of materials, however, it is necessary to credit Stores Control Account with *actual* quantities at standard prices.

For Accounting Method I the credit to Stores Control Account is for actual quantities at actual prices. The corresponding debit to Work-in-progress Account is also at Actual Cost. The variances are then shown in the Work-in-progress Account.

The closing stocks of raw materials under the two methods of accounting are:

> Method I   £401.00
> Method II £435.00

The difference of £34·00 is the additional amount added to the price variance by calculating the variance when the materials were received, instead of when used. Under Method I there is a favourable Material Price Variance of £12·00, whereas, for Method II the variance is £46·00. The addition, therefore, as indicated, is £34·00.

NOTE 4

Direct wages for January are:

	Actual	*Standard*
	£928·40	£960·00

The Labour Cost Variance is, therefore, £31·60 (favourable), which may be analysed, as under Method I, into:

Labour Efficiency Variance	£40·00	(favourable)
Labour Rate Variance	£8·40	(unfavourable)

The entries are similar to those shown for direct materials. As will be appreciated, there is no question of valuing labour "stocks," so the treatment of direct labour is probably more straightforward than that for direct material. In summary form the entries are:

Debit: Direct Labour Control A/c   £928·40 ⎱ Actual Cost
Credit: Cost Ledger Control A/c   £928·40 ⎰

then:

Debit: Work-in-progress—D/Labour
     (Standard hours × Standard Rate) ⎱ £960·00
Debit: Labour Rate Variance   £8·40
Credit: Direct Labour Control A/c (Actual Cost) £928·40
Credit: Labour Efficiency Variance   £40·00

NOTE 5

Factory Overhead for January is as follows:

	Actual	*Standard*
	£600·00	£480·00

The Overhead Cost Variance is, therefore, £120, made up as shown below:

	Unfavourable	*Favourable*
Overhead Budget Variance	£100·00	
Overhead Volume Variance	£40·00	
Overhead Efficiency Variance		£20·00

Following the procedure, already explained, the entries are:

Debit: Factory Overhead Control A/c   £600·00 ⎱ Actual Cost
Credit: Cost Ledger Control A/c   £600·00 ⎰

then:

Debit: Work-in-progress A/c—Overhead (Standard hours × Standard Overhead Rate)	}	= £480·00
Debit: Overhead Budget Variance		= £100·00
Debit: Overhead Volume Variance		= £40·00
Credit: Factory Overhead Control A/c		= £600·00
Credit: Overhead Efficiency Variance		= £20·00

NOTE 6

The cost of the work completed is transferred to Finished Goods Account and then the cost of goods sold is transferred to Cost of Sales Account.

SPECIAL NOTE.—With the exception of the Material Price Variance the variances, it will be noticed, are identical under both Methods of Accounting.

EXAMINATION QUESTIONS

1. From the following figures (Standard, except where otherwise stated) relating to a month's activities draw up the various Control Accounts required, showing for the period the profit and the total variances from Standard:

		£	£
Stock brought forward—	steel bars	7000	
	pressings	5000	
	tools	1000	
	consumable stores	2000	
			15,000
Work-in-progress brought forward			11,000
Direct wages—	machine shop	3000	
	assembly shop	7000	
	tool room	2000	
			12,000
Overheads—	machine shop	6000	
	assembly shop	3500	
	tool room	3000	
			12,500
Sales (actual)			42,000

	Actual £	Standard £	
Purchases—			
steel bars	6140	6000	
pressings	6090	6000	
tools	1050	1000	
consumable stores	1020	1000	
	14,300		14,000

Issues from stores—
    steel bars to machine shop   6500
    pressings to assembly shop   5500
    tools   500

	£	
Consumable stores—		
Machine shop	750	
Tool room	250	
	———	1000
		13,500
Production—		
Machine shop		20,500
Assembly shop		16,750
Scrapped work-in-progress—		
Machine shop	750	
Assembly shop	250	
	———	1000
Work-in-progress carried forward		12,000
Cost of Sales		35,250
Allocation of tool room costs—		
Machine shop	5000	
Assembly shop	750	
	———	5750

NOTE.—Total variance only is required and no attempt should be made to analyse by causes.

(I.C.W.A.)

2. Draw up a Material Control Account, using Standard Costs, for any industry with which you are familiar. Give specimen entries and explain those by means of which the material is charged to the product. By what means do you draw attention to variances?

(I.C.W.A.)

3. Under a system of integrated accounts, draw up a detailed organisation chart for a purchasing department.

(I.C.W.A.)

CHAPTER 11

ACCOUNTING FOR STANDARD COSTS: BASIC STANDARD COSTS

THE Question * used to illustrate Accounting Methods I and II for Current Standard Costs will again be answered, but this time to show the principles relating to Basic Standard Costs. Before the Answer is shown, however, it would seem advisable to summarise the characteristic features of a Basic Standard Costing System. These are as follows:

1. Standard Costs are set, based on either "Ideal" or "Expected" conditions. The class of conditions chosen depends upon the opinion of the cost accountant and other responsible officials.
2. Once determined, the Standard Costs usually remain in force for a number of years.
3. Standard Costs and Actual Costs are recorded, side by side, for both debits and credits.
4. Ratios are used to indicate the relation between Actual and Standard Costs. These ratios, often shown as percentages, indicate the degree of efficiency achieved.

   Obviously, however, if particular Basic Standard Costs have been in operation for a long period the "efficiency" or "inefficiency" portrayed by comparison of Standard and Actual may not be very edifying. If conditions have changed out of all recognition to the Basic Standards, management may not be interested in efficiency as indicated by Basic Standard Costs, but instead will turn to Current Standard Costs which reflect present-day conditions.
5. In the example given below Actual Cost in some cases is obtained by multiplying Standard Cost by the appropriate Ratio. Thus the issues of materials for "Actual" are obtained from £575 × 0·9843.

The chief arguments put forward in support of using Basic Standard Costs are:

(a) A disadvantage associated with Current Standard Costs—the need to revise Standards with changes in conditions—is overcome. This fact reduces the costs of operating the standard costing system.
(b) Stocks are shown at Actual as well as Standard Costs, therefore there is no discord on the matter of stock valuation for the purpose of Final Accounts.

* In Chapter 9.

(c) Statistical trends are readily apparent, so much useful information for policy-making and planning becomes available.

(d) By the use of Ratios a measure of efficiency, which can be linked up with, say, an incentive-payments scheme, can be obtained.

Obviously, as will be apparent from examples of the number of the two types of system seen in practice, Current Standards have more to offer. Although these advantages are present in a Basic Standard Costing System, a greater number of business enterprises adopt a Current Standard Costing System because the aim is to measure deviations from *current*, not *past*, efficient performances. Moreover, such a system is usually simpler to operate and, where Budgetary Control is being used, lends itself more readily to making full use of the budget figures, thus reducing the work of setting Standards; this is perhaps especially so for Expected Standard Costs.

A complete Current Standard Costing System aided by a diluted form—to suit particular requirements—of Basic Standard Costs will ensure that the benefits of both systems are available. Some accounting systems, it should be noticed, show only Actual Costs in the books of account, but keep statistical records of Variances and Standards. The latter may be Basic or Current Standards. Obviously, a full double-entry is desirable, but in some circumstances, such as when job costing is operated, a compromise will have to be adopted.

ANSWER

Cost Ledger of the O.M. Co. Ltd.
(Basic Standard Costs)

Dr.   Stores Control Account   Cr.

	£ Actual	£ Standard	Ratio		£ Actual	£ Standard	Ratio
Balances	450·00	450·00	1·0000	Issues to Work-in-progress			
Purchases	514·00	560·00		Balances c/d	548·80	575·00	0·9545
					415·20	435·00	
	£964·00	£1010·00	0·9545		£964·00	£1010·00	
Balances b/d	£415·20	£435·00	0·9545				

NOTES

1. In this, and later accounts, in this chapter, the prefixes "To" and "By" have deliberately been omitted.

2. The Material Cost Ratio is found by dividing the Actual Cost by the Standard Cost:

$$\frac{£964·00}{£1010·00} = 0·9545 *$$

3. Actual issues to production are found by multiplying the Standard Cost for actual usage by the Cost Ratio, *i.e.* £575 × 0·9545 (see (6) below).

* It may be felt that seven or eight figure ratios are necessary. Before reaching any conclusion see p. 128 later in this Chapter.

4. The figures in the account are obtained as follows:

Balances (Dr.)—simply the amounts brought forward from the previous month. Actual and Standard Costs are identical.

Purchases: 1200 pieces of "A."
              5000 lengths of "M."

Actual Cost given in Question = £514·00	
Standard Cost of Actual quantities = "A"	£60
"M"	£500
	£560

Issues—explained in (3) above.
Balances (Cr.)—the amounts left in the account.

5. The Material Price Variance may be found:

	£
Standard Cost of issues	575·00
Actual Cost of issues	548·80
	£26·20 (favourable)

6. The £575·00 is for *Actual* quantities so a direct debit to Work-in-progress Account is not possible. Instead, the £575·00 is debited to the Cost Ledger Control Account. The latter account is then credited and Work-in-progress Account—Material, debited, with the cost of the *Standard* quantities of materials for work actually achieved.

7. Because the Material Cost Ratio calculation has not been taken beyond four figures after the decimal point, the Issues and Balances carried down (Actual Costs) have had to be "adjusted," thus arriving back at the total of £964·00.

Dr.			*Work-in-progress Account—Materials*				Cr.
	£ Actual	£ Standard	Ratio		£ Actual	£ Standard	Ratio
Stores Control and Cost Ledger Control				Finished Goods Balances c/d	504·90 43·90	506·00 44·00	0·9978
	548·80	550·00	0·9978				
	£540·80	£550·00	0·9978		£548·80	£550·00	0·9978
Balances b/d	£43·90	£44·00	0·9978				

NOTES

1. The debit entry is for the issues to production.
(STD. = 1000 pieces of "A" at £0·05 and 5000 lengths of "M" at £0·10)

2. The Finished Goods figure is obtained as follows:
460 units × £1·10 (Standard Cost)

= £506, which, multiplied by the Material Cost Ratio, gives the Actual Cost of £504·90

3. The Cost Ratio is $\dfrac{£548·80}{£550} = 0·9978$.

4. The Material Usage Variance is:

	£
Standard Cost of issues	575
Standard Cost of Standard issues	550
	£25 (unfavourable)

5. Again the Finished Goods and Balances (Actual Cost figures) have had to be adjusted.

Note carefully that the debit is for the standard *not* actual usage.

Dr. *Direct Labour Control Account* Cr.

	£ *Actual* £928·40		£ *Actual* £928·40
Cost Ledger Control		Work-in-progress—Labour	

Dr. *Work-in-progress Account—Labour* Cr.

	£ *Actual*	£ *Standard*	*Ratio*		£ *Actual*	£ *Standard*	*Ratio*
Direct Labour Control and Cost Ledger Control				Finished Goods	889·70	920·00	0·9671
				Balances c/d	38·70	40·00	0·9671
	928·40	960·00	0·9671				
	£928·40	£960·00			£928·40	£960·00	
Balances b/d	£38·70	£40·00	0·9671				

NOTES

1. The Labour Cost Ratio is $\dfrac{£928·40}{£960·00} = 0·9671$.

2. Since 480 units have been produced the standard number of hours is 1920, *i.e.* (480 × 4 hours).

The Standard Cost is, therefore, £960 (1920 × £0·50 the standard rate). The Actual Cost is the total wages paid.

3. The Labour Cost Variance is clearly £960·00 − £928·40

$$= £31·60 \text{ (favourable)}.$$

Dr. *Factory Overhead Control Account* Cr.

	£ *Actual* £600·00		£ *Actual* £600·00
Cost Ledger Control		Work-in-progress—Overhead	

Dr. *Work-in-progress Account—Factory Overhead* Cr.

	£ *Actual*	£ *Standard*	*Ratio*		£ *Actual*	£ *Standard*	*Ratio*
Factory Overhead Control	600·00	480·00	1·25	Finished Goods	575·00	460·00	1·25
				Balances c/d	25·00	20·00	1·25
	£600·00	£480·00			£600·00	£480·00	
Balances b/d	£25·00	£20·00	1·25				

NOTES

1. An alternative method of charging "Actual Overhead Cost" is to take the actual hours at the standard overhead rate, *i.e.* 1840 × £0·25 = £460. If this method is adopted there will be a balance in the Factory Overhead Control Account for under—or over—absorbed overhead.

2. The difference between Actual hours × Standard rate (applied overhead) £460, and Standard hours × Standard rate (standard overhead) £480, gives the favourable Overhead Efficiency Variance (£20).

Dr.   *Finished Goods Account*   Cr.

	£ Actual	£ Standard	Ratio		£ Actual	£ Standard	Ratio
Work-in-progress A/cs:				Cost of Sales A/c and Cost Ledger Control	1712·70	1640·00	1·0443
Material	504·90	506·00	0·9978	Balances c/d	256·90	246·00	
Labour	889·70	920·00	0·9671				
Overheads	575·00	460·00	1·2500				
	£1969·60	£1886·00	1·0443		£1969·60	£1886·00	
Balances b/d	£256·90	£246·00	1·0443				

NOTES

1. All the debit entries are transfers from the Work-in-progress Accounts.
2. The Cost Ratio is found by the following:

$$\frac{£1969·60}{£1886·00} = 1·0443.$$

Dr.   *Cost of Sales Account*   Cr.

	Actual
Finished Goods A/c	£1712·70

Dr.   *Cost Ledger Control Account*   Cr.

	£ Actual	£ Standard	Ratio		£ Actual	£ Standard	Ratio
Stores Control	—	575·00		Stores Control	450·00	450·00	
Finished Goods	—	1640·00		" "	514·00	560·00	
Balances c/d	2492·40	785·00		Work-in-progress A/c—Material	—	550·00	
				Work-in-progress A/c—Labour	—	960·00	
				Work-in-progress A/c—Overhead	—	480·00	
				Direct Labour Control A/c	928·40		
				Factory Overhead Control A/c	600·00		
	£2492·40	£3000·00			£2492·40	£3000·00	
				Balances b/d	£2492·40	£785·00	

NOTES

1. The procedure for Actual Costs is as already described for Current Standards, *i.e.* any transactions which originate in the financial accounts will have to have a debit or credit in the Cost Ledger Control Account as well as a corresponding entry in another account, *e.g.* Stores Control Account. In effect, therefore, the Cost Ledger Control Account is used to make the Cost Ledger self-contained.

2. The account serves a similar purpose for Standard Costs. For integrated accounting, when Creditors and Debtors Control Accounts are used, there will be no need for a Cost Ledger Control Account to "balance" Actual Costs. One will still be required for Standard Costs. The name usually given to this account when it contains Standard Costs only is the "Standard Cost Clearing Accounts."

Trial Balance

	Dr. £ Actual	Cr. £ Actual	Dr. £ Standard	Cr. £ Standard
Stores Control A/c	415·20		435·00	
Work-in-progress A/cs:				
Material	43·90		44·00	
Labour	38·70		40·00	
Overhead	25·00		20·00	
Finished Goods	256·90		246·00	
Cost of Sales	1712·70			
Cost Ledger Control		2492·40		785·00
	£2492·40	£2492·40	£785·00	£785·00

FURTHER VARIANCE CALCULATIONS FOR THE O.M. CO. LTD., PROBLEM

The Material Price Variance may be found from the Stores Control Account (£26·20). Alternatively, it may be found by multiplying the price ratio deducted from 1 by the Standard Cost of the actual issues, *i.e.* (1·0000 − 0·9545) × £575 = £26·16. The slight discrepancy is brought about by the fact that the ratio has been left at five figures. Taken further, this will reduce the difference between 1·0000 and the price ratio which, in turn, will account for the £0·04. The variance is favourable.

Material Usage Variance

This variance may be obtained from the accounts. It is the Standard Cost for Actual usage, £575, minus the Standard Cost for Standard usage, £550, to give a variance of £25.

The Material Usage Ratio can be found by the formula

$$\frac{\text{Standard Cost of Material Used}}{\text{Standard Cost of Material for Actual Production}}$$

$$i.e. \ \frac{£575}{550} = 1·0455$$

Using this ratio, the Material Usage Variance may be found:

$$(1·0455 − 1·000) × £550 \ (\text{Standard Cost})$$
$$= £25 \ (\text{unfavourable}).$$

Labour Rate Variance

A Labour Rate Ratio may be calculated as follows:

$$\frac{\text{Actual Rate per hour}}{\text{Standard Rate per hour}}$$

Using the information given in the Question, the ratio may be found:

$$\frac{£0·51}{£0·50} = 1·020$$

If the difference between the ratio and 1·0000 is multiplied by the standard labour cost the Labour Rate Variance may normally be found. In the particular problem being dealt with, only 840 hours were at the higher rate, so it is necessary to adjust the apparent variance to allow for this fact. The calculation 0·020 × £960 results in an unfavourable variance of £19·20, which would be correct if all the hours had been paid for at the £0·51 rate.

The adjustment may be made by dividing the variance by the standard hours and multiplying by the actual hours for which the higher rate was paid,

$$i.e. \ \frac{£19·20 \times 840}{1920} = \underline{\underline{£8·40}} \text{ (unfavourable).}$$

Labour Efficiency Variance

The calculation of the Labour Efficiency Ratio presents no difficulty:

$$\frac{\text{Actual Direct Labour Hours}}{\text{Standard Direct Labour Hours for Actual Production}}$$

$$\frac{1840}{1920} = 0·9583.$$

Again, the difference between the ratio and 1·0000 is multiplied by the standard labour cost, *i.e.* 0·0417 × £960 = £40 (approx.) (favourable).

NOTE.—The Efficiency Ratio shown above is obtained by dividing actual hours by standard. This is all very well for portraying a change in cost, but is not accurate for showing a change in efficiency. Accordingly, to calculate a *true* Efficiency Ratio it will be necessary to divide standard hours by actual hours, *i.e.* 1920 ÷ 1840.

As shown earlier, the Labour Cost Variance is £31·60 (favourable). Obviously, in attempting to arrive at this figure from the rate and efficiency variance there will be a discrepancy, but this is to be expected, for the use of ratios implies a certain loss of accuracy. The use of seven- or eight-figure ratios which would give greater accuracy is not normally justified. When a ratio is calculated to cover the material prices of different classes of materials, or the same classes even, there is in effect, an "averaging" of the prices paid, the ratio showing what has happened—average prices have been lower or higher than standard prices—over a period of time. This, in itself, introduces a loss of accuracy, which no subsequent refinements are likely to overcome.

Overhead Cost Variance

This may be found as follows:

(1·25 − 1·00) × £480 (Standard Overhead for Actual Production)
$$= \underline{\underline{£120}} \text{ (unfavourable).}$$

Overhead Budget Variance

This may be found directly from the question, *i.e.* £600 − £500
$$= \underline{\underline{£100}} \text{ (unfavourable).}$$

Overhead Efficiency Variance

The Overhead Efficiency Ratio is found as follows:

$$\frac{\text{Actual}}{\text{Hours}} \times \frac{\text{Standard}}{\text{Rate}} \div \frac{\text{Standard}}{\text{Hours}} \times \frac{\text{Standard}}{\text{Rate}}$$

$$= \frac{£460}{£408} = 0.9583.$$

NOTE.—See Labour Efficiency Ratio for alternative method of calculating the Overhead Efficiency Ratio.

The variance is $(1.0000 - 0.9583) \times £480 = \underline{£20 \text{ (approx.)}}$ (favourable).

Again there is a discrepancy; if, however, 0.0416666 is used (instead of 0.0417) the result will be the £20.

NOTE.—The remarks made in connection with the Labour Efficiency Ratio apply here. That is, to obtain a true measure of change in efficiency it will be necessary to divide Standard by Actual.

Overhead Volume Variance

The Overhead Volume Ratio may be found by the following formula:

$$\frac{\text{Actual Direct Labour Hours}}{\text{Budgeted Direct Labour Hours}}$$

$$= \frac{1840}{2000} = 0.9200$$

Clearly the Volume Variance may be obtained by calculations similar to those shown above. Thus:

$$(1.000 - 0.9200) \times \text{Budgeted Overhead } £500$$
$$= 0.08 \times £500$$
$$= \underline{£40 \text{ (unfavourable)}}$$

OBSERVATIONS ON VARIANCES AND BASIC STANDARDS

That variances from Basic Standards will be of limited value for cost control was noticed at the beginning of this chapter. For this reason the variances in terms of £ are not always calculated; instead, the ratios or percentages are shown, these indicating to management the upward or downward trend of efficiency, rates and prices and the extent of the changes. Variances from Current Standards may be small in size and, accordingly, call for no serious thought. Taken over a long period —say four or five years—they may be of significance, yet with Current Standards all but the final year's figures will have been written off. When a Basic Standard Costing system is used long-term changes will be apparent, and the reasons for them may be equally apparent. Any variations in the profits earned over a long period may be explained from the ratios or percentages. Current Standard Variances will show why the *present* profits are not in accordance with budgeted plans.

In the example given, when a ratio is above 1·0000 this means that the Standard Cost has been exceeded. Thus the ratio 1·0455 for material usage indicates that there was a 4·55% increase in usage (above Standard) for the production actually achieved. A ratio of less than unity will usually indicate that less than the Basic Standard Cost has been expended.* In this connection, however, care should be exercised when dealing with efficiency ratios. With increased efficiency (Actual greater than Standard) the true efficiency ratio will be above 1·0000, yet the Actual Cost will be less than Standard Cost.

The Question answered above portrayed a system which is much simpler than any likely to be found in practice. Even with this much simplified problem though, the student will appreciate that the calculation of the ratios and a full understanding of their nature are attended with difficulties and are strong objections against the use of Basic Standard Costs. Moreover, the fact that there are many different ways adopted for calculating the ratios and for recording the information in the books of account makes a clear understanding more difficult. The illustrations given above are intended merely to outline the principles, and not to explain the different practices that may be followed.

EXAMINATION QUESTIONS

1. (a) Who should participate, and what part should each play, in setting standards?

    (b) For a mechanised process requiring a group of differently graded operatives tabulate possible reasons for deviations from the labour standard. Show how these deviations are differently treated when setting the standard according to whether (i) perfect, or (ii) attainable performance is the aim.

                                                                      (*I.C.W.A.*)

2. What do you understand by a flexible budget?

What degree of flexibility applies to the following:

    (a) shop supplies;
    (b) indirect labour;
    (c) repairs to plant and machinery;
    (d) electrical power?

Write a short note on each of the above, relative to

    (i) a short period of 1–3 months;
    (ii) a long period of 12 months.

                                                                      (*I.C.W.A.*)

3. What are the essential differences between budgeting and forecasting? Illustrate their relationship by examples from one or more industries.

* An exception is the Overhead Volume Variance. Actual hours *less* than standard hours means that the variance is *unfavourable*.

CHAPTER 12

CONTROL OF STORES USING ACTUAL COSTS

THERE should be effective control of all receipts and issues of materials and parts kept in a Stores. This control, as far as possible, should be achieved automatically as part of a routine system.

It will be obvious that the initial planning of a system is of the utmost importance. The stages involved, and possible procedure, may be summarised:

1. Initiation of Purchase Order. This is done by—

   (a) Purchase Requisition from Stores, or Production Planning (when a Schedule programme is followed), or
   (b) Purchase Requisition from the department requiring material not normally stocked.

2. Preparation and issue to Supplier of Purchase Order.
3. Receipt of materials into Stores. The recording involved is:

   (a) Entries on Goods Inwards Sheet or Note.
   (b) After inspection, where necessary, the preparation of a Returned to Supplier Form or Rejection Report which is sent to the Purchasing Department so that arrangements can be made for the return of the materials to the Supplier.

4. Details of materials received are entered on Bin Cards held in the Stores and/or on the Stores Record in the Material Control Office. This is done from the Stores copy of the Goods Inwards Sheet.
5. Invoice received from Supplier and passed for payment by the Purchasing Officer.

   Before being certified, "in order for payment," the invoice is checked—quantities, prices, etc.—by reference to a copy of the Purchase Order, already entered up from the Goods Inwards Sheet.

6. Invoice sent to Accounts Department for payment, being used as a medium for entering up the Stores Ledger.

ADMINISTRATION OF STORES

The principal departments concerned with the Stores and Stores Records are:

(a) Material Control * Department.

* The term "material control" is also used to describe the planned flow of materials in a factory.

131

(*b*) Purchasing Department.

(*c*) Accounts or Costing Department.

The functions of these, so far as they affect storekeeping, are now discussed.

MATERIAL CONTROL DEPARTMENT

A modern practice, which recognises the importance of Stores control, is the creation of an executive position to cover all the responsibilities which arise from the usage, in production, of large quantities of materials. The title is, appropriately, that of Material Controller. Often the responsibilities of this executive extend to being in charge of the administration of the Stores, the section responsible for initiation of Purchase Requisitions (which may be done in the Stores or in a Material Control Office), and the Purchasing Department. In some organisations, however, the Material Controller may be nothing more than a Stores Manager, being in a junior capacity under the Purchasing Officer.

As will be apparent, irrespective of the exact extent of the Material Controller's duties he will normally be held responsible for the execution of the policy of the business as regards the extent to which stocks are to be carried. If the stock of each material is to be kept to an absolute minimum, without production stoppages, then a systematic procedure will be essential. Much of the skill of carrying minimum stocks may be regarded as the initiation of the Purchase Requisition at the correct time. If this is sent to the Purchasing Department too early, excess stocks may result; if too late, there may be a hold-up in production owing to a shortage of the material concerned. Obviously, a routine which enables Purchase Requisitions to be completed at the right time is essential: this can now be examined.

Initiation of Purchase Requisition

As already indicated, the Purchase Requisition may be initiated by the Stores or by a Material Control Office—depending on the particular organisational pattern adopted. In addition, materials and parts not normally held in stock may be requested, on a Purchase Requisition, by Heads of Departments, *e.g.* Maintenance materials may be requisitioned by the Maintenance Engineer. This second method involves authorisation of the purchase by, say, the Works Manager, although for small purchases the Maintenance Engineer will normally have the necessary authority. If a Maintenance Stores, quite separate from the Production Materials Stores, is considered necessary, records will normally have to be kept as for ordinary storekeeping, *i.e.* Bin Cards and Stores Ledger. The Production Planning Department may also be concerned with requisitioning. An outline of the normal procedure will now be covered.

The two principal methods used to enable Purchase Requisitions to be initiated are as follows:

1. *By schedule.*—Production requirements of materials are estimated and a "provisional schedule" drawn up. Possibly orders are placed on suppliers with a provisional delivery date stated. Later, when it is more apparent that the estimated materials *will* be required, a "frozen schedule" comes into operation. The delivery date then becomes quite positive and the supplier is notified to that effect. The system can be varied, of course, to suit the particular business concerned. What is essential is that there is a definite programme of production of a standardised product—usually on a large scale. The Production Planning Department will often be responsible for notifying the Purchasing Department of schedule requirements.

2. *By the minimum–maximum method.*—From a practical point of view this method has a wider application than the Schedule system, and is, therefore, probably of greater importance.

This second method is now examined.

Minimum, maximum and re-order levels

For each kind of raw material part or component it is possible to estimate a "maximum," and a "minimum," stock level; between these two will lie a level which, in practice, will tend to be the stock carried.

The maximum quantity will be fixed by taking into account such matters as those shown below.

(a) The storage facilities available and the physical nature of the product. Where deterioration takes place or there is danger of obsolescence, or space is limited, other things being equal, the smaller will be the stock carried.

(b) The ordering of economic quantities. An expensive special pattern or tool may be required for the production of a component and, if so, this fact will be reflected in the price quoted by the supplier. The practice usually followed by a manufacturer is to "cover" the special pattern or tool by including its cost in the quotation: obviously the larger the number of units included in a quotation, the smaller will be the share, *per unit*, of the fixed cost of the special pattern or tool. The greater this fixed cost, the larger will tend to be the economic ordering quantity, which, in turn, will be reflected in the maximum stock level.

(c) Possible price fluctuations. There will be a tendency to hold larger stocks when prices are rising or are likely to rise.

(d) The rate of consumption. Where 50 units are likely to meet production requirements for the next ten years there would be no justification for carrying 500 units, even if the ordering of such a quantity would mean some reduction in the initial cost per unit.

(e) Availability of cash to pay for purchases and, later, capital to be locked up in the form of stock. Excess stock carrying implies that the business is not making the most efficient use of its resources: cash should not be "frozen" in this way, especially if there are profitable outlets for its use.

All these factors require to be considered; the best solution of one may conflict with the best solution for another. Thus the storage space which could conveniently be made available, may be sufficient to store only 1000 units of a certain product. Suppose the price to be paid for the 1000 units was £0·50 each, but that if a quantity of 4000 were to be purchased the price would be £0·25 each, then, provided 4000 units would be consumed within a reasonable period, a decision would have to be made which considered these two conflicting circumstances. Possibly a minor re-organisation of the Stores would make available sufficient space to store the 3000 extra units. From this it will be clear that in fixing the maximum stock level no single factor will be considered, but all relevant matters will be taken into account and a compromise adopted. One factor may, needless to say, carry much greater weight than another, depending upon the circumstances; if there is a shortage in the supply of an *essential* material this fact, until the supply position improves, will tend to be the main influence in fixing the maximum stock level of such material. From what has been observed, it should be apparent that a maximum stock level cannot be fixed with any degree of permanency, for when circumstances change the level will probably need revising.

The minimum-stock figure will normally be fixed after due regard has been given to the purchasing time-cycle; that is, the period normally taken to obtain a specified material, counting from the date of placing the purchase order to the expected date of the receipt of the material in the Stores. The reliability of the supplier will have to be considered when arriving at the "normal period," due allowance being made for any likely delay. The rate of consumption is extremely important. In connection with maximum stock it was noted that supplies should not generally be carried for long periods. The minimum stock level, from the viewpoint of consumption, is set to ensure that production is never at a standstill. If average production is maintained and the purchase orders are placed in good time the stocks should not fall below the minimum level. A small margin of safety to cover normal fluctuation in usage, should, of course, be allowed when making the calculations.

In addition to minima and maxima the question of the correct re-order levels should also be given attention. In some cases a re-order level will coincide with the minimum stock level, but this is not always the case. To ensure that the purchase order is initiated in good time a re-order level, which is above minimum level, may be fixed. This is likely to be so when the minimum level is at its lowest possible point, say to cover two weeks' production. Should there be an unexpected increase in the usage rate or an unforeseen delay in delivery, reliance on minimum stock level, to initiate a purchase order, may result in loss of production. To avoid this occurrence, a percentage, the size depending upon the circumstances, will be added to minimum stock level, to arrive at re-order level.

An example of the sort of calculation involved in arriving at the three stock levels, once the relevant details have been considered, can be given thus:

Data Relating to Part No. 400–201. Adjustment Wheel

Purchasing Time Cycle (*i.e.* period covered from date of order to delivery)	=	30 days
Average Daily Rate of Consumption	=	50 units per day
Maximum No. of Units Consumed during a 30-day period	=	2000 units
Minimum No. of Units Consumed during a 30-day period	=	1200 units
Standard Order Size (*i.e.* size of order: fixed after considering such factors as price, transport costs and storage space available)	=	3000 units

The above information may be obtained from the stock records, or be estimated by making trial production runs and referring to relevant production records. Minimum and Maximum stock levels can be calculated as follows:

Minimum stock level

Largest number of units consumed during a 30-day period	= 2000
Less Average requirements for the Purchasing Time Cycle 30 × 50	= 1500
Minimum level is therefore:	500

Maximum stock level

Largest number of units consumed during a 30-day period	= 2000 (Re-order level) *

* *Re-order level.* Since there is a possibility of 2000 units being consumed within a period of 30 days—which is also the Purchasing Time Cycle—it will be clear that the re-order level is 2000 units. If an ordering point is fixed below 2000 units there will be a danger that stocks will be consumed before a replenishment is received.

Less Minimum consumption for a 30-day period = 1200

$$\underline{800}$$

Add Order to be received (Standard Quantity) = 3000

$$\underline{3000}$$

Maximum level is therefore: $\underline{\underline{3800}}$

This method of arriving at the three levels is not to be regarded as the only one used. There are others, some probably less accurate, some more "scientific." The object of showing the method in question is to illustrate the principles involved.

THE PURCHASING DEPARTMENT

The Purchasing Department is headed by the Purchasing Officer or Buyer. Briefly, his routine work involves responsibility for the following functions:

1. Upon receipt of a Purchase Requisition to understand clearly what materials are required.
2. To be aware of possible sources of raw materials or supplies.
3. From the possible sources to obtain full details and prices of the items covered by the Purchase Requisition. Obviously, for items which are purchased regularly, it will be unnecessary to obtain a quotation for each new request. Instead, quotations may be obtained every few months, or other suitable period.
4. To select the supplier offering the best terms and conditions. Price will not be the only consideration in the choice, for often delivery is more important. However, other things being equal, price should be the deciding factor.
5. To place a Purchase Order with the supplier selected.
6. To obtain acknowledgment of the Purchase Order from the supplier.
7. To ensure that the delivery promise is kept. Normally a "progressing" or "follow-up" system is employed.
8. Upon receipt of the goods to receive a Goods Inwards Sheet from the Receiving Department. Details of quantities received are entered on the copy Purchase Order. This is a duplicate of the one sent to the supplier with the addition of a printed "box," suitably ruled and headed, so that date of receipt, Goods Inwards Sheet number, and quantities may be entered. Later, when the supplier's invoice is received, the price can be checked with the price originally quoted, and the quantities invoiced compared with those shown as having been received, before the invoice is passed for payment.
9. To return goods which are not according to specification or, alternatively, reach some agreement with the supplier on payment.

10. When an invoice is received to check quantities, prices, and other relevant details, then authorise for payment.
11. To send the invoice, duly authorised and showing the account to be charged, to the Accounts Department.

THE ACCOUNTS OR COSTING DEPARTMENT

Payment for the goods is made within a reasonable time of receiving the approved invoice from the Purchasing Department. Details of those items which go into the Stores have to be entered into the Stores Ledger, usually one sheet or card being reserved for each type or grade of material. At the end of each four-weekly accounting period the totals are posted to the Stores Control Account in the Cost Ledger. The invoices are thus the principal source of debit entries in the Stores Ledger and Stores Control Account.

The other key documents are Material Requisitions and Material Return Notes. Each issue from Stores must be authorised by a Material Requisition which has been signed by a responsible official. Similarly, any returns of materials to Stores have to be covered by a Material Return Note. Both are essential for effective control. The Requisitions provide the credits and the Notes the debits for the Stores Ledger and Stores Control Account.

The method for pricing the materials, so that requisitions may be evaluated, is normally taken from the following:

1. Average price

The most usual average adopted is that which, when being calculated, considers the quantities purchased, this being called the "weighted average price." After each new purchase is received the new average price is calculated by the formula:

$$\frac{\text{Stores Ledger Cost Balance of Material}}{\text{Total Units in Stock}}$$

Both the cost balance and the units will include the *new* purchases.

2. First in, first out price (FIFO)

For the purpose of pricing stores it is assumed that the materials received first are issued first. This conforms with what should, in practice, occur, for if the earliest purchases are used before later ones there will be less chance of deterioration. Needless to say, although this relation between actual usage and issue price is desirable, it may not always be achieved.

3. Last in, first out price (LIFO)

In this case the price paid for the last purchase is used until a quantity equal to that purchase has been issued, then the price is changed to the one paid for the most recent purchase. The price charged will tend, when prices are rising, to be equal to current price. Thus as much as possible of actual cost is being charged against production, and profit is kept as realistic as possible. Stock is valued at a low, conservative figure.

If controls are to be effective there must, obviously, be some means of ensuring that book figures and actual figures agree. Unless this is done, there will come a time when the records kept are valueless. A complete physical stocktaking may be accomplished only at considerable expense and, usually, when the producing departments are not operating. An alternative approach, which is now adopted by most progressive concerns, is discussed below.

PHYSICAL STOCKTAKING AND THE PERPETUAL INVENTORY SYSTEM

For a number of reasons it is usual to obtain detailed information on the quantities and values of stocks carried. From a purely financial point-of-view there is the necessity to calculate the values of stocks carried for the Balance Sheet and Profit and Loss Account; to effect insurance covers; to calculate the rate of turnover of particular items and to ensure maximum economy in stock carrying.

Physical stocktaking has many disadvantages. Production may have to come to a standstill and, in addition, great expense may be involved in counting each class of stock, especially where overtime working is involved for a number of days. There are thus the extra expenses of carrying out the stocktaking and, also, the loss in production. The latter should not, however, be over-emphasised, for the period can provide an opportunity for plant and machinery to be overhauled and cleaned.

To avoid *frequent* physical stocktakings the Perpetual Inventory System may be used. This is a method which uses planned procedures and specially designed forms *to show, at any time, the stock on hand,* both as to quantity and value, for each item of material or each part. If a Stores Control Account is maintained in the Factory or Cost Ledger it should be possible to furnish without delay the total value of the stocks carried. The System usually takes the following form:

1. Bin Cards in the Stores which show the volume or number of items on hand. One card is normally kept for each different type or size of material or part.

   Some authorities, it should be noted, consider Bin Cards an unnecessary duplication of the Stores Ledger. There is much to be said for this view and, certainly, there is great difficulty in ensuring that the entries made on the cards are accurate and up to date, especially when the person handling the physical goods also maintains the records. However, the initiation of Purchase Requisitions usually requires that a record is kept in the Stores or in a Material Control Office. For this reason the extra record can be justified.

2. A Stores Ledger with an account for each size or quality of a particular material or part is kept in the Accounts or Costing Department.

3. Control Accounts are maintained in the Factory Ledger. The Stores Control Account will show the value of the stocks held.

4. A number of items of stock are counted, weighed, or gauged daily, and any discrepancies between the physical count and the figures shown by the Bin Cards and Stores Ledger are investigated. Some differences may be due to clerical errors, others to normal causes (losses in cutting or breaking bulk), whereas some may be a result of inefficient storekeeping (wrong quantities issued, wastage and breakage, pilfering, and loss of items through wrong labelling or location).

The differences are written off, or brought on to, the records. Forms suitably ruled and put into pad form can be used both for the actual count and for adjusting the Bin Card, Stores Ledger, and Factory Ledger. The counting can be done by Stores auditors, and any discrepancies, once investigated, should be brought to the attention of the official in charge of the Stores and appropriate records, who can then authorise the adjustments in the records to be made.

CONTINUOUS STOCKTAKING

Wherever possible, each item of stock should be counted a number of times—generally speaking, at least twice—each year, in addition to the annual physical stocktaking. The number of items of stock can be divided by the number of working days to give an average daily count. Provided the items do not differ considerably, as regards ease of counting, the average daily count should indicate the number of staff required to carry out the Continuous Stocktaking. To minimise the work, items may be counted when the stock is low. The "requests" for stocktaking, by preparation of the form already mentioned for stock checking, may be carried out by the appropriate clerk who raises the Purchase Requisition; that is, when the stock is at re-order level.

Besides furnishing accurate records of stocks, which facilitates the preparation of monthly profit and loss statements, Continuous Stocktaking can claim the following advantages:

1. By adopting a system of checking items without notice an efficient control over stocks is exercised. Storekeepers will tend to take great care, and pilfering should be kept to a minimum.

2. Because stocks are counted by degrees, more time can be spent, and greater accuracy result, than when a complete physical stocktaking is carried out.

3. Incipient defects in the Stores system can be rectified before much damage through loss or irregular practices has occurred.

4. Slow-moving stocks can be noted and, where necessary, action taken to prevent excessive accumulation of stocks. Possible action may be the amendment of re-order levels or the marking of the material requisitions to the effect that the oldest stock must be issued first, thus reducing the danger of deterioration.

POSSIBLE WEAKNESSES OF STORES CONTROL WITH ACTUAL COSTS

The above description, though brief, should serve to illustrate that purchasing, receiving, issuing, and accounting for Stores can be done in a systematic manner, thus achieving a high degree of control. Not to be forgotten, however, are the following possible weaknesses of any system which adopts Actual Costs:

1. Not all systems using Actual Costs achieve the degree of efficiency suggested above.

   Often purchasing, receiving, and issuing are accomplished in a haphazard fashion. There may be no Perpetual Inventory and Continuous Stocktaking System, with the result that book figures and actual physical figures rarely agree. Too frequently a proper Stores organisation is neglected, the emphasis being on organising the shop-floor activities. The responsibility for the Stores is often delegated to a production foreman, on a part-time basis, with the result that, in the case of dispute, the producing department gets its own way. To be able to carry out his work effectively the storekeeper should have similar status to a foreman and be directly responsible to the Material Controller, Purchasing Officer, or Accountant.

2. Before Standard Costs are set *all* functions are examined and, where necessary improved, thus obtaining maximum efficiency. Even if a system recording Actual Costs is reasonably efficient it can usually be made more efficient by careful examination of all relevant functions.

3. There is no attempt to segregate, as part of an "automatic" process, excess usage from normal usage, thus controlling the quantities of materials used.

4. The prices paid are accepted as being normal and quite outside the control of anyone employed by the business concerned.

5. There is a great deal of clerical work required to calculate prices, and when actual prices are used (LIFO or FIFO) there may be wide variations in unit costs, between identical products, made within hours of each other.

Standard costing is an integral part of modern, planned management. All methods and routines fit in with, and are co-ordinated with, other aspects of production planning and control. It is for this reason and the disadvantages of Actual Costs, listed above, that a system of control which uses Standard Costs is to be preferred. This is covered in the next chapter.

EXAMINATION QUESTIONS

1. Outline the procedure you recommend to avoid the accumulation of obsolete items of stock. Indicate how the cost accounts are affected by the various arrangements you advocate.

(I.C.W.A.)

2. What factors should be taken into consideration in fixing maximum and minimum stock levels for raw materials? In what circumstances, and at what periods would you suggest a revision of the levels? How are ordering quantities affected (if at all) by these levels?

(I.C.W.A.)

3. What do you understand by the term "Material Control"? Comment fully on this function, and indicate its importance in Cost Control.

(I.C.W.A.)

4. Discrepancies are frequently found between actual stocks and book stocks in a certain factory.

Itemise the possible causes of these discrepancies from receipt of goods to despatch of product. Indicate the safeguards you would recommend at each stage.

(I.C.W.A.)

5. On examining the stores control of a manufacturing business you discover that:

    (*a*) foremen often quote wrong job numbers on material requisitions causing incorrect charges to the jobs;

    (*b*) the issue of materials in excess of quantities needed for a job is permitted provided a requisition is received.

Outline a system which would overcome these irregularities.

(I.C.W.A.)

6. In dealing with material costs, outline the advantages and disadvantages of using Standard Cost methods.

(I.C.W.A.)

7. Design a material issue requisition suitable for use in a general stores. Outline briefly the procedure for authorising these documents.

(I.C.W.A.)

8. Your managing director wishes to reduce the investment in stocks and stores as disclosed by a recent Balance Sheet and asks you to investigate and report. List the type of information you would submit and the factors to which you would draw attention.

(I.C.W.A.)

9. Describe: (a) perpetual inventory, and (b) continuous stocktaking. State the relationship between the two and the advantages and disadvantages of the latter.

(I.C.W.A.)

10. List the steps whereby:
(a) a supplier's invoice is passed for payment;
(b) an invoice to a customer follows an instruction to the despatch department to send goods.

(I.C.W.A.)

11. (a) Distinguish between slow-moving, dormant and obsolete stocks.
(b) What principles would you follow in pricing these stocks for stock-taking purposes?
(c) What practical steps should be taken to minimise the losses and costs arising from the existence of these stocks?

(I.C.W.A.)

12. (a) Within the context of materials accounting, enumerate the steps which have to be taken to install variance analysis procedure.
(b) In a manufacturing process the following standards apply:

Standard price: Raw material A   £1 per lb.
          ,,   ,,   B   £5 ,, ,,
Standard mix: 75% A; 25% B (by weight).
Standard yield (weight of product as percentage of weight of raw materials): 90%.

In a period, the actual costs, usages, and output were as follows:

Used: 4,400 lbs. A, costing £4,650.
      1,600 ,, B, ,,   £7,850.
Output: 5,670 lbs. of products.
The budgeted output for the period was 7,200 lbs.

Prepare an operating statement, showing how the material cost variance is built up, and give activity and yield percentages.

(I.C.W.A.)

13. Outline the effects of rising prices in relation to pricing of issues, and stock valuation.

(I.C.W.A.)

14. (a) Design a stock record card.
(b) Show by means of a chart how information relating to materials flows from the sales office, through production control, stock control, stores, accounts department, and purchasing office to a supplier of raw materials (or components). (Assume that products are made after receipt of a customer's order from raw materials and components which are stocked.)

(I.C.W.A.)

CHAPTER 13

CONTROL OF STORES USING STANDARD COSTS

THE previous chapter briefly covered the control of Stores when Actual Costs are adopted. Only an outline of the usual procedures was given, and examples of the forms used were deliberately omitted. The object was to show the principles involved, without unnecessary detail. In this chapter the differences between the system for Actual Costs and the one for Standard Costs will be explained.

Much of what has already been said in the previous chapter will also apply to a system for Standard Costs. This system, in connection with the control of materials, will be discussed under the following headings:

1. Organisation of the Stores, Purchasing, and Costing (or Accounts) Departments.
2. Setting of Standard Costs for Materials.

   (a) Quantities of Direct Materials.
   (b) Prices of Direct Materials.

3. Procedures for Pricing Invoices, Material Requisitions, and other forms and isolation of variances.
4. Ensuring that Book Stocks and Actual Stocks agree and valuation of stocks.

These can now be examined.

ORGANISATION

Efficient organisation of *all* functions concerned with purchasing and using materials is essential. One of the first essentials of control is to define the precise responsibilities of each executive, departmental manager, foreman, or supervisor. Procedures are formulated and put into written, specific form. Everyone concerned is notified, and the necessary records and forms are drafted. Once the framework has been developed, the data accumulated by the accountant provide the basis of the control.

ORGANISATION OF THE STORES

Lay-out of the Stores should receive attention before any attempt is made to set Standard Costs. The nature of the materials and other

143

goods to be stored, including the sizes or dimensions, and quantities to be normally carried, will influence any decisions made. The bins, racks, and shelves should be the ones most suitable for the items to be stored; haphazard location must be avoided. Considerations involved in selecting the most suitable places for storing the various items are:

1. Quantity and weight of item.
2. Frequency of use.
3. Difficulty of handling.
4. Special problems inherent in the material, *e.g.*

    (*a*) Location of highly inflammable materials must take account of necessary safety measures.
    (*b*) Some materials may perish quickly.
    (*c*) Valuable materials have to be kept in a place of safety.

5. Accessibility.

In particular, the aisles should be so arranged that handling costs are kept to a minimum. The fullest use has to be made of handling equipment such as conveyors, fork-lift trucks, and similar vehicles.

Receiving materials

When materials are received their description should immediately be entered on a Goods Inwards Sheet. They are then inspected and, if found to be according to specification, transferred to the producing department—covered by Requisition—or to the appropriate rack or bin. When there is danger of deterioration the use of coloured tags can show which batch should be used first.

In the Receiving Section of the Stores the following matters should be given attention:

1. Unloading and handling equipment should be efficient.
2. Unnecessary handling has to be avoided; in particular—

    (*a*) If two or more men are manually moving materials, the possibility of substituting a machine must be examined.
    (*b*) Inspection, if possible, should be performed on the spot, thus avoiding excessive movement of materials.
    (*c*) Materials should not be packed into containers only to be unpacked and put into other containers when being stored away.

3. Production hold-ups have to be avoided.

Material which is urgently required by producing departments should, upon being received, be given priority treatment, and not be delayed by having it waiting its turn for inspection and booking-in. The actual storing of the materials should also receive careful consideration. The most important factors affecting location have already been mentioned.

So that items, once stored, can be readily located, it is necessary to focus attention on a number of important points:

1. Each size or grade of a material should be booked on a Bin Card.
2. All Bin Cards should be given a suitable number, and the same number should appear on the bin, rack, or shelf.
3. Each size or grade of material should be given a code number, symbol, or other mark of identification.
4. All materials should be labelled or a named diagram, on the bin, should clearly illustrate what item is being stored in that particular bin.
5. So that no confusion can possibly arise, the numbering of the bins should follow a logical sequence.
6. A map or other diagrammatic representation should be used to indicate clearly how the Stores is laid out and where materials are to be located. Often an index by materials' names and/or codes will be helpful.

Coding of materials

The use of code numbers, letters, or symbols will usually result in more efficient storekeeping. The advantages claimed for coding are as follows:

1. Economy of space in writing out requisitions, reports, and other forms.
2. Less time is required to complete requisitions, etc.
3. The true identity of materials is hidden when secrecy is necessary.
4. Ambiguity is avoided, for the symbol used denotes one thing only and no other; this allows less opportunity for error to occur in the issue of materials, and in pricing.
5. Management accounting, especially punched card accounting and computers, requires numbers to be employed.

There are disadvantages, the chief being the danger of transposition when figures are used and the fact that employees have to be trained to recognise the codes.

Clearly the choice of symbol requires great care. Its features must be such that there is no danger of confusion one with another and, moreover, should clearly indicate the class of materials to which the code relates. Flexibility of a system of coding is essential, and this may be obtained by the use of hyphens or decimal points. If possible, the symbols adopted should be an aid to memory, thus requiring shorter training time for new employees and also reducing the possibility of error.

There is a number of systems in use, and these may be summarised as follows:

1. *Numerical.*—Numbers are used to identify, and may be whole numbers or decimals. They are useful for identifying components, *e.g.* Part No. 102-20 may show that the part is No. 20 for product No. 102.
2. *Alphabetical.*—Each material is suggested by the use of letters.
3. *Mnemonic.*—This is similar to the alphabetical symbol. The difference is that the letter, or letters, used can be clearly identified with the particular material, *e.g.* SS may mean Stainless Steel.
4. *Signals, Colours, or Signs.*—These may be useful for classifying materials into broad divisions. Different types of steel may be indicated by different colours. Bins can display the colours, thus aiding identification.
5. *Combination* of two or more of the others.

Generally, all materials have to be classified into main groups, then sub-groups, and finally further subdivided according to characteristic, such as grade or size. "Steel" may be a main group, "mild steel" a secondary group, "steel sheet" a sub-group, and the thickness the characteristic. There is no hard-and-fast rule that can be followed when choosing the most suitable code: the requirements of the business will determine the one to use. If few materials are stored, then a simple classification may be possible. When a multitude of items, of various types, are held, a more complex system will be necessary. For most modern concerns, manufacturing a number of products, a combination of the mnemonic and numerical methods may be necessary, a decimal system being used when the number of items in each class is large.

The issue of materials

Issues from Stores should be covered by duly authorised Material Requisitions or, where a large number of different materials are covered by the one form, by Material Specifications. In a small business the form may be signed by a foreman, whereas in a large concern it will be authorised at the time of issue by the Production Planning Department.

For a *complete* standard costing system (Accounting Method II) there is a need to have two different types of Requisition, viz.:

1. Standard Material Requisition; which covers standard quantities for the number of products to be made.
2. Excess Material Requisition, which covers any extra materials, *i.e.* the standard usage is exceeded. This should be of a distinctive colour, thus clearly distinguishing it from the Standard Material Requisition.

Examples of the rulings for the requisitions are given in Figs. 13, 14, and 15, though these will, of course, be varied to meet the specific needs of the business concerned.

STANDARD MATERIAL REQUISITION. No.............

Date............ Prod. Order No.............

Part No..................... No. Off.........

Code	Material Description	Qty (Std.)	Unit price (Std.)	Value £

Issued (Stores) .... Authorised ....

Rec'd by (Worker) .... Stores Ledger Folio.............

FIG. 13.—*Standard Material Requisition*

NOTES

1. The form will be partially completed by the Production Planning Department at the same time as the Production Order.
2. Upon issue of the materials the form is signed by the worker and given to a storekeeper.
3. The storekeeper initials the form and it then goes to the Stores clerk for details to be entered on the Bin Card.
4. It is finally sent to the Costing Department, where it is priced, valued, and entered in the Stores Ledger. All the requisitions are then summarised and a total posted to the Stores Control Account.

The fourth stage (Note (4)) can be much simplified by the elimination, from the form, of the unit price and value. Instead, quantities only are entered in the Stores Ledger, and these quantities are then summarised on a Materials Issued Analysis Sheet. At the end of each month the quantities can be multiplied by the standard price to give a total value for issues made. A posting can then be made to the Stores Control Account in the Factory Ledger.

An example of a requisition which covers quantities only is shown in Fig. 14.

STANDARD MATERIAL REQUISITION. No.............

Date............   **Prod. Order No.**.............

                        Part No......................   **No. Off**.........

Code	Material Description	Quantity (Std.)

Issued (Stores) ....   **Authorised** ....

Rec'd by (Worker) ....   **Stores Ledger Folio** ....

FIG. 14.—*Standard Material Requisition* (*Alternative*)

NOTES

1. Because the price and value columns are omitted there can be a great saving in time and effort brought about because:

   (a) Prices do not have to be entered on the requisitions.
   (b) Values (prices × quantities) do not have to be calculated.
   (c) Values of issues do not have to be entered in the Stores Ledger or on a Materials Issued Analysis Sheet to arrive at the totals for the month.

2. Offsetting the reduction in work are the following:

   (a) Calculation of values, from a Materials Issued Analysis Sheet for month-end posting to Stores Control Account and, from balances (quantities) in the Stores Ledger, is necessary.
   (b) Values must be entered in the Stores Ledger each month.

Despite the disadvantages mentioned in Note 2, the savings can be quite considerable. There may be hundreds, or even thousands, of issues made in one month, and avoiding a calculation for each one cannot but result in a saving. Care must be taken, however, to "stagger" the calculations in the Stores Ledger. In some circumstances it may be necessary to sectionalise the Ledger and programme the calculations so that they do not all have to be packed into a few hectic days at the end of each month.

SPECIAL NOTE.—As already stated, in connection with the Accounting for Standard Costs, Accounting Method I keeps the materials at Actual Costs. The variances, both for price and usage, are calculated when an issue is made. Accordingly, much of what has been said will not apply to Accounting Method I. Issues in this case are made at Actual prices, thus crediting Stores Control and debiting Work-in-progress, at Actual Cost. The requisitions will usually, therefore, have to be priced at Actual prices. "Standard" and "Excess" Requisitions may still be adopted, thus facilitating the calculation of usage variances. An example of an Excess Material Requisition may take the form shown in Fig. 15.

EXCESS MATERIAL REQUISITION. No............				Variance Calculation (unfavourable)
Date............ **Prod. Order No.**				
Part No. .... **No. Off.**				
Code	Material	Quantity	Price (Std.)	Value £
				£

Issued (Stores) .... **Authorised** ....

Rec'd by (Worker) .... **Stores Ledger Folio**...........................

                                             Variance Analysis Sheet Folio............

Reasons for Excess ....
....

FIG. 15.—*Excess Material Requisition*

NOTES

1. Only when the foreman is fully satisfied that the extra materials are warranted should he authorise the issue.

2. The reasons for requiring the extra materials should be stated.

3. Unfavourable variances can be calculated by reference to the Excess Materia Requisitions. These variances can then be summarised to arrive at total variances for each day, week, month, or other period.

When materials are returned to Stores, for whatever cause, they should be covered by a Material Return Note. Once again it will be necessary for the reason for the action to be clearly stated on the form. In particular, it will be necessary to distinguish between materials that remain in their original form and those which have changed or are not according to the required specification. Examples of the latter are those materials which have been worked upon and have then been rejected or those which are defective, making them unsuitable for the product being manufactured.

	MATERIAL RETURN NOTE. No............			
Date............	Prod. Order No.............			
	Part No......................		No. Off.........	
Code	Material	Quantity	Unit price	Value £
				£

Rec'd by (Stores) ....   Authorised (Foreman) ....

                                     Variance Analysis Folio ....

Returned by (Worker) ....   Stores Ledger Folio ....

Fig. 16.—*Material Return Note*

NOTES

1. If materials are returned because they were issued for a Production Order which has now been cancelled, then the Material Return Note acts as a cancellation of the original Standard Material Requisition. There is thus no direct material charge made.

2. When material has been spoilt the cost can be charged to the good products simply by showing the *actual* number of good units produced and *total* cost. This is done for normal wastage only.

3. As an alternative to (2) the overhead cost can be increased by the cost of the spoilt material.

4. Scrap, resulting from normal production, may be sold and the value used to reduce the direct cost of specific products or to reduce overhead costs.

If materials are returned because there has been a saving in usage, then a favourable variance will result. In any other circumstances, such as when material is spoilt, the procedure followed will depend upon the reason for the return. Generally speaking, either the direct production costs will be increased or the cost will be charged to an appropriate standing-order account.

When the expected production is achieved and there is scrap left (short-ends or shavings), depending upon the value involved, the proceeds from selling the scrap may be credited against the direct material cost or to a standing-order account opened for that purpose, thus reducing the manufacturing overhead costs.

One form only (the Material Return Note) may be used to cover all returns, the various reasons being stated so that a full analysis can be made. Alternatively, a number of different forms may be introduced. There may be a Scrap Return Note, a Spoiled Material Return Note, and so on. Clearly, additional forms should be introduced only if warranted by increased efficiency.

A ruling for the Material Return Note is given in Fig. 16.

Completion of Purchase Requisition *

The methods already described for use with Actual Costs, will apply for Standard Costs. Use of the method which requires a Purchase Requisition to be completed when a re-order level is reached is likely to give good results. The total cost of running the Stores has to be considered, but this is not the only important matter. Unfortunately, some of the costs are difficult to measure or, if they can be measured, cannot be related to a specific cause. Why an excessive quantity of a certain material is being carried in stock may not be the fault of the Stores at all. Often the Chief Storekeeper works on information given, only to find at a later date that plans have been changed, the reason for the change going right back to the consumer.

As with all service cost centres, the Stores is very much in the hands of the producing cost centres. The service has to be there so that production never comes to a standstill. Accordingly, provided re-order, maximum, and minimum levels are carefully fixed and amended when necessary, although a certain degree of discretion must be exercised, the Storekeeper cannot really be held responsible for many of the under- or over-purchasing mistakes that are bound to arise. In any event, there should be authorisation by some higher-ranking official, such as the Material Controller, who will know of any possible moves to change style of product or policy. The act of countersigning, provided this does not develop into a mere formality, should ensure that, within broad limits, no excessive quantities of materials are being purchased.

* Example shown later, FIG. 18.

One of the main problems likely to arise is the keeping of maximum–minimum and re-order levels at figures which reflect *current* requirements. Any introduction of new products or cancellation of old lines must be promptly related to material requirements and the three levels, shown on the Bin Cards, amended without delay. In short, there has to be a definite liaison between Production Planning and Stores.

To make sure that no unauthorised types of material are carried in the Stores there should be a rule that purchase requisitions for materials, not previously stocked, are not to be initiated unless authorised beforehand by the Production Engineer or other responsible official. It is quite a usual practice to have an Authorised Materials List, which shows the materials which can be stocked; amendments to the list have to be authorised. In this way the most suitable materials are stocked, and no others, thus keeping costs to a minimum.

Conclusion on storekeeping

Inevitably, a certain amount of "overlapping" occurs in the above description, some of the functions not relating to storekeeping alone. This makes investigation into all functions more essential, for, obviously, if the storekeeping is not efficient, other departments will be affected. As stated, the corrective action should be taken before any attempt is made to set the Standard Costs.

ORGANISATION OF PURCHASING DEPARTMENT

The description already given for Actual Costs will cover the procedure necessary for Standard Costs. Once again, the principal difference is likely to be that an improvement in efficiency is deliberately aimed at, before the Standards are set.

Comparison of Budgeted and Actual Costs should indicate the degree of efficiency actually attained. However, it should be remembered, as with storekeeping, that many apparent purchasing inefficiencies may be the result of faulty functioning in other departments. Nevertheless, some attempt at measuring results with costs has to be attempted.

ORGANISATION OF COSTING OR ACCOUNTS DEPARTMENT

So far as control of material receipts and issues is concerned the organisation may be on similar lines to those now to be described. The problems involved are as follows:

1. Materials must have actually been received before payment is made. Obviously this can be done only by having appropriate forms and procedures, and by clearly defining by name the person or persons authorised to "pass" invoices for payment.

2. Adequate control must be maintained over materials in the Stores, and when these are received into, or issued from, the Stores.

3. An accurate record must be kept of all external and internal transactions, both as to quantities and prices.

The Cost Accountant will normally be called upon to design all necessary forms and, after consultation with other executives and general management, to issue written procedures. Some essential forms have already been illustrated earlier in this chapter; other important ones will now be shown.

1. Goods Inwards Sheet

A Goods Inwards Sheet is illustrated in Fig. 17. Instead of a sheet a "Note" may be used one item, or items, appearing on *one* purchase order, being recorded. This has advantages over a sheet containing a

GOODS INWARDS SHEET. No.........					
Received From	Qty or weight	Part No.	Description	Purchase Order No.	Remarks

Rec'd by .... Date ....

Stores Ledger Folio .... Checked by ....

FIG. 17.—*Goods Inwards Sheet*

NOTES

1. All receipts are entered on the Goods Inwards Sheet.

2. The number of copies will vary according to the particular system adopted, but three copies should be adequate.

3. The Purchasing Department compares the details with the Purchase Order and record them, so that, when an invoice is received, the amount charged can be verified as being correct.

4. When Accounting Method II is adopted (raw materials at Standard Cost) the Goods Inwards Sheet is the basic document from which receipts are entered in the Stores Ledger.

mixed lot of items. The Goods Inwards Notes can be sorted into a definite sequence either by Purchase Order number or by types of material. In this way clerical procedure can be speeded up and, if necessary, a number of clerks can work on the Notes, one not being held up by the other. Under some systems a preference is shown for attaching the Goods Inwards Note, duly signed by a storekeeper, to the appropriate invoice, thus providing a further safeguard against paying twice for the one account.

The concern is with quantities only, so the entries in the Stores Ledger can be made without having to wait for an invoice to be sent. Often, with systems using Actual Costs only, discrepancies between Bin Cards and the Stores Ledger arise because the entries in the latter are to be made from an invoice, which has not yet been received, whereas the entries on the Bin Cards have been made from the Goods Inwards Sheets. These are further examples of advantages to be gained from the use of a complete system of Standard Costs.

2. Purchase Requisition (*Fig. 18*)

PURCHASE REQUISITION. No.........				
Date............				
To Purchasing Dept.			From............................Dept.	
Code	Material Description	Quantity	Delivery Required	Remarks
Signed (Storekeeper) .... Authorised (Material Controller)				

FIG. 18.—*Purchase Requisition*

NOTES

1. The Purchase Requisition will normally be completed by the Stores clerk when stocks carried reach the re-order level. It may, however, be used by other departments when indirect materials, not held by the Stores, are required.

2. Additional columns are often provided. There may be a column for the purchase order number and columns for price and value. The latter may be used to show the extent of future purchase commitments—essential for budgeting.

3. The Purchasing Department will order goods only when authorised by a Purchase Requisition.

3. *Returned to Supplier Form* (*known also as Rejection Report*) (*Fig. 19*)

RETURNED TO SUPPLIER FORM				
No............. Date............				
The following materials have today been returned to:				
....				
....				
....				
Code	Description	Unit Price	Value	Reason
Signed (Storekeeper or Inspector)............................				

FIG. 19.—*Returned to Supplier Form* (*or Rejection Report*)

NOTES

1. When materials do not agree with the required specifications or sample this form is completed and the materials are returned to the supplier.

2. Copies are sent to the Purchasing Department and Accounts Department.

3. The original entries on the Goods Inwards Sheet will, by this time, have been entered on the Bin Cards, in the Stores Ledger, and on the Summary used to build up the total for posting to the Stores Control Account. Entries will also have been made on the copy of the purchase order, held in the Purchasing Department.

4. Upon receiving the Returned to Supplier Form, the Purchasing and Accounts Departments will make entries which will cancel those listed in (3).

SETTING OF STANDARD COSTS FOR MATERIALS

The setting of Standard Costs for materials, the procedures for pricing, the isolation of variances, and the control and valuation of stocks are of such importance that they will be given special consideration.

As already stated, the setting of Standard Costs should not be attempted before all functions have been examined and made efficient. Once this has been done there are two problems:

1. Determination of standard quantities.

2. Fixing of standard prices.

STANDARD QUANTITIES

A clear understanding of the product to be manufactured is essential. Once the chemists or engineers have decided the types and qualities of materials which are to go to make the product, these are entered on a Product Specification Sheet which is an analysis, along broad lines, of a product. All the main features are listed.

The next stage is the *detailed* listing of all the materials. This is done on a Standard Material Specification (Fig. 20), which is also known as a Bill of Material.

STANDARD MATERIAL SPECIFICATION. No..........

Description of Product .... **Date............**

....

Part No. ....

Code or Part No.	Material Description	Quantity or No. per Product	Remarks

Prepared by ....
Checked by ....

FIG. 20.—*Material Specification*

NOTES

1. In practice, the Material Specification may be quite long. All assemblies and sub-assemblies, where appropriate, will be shown.

2. The Material Description will be standardised, the most suitable type and quality being selected.

3. The Standard Quantities of material, per product, will be shown. These will be determined by technical experts from past records or by building prototypes and conducting test runs. Included in the quantities will be amounts to cover waste. That this allowance will vary according to the type of Standard Cost being adopted has already been noticed in previous chapters.

4. The Standard Material Specification can be used as an authorisation for the issue of materials. This will be so when all the materials can conveniently be issued together. In some cases the specification will have to be divided into convenient material batches—usually dictated by technical considerations, such as when one process is completed before additional materials, which are required in the second process, are issued. As will be appreciated, a Material Requisition may be "part" of a Material Specification.

Before a particular specification is adopted the cost and profit aspects have to be considered. The technical experts may, in an endeavour to produce a top-grade product, suggest the use of costly materials. Sales considerations and a desire to earn an adequate margin of profit will often require that cheaper grades of materials be used. The individual business has, frequently, to accept the price ruling in the market and has little or no say in its determination. For this reason the accountant should be called upon to evaluate a number of specifications and determine the most profitable one, before a final decision is made.

Once adopted, the Standard Material Specification will not, without special authorisation, be amended. If the quantities have been accurately determined any deviations will mean that the anticipated efficiency is not being realised. Under or excess usage should be made the subject of investigation, for it is only in this way that maximum efficiency is achieved.

STANDARD PRICES

The standard prices for materials should be fixed by the Purchasing and Accounts Departments. The detailed work may be left to the former department, while the latter is held responsible for ensuring that established procedures are recognised when the standard prices are fixed. The prices paid in the past may be inadequate Standards for the future. Accounting procedure followed may, or may not, require that Stores and handling charges be included in price. Anticipated shortages in the Stores, due to normal losses from shrinkage or from cutting, may be covered by inflating the issue price; alternatively, the cost may be included as part of the costs of the Stores (*i.e.* in the overhead costs). All these matters can influence the size of the standard prices.

Costing of products and the valuation of stocks are very much affected by the choice of standard prices. These are the responsibility of the accountant, and he is thus vitally interested in the fixing of fair and reasonable prices. Since the Purchasing Agent is normally asked to explain Material Price Variances, it is inevitable that he, too, should be concerned with the setting of standard prices. The type of Standard being adopted will affect the estimate made. If an Ideal Standard is used the standard prices will tend to be below the actual prices paid. When the standard prices are set it will be assumed that economical quantities are purchased, that orders are placed in good time (avoiding the penalty of high prices for "rush" orders) and that all discounts are taken. Since the reasons for changes in prices cannot always be regarded as the responsibility of the Purchasing Agent, when Ideal Standards are employed, the variances tend to lose much of their usefulness.

With Expected Standards, a number of possible approaches to the setting of standard prices is possible. If large stocks of materials are being carried and, up to the present time, actual prices have been adopted (LIFO or FIFO), then the standard prices may be taken as being those actual prices. On the other hand, when existing stocks are not likely to cover a long period a forecast of future trends is essential. Generally speaking, a period of a year is likely to be quite long enough to cover when forecasting prices. In some circumstances a period of six—or even three—months may be regarded as a quite adequate gap over which an estimate can safely be made. However, because of the large amount of work involved in setting standard prices, for all practical purposes a year is likely to be the most acceptable period. Any interim adjustments can be dealt with by the use of a Price Revision Variance. To avoid fluctuations in material charges to production there is a strong case for using an estimated average price. Even when there are wide fluctuations in actual prices it is possible, provided the average covers anticipated "ups and downs," to introduce a stabilising influence which may in the long run be beneficial to the business. Pricing can be made simpler and more easy to understand by all concerned. The important fact to remember is that the standard prices should be the best possible estimate of what prices are likely to be over a stated period, usually a year.

If Basic Standards are adopted the choice of standard prices is, obviously, not such an important matter. Either Ideal prices or Expected prices may be taken: the essential thing is to have a clear understanding of what *is* being used. The stocks are, of course, valued at Actual Cost which can be—and usually is—taken for all accounting purposes when Basic Standards are adopted.

PROCEDURES FOR PRICING AND ISOLATION OF VARIANCES

The following forms have to be priced as part of the normal accounting routine:

1. Invoices from suppliers.
2. Material Requisitions (or Specifications) and Return Notes.
3. Returned to Supplier Forms.
4. Stock Check Forms.

A routine system, with suitably ruled forms, must be established. The precise way in which it will operate depends upon the circumstances, in particular, the nature of the business involved. Whether Accounting Method I *or* Method II is adopted is of great significance.

ACCOUNTING METHOD I

With Accounting Method I the raw materials are kept at Actual Cost, so the procedure followed, as regards invoices, can follow the lines used for a system using Actual Costs only. When the invoices have been "passed for payment" they are entered in a Purchases Book. Detailed entries in the Stores Ledger are then made. If average prices are used to charge out issues made it will be necessary, after each new receipt is entered in the Stores Ledger, to calculate a new average price.

To facilitate rapid pricing of requisitions and other forms, a Price Book, or Price Sheets, will be found to be quite useful. The materials can be arranged in code number, part number, or alphabetical order. As each requisition, return note, or other form is received, each item on it will have to be priced by reference to the Price Book. The quantities are then multiplied by the prices and the entries made in the Stores Ledger. A Summary is made daily, weekly, and monthly of all issues from, and returns to, Stores so that a posting may be made to the Stores Control Account at the end of the month. The total of balances from the Stores Ledger should, of course, be equal to the total balance on the Stores Control Account.

When stock counts are made the details may be entered on a Stock Check Sheet. Any differences between actual and book figures will have to be valued and the Stores Ledger and Stores Control Account adjusted.

Transfers from the Work-in-progress Accounts are made at Standard Cost: any balances, after considering unfinished work, are variances. These facts have already been covered in the chapters which deal with the procedures for Accounting for Standard Costs. Price variances are not revealed until material is actually used.

ACCOUNTING METHOD II

With the complete system, the price variances are brought to light as soon as an invoice is received. A suitably ruled Purchases Book, an example of which was given earlier, allows the variances to be calculated each day.

The Stores Ledger may record quantities only, thus eliminating a considerable amount of clerical work which would otherwise be required for pricing. Evaluation of the balances is accomplished by multiplying the quantities with the standard prices.

For the Stores Control Account some kind of Summary of issues and receipts will be essential. The Purchases Book will provide the principal debit entries. For the issues and returns of materials a Summary of quantities should be possible. When each Standard Material Requisition or other form is received into the Costing Department it will be entered in the Stores Ledger. A Materials Issued Analysis Sheet of stores showing material code numbers and quantities involved may be compiled and then, at the end of each month, the total quantities of each type of material may be ascertained and priced.

ENSURING THAT BOOK STOCKS AND ACTUAL STOCKS AGREE; VALUATION OF STOCKS

The Perpetual Inventory and Continuous Stocktaking systems have already been described in the previous chapter: with Standard Costs these systems may be regarded as being an indispensable aid to control. Unless actual and book figures coincide, there can be no confidence in the methods used.

Any gains or losses in physical quantities must, of course, be covered in the costs. The reasons for the differences between book figures and the actual count determine the subsequent treatment in the books of account. These discrepancies may be classified into:

1. Those due to clerical or related mistakes. Examples are:

   (a) Issues, receipts or returns not posted.

   (b) Clerical errors in posting (wrong figures or to wrong account).

   (c) Loss of material requisitions or other forms.

2. Faulty handling of the material itself. Examples are:

   (a) Incorrect quantities received into, or issued from, the Stores (i.e. physical quantities different from quantities shown on forms).

   (b) Loss of material, due to one or more of the following reasons—

   Shrinkage (e.g. due to evaporation or seepage).
   Breakage.
   Careless handling causing damage.
   Theft.
   Deterioration.
   Misplacement causing loss (e.g. placing in wrong bin).

Accuracy in counting and recording of the counts when made is absolutely essential. Many errors arise because of incorrect identification of materials. Materials with similar names are confused and as a result the physical quantities relating to other materials are entered on the Stock Check Sheet. Obviously, there can be little chance of agreement between actual and book figures if different species are being compared. As already indicated, the use of codes or symbols will make identification more certain. An example of a Stock Check Sheet is given in Fig. 21.

Before any action is taken with losses or gains, it will be essential to investigate and find out why they have occurred. Many differences may, of course, be negligible, being the result of minor failings in the system. The quantity of items gained or lost will not be the only guide to the action to take on any difference disclosed. A loss of one unit, if of considerable value, will usually call for a prompt and thorough investigation. To reduce errors to a minimum the Stores auditors should be experienced men. Also, they should be directly responsible to the accountant, thus minimising the possibility of collusion with someone employed in the Stores.

STOCK CHECK SHEET. No.........								
Date of Count	Code	Material Description	Quantities				Reasons for Loss or Gain	
			Actual	Bin Card	Stores Ledger	Loss or Gain		
Stores Auditor			**Material Controller**					
			Accountant					

FIG. 21.—*Stock Check Sheet*

NOTES

1. In practice, the ruling of this form will tend to vary considerably to meet the needs of the particular business.

2. The Code and Description columns may be completed by a Stores Records clerk, a Stores Ledger clerk, or the Stores auditor himself.

3. The Date of Count and Actual quantity will be written on the form by the Stores auditor.

4. If the Actual quantity is different to the Bin Card quantity, once the correction is authorised, the Actual quantity can be entered on the Bin Card. A possible procedure is to rule a line after the last entry on the card and then enter the new quantity, showing, of course, the date and the Stock Check Sheet number. A different-coloured ink from that used for normal entries is to be preferred for entering the new figures.

5. The Stores Ledger and Loss or Gain columns are completed by the Stores Ledger clerk. Any loss or gain, when authorised, has to be written off or added respectively in the Stores Ledger. The figure is thus the difference between the Actual count and Stores Ledger quantity. These differences are summarised so that a total may be posted to the Stores Control Account. On the Stock Check Sheet plus or minus signs, or black and red figures, may be used to denote which are gains and which are losses.

6. If necessary, unit prices and total values may also be shown on the form. These are unnecessary when the Stores Ledger shows physical quantities only.

DISPOSAL OF THE STOCK DIFFERENCES

At the end of each month it will be necessary to dispose of the total stock loss (or gain). How this will be done has to be determined *before* the Standard Costs are set. The first question to be decided is: how are the shortages to be classified—which may be regarded as "normal" and which "abnormal"?

Normal shortages are clearly part of the costs of manufacturing, and as such may be included in the Standard Costs. The size of the allowance to cover these shortages will, naturally, be influenced by the type of Standard being adopted.

Some accountants advocate the use of an inflated standard price, others the inclusion of an allowance in manufacturing overhead costs. Both methods recognise that the shortages are a true cost of production.

The use of inflated prices to cover shortages, although theoretically sound, may in practice be difficult to apply. Only certain types of materials may incur losses, and yet an attempt will have to be made to inflate all prices. A percentage may be applied to all basic prices, but, unless very similar types of materials are stocked, the additions are unlikely to represent responsibility for shortages which arise: calculation of *actual* prices for comparison with standard prices will not be easy. If estimates are added to cover average actual losses, notional figures are introduced, which do little to further cost control. This sort of problem has to be faced with all indirect costs, and especially when they arise at irregular intervals. With a direct cost there is a definite Actual Cost, which can be compared with its matching Standard Cost, and any difference will be a significant variance.

From what has been said, it will be apparent that a charge to overhead costs is likely to give better results than when an inflated price is used. A month-ending journal entry to cover the stock adjustment may be as follows:

	Dr.	Cr.
	Dr.	*Cr.*
Stock Shortage Account	Dr. £xx	
To Stores Control Account		£xx

The charge for stock shortages is thus included in overhead costs, both Actual and Standard.

If a shortage or loss arises from an abnormal cause it is better taken to a special loss account, and not included in the cost of the product. Accordingly, Standard Costs do not include abnormal losses. If, due to unusual weather conditions, there is a rapid deterioration of a material, with the result that it is no longer fit for use, then the cost would be transferred to an appropriately named loss account. This procedure follows the well-established rule in costing that any unusual or abnormal occurrence should, so far as production costs are concerned, be treated as a loss and taken to Costing Profit and Loss. With Standard Costs, any "cost" which is abnormal finds its way to Costing Profit and Loss as part of the appropriate variance.

VALUATION OF STOCKS

The valuation of stocks is very much a part of the problem of how to dispose of cost variances. Because of its importance, a later chapter has been devoted to the considerations involved.

The now generally accepted rule for stock valuation is to take Cost or Market Value (or one of the other acceptable descriptions), whichever is the lower. With Standard Costs the question which must inevitably arise is: what is the meaning of "Cost"? Is it to be the Actual Cost, which also includes inefficiencies or losses (not true costs at all) or Standard Cost? Does the fact that a higher than normal price had to be paid for materials make them any more valuable than the same materials for which the usual price was paid? This sort of situation can arise when, for example, materials are obtained from a new supplier without requesting a quotation, the main purpose being to obtain speedy delivery irrespective of cost. Certainly, an argument can be put forward for adopting Actual Cost for valuation purposes. It can be suggested that since, in the example, the materials *had* to be obtained so that some could be used immediately, Actual Costs are very much a realistic reflection of operating conditions and, therefore, are the true costs. On the other hand, in favour of Standard Costs, it can be stated that provided plans are made in good time and acted upon (*i.e.* there is efficient management), the "rush orders" should be quite unnecessary.

Without dwelling on arguments for, or against, the use of Standard Costs for valuation purposes, there is a strong case for their use in avoiding the complications arising from conversion of Standard Costs to Actual Costs and in ensuring that full advantage is taken of all savings in clerical costs. If Standard Costs are not accepted as the real costs they lose many of their advantages and their significance.

The normal conventions of accounting should still be followed when adopting Standard Cost as "Cost" for valuation purposes. Only those items which have a realisation value should be included in a stock valuation. Any obsolete, slow-moving, or unsaleable stocks will thus have to be revalued at more realistic prices, or written off altogether. Needless to say, a method of valuation, once adopted, should be used consistently.

As will be appreciated, the above remarks apply to a complete system of Standard Costs. When Accounting Method I is adopted the raw materials are kept at Actual Cost, so if this is to form the basis of valuation, no problem arises. Since Actual Cost *will* usually be taken, this matter need not be pursued further.

THE STORES LEDGER AND BIN CARDS

The chapter would be incomplete without an illustration of a typical ruling for a Stores Ledger and a Bin Card. Under the Perpetual Inventory system it is necessary to be able to see, at any time, the balance of stock on hand; accordingly the rulings given enable this objective to be achieved. Fig. 22 illustrates a sheet from the Stores Ledger; the Bin Card (Fig. 23) is very similar, the principal differences being the exclusion of the unit price and value columns and the inclusion of Purchase Order details.

STORES LEDGER. Folio.........

Code ....   Unit..............   Max. ....

Description ....   Min. ....

Std. Price ....   Re-ordering Point ....

Date Price Fixed ....

Date	Reference	Received (Quantity)	Issued (Quantity)	Balance (Quantity)	Std. (Price)	Value £

FIG. 22.—*Stores Ledger*

NOTES

1. A separate sheet or card is maintained for each grade or type of material or part.

2. The ruling assumes that accounting Method II is being used, quantities only being recorded, the value of the balance being obtained when needed by multiplying quantity by standard price.

3. The Received column is for all debit items, the sources of which will be:
    (*a*) Goods Inwards Sheets.
    (*b*) Material Return Notes.
    (*c*) Stock Check Sheets (stock gains).

4. The Issued column is for all credit items the sources being:
    (*a*) Standard Material Requisition (or Specification).
    (*b*) Excess Material Requisition.
    (*c*) Returned to Supplier Form (or Rejection Report).
    (*d*) Stock Check Sheets (stock losses).

BIN CARD. Folio.........								
Code...........................				Max........................				
Description..............................				Min........................				
				Re-order Level.................				
Purchase Order Details				Receipts and Issues				
Date	P.O. No.	Qty	Delivery	Date	Reference	In	Out	Balance

FIG. 23.—*Bin Card*

NOTES

1. This record is kept in the Stores; there is one card for each grade or type of material.

2. So that the recording of receipts and issues and the initiation of Purchase Requisitions are carried out correctly it is advisable to have properly trained clerks and a suitably equipped office attached to, or within, the Stores. The storekeeper should not be expected to perform the clerical duties.

3. A duplicate set of records is sometimes kept in the Material Control Office or Stores Records Office. In this case, the raising of Purchase Requisitions is not done in the Stores, but in the office, away from the Stores, possibly in the administrative block of the factory. Unless there are special reasons for this additional set of records, it will be found that the Stores Office plan ((2) above) will be a much more efficient and cheaper arrangement.

EXAMINATION QUESTIONS

1. State the advantages and disadvantages of using standard prices for issuing materials from stores.

(*I.C.W.A.*)

2. (*a*) Design a materials cost-analysis form, and enter suitable figures from the detail given below:

Production for period   192 units

	Material X	Material Y
Standard price per ton	£24·00	£32·00
Actual price paid per ton	£22·80	£30·80
Actual usage	16 tons	13 tons

The standard production for the period represented by the above figures is 400 units, for which the standard quantity allowances for materials are 30 tons of X and 25 tons of Y.

(b) Using the appropriate four columnar totals from your entries on the form, show the journal entries applicable to production, materials, and variance accounts.

(I.C.W.A.)

CHAPTER 14

CONTROL OF LABOUR COSTS

WITH Standard Costs the control of labour costs will, inevitably, follow similar lines to those adopted for a properly organised Actual Costs system. There is, however, an important difference between the two systems. With Standard Costs there is a planned approach to improving efficiency before the Standards are actually set. An objective measure of achievement is therefore provided. Another important difference is the aim to reward the worker on the basis of work done, preferably calculated by considering standard hours. Certainly the high degree of standardisation likely to be achieved in the methods of production and in components should allow an incentive plan to operate. Another point to remember is that the provision of an incentive should ensure that the standard times set are actually achieved.

The observations made earlier on the calculation and analysis of variances envisaged that the method of calculating wages would be based on hourly rates. Accordingly, both a rate and time variance were calculated. If some form of incentive plan is operated a modified form of variance calculation may be necessary. With piece rates, for example, the concern will be with the number of "pieces" and not the hours worked.

Because direct labour costs can be controlled more effectively than indirect labour costs the former has been given greater attention, both in text-books and in practice. Better supervision, "machine-pacing" and standardisation of operations, have made maximum control possible. Nevertheless, some attempt has to be made to keep indirect labour costs within the limits laid down by the Standard Costs. In this chapter the emphasis will be on direct costs, although some matters will also affect indirect labour costs, and in this case the fact will be stated. The main features of a plan for control of labour costs are shown below:

1. Determination of work to be done distinguishing:

    (a) Direct work (*i.e.* that which directly results in products being made).

    (b) Indirect work (*i.e.* that performed as a necessary aid to the efficient carrying out of direct work).

2. Setting of standard times for all operations to be performed by direct workers and where possible, and practicable, for work to be done by indirect workers.

3. Determination of the correct grade of labour to be employed on each operation and on indirect work and, as a corollary, the wages rates to be paid.

4. The timing of workers both as regards:

    (a) Attendance (*i.e.* time spent at the factory).
    (b) Effectiveness (*i.e.* time spent on productive work).

5. The calculation and payment of wages.
6. Isolating and reporting labour variances.

These matters are discussed below.

DETERMINATION OF WORK TO BE DONE

In total, the work to be done will be determined from the production programme, based on estimated sales. The adoption of a system of Budgetary Control is recommended for all businesses that are using, or are about to use, Standard Costs. Usually, therefore, the production budget will form the background to any planning for labour requirements.

To bring all work into terms of a readily understood common unit, which may be used as a basis for assessing labour requirements and calculating wages, it is necessary to use the "standard hour." This refers not to time only, but to the amount of work that should be done within one hour. Naturally, certain important matters have to be considered before the standard hour can be determined. The conditions to be taken for setting the Standard Costs will also have to be taken into account when fixing the standard hour. If ideal conditions are assumed, more work should be done than when expected conditions are taken.

All functions have to be made efficient before any attempt is made to determine the standard hour. Plant lay-out should receive special attention. There should be no doubling-back, or delays, of work-in-progress: at all times an even flow of work, without bottlenecks, is the aim. Methods study should be employed to find out the best ways of performing work. Tools and equipment should be the most suitable for the purposes for which they are used and, moreover, kept in a condition which consistently allows good work to be performed.

For each type of product two important forms will usually be necessary. These are:

1. A Process Chart (Fig. 24), which indicates how the product is to be manufactured, naming and possibly illustrating each part, and showing the plan for the materials and parts to flow from one operation to another. This chart will be useful when determining

Part No. 300-120

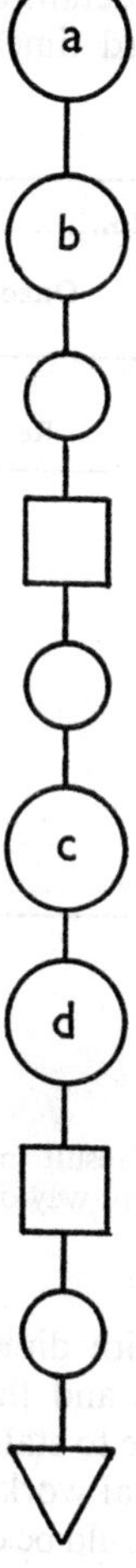

NOTES

1. Common symbols used in Process Charts are:

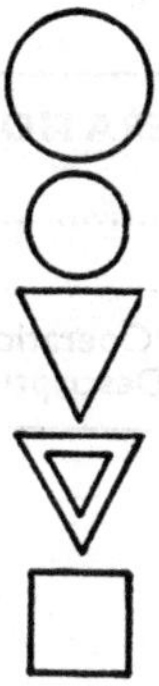

◯ = An operation.

◯ = A move.

▽ = A permanent storage.

▽ = A temporary storage.

☐ = An inspection.

2. Every movement in preparing for, carrying out, and completing necessary work is set out on the chart. All possible detail is therefore included. In this way the best sequence of operations can be obtained, any wasteful movements being eliminated.

3. The "Key" would give details of each operation involved: "a" is the first operation, "d" is the last.

4. The times involved may also be shown.

5. Inclusion of the number of feet, materials etc., have to travel, will often prove useful. Comparisons of alternatives can be made only when all information is shown.

Key to Operations:
a = ... ⎫
b = ... ⎬ Details of operation
c = ... ⎭ would be given
d = ...

FIG. 24.—*Process Chart* (with Notes).

the best sequence of operations, when charging the product with the overhead costs for each cost centre involved, and when preparing the Standard Operation Schedule.

2. A Standard Operation Schedule (Fig. 25), which details by number and name the operations required. The standard times for each operation are also included on the schedule.

Operation No.	Machine or Cost Centre	Operation Description	Standard Time	Remarks

STANDARD OPERATION SCHEDULE. No.........

Product (or Component).............................   **Date**............

FIG. 25.—*Standard Operation Schedule*

NOTES

1. The Schedule may be prepared from the Process Chart.
2. Any deviations from procedures laid down will usually result in a variance arising. This is so because the Schedule shows the most efficient way of producing the particular components.

At the present time, the concern is, of course, with direct labour. When the standard times for all products are listed, and the number of each type of product is considered, it will be possible to state the total standard hours per week. This, divided by the normal working hours per worker for a week, will show how many workers should be employed.

Similar procedures can be followed for indirect labour. The determination of "work units" has already been covered. This involves the determination of suitable measures for indirect work, so that a standard hour may be fixed. To repeat an earlier example, the square yards of floor that can be swept by one man in one hour may be calculated, and this can then form the basis for estimating the indirect man-power requirements.

Once the plant lay-out, methods, procedures, and other relevant matters have been considered and the most efficient plan of operation determined, the standard times, for all operations, have to be set. This has to be done to be able to see how much work should be performed in one hour (the standard hour).

SETTING OF STANDARD TIMES

Each operation should be timed. This may be achieved by:

1. Test runs, making use of time studies to determine the time for each operation.
2. Past records.

Time studies ensure that the times set are accurate. Moreover, such times are arrived at objectively and are not unduly influenced by personal bias. The best manner of performing work is found by the use of motion studies, and then each operating cycle is divided into distinct elements, times being set for each. To these times are added allowances to cover relaxation, unavoidable delays and fatigue, the total time then showing the expected performance of an average operator; because these allowances are made, the worker concerned should be able to achieve consistently the standard times, without excessive exertion or deterioration in health.

Needless to say, care must be taken in selecting the average operator. He should be one who is skilled in his trade or occupation and who will give a performance which can be relied upon.

Past records not based on time studies, or test runs which are not timed scientifically, are unlikely to give satisfactory results and should thus be avoided.

The work envisaged, to which the above procedures will relate, is of a standardised nature and is made up of operations which, taken together, go to make a product. Thus in an engineering works, for example, a component may go through various stages, metal being cut to suitable sizes, then shaped, drilled, and put through other operations until, finally, it is "finished." With chemical processing, flour milling, or similar industries, detailed time studies may be unnecessary: the volume of production is largely determined by the capacity and speed of the machines used.

THE CORRECT GRADE OF WORKER AND APPROPRIATE WAGE-RATE

These matters have already been mentioned in the Chapter on Setting Standard Costs. It was shown that, for effective cost control, the determination of the correct grade of worker is extremely important. The fixing of the wage-rate is, of course, part of the same problem: one cannot be divorced from the other.

Job evaluation should be adopted for determining the category or grade into which work, and consequently workers, fall. Only in this way can operations be understood and evaluated. The duties and responsibilities attaching to "key" jobs are assessed and given points values. From these, on a relative basis, all other jobs may also be evaluated. Provided a fair assessment of each job is made there should be greater satisfaction among workers: one will not feel that he is being undervalued while another is overvalued.

Each job is analysed into basic requirements, such as skill required, responsibility, physical or mental effort needed, and the working conditions attaching to it. Different plans show variations in the way the "requirements" are classified, but the principles followed in all cases are similar. Thus, for example, "skill" may be awarded points varying from, say, 1 to 40 in number, "responsibility" from, say, 1 to 50, and so on. The result of analysing four different jobs may take the form shown in Fig. 26.

JOB ANALYSIS

Job No.	Job Requirements				Total Points Awarded
	Skill	Responsibility	Physical Effort	Working Conditions	
1	20	30	15	40	105
2	30	40	20	30	120
3	40	25	30	40	135
4	15	30	20	20	85

FIG. 26.—*Job Analysis*

The points are awarded on a relative basis. By carefully considering the degree of skill, etc., required, production men can determine scientifically the relation of one job to another. Hourly rates can then be fixed according to total points values. Thus 100 points may warrant 4s. per hour, and each addition or reduction of, say, 5 points, may add or reduce the hourly rate by one halfpenny. In this way, jobs are graded and evaluated: at all times the rate of pay depends upon the work done, rather than upon the particular person involved. The wages of both direct and indirect workers may be determined in this way. Needless to say, the support of workers and their unions is essential if job evaluation is to succeed.

THE TIMING OF WORKERS

A man may be required to attend a factory for, say 44 hours each week. During that time he should be *effectively* employed. Only appropriate controls and the keeping of suitable records will ensure that this essential objective is achieved.

Control of both direct and indirect workers should receive attention. The procedure for administrative and clerical workers is discussed in a later chapter.

GENERAL OBSERVATIONS

The employment of suitable labour is normally the responsibility of the Personnel Department—who deal with all formalities—and the official in charge of the department requiring the worker being engaged.

The worker is usually required to complete a form of application on which he must state all personal, and experience, particulars. An interview then follows. Upon being engaged he may be expected to sign an agreement which requires him to comply with the regulations governing conditions of employment.

In the Personnel Department suitable records are maintained for each man or woman. The date of commencement, grade or occupation, rate of pay, upgradings, and other relevant details are all recorded.

Each service cost centre and producing cost centre is given a distinctive number and is allocated a block of "clock numbers," the size of which depends upon the number of workers to be employed, remembering that flexibility is essential. Thus Cost Centre "A" may be given code number 1, and clock numbers 1–99. Number 1/1 will therefore indicate worker number 1, say, L. Davies, who works in "A" Cost Centre. Cost Centre "X" may be No. 2, with clock numbers 100–149, and all other cost centres will be given code numbers and clock numbers.

These numbers become an essential part of the system. All documents relating to a worker will bear a hyphenated number to show department and "identity." Wages sheets are so laid out that departmental and cost-centre wage totals are shown as part of a routine.

RECORDING ATTENDANCE TIMES

All workers should be given a clock card so that comings and goings may be mechanically recorded by use of a time recorder. There are other methods, but these are now outmoded and, because of their inefficiencies, should not be tolerated. The advantages claimed for card time recorders may be summarised as follows:

1. The worker makes the record himself, so he cannot, afterwards, dispute its accuracy.

2. Time recorders can be operated quite rapidly, so delays are minimised.
3. Clerical work in the Wages Office is simplified. For example, there is no question of having to write up an attendance book, and any lateness or overtime may be shown automatically by the time recorder printing in a different-coloured ink—say red instead of black.
4. In suitable cases the same clock card may be used to record both attendance time and times spent on operations (effective time).
5. There is greater accuracy and a much more legible record.

Time recorders, at one time situated near the factory gates, are now often to be found in each department. This avoids time being lost between the gate and place of work.

At the end of a week the total time shown on an attendance card should be reconciled with the worker's total, effective time. When both times are collected on the one record, no difficulty should be experienced. When separate records are necessary, such as, for example, when a worker performs operations on batches of different types of components, the totals from the two records have to be brought together and compared.

Irrespective of the method used for recording times, it will be necessary to have idle or lost time segregated from normal production time and have it explained.

RECORDING OF EFFECTIVE TIMES

How effective time is to be recorded will depend upon the manufacturing processes involved. It is possible to distinguish two types of system:

1. Where flow production operates.

   Irrespective of the precise nature of what is being done, there is a continuous repetitive sequence of operations or processes, resulting in one product or a range of similar products being made.
2. A number of different products is manufactured and flow production is impossible.

   Each product, or batch of products, requires a number of operations to be performed. These do not, however, follow a definite pattern. Accordingly, as each operation is performed, the time of starting and then the time of completion have to be recorded.

An example of the first type is to be found in process industries and in the so-called mass-production industries. The second may be illustrated by reference to batch production of components in light engineering.

With (2) a separate time card will normally be essential. For each operation the commencing and finishing times will have to be recorded. Any "non-productive" time will also be shown on the card kept for each worker.

Since, with (1), each worker will normally be engaged on making the same product, or part of a product, and the pace is set by the machinery and equipment being used, then the attendance time will, excluding stoppages due to breakdowns or hold-ups, be the same as the effective time. There may be no necessity to time individual operations because identical products are being produced. If, however, different "inputs" have to be timed this may be done on the card used to record attendances or on a work sheet kept by the foreman. The latter is quite a normal practice: the time is booked for the team or gang and not for each individual. Any lost time should, of course, be recorded separately.

Indirect workers may be required to record attendance times only. However, for effective control, it is advisable for details of work done, and times taken over each part of it, to be recorded. Time sheets, especially for maintenance and other "roving" personnel, are, therefore, usually essential.

The accountant, when planning a system for timekeeping, should ensure that regulations, made known to all workers, are actually observed. The intentional stamping of another person's clock card may be grounds for instant dismissal, but this fact does not always deter workers from carrying it out. If daily observations of workers, arriving and leaving, cannot be made, at least fairly regular checks can be managed. A rule to be rigidly observed is that relating to the printing of times. Unless times of arrival and leaving are printed by the time recorders they are, in the absence of very exceptional circumstances, open to suspicion and should not therefore be recognised. This is essential to ensure that workers are paid only for what they do and that the times are accurate. To spend large sums of money on installing a system of standard costing only to allow it to become virtually ineffective by malpractices in timekeeping is quite ludicrous. Only by insisting on efficiency in *all* phases of the system can maximum efficiency be achieved.

THE CALCULATION OF WAGES AND ORGANISATION FOR PAYMENT

The calculation of a man's wages will be very much affected by the scheme of payment in operation, the two principal forms of which are as follows:

1. Payment according to time worked.
2. Payment according to work done.

There are many variations of these and, in Great Britain, it is quite usual for a minimum-wage plan to operate so that even when paid by results the worker is still guaranteed a certain wage.

With standard costing the aim should be to pay on work done. Usually, with direct workers, there will be no difficulty in accomplishing this end: a direct connection can often be established between the quantity of work done and the payment made. Sometimes the quantity is dictated by the pace of a machine or by technological factors, the workers having no influence, except in an indirect way, on the volume of output. In such cases an incentive method of payment based on quality may be possible. Clearly, only when the worker can improve quality by the way he exercises his skill, and when the differences in quality are important from a commercial standpoint, will an incentive payment based on quality be a practical proposition. Quantity is, therefore, the most usual measure for determining the payments to be made.

Generally speaking, the best incentive is a personal one; that is, one which is paid to an individual for work he has himself performed. To earn a certain wage he knows how many units he has to produce. Provided the incentive is strong enough, a worker will therefore produce at a consistently high level.

If the responsibility for output cannot conveniently be traced to individual workers (and this is so when the work is done on a conveyor), then a group incentive will usually have to operate. That is to say, the output of a group of workers will be measured, and any total payment above basic earnings will be divided equally among them. Although the incentive is not as strong as that provided by an individual scheme, there are circumstances where it can give good results. If all workers are of approximately the same ability, close co-operation may result, thus achieving a high level of output. Needless to say, any loitering or slackness by one or more individuals may destroy the essential feeling of mutual trust.

CHOICE OF INCENTIVE SCHEME

There can be no suggestion of one ideal incentive scheme, even for Standard Costing. The plan to adopt is the one most suitable for the particular requirements of the business concerned. However, if possible, full use should be made of the Standard Costing data: in particular, the standard times should be fully utilised.

The scheme should be simple to understand and operate, and acceptable to workers and management. Accordingly, complicated schemes requiring many clerks to operate them are likely to prove both too costly and of limited value. A fact now established is that an effective scheme need not be complicated; indeed, the simpler the better.

The interests of both the workers and the business must be considered. A good reward for the former is essential. This the business will be able to afford, for with an efficient incentive scheme a larger volume of output for the same fixed overhead cost will mean a reduced unit cost per product and, moreover, since *total* output will tend to be greater, there will tend to be additional profit. The business cannot, however, afford to be over-generous, or the result will be a loss on trading or, if not so catastrophic, a greatly reduced profit, which will not allow a reasonable return on capital invested. A compromise between a cheap-labour policy, on the one hand, and over-payment, on the other, has to be adopted.

Even when a minimum wage is not legally obligatory, there appears to be merit in its payment. Its existence gives a worker more "security." Days when he is not at his best, or when work is delayed, or when a man is in the process of being trained, may mean that less than standard output is produced. Often the reason may not be the fault of the individual worker concerned, so it would be unfair for him to be penalised.

The "minimum wage" is usually nothing more than a "minimum hourly rate," for the worker is paid only for the time he is actually in attendance at the factory. Stating work in terms of standard hours allows calculation of wages, whether minimum or otherwise, to be readily calculated. If a worker is unable to produce sufficient units to earn the minimum wage (minimum rate × hours attended), then a make-up allowance will have to be given. When a worker completes work evaluated at, say, 50 standard hours, in 44 hours, then he will be paid at the appropriate rate for the 50 hours.

For a successful scheme, the setting of the minimum hourly rate is extremely important. If a real incentive is to be present, there should be a differential between the ordinary rate and the incentive rate. The man earning a minimum wage is thus paid at a lower rate and receives a lower wage than a man who works hard enough to earn a bonus. Payment of the higher rate should result in all workers aiming for standard or above-standard output. The power of the incentive has to be maximised. Those workers who will work hard should be encouraged to do so. If, when the time studies are carried out, the average worker is considered, then the exceptional worker should be able to earn quite large bonuses. Earnings may thus be 25% or more above basic earnings, and large outputs inevitably result.

Many accountants are now against the adoption of premium bonus schemes, where both worker and employer share in the savings in time. Typical examples are the Halsey and Halsey–Weir schemes. The argument put forward for sharing any saving in time is based on the view that because he provides modern up-to-date equipment which allows the worker to operate quicker and more efficiently, the employer is partly responsible for a bonus being earned. For example, if the standard time for a task is 4 hours, but the worker takes 3 hours, the 1 hour saved may be shared, say, equally between employee and employer. Labour troubles may arise from this sharing when comparable results, in terms of output and costs, can be obtained from much simpler and more acceptable schemes.

A brief outline of a typical scheme for paying individual workers on the basis of work done is given below:

1. The manufacturing operations involved in making the products are examined, made efficient, and then timed. The standard time for each product is thus determined.

2. Two rates of pay operate—

   (a) The normal rate, paid when the worker achieves normal efficiency, *i.e.* produces at least the same number of "standard hours" as actual hours worked.

   (b) The minimum rate, paid when the worker fails to achieve the standard output.

3. Failure to achieve standard output means that the actual hours worked are paid for at a lower rate.

The rate for 2 (*a*) may be, say, £0·50 per hour and for 2 (*b*) £0·45 per hour. There is thus a definite incentive to reach the output which pays the higher rate.

For the industrious worker there will be every encouragement for him to work hard. For each standard hour completed, irrespective of the actual hours worked, he will be paid at £0·50 per hour. Provided the standard hour is not made too difficult to achieve, a good bonus will be earned, even by the average worker.

When the reason for failure to achieve standard output is outside the control of the worker it may be felt that he should not be penalised. In such case, the normal rate of £0·50 will be paid for time unavoidably lost. Thus if a machine breaks down, or there is a delay waiting for tools, or for materials, or because another "feeder" machine has broken down, credit for the actual time lost, in terms of standard hours, may be given. If, for example, the normal working week consists of 44 hours and a worker unavoidably loses 6 hours, then, provided he produces the equivalent of 38 standard hours or more, he will be paid at the higher rate. If, however, he manages less than the 38 hours the 44 hours will be paid at the lower rate of £0·45. An example, to illustrate the principle, is given on the next page. Failure to achieve normal efficiency will result in a variance.

Example of principle

Product Y made.
Operation of 10 minutes (standard time on each).
The "standard hour" is, therefore, 6 units.

Weekly production of Y by two workers is:

$$\begin{array}{ll} \text{M. Cole} & \text{300 units} \\ \text{S. Strutt} & \text{260 units} \end{array}$$

The wages earned are as follows:

$$\begin{array}{l} \text{M. Cole 50 hours at £0·50} = \text{£25·00} \\ \text{S. Strutt 44 hours at £0·45} = \text{£19·80} \end{array}$$

Because the second man produces less than the standard output (44 standard hours) he is paid the minimum wage.

ROUTINE FOR CALCULATING WAGES AND SHOWING VARIANCES

The wages for each worker have to be calculated and entered on a Wages Sheet. The latter is usually divided, or a number of sheets used, so that the total wages for each cost centre can, as a matter of routine, be obtained. This facilitates the preparation of statistics relating to wages and labour.

If, as far as possible, the isolation of variances is made part of the normal routine procedures there is obviously minimisation of clerical costs. All forms should, therefore, be designed with this purpose in mind.

With Standard Costing it is necessary to show:

(*a*) Variances in wage-rates.
(*b*) Variances in labour times.

Variances in direct wage-rates may be shown weekly on the Wage Sheets. Alternatively, a separate Variance Analysis Sheet may be used. The work involved should not be great, for only when the actual rate and standard rate do *not* coincide will details be recorded. The routine for showing the Labour Efficiency Variance is explained below.

Before turning to an example of a Wages Sheet it should be appreciated that the procedures adopted for arriving at the wage due to each employee will vary from one business to another. Whether workers are paid according to time worked or volume of output will most certainly affect the detailed procedures followed. If on "time," all calculations and deductions relating to a man's wage may be done on the attendance time card, the important information simply being transferred to the Wages Sheet. When the wages are based on individual output,

WAGES SHEET

Week Ended..............

(1) Clock No.	(2) Name	Department		(5) Gross Pay	(6) Deductions	(7) Net Pay	(8) Employer's Nat. Ins.	Rate Variance Analysis			
		(3) Hours Worked	(4) Rate					(9) Std. Rate	(10) 4 minus 9	(11) Actual Hours	(12) Rate Variance (10 × 11)

FIG. 27.—*Wages Sheet*

NOTES

1. A complete batch of Wages Sheets would show details of wages of all cost centres or departments.

2. As with previous rulings, the one given shows possible headings. There will be variations to suit particular circumstances.

3. The "Hours Worked" in column (3) may be replaced by "Standard Hours," "Pieces" or some other basis of payment. The rate, in such cases, will be the rate per standard hour, per piece, or other basis.

Operation Time Cards, Piece-rate Tickets, or other means must be used for obtaining the necessary information.

When an incentive scheme of payment is in operation rate variances, as already defined, may not arise. This is so because each worker, provided he works sufficiently hard enough to earn a bonus or other extra payment, will be on a rate which is determined by output and not time worked. Where, however, different rates apply for different levels of output there is a problem of deciding which rate is to be regarded as the standard rate. Some criterion, such as "100% efficiency" may be taken. Alternatively, if it is felt that a reasonably hard-working man can earn a 25% bonus, then there may be merit in fixing the standard rate at around 125%. In this way the Labour Rate Variance will show deviations from a realistic standard.

Irrespective of the method of payment that is adopted, a clear understanding of all its aspects will be essential. Some schemes may give an increase in *unit* costs with a larger output, whereas others may show that unit cost decreases as output increases.

A Wages Sheet is shown in Fig. 27. Clearly, if a rate is fixed for each class or grade of work, then a rate variance should not *normally* arise. If a lower-paid worker is temporarily transferred to a higher-grade operation, then his rate of pay will usually be increased: there will, therefore, be no rate variance. There may, however, be a case of a higher-paid employee being required temporarily to do a lower grade of work. If so, it is quite likely that his *normal* rate of pay will have to be paid, so a variance will arise. If strict control over rates is to be achieved a very close watch will have to be kept on transfers from one type of work to another. Arbitrary transfer, without good reason, will have to be opposed and prevented.

LABOUR RATE VARIANCE ANALYSIS SHEET

Instead of showing the difference in wage-rates on the wages sheets, they may be given on a special form, designed for the purpose. An example is given in Fig. 28; the entry given should make the form self-explanatory.

LABOUR UTILISATION

The effective employment of labour, indicated by the degree of success with which standard times (or outputs) are achieved, has also to be brought to light as part of the ordinary routine.

Much of this work may be left to the Production Planning Department. For example, a routine may be established which requires standard times to be entered on Production Orders. Any additional times required can then be covered by supplementary time tickets, signed by

LABOUR RATE VARIANCE ANALYSIS SHEET

Week Ended.................................

Finishing Dept.

Clock No.	Name	Actual Rate	Std. Rate	Actual Hrs × Diff. in Rates	Rate Variance	Reasons
51	Smith M.	£0·50	£0·49	40 at £0·01	£0·40	Award of Merit Rate agreed with Union
				Total Variance		

FIG. 28.—*Labour Rate Variance Analysis Sheet*

NOTES

1. To be able to give details to foremen and other personnel it will usually be necessary to have a sheet which is quite distinct from that used for the wages.

2. A combined Rate *and* Efficiency Report may be prepared. The main disadvantage of adopting this idea is to be found in the fact that rate variances may conveniently be reported upon weekly (often uncontrollable), whereas efficiency is better watched on a daily basis (usually controllable).

the foreman of the department concerned. The very fact that a worker has to obtain permission to take extra time should act as a deterrent to taking longer than the standard time.

The Wages or Costing Department may make provision for entering standard times on Operation Time Cards (Fig. 29). This may be done daily and any variances isolated.

The Labour Efficiency Variance Analysis (Fig. 30) is a very important form. Prompt preparation and presentation to foremen and other departmental managers can do much to control labour costs. As will be appreciated, it is a summary statement, showing the efficiency variances for a *number* of employees. The Operation Time Card covers *one* employee only. The aim should be to show foremen the variances for the day, early next morning.

The daily efficiency achieved by each worker may also be shown in a Labour Efficiency Report (Fig. 31). In the example given below a comparison is made between output achieved in terms of standard hours and actual hours worked. In the final column the percentage efficiency achieved is also given.

OPERATION TIME CARD

Clock No. ....

Name ....

Date...................

Department ....

(1) Production Order No.	(2) Operation	(3) Standard			(4) Actual			(5) Labour Variance		(6) Remarks
		Time	Rate	Amount	Time	Rate	Amount	Hours	Amount	

Fig. 29.—*Operation Time Card*

NOTES

1. The ruling shown envisages that times of commencing and finishing are shown on the back of the card or on a separate time ticket. There should be no difficulty experienced in adapting the card to meet all circumstances. A time recorder may be used for recording starting and finishing times on the back of the Operation Time Card.

2. The variance shown will relate to both Rate and Efficiency and thus be a Labour Cost Variance. If it is desirable to show Efficiency only, the Actual Rate (column (4)) may be substituted by the Standard Rate, thus calculating only the difference in hours and not any difference in rate. This information may, however, be shown on a Labour Efficiency Variance Analysis (Fig. 30).

LABOUR EFFICIENCY VARIANCE ANALYSIS

Department............................   Date............

Clock No.	Name	Operation	Actual Time	Std. Time	Varia-tion in Time	Std. Rate	Labour Efficiency Variance £	Remarks
			Total Labour Efficiency Variance					

FIG. 30.—*Labour Efficiency Variance Analysis*

NOTES

1. This analysis form provides a means of controlling each worker's efficiency.

2. Daily presentation will enable the foreman concerned to investigate abnormal operation times, therefore maintaining anticipated efficiency.

LABOUR EFFICIENCY REPORT

Department............................   Date............

Clock No.	Name	"Standard Hours" Produced	Actual Hours Worked	% Efficiency Act. to Std.	Remarks

FIG. 31.—*Labour Efficiency Report*

NOTES

1. Daily efficiency is shown in the Percentage column.

2. This Report may be used as a basis for an incentive-payments scheme. A weekly summary may be useful.

There is thus provided an overall measure of efficiency. The percentage shown for each man is known as the Efficiency Ratio: a useful guide to labour efficiency.

PAYMENT OF WAGES

Wages can be paid by one of the following methods:

1. The net wage can be handed to each employee by the pay clerk, no receipt being obtained.
2. Upon handing over the wage, the pay clerk gets each employee to sign the Wages Book, which acts as a receipt.
3. A special book, having one page for each man, to cover, say, six months may be used as a receipt book.
4. The time card can be used as a receipt. This is likely to give the best results.

PREVENTION OF FRAUD

To prevent fraud by dishonest employees an efficient system of internal check should be adopted. The fundamental principle of internal check is that one clerk checks the work of another.

In addition, other precautions may be taken. To assure that the payroll is not "padded," employees can be identified each time they collect their wages. If employees are not identified at each pay day this should be done at least periodically and without notice. Another point to watch is that the person or persons making up the wages sheets do not carry out the actual paying functions. From time to time the personnel engaged in paying out the wages should be changed and transferred to the preparation of the wages sheets.

Other points to watch:

1. Overtime should have special authorisation from the foreman, and overtime on time cards should be compared with the special authorisations.
2. Employees leaving the factory before finishing time should have a pass-out signed by the foreman.

EXAMINATION QUESTIONS

1. Where Standard Costing is used, what cost variances may be attributed to labour? Differentiate between the variances due to the efficiency of the actual labour force and those due to the faulty use of labour by management.

(*I.C.W.A.*)

2. To what considerations would you have regard in setting a piece-work rate for a machine operation?

(*I.C.W.A.*)

3. What records relating to labour do you consider (a) necessary, (b) desirable, for the efficient conduct of a business? List and describe briefly the contents of each record.

(I.C.W.A.)

4. In what circumstances should overtime premiums be charged to direct wages or overhead? Explain your views.

(I.C.W.A.)

5. Job evaluation is to be used as the basis of the wages structure for a firm employing over 1000 production and ancillary workers. List *six* evaluation factors which might be used in such a scheme giving a brief definition of each.

(I.C.W.A.)

6. As cost accountant of a large company you are charged by the financial controller with the task of ensuring that the system of computing earnings, the payroll routine and the payment of wages is adequate. List the internal checks which you would perform. What types of deliberate fraud would you need to guard against?

(I.C.W.A.)

7. Describe the preparation of the direct wages element of a production cost budget both with and without the advantage of a Standard Costing system. In establishing Standard direct wages rates what information is required from the planning department and how would it obtain this information?

(I.C.W.A.)

8. How would you measure "employee performance" of the following grades of labour:

(a) Warehouse packers.
(b) Stores labour.
(c) Internal transport personnel.

(I.C.W.A.)

9. Output per man-hour is regarded as a most valuable guide to the productivity of labour. What other criteria are available to measure productivity? Explain briefly their operation, value and limitations.

(I.C.W.A.)

10. Distinguish between (a) efficiency ratio, and (b) activity ratio. Illustrate your answer with an example of each ratio for each shop using the following figures:

Cutting shop:

	Unit *x*	Unit *y*
Budgeted output	36,000 units	8,000 units
Standard minutes per unit	10	15
Actual clocked time	12,500 hours	
Actual output	30,000 units	20,000 units

Finishing shop:

Budgeted man-hours	8,400, standard
Actual man-hours	7,200, clocked
Standard man-hours	7,560, produced

(I.C.W.A.)

CHAPTER 15

INTEGRATED ACCOUNTS AND STANDARD COSTING

In previous chapters the Accounting for Standard Costs was covered. The method adopted was based on the assumption that both a Cost and Financial Ledger were kept. This is often so when factories, situated some distance from the head office of a concern, keep their own detailed records. All matters affecting the individual factory are kept in that factory's Cost Ledger, whereas a complete set of financial records, possibly for a number of factories, is maintained in the form of a Financial Ledger.

Both the information provided by the factory records and that shown in the financial records serve a useful purpose. The cost accounts serve the local management and assist head-office management in formulating policy. There is a legal obligation for companies to supply information to shareholders, so the use of the financial records is quite obvious. There is no doubt whatsoever that, in some circumstances, the two sets of records can be justified.

Clearly, however, to some extent there is a certain amount of duplication. Information in the financial books is the same as that in the costing records, the main difference being in the way the information is classified for the purpose of recording. If the records can be so arranged that *both* the financial and the costing requirements are covered there will clearly be a saving in clerical costs. Furthermore, since only one set of records will be kept, there will be no problem of reconciliation of cost and financial figures.

If the factory and head office are situated together there will be no difficulty in having one ledger to cover all requirements. If factories are situated over a wide area and detailed local records are necessary there are complications. Cost analysis is possible on analysis sheets, reports, and statements, but to achieve a high standard of accuracy it is normally essential to operate records on a double-entry principle. Before attempting to introduce the single complete record—known as "integrated" or "integral" accounts—some means of ensuring that the necessary degree of accuracy is achieved will, therefore, be essential. A very carefully planned routine with internal checks may solve the problem. However, care will have to be exercised to ensure that the routine does not cost as much as the keeping of a separate Cost Ledger, otherwise there may be little justification for integrated accounts. There can be no hard-and-fast rule laid down: the system which best serves management, at reasonable cost, should be the one to adopt.

DETAILS OF THE SYSTEM OF INTEGRATED ACCOUNTS

The procedures followed are very similar to those adopted for a separate Cost Ledger. Naturally, there will be the addition of financial items—capital, liabilities, and assets all have to be recorded, as well as the day-to-day costs. In general, however, the classification of accounts follows the pattern adopted for costing purposes. To avoid the detailed analysis of expenses usually found in the nominal ledger and, at the same time, to build up the totals for charging to Work-in-progress and Finished Goods, detailed analysis of costs on Production Cost Sheets will be essential. The recording on these sheets is known as "third entries," a term which, from a student's point of view, is rather misleading, for all that is involved is the keeping of detailed records, for primary and overhead costs, that are *not* part of the double-entry system. "Summarising of costs," or a similar term, is a much better description of the work done.

The principal accounts required for an integrated ledger are as follows:

1. A Stock Account for each of the following—

(*a*) Raw Materials, which is debited with the opening stock and purchases, and credited with any issues of materials.

(*b*) Work-in-progress, which is debited with opening stock and production charges, and credited with the cost of articles finished, any closing stock being carried down to the next period.

(*c*) Finished Stock (or Finished Goods Account), which is debited with goods finished (the credit is to Work-in-progress) and credited with the cost of sales made for a period.

That the Work-in-progress Account is often divided according to the elements of cost has already been noticed (Chapter 8). When a number of cost centres are involved the debits may come to the Work-in-progress Account *via* an individual account which is kept for each cost centre.

The Stock Account and Purchases Account, normally to be found in the financial ledger, are replaced by the above stock accounts.

2. Cost of Sales Account

The cost of the goods sold is debited to a Cost of Sales Account the corresponding credit entry being to Finished Goods Account. With Standard Costs, as will be shown below, any Sales Variance may be shown in a Sales Control Account, a debit at Standard Cost being made to the latter Account, the credit being to Cost of Sales Account.

3. Asset Accounts

Separate accounts for Buildings, Machinery, Furniture, etc., are all maintained in the normal way. Any capital expenditure costs, such as own materials from Stores, or own labour erecting Plant and Machinery, will have to be debited to the appropriate asset account, the credit being to a producing or service cost centre account. Details of such charges will emerge from the summarising of costs (third entries).

4. Control Accounts for Debtors and Creditors

These accounts show, in total, the credit dealings with customers and suppliers. Personal Ledgers would also be maintained and, at a specified time, the total of the balances in the Sales Ledger should be equal to the balance in the Debtors Control Account, and the total of the balances in the Purchases Ledger should coincide with the balance in the Creditors Control Account.

5. Cash or Bank Account

All receipts are debited and payments credited.

6. Accounts for Prepayments and Amounts Due but not Paid

If an expense has been paid, say, for the next six months, the integrated ledger will show an account, possibly in columnar form, which includes, with others, this particular prepayment. The amount actually prepaid may be debited to the Prepayment Account and credited to, say, the Overhead Control Account. In this way, only the expense for the one period is charged to the Work-in-progress Account.

If an expense is due but has not been paid, an Expenses Due Account may be credited and the Overhead Control Account may be debited. This is done for each period. When the amount due is paid it will be necessary to credit the Bank Account and debit the Expenses Due Account or adjust through the Overhead Control Account.

The notes on control accounts below (7) are pertinent to this matter.

7. Control Accounts for Direct Wages and Overhead Costs

These are "clearing accounts." When actual payments are made the Cash or Bank Account is credited and the appropriate control account is debited. Thus the total of the direct wages paid will be debited to a Direct Labour Control Account.

At the end of the month the transfers to the Work-in-progress

Accounts are made by crediting the appropriate control accounts and debiting the Work-in-progress Accounts. As will be appreciated, the actual payments made in a period will not agree with the appropriate expenditure to be charged to that period. Accordingly, to make adjustments, accounts discussed under heading (6) above will be necessary.

The debits to Work-in-progress Accounts may be made *via* intermediate accounts. These are discussed below.

8. Departmental Accounts

An Account may be maintained for each cost centre. In this way it is possible to see how much is being spent by individual departments, thus locating responsibility and maximising control over costs.

OBSERVATIONS ON ACCOUNTS AND PROCEDURES

The brief remarks on the necessary accounts should have indicated that the principles followed for integrated accounting are, as already stated, similar to those adopted when separate cost and financial ledgers are maintained. Accordingly, if the student has studied, and understands, the procedures covered in Chapters 9 and 10 he should have little difficulty in mastering the techniques now being explained.

With the Cost Ledger all transactions which arise in the financial books have to be brought into the double-entry system by making a matching entry, to one made in a cost control account, in a Cost Ledger Control Account. In the integrated system both the debit and the credit entry appear in the one ledger. There is, therefore, no question of having a Cost Ledger Control Account: the ledger is self-contained.

On the remaining pages in this chapter two questions, with solutions and explanatory notes, are given. It is recommended that the student works through these and then proceeds to answer similar questions from past examination papers. Only in this way can the required degree of proficiency be attained.

SPECIAL NOTE.—Later in this chapter the Control Accounts for Wages and Overhead Costs will be superseded by a "Cost Control Account." In this Account, Actual Costs are debited and then Standard Costs are transferred to the Work-in-progress Account or Cost of Sales Account. A full explanation of the principle involved is given on pages 206 to 210.

QUESTION ON INTEGRATED ACCOUNTING

Trial Balance of the O.M. Co. Ltd.

January 29th, 19...

	Dr. £	Cr. £
Stores Control	435·00	
Work-in-progress A/cs— £		
Material 44		
Labour 40		
Overhead 20		
—	104·00	
Finished Goods	246·00	
Cost of Sales	1,640·00	
Material Price Variance		46·00
Material Usage Variance	25·00	
Labour Rate Variance	8·40	
Labour Efficiency Variance		40·00
Overhead Budget Variance	100·00	
Overhead Efficiency Variance		20·00
Overhead Volume Variance	40·00	
Debtors Control A/c	400·00	
Creditors Control A/c		822·40
Share Capital A/c		7,500·00
Bank A/c	6,000·00	
Land and Buildings	3,000·00	
Plant and Machinery	2,000·00	
Profit and Loss Balance		4,570·00
Depreciation on Plant and Machinery total to date		1,000·00
	£13,998·40	£13,998·40

This is the closing Trial Balance, with additions, of the exercise which illustrates Accounting Method II given in Chapter 10.

It will be recalled that one component is produced and the Standard Costs of this Part, as taken from the Standard Cost Card, have been given on p. 97.

Accounting Method II—both debits and credits to Work-in-progress Accounts at Standard—is used.

The Company has now decided to operate an integrated accounting system. Standard selling costs and sales are to be a feature of this new and more comprehensive system.

Some idea of the difference in the accounts classification of a system which has *separate* cost and financial ledgers and an Integrated system may be obtained from a comparison of the Trial Balance given above with the one given on page 115.

The transactions for February, along with any necessary notes, are shown below.

Material purchased on credit

	Actual £	Standard £
1600 pieces of "A" at £0·05 each	80·00	80·00
6000 lengths of "M" at £0·11 each	660·00	600·00

Material issues to production

1250 pieces "A."
6200 lengths "M."

Direct wages paid

Cheque for Wages and National Insurance = £1000.
P.A.Y.E. deducted from Wages = £150.

The number of hours actually worked was 2300. A rate of £0·50 per hour was paid.

Factory overhead costs

	Actual £	Total Standard
Depreciation on Plant and Machinery (for one month)	12·50	
Indirect Labour:		£580·00
Producing Dept. O.P.	40·00	(*i.e.* 580 units equivalent
Service Dept. R.M.	100·00	production at the Over-
Office Salaries	200·00	head Cost of £1 each.)
Sundry Purchases—Supplies, etc.:		
Producing Dept. O.P.	75·00	
Service Dept. R.M.	50·00	
Office	10·00	
Indirect Materials Dept. O.P.	60·00	
Indirect Materials Dept. R.M.	96·00	

All payments have been made by cheque.

Production for period (*units*)

	Complete	In Progress
Materials	560 + 40 *	40 (fully complete)
Labour	560 + 40 *	40 (half complete)
Factory Overhead	560 + 40 *	40 (half complete)

NOTE.—Strictly speaking, the 40 units from January *completed* in February, should have been brought into the calculation for the Standard Cost, but for simplicity have been ignored. This also applies to labour costs.

* From January Work-in-progress.

The balances on the Work-in-progress Accounts, based on the above "equivalent production," are as follows:

		£	£
Materials	$40 \times 1·10 =$		44·00
Labour	$20 \times 2·00 =$		40·00
Overhead	$20 \times 1·00 =$		20·00

Sales and selling and distribution costs (2 periods)

900 units at £7 each sold on credit.
Standard sales for the same 2 periods are 950 units at £7·25 each.

Selling and distribution costs paid by cheque:

Actual	Standard
£	£
162·00	150·00

Credit transaction payments

Payments to Suppliers for Materials purchased = £600.
Payments from Customers = £3850.

Summary of variances for period

	Unfavourable	Favourable
	£	£
Material Price Variance	60·00	
Material Usage Variance	22·00	
Labour Rate Variance	—	—
Labour Efficiency Variance		4·00
Overhead Budget Variance	143·50	
Overhead Efficiency Variance		25·00
Overhead Volume Variance		35·00
Selling and Distribution Costs (2 Periods)	12·00	
Sales Volume Variance * (i.e. "Loss" of Units)	362·50	
Sales Price Variance * (due to obtaining £0·25 per unit less than standard price)	225·00	

Additional information

There are four principal departments:

(a) Producing Department OP.
(b) Service Department RM.
(c) Office.
(d) Selling and Distribution.

* These variances may be calculated so as to show:

(a) differences in total Actual, and total Standard revenue; or
(b) differences in profit (Actual and Standard).
See Chapter 19 for a fuller description.

REQUIREMENTS FOR PERIOD ENDED FEBRUARY 25TH

From the above information you are required to show:

1. Ledger Accounts.
2. Costing Profit and Loss Account and Profit and Loss Statement; showing clearly the total Standard and Actual Profits for the two Periods.

SPECIAL NOTE.—In practice, much larger figures than those shown above would be encountered. The principles will, however, remain the same.

ANSWER USING INTEGRATED ACCOUNTING

Once again a suggested solution is shown, with explanatory notes as were given in the solution to the question on Current Standard Costs (Method II) in Chapter 10. As there, for ease of reference, the number of the Note explaining an entry will be given in the folio column of the ledger. At the top of each account (A) = Actual Cost, (S) = Standard Cost.

NOTE 1

The first step is the posting of the opening balances to the various accounts in the ledger.

NOTE 2.—MATERIAL PURCHASES

With the particular method of accounting to be adopted the Stores Control Account is kept at Standard Cost. Accordingly, the following entries reflect this fact:

		Dr.	Cr.
Stores Control A/c	Dr.	£680·00	
Material Price Variance A/c	Dr.	£60·00	
To Creditors Control A/c			£740·00

NOTE 3.—ISSUE MADE TO PRODUCTION

To take care of the *actual* usage the necessary entries are:

		Dr.	Cr.
Department OP	Dr.	£682·50	
To Stores Control A/c			£682·50

The concern is, of course, with actual issues at standard prices.

Only the Material Usage Variance remains to be isolated, and this may be done as shown below:

		Dr.	Cr.
Work-in-progress A/c—Material	Dr.	£660·00	
Material Usage Variance A/c	Dr.	£22·50	
To Department OP			£682·50

The variance is made up of 50 units of "A" at £0·05 and 200 lengths of "M" at £0·10.

SPECIAL NOTES.—For simplicity the Question deals with one producing department only. If there is a number of such departments an account would have to be opened for each one. Rather than over-burden the Ledger proper with a great number of departmental accounts, it is possible to show them only as part of the third entries: some systems of integrated accounting follow this principle.

The Wages and Overhead Control Accounts shown below may be felt to be unnecessary, being merely a duplication of the Producing Department Account. This, to some extent, is quite true, and the omission of these intermediate accounts would be quite permissible—valuable time could be saved. They are included in the Solution to keep it as near as possible to the one given earlier in Chapter 10.

NOTE 4.—DIRECT WAGES

The record for the actual payment and to show the amount due to the Commissioners of Inland Revenue for P.A.Y.E. Income Tax is:

		Dr.	*Cr.*
Wages Control A/c	Dr.	£1150·00	
To Bank A/c			£1000·00
„ P.A.Y.E. Income Tax A/c			£150·00

When the Income Tax is paid that account will be debited, the Bank Account being credited.

To charge the wages to production the entries are:

		Dr.	*Cr.*
Department OP	Dr.	£1150·00	
To Wages Control A/c			£1150·00

Following this entry, it is necessary to isolate the Labour Efficiency Variance, which may be accomplished as follows:

		Dr.	*Cr.*
Work-in-progress A/c.—Labour	Dr.	£1154·00	
To Department OP			£1150·00
„ Labour Efficiency Variance			£4·00

NOTE 5.—FACTORY OVERHEAD COSTS

In the Ledger the concern is with total costs. Since all the accounts for overhead costs have been settled by cheque, the credit entry is clearly to the Bank Account and the debit to the Factory Overhead Control Account. The charges to the departments concerned will be effected by debiting appropriate departmental accounts and crediting, in total, the Factory Overhead Control Account. The final step is the isolation of the overhead variances. In summary form the entries are thus:

		Dr.	*Cr.*
(a) Factory Overhead Control A/c	Dr.	£643·50	
To Bank A/c			£631·00
„ Depreciation—Plant and Machinery			£12·50

This is to record the payment of the overhead costs and to show how depreciation is dealt with in the accounts.

		Dr.	Cr.
(b) Department OP	Dr.	£397·50	
Department RM	Dr.	£246·00	
To Factory Overhead Control A/c			£643·50

This transfers the overhead costs to the departments concerned. Office expenses, in the absence of instructions to the contrary, have been taken direct to the producing department.

		Dr.	Cr.
(c) Department OP	Dr.	£246·00	
To Department RM			£246·00

This transfers the service department's costs to the producing department

		Dr.	Cr.
(d) Work-in-progress A/c—Overhead	Dr.	£580·00	
Overhead Budget Variance A/c	Dr.	£143·50	
To Department OP			£643·50
„ Overhead Efficiency Variance A/c			£5·00
„ Overhead Volume Variance A/c			£75·00

The variances are thus isolated. Not enough information is available to show separate variances for service and producing cost centres. This has been done deliberately to avoid complications.

NOTE 6.—TRANSFER OF COSTS OF FINISHED GOODS FROM WORK-IN-PROGRESS ACCOUNTS

The closing balances on the Work-in-progress Accounts may be entered and carried down to the next period. These figures are given in the Question.

Any "differences" on these Accounts will, of course, be the cost of finished goods which are transferred to the Finished Goods Account.

NOTE 7.—SALES

Goods sold in the two periods (January and February) are 900 units.

The cost of sales for January has already been debited to the Cost of Sales Account, so only the cost of the *difference* has now to be dealt with. This may be covered by:

		Dr.	Cr.
Cost of Sales A/c	Dr.	£2050·00	
To Finished Goods A/c			£2050·00

Being 500 units at £4·10 each (being total standard cost).

The standard sales for the two periods are covered by the following entry:

		Dr.	Cr.
Sales Control A/c	Dr.	£6887·50	
To Cost of Sales A/c			£6887·50

This is to record the standard sales of 950 units at £7·25 each. An alternative method of showing Sales is to debit the actual number sold (900 in example) at the standard price: the total would thus be £6525. With the latter way, the Cost of Sales Account is concerned with the costs *and* sales of 900 units and not with the costs of 900 units and the sales of 950 units.

The *actual* sales are covered by:

		Dr.	Cr.
Debtors Control A/c (Actual Cost)	Dr.	£6300·00	
Sales Price Variance A/c	Dr.	£225·00	
To Sales Control A/c (*Actual* at Standard Price)			£6525·00

As will be noticed, the Sales Price Variance is isolated in the above entry. The falling off in the volume of sales may be introduced into the books by the following:

		Dr.	Cr.
Sales Volume Variance A/c	Dr.	£362·50	
To Sales Control A/c			£362·50

NOTE 8.—SELLING AND DISTRIBUTION COSTS

To record the *actual* payment for the selling and distribution costs the entry would be:

		Dr.	Cr.
Selling and Distribution Costs A/c	Dr.	£162·00	
To Bank A/c			£162·00

Then the total variance may be recorded by the entry shown below:

		Dr.	Cr.
Cost of Sales A/c	Dr.	£150·00	
Selling and Distribution Costs Variance A/c	Dr.	£12·00	
To Selling and Distribution Costs A/c			£162·00

NOTE 9.—PAYMENTS FOR CREDIT TRANSACTIONS

Payments to suppliers will be recorded by debiting Creditors Control Account and crediting the Bank Account.

Payments from customers are dealt with by debiting the Bank Account and crediting Debtors Control Account.

NOTE 10.—TRANSFER OF VARIANCES TO COSTING PROFIT AND LOSS

The balance on the Cost of Sales Account will represent the Standard Profit. This is now transferred to Costing Profit and Loss Account.

All variances may then be debited or credited to the Costing Profit and Loss Account, thus arriving at the Actual Profit. Reference to the chapter covering stock valuation and the disposition of variances will enable the student to see that the transfer of variances to Profit and Loss, while quite usual, is not invariably followed.

Profit and Loss Statement

The Costing Profit and Loss Statement is much more informative to management than is the orthodox Trading and Profit and Loss Account. Not only does it show what has happened, but, also, what should have happened. Failure to achieve expected sales, or excess spending in relation to results is clearly shown. The appropriate action to take, to correct adverse tendencies, may be determined after careful study of the Profit and Loss Statement and detailed information on particular aspects—usually those not proceeding according to plan.

Special note on summarising of costs (third entries)

The third entries have been kept to a minimum. In practice, these functions will, of course, be quite extensive, but in a question of the type given there is very little scope for "collecting" costs according to function or other basis; this is for the simple reason that the costing aspect has already been covered— a fact confirmed by totals being given. Only the separation of the overhead costs according to whether incurred by producing, service, or office departments can thus be attempted.

Trial Balance

A Trial Balance is not specifically requested, but for *all* questions, if time permits, this is essential. In the solution given a Trial Balance has been extracted.

The accounts are balanced and, where appropriate, the balances are carried down to the next period.

Ledger of The O.M. Co. Ltd.

Dr. (S)		Stores Control Account		(S) Cr.
		£		£
Jan. 29 To Balance	N.1 b/d	435·00	Feb. 25 By Dept. OP N.3	682·50
Feb. 25 ,, Creditors Control	N.2	680·00	,, 25 ,, Balance c/d	432·50
		£1115·00		£1115·00
Feb. 26 To Balance	b/d	£432·50		

(S)		Work-in-progress Account—Material		(S)
		£		£
Jan. 29 To Balance	N.1 b/d	44·00	Feb. 25 By Balance N.6 c/d	44·00
Feb. 25 ,, Dept. OP	N.3	660·00	,, 25 ,, Finished Goods N.6	660·00
		£704·00		£704·00
Feb. 26 To Balance	b/d	£44·00		

Dr. (S)   *Work-in-progress Account—Labour*   (S) Cr.

			£				£
Jan. 29	To Balance	N.1 b/d	40·00	Feb. 25	By Balance	N.6 c/d	40·00
Feb. 25	To Dept. OP and Efficiency Variance	N.4	1154·00	,, 25	,, Finished Goods	N.6	1154·00
			£1194·00				£1194·00
Feb. 26	To Balance	b/d	£40·00				

(S)   *Work-in-progress Account—Overhead*   (S)

			£				£
Jan. 29	To Balance	N.1 b/d	20·00	Feb. 25	By Balance	N.6 c/d	20·00
Feb. 25	,, Dept. OP and Variance A/cs	N.5(d)	580·00	,, 25	,, Finished Goods	N.6	580·00
			£600·00				£600·00
Feb. 26	To Balance	b/d	£20·00				

(S)   *Finished Goods Account*   (S)

			£				£
Jan. 29	To Balance	N.1 b/d	246·00	Feb. 25	By Cost of Sales A/c	N.7	2050·00
Feb. 25	To Work-in-progress:	N.6		,, 25	,, Balance	c/d	590·00
	Material		660·00				
	Labour		1154·00				
	Overhead		580·00				
			£2640·00				£2640·00
Feb. 26	To Balance	b/d	£590·00				

(S)   *Cost of Sales Account*   (S)

			£				£
Jan. 29	To Balance	N.1 b/d	1640·00	Feb. 25	By Sales Control	N.7	6887·50
Feb. 25	,, Finished Goods	N.7	2050·00				
,, 25	,, Selling and Distribution Costs	N.8	150·00				
,, 25	,, Costing Profit and Loss A/c	N.10	3047·50				
			£6887·50				£6887·50

(A)   *Debtors Control Account*   (A)

			£				£
Jan. 29	To Balance	N.1 b/d	400·00	Feb. 25	By Bank	N.9	3850·00
Feb. 25	,, Sales Control	N.7	6300·00	,, 25	,, Balance	c/d	2850·00
			£6700·00				£6700·00
Feb. 26	To Balance	b/d	£2850·00				

Dr.   (A)   *Creditors Control Account*   (A)   Cr.

		£			£
Feb. 25 To Bank	N.9	600·00	Jan. 29 By Balance	N.1 b/d	822·40
,, 25 ,, Balance	c/d	962·40	,, 25 ,, Stores Control and Material Price Variance	N.2	740·00
		£1562·40			£1562·40
			Feb. 26 By Balance	b/d	£962·40

Share Capital Account   (A)

			Jan. 29 By Balance	N.1 b/d	£7500·00

(A)   *Bank Account*   (A)

		£			£
Jan. 29 To Balance	N.1 b/d	6000·00	Feb. 25 By Wages Control	N.4	1000·00
Feb. 25 ,, Debtors Control	N.9	3850·00	,, 25 ,, Factory Overhead Control	N.5(a)	631·00
			,, 25 ,, Selling and Distribution	N.8	162·00
			,, 25 ,, Creditors Control	N.9	600·00
			,, 25 ,, Balance	c/d	7457·00
		£9850·00			£9850·00
Feb. 26 To Balance	b/d	7457·00			

(A)   *Land and Buildings Account*

Jan. 29 To Balance	N.1 b/d	£3000·00

(A)   *Plant and Machinery Account*

Jan. 29 To Balance	N.1 b/d	£2000·00

Profit and Loss Balance Account   (A)

					£
			Jan. 29 By Balance	N.1 b/d	£4570·00

Depreciation on Plant and Machinery Account   (A)

					£
			Jan. 29 By Balance	N.1 b/d	1000·00
			Feb. 25 ,, Factory Overhead Control	N.5(a)	12·50
					£1012·50

(A)   *Service Department RM*   (A)

Feb. 25 To Factory Overhead Control	N.5(b)	£246·00	Feb. 25 By Dept. OP	N.5(c)	£246·00

Dr.   Cr.

(A)			*Producing Department OP*	(A)	
		£			£
Feb. 25 To Stores Control A/c	N.3	682·50	Feb. 25 By Work-in-progress Material and Usage Variance	N.3	682·50
,, 25 ,, Wages Control	N.4	1150·00	,, 25 ,, Work-in-progress—Labour	N.4	1150·00
,, 25 ,, Factory Overhead Control	N.5(*b*)	397·50	,, 25 ,, Work-in-progress—Overhead and Variance A/cs	N.5(*d*)	643·50
,, 25 ,, Dept. RM	N.5(*c*)	246·00			
		£2476·00			£2476·00

(A)			*Wages Control Account*	(A)	
Feb. 25 To Bank A/c and P.A.Y.E.	N.4	£1150·00	Feb. 25 By Dept. OP	N.4	£1150·00

			P.A.Y.E. Income Tax	(A)	
			Feb. 25 By Wages Control A/c	N.4	£150·00

(A)			*Factory Overhead Control Account*	(A)	
		£			£
Feb. 25 To Bank and Depreciation	N.5(*a*)	643·50	Feb. 25 By Dept. OP	N.5(*b*)	397·50
			,, 25 ,, Dept. RM	N.5(*b*)	246·00
		£643·50			£643·50

(S)			*Sales Control Account*	(S)	
		£			£
Feb. 25 To Cost of Sales	N.7	6887·50	Feb. 25 By Debtors Control and Price Variance	N.7	6525·00
			,, 25 ,, Sales Volume Variance	N.7	362·50
		£6887·50			£6887·50

(A)			*Selling and Distribution Costs*	(A)	
Feb. 25 To Bank A/c	N.8	£162·00	Feb. 25 By Cost of Sales and Variance A/c	N.8	£162·00

			Material Price Variance Account		
		£			£
Feb. 25 To Creditors Control A/c	N.2	60·00	Jan. 29 By Balance b/d	N.1	46·00
			Feb. 25 ,, Profit and Loss A/c	N.10	14·00
		£60·00			£60·00

Dr.   *Cr.*

Material Usage Variance Account

		£				£
Jan. 29 To Balance	N.1 b/d	25·00	Feb. 25 By Profit and Loss A/c	N.10		47·50
Feb. 25 ,, Dept. OP	N.3	22·50				
		£47·50				£47·50

Labour Rate Variance Account

Jan. 29 To Balance	N.1 b/d	£8·40	Feb. 26 By Profit and Loss A/c	N.10		£8·40

Labour Efficiency Variance Account

		£				£
Feb. 25 To Profit and Loss A/c	N.10	44·00	Jan. 29 By Balance	N.1 b/d		40·00
			Feb. 25 ,, Work-in-pro-gress—Labour	N.4		4·00
		£44·00				£44·00

Overhead Budget Variance Account

		£				£
Jan. 29 To Balance	N.1 b/d	100·00	Feb. 25 By Profit and Loss A/c	N.10		243·50
Feb. 25 To Work-in-pro-gress—Over-head	N.5(d)	143·50				
		£243·50				£243·50

Overhead Efficiency Variance Account

		£				£
Feb. 25 To Profit and Loss A/c	N.10	25·00	Jan. 29 By Balance	N.1 b/d		20·00
			Feb. 25 ,, Work-in-pro-gress-Over-head	N.5(d)		5·00
		£25·00				£25·00

Overhead Volume Variance Account

		£				£
Jan. 29 To Balance	N.1 b/d	40·00	Feb. 25 By Work-in-pro-gress-Over-head	N.5(d)		75·00
Feb. 25 ,, Profit and Loss A/c	N.10	35·00				
		£75·00				75·00

Sales Volume Variance Account

Feb. 25 To Sales Control A/c	N.7	£362·50	Feb. 25 By Profit and Loss A/c	N.10		£362·50

Dr.

Sales Price Variance Account

Cr.

Feb. 25 To Sales Control	N.7	£225·00	Feb. 25 By Profit and Loss A/c	N.10	£225·00	

Selling and Distribution Costs Variance

Feb. 25 To Selling and Distribution Costs	N.8	£12·00	Feb. 25 By Profit and Loss A/c	N.10	£12·00	

Costing Profit and Loss Account

			£			£
Feb. 25 To Material Price Variance	N.10	14·00	Feb. 25 By Cost of Sales A/c	N.10	3047·50	
,, 25 ,, Material Usage Variance	N.10	47·50	Labour efficiency Variance	N.10	44·00	
,, 25 ,, Labour Rate Variance	N.10	8·40	,, 25 ,, Overhead Efficiency Variance	N.10	25·00	
,, 25 ,, Overhead Budget Variance	N.10	243·50	,, 25 ,, Overhead Volume Variance	N.10	35·00	
,, 25 ,, Sales Volume Variance	N.10	362·50				
,, 25 ,, Sales Price Variance	N.10	225·00				
,, 25 ,, Selling and Distribution Costs Variance	N.10	12·00				
,, 25 ,, Actual Profit	c/d	2238·60				
		£3151·50			£3151·50	
			Feb. 26 By Balance	b/d	£2238·60	

Trial Balance of The O.M. Co. Ltd.
February 25th, 19...

		Dr. £	Cr. £
Stores Control Account		432·50	
Work-in-progress Accounts	£		
Material	44		
Labour	40		
Overhead	20		
	—	104·00	
Finished Goods		590·00	
Debtors Control Account		2,850·00	
Creditors Control Account			962·40
Share Capital Account			7,500·00
Bank Account		7,457·00	
Land and Buildings		3,000·00	
Plant and Machinery		2,000·00	
Profit and Loss Balance			4,570·00
Depreciation on Plant and Machinery			1,012·50
P.A.Y.E. Income Tax			150·00
Costing Profit and Loss Account			2,238·60
		£16,433·50	£16,433·50

Summarising of Costs (*Third Entries*)

Factory Overhead Costs Incurred: February

	Dept. OP £	Dept. RM £	Office £
Depreciation	12·50		
Indirect Labour	40·00	100·00	
Materials	60·00	96·00	
Salaries			200·00
Sundry Purchases: Supplies	75·00	50·00	10·00
	£187·50	£246·00	£210·00

The totals form the basis of the ledger entries to departmental accounts (see Note 5(*b*) above, page 196).

The O.M. Co. Ltd.

Costing Profit & Loss Statement

Periods: January and February

	£	£
Standard Sales 950 units at £7·25 each		6887·50
Less Standard Cost of Sales:		
Factory 950 × £4·10	3895·00	
Selling and Distribution	150·00	4045·00
Standard Profit =		£2842·50
Less Unfavourable Variances:		
Sales Volume	362·50	
Sales Price	225·00	587·50
		£2255·00
Material Price	14·00	
,, Usage	47·50	
Labour Rate	8·40	
Overhead Budget	243·50	
Selling and Distribution	12·00	325·40
		£1929·60
Add Favourable Variances:		
Overhead Efficiency	25·00	
Overhead Volume	35·00	
Labour Efficiency	44·00	104·00
		£2033·60

Reconciliation with Costing Profit and Loss Account

		£
Profit per Statement above	b/d	2033·60
Add Cost deducted for 50 units not sold, at £4·10 each		205·00
Actual Profit* =		£2238·60

* In the ledger the Factory costs covered 900 units actually sold. This is correct—the full difference in Sales £587·50 has been deducted, so it is wrong to deduct also the cost of producing the sales. Accordingly, the actual profit may be taken as £2238·60. Had *actual* sales, at the standard price, been taken, the cost of sales would also relate to actual sales, thus avoiding the necessity to add back any cost deducted for sales not obtained. An example, in summary form, is given below. The use of that type of Profit and Loss Statement, because of its lack of detail, is not to be recommended.

Costing Profit and Loss Statement

(Summarised)

Periods: January and February

	£	£
Sales: *Actual* Volume at Standard Price } 900 × £7·25		6525·00
Less Standard Cost of Sales:		
Factory } 900 × £4·10	3690	
Selling and Distribution	150	
		3840·00
Standard Profit =		£2685·00
Less Unfavourable Variances		550·40
		£2134·60
Add Favourable Variances		104·00
Actual Profit =		£2238·60

NOTE.—Obviously, the Sales Volume Variance will not be included in the total for unfavourable variances. Actual sales have been taken, so to deduct the variance due to loss in sales would be incorrect. A footnote, to show the effect of the failure to achieve Standard sales, would, of course, be appended to the Statement.

Many accountants would prefer to defer the writing off of Variances, especially overhead variances, until the end of the accounting year. From month to month, overhead variances may cancel each other out.

PROFIT VARIANCE

At this stage it is convenient to mention that any variation between the budgeted profit and actual profit is known as a *profit variance*. In effect, it is a composite variance which is made up of a number of other variances. These can be seen from the profit and loss statements shown above, and are as follows:

1. Manufacturing variances for labour, material and overhead as described earlier (Cost of Sales Variances).

   It will be seen that the standard cost of sales is £4·10 per unit produced. The differences would be ascertained for the separate elements of cost. In addition, the selling and distribution costs would be included in the cost of sales.

2. Administration costs variances.
3. Research and development costs variances.
4. Sales margin variances which are considered further in Chapter 19.

ANALYSIS OF PROFIT VARIANCE

The budgeted profit, also known as the "target profit," should be established in advance of the specific financial year to be covered by the budgets. Many factors would be considered, including the "cost of capital" and an adequate return on capital employed.* Once established, the target profit should be earned *provided* the plans represented by the various budgets are achieved. If, say, actual production costs are in excess of standard costs, then these will be a reduction in the profit earned.

When analysing the profit variance an attempt should be made to locate the *reasons* for the failure to achieve the target established. The precise requirements will vary to suit the particular business. Besides the analysis given above on the profit and loss statements a Profit Variance Analysis Report may be completed along the lines shown in Fig. 32. Chapter 19 covers the sales variance analysis more fully.

FURTHER DETAILS OF SYSTEM OF
INTEGRATED ACCOUNTS

The above Question and Solution have been developed along the lines previously explained for a separate Cost Ledger. They may, therefore, be regarded as "transitional"; the next Problem attempts to limit the double-entry accounting, but to extend the summarising of costs (the third entries).

Students often have difficulty in determining which items are *part of*

* For a detailed explanation see J. BATTY, *Management Accountancy*, Macdonald and Evans.

The R.M. Co. Ltd.   Date............

PROFIT VARIANCE ANALYSIS REPORT

Period: 6 months to 30th June, 19...

Product: Buildo

	£
Capital Employed: *i.e.* total assets used in the business	500,000
Target Profit for period: 20%	100,000
Actual Profit for period	92,000
Profit Variance (unfavourable) =	£8,000

REASONS FOR VARIANCE:

	£	£
Reduction in Sales Volume		1,500
Extra fixed costs: production	2,000	
selling	1,600	
distribution	300	
administration	1,000	
		4,900
Extra variable costs: production	1,800	
selling	700	
		2,500
		8,900

Addition to Profit (favourable variances):

	£	£
Increase in selling prices	400	
Improved sales margins	200	
Reduction in sales allowances	300	
		900
		£8,000

Action Recommended/Carried Out:

 1. Economies in production costs to be sought: value analysis being instigated.
 2. Greater volume of sales necessary, but selling costs should be controlled with more vigour. Report awaited on provision of incentive scheme for rerematives.

FIG. 32.—*Profit Variance Analysis Report*

the double-entry system and which go towards making totals, to enable the necessary accounting entries to be made. A clear understanding of the nature of each transaction will normally overcome this difficulty.

Each transaction may be viewed from two aspects. There is the financial side which is concerned with paying out, and receiving, money. This category includes credit dealings, for they have, eventually, to be settled by transfer of money, or money's worth. In exchange for goods or services, payments are made. Alternatively, for supplying goods or services, payments are received. There is a twofold function, so, naturally, a double-entry, in the books of account, is quite straight-forward.

The costing aspect deals with the internal functioning of the business. Division of cost according to the following is essential:

1. Elements; *i.e.*
    (*a*) Direct Material.
    (*b*) Direct Labour.
    (*c*) Overhead.

2. Functions:
    (*a*) Manufacturing divided into:
        (*i*) Producing Cost Centres.
        (*ii*) Service Cost Centres.
    (*b*) Administration.
    (*c*) Selling and Distribution.
    (*d*) Research and Development.
    (*e*) Producing assets (*i.e.* Capital Expenditure).

Costs are analysed according to the above functions. Once totals have been accumulated, for each functional department, transfers between them have to be made.

In summary form the procedures are as follows:

1. Take the financial aspect of a transaction and complete the double entry, *e.g.* Paid Wages, then debit Wages Control Account (or Cost Control Account) and credit Bank Account. There is thus a double-entry in the Ledger.
2. Consider the transaction in (1) from a costing point of view. Decide: Is the cost direct or indirect, and which department is responsible for its being incurred?

Having answered the above question, it will be possible to analyse the cost concerned and to include it under the appropriate functional headings. Thus the example given under (1), the payment of Wages, may be considered. Wages may be divided into those which are direct and those which are indirect: if the total paid is, say, £5000, this may consist of £3500 direct wages and £1500 indirect wages. The £3500 would be entered on the Production Department's Direct Cost Sheet and the £1500 on the Production Department's Indirect Cost Sheet. There is no entry made in the Ledger.

3. At the end of each accounting period (4 or 5 weeks) the Cost Sheets are totalled and the totals form the basis for a double-entry in the Ledger. The following entries are examples:

Direct Production Costs (total from Cost Sheet)
    Debit: Work-in-progress Account.
    Credit: Cost Control Account.

Indirect Production Costs (total from Cost Sheet)
> Debit: Work-in-progress Account.
> Credit: Cost Control Account.

Administration Costs (total from Cost Sheet)
> If to form part of Cost of Work-in-progress then:
>> Debit: Work-in-progress Account.
>> Credit: Cost Control Account.

> If to be regarded as a "period cost" being charged only against goods sold in a period:
>> Debit: Cost of Sales Account (or Profit and Loss).
>> Credit: Cost Control Account.

Selling and Distribution (total from Cost Sheet)
> Debit: Cost of Sales Account.
> Credit: Cost Control Account.

Research and Development (total from Cost Sheet)
> Method (1)
>> Debit: Work-in-progress Account.
>> *or* Cost of Sales Account.
>> *or* Profit and Loss Account.
> Credit: Cost Control Account.

> Method (2)
>> Debit: Research and Development Account (Deferred Revenue).
>> Credit: Cost Control Account.

> Then, periodically, write off a percentage as under Method (1).

Capital Expenditure (total from Cost Sheet)
> Debit: Appropriate Asset Account.
> Credit: Cost Control Account.

4. As part of (3) isolate the variances in the accounts. The Cost Control Account will have been debited with Actual Costs, which will, of course, include the variances. Totals under (3) will be Actual Costs, so if the Cost Control is credited with these totals there will be nothing left in the Cost Control Account; *i.e.* all costs will be transferred to Work-in-progress Account or other account.

However, the very important fact that the corresponding debits (*i.e.* transfers to Work-in-progress) must be at Standard Cost, has to be remembered. Accordingly, if there is an unfavourable variance a variance account will be debited, the Work-in-progress Account (or other account) will be debited, and a corresponding credit entry, equal to the two debits, will be made in the Cost Control Account.

SPECIAL NOTE.—The Material Price Variance will have to receive special attention. The Creditors Control Account will have to be credited with Actual Cost and Stores Control Account debited with Standard Cost. Any difference, due to paying a price different from the standard price, will appear in the Material Price Variance Account.

The observant student will already have noted, in connection with Accounting for Standard Costs (Accounting Method II), that the isolation of the price variance, when purchases are made, has two important effects, which are, briefly, as follows:

1. Unless the purchases and usage coincide, the Price and Usage Variance will *not* agree with the figure for the Material Cost Variance which is calculated on usage only. (See first paragraph, Chapter 7, Calculation of Principal Manufacturing Variances.)
2. The Material Price Variance will relate to purchases and not usage. Accordingly, if the price variance is written off each period there will not be a correct "matching" of costs and variances.

With the problem to be answered, it will be seen that the Material Price Variance does not appear in the Cost Control Account, whereas all other variances are included in that account.

Explanatory notes, on the Question given below, have been kept to a minimum. It is hoped that, by this time, the student will be able to work through the example without difficulty.

QUESTION ON INTEGRATED ACCOUNTING

Trial Balance of Bradley & Co. Ltd.
January 1st, 19...

	Dr. £	Cr. £
Land and Buildings	200,000	
Plant and Machinery	60,000	
Depreciation on Plant and Machinery		10,000
Stores Control Account (at Standard Cost)	50,000	
Finished Goods (at Standard Cost)	30,000	
Debtors Control Account	40,000	
Creditors Control Account		24,000
Work-in-progress Account (at Standard Cost)	12,000	
Bank Account	18,000	
Share Capital		300,000
Profit and Loss Account		76,000
	£410,000	£410,000

TRANSACTIONS FOR JANUARY

Wages paid by cheque:

Net Wages	£10,000
National Insurance Stamps	£540

P.A.Y.E. Deductions	£500

Credit Purchase of Materials (Actual Cost):

Taken to stock	£10,000
Taken direct to products	£200
Sundry Materials for use in the factory	£2,000
Sundry Materials for Selling and Distribution	£1,000
Sundry Materials for Administration	£600
Material Price Variance (unfavourable)	£1,300

Materials Issued to Production (Actual Quantity at Standard Prices)	£11,300
Material Usage Variance (Direct Materials) (unfavourable)	£800
Indirect Materials issued to Production (at Standard Prices)	£900
Direct Wages	£9,040
Factory Indirect Wages	£2,000

Salaries paid:

Selling and Distribution	£1,200
Administration	£2,000

Expenses paid:

Factory	£1,100
Selling and Distribution	£800
Administration	£200

Depreciation for Month (Plant and Machinery)	£300
Rates Prepaid (Factory £300, Administration £50, Selling and Distribution £50) included in Expenses paid, given above	£400
Rent Accrued Due—Warehouse (Distribution)	£200
Labour Rate Variance (unfavourable)	£100
Labour Efficiency Variance (unfavourable)	£300

Factory Overhead Variances:

Budget (unfavourable)	£100
Efficiency (unfavourable)	£150
Volume (favourable)	£50

Balance on Work-in-progress Account, January 28th	£11,500

Sales for Period:

Actual	£50,000
Standard	£55,000
Stock of Finished Goods at January 28th	£20,000

There are no Selling, Distribution and Administration *Costs* Variances

Sales Price Variance (unfavourable)	£5,000
Payments to Creditors	£22,000
Received from Debtors	£45,000

You are required, at January 28th, to show the ledger accounts and, to prove the accuracy of your work, to take out a Trial Balance.

The following matters have also to be considered when preparing your answer:

1. One Work-in-progress Account only is kept. Both debits and credits are at Standard.
2. Summarising of the costs according to functional responsibility (Factory, Selling and Distribution, and Administration) has to be shown *outside* the double-entry system.
3. A Cost Control Account is to be opened through which all costs are to go.
4. Administration Costs are to be charged to Work-in-progress.

SOLUTION

Ledger of Bradley & Co. Ltd.

(S) = Standard Cost
(A) = Actual Cost

Dr.   Cr.

(A)   *Land and Buildings Account*   A)

Jan. 1 To Balance	b/d	£200,000

(A)   *Plant and Machinery Account*

Jan. 1 To Balance	b/d	£60,000

Depreciation: Plant and Machinery   **(A)**

		£
Jan. 1 By Balance	b/d	10,000
„ 28 „ Cost Control		300

(S)   *Stores Control Account*   **(S)**

		£			£
Jan. 1 To Balance	b/d	50,000	Jan. 28 By Cost Control A/c		11,300
„ 28 „ Creditors Control		8,700	„ 28 „ Cost Control A/c		900
(£10,000 − £1,300)			„ 28 „ Balance	c/d	46,500
		£58,700			£58,700
Jan. 29 To Balance	b/d	£46,500			

NOTE.—Credits represent *actual* usage at standard prices.

Dr.   Cr.

(S)   *Finished Goods Account*   **(S)**

		£				£
Jan. 1 To Balance	b/d	30,000	Jan. 28 By Cost of Sales A/c			38,390
,, 28 ,, Work-in-progress		28,390	,, 28 ,, Balance	c/d		20,000
		£58,390				£58,390
Jan. 29 To Balance	b/d	£20,000				

NOTE.—Transfer to Cost of Sales Account is "difference" after entering stock at January 28th.

(A)   *Debtors Control Account*   **(A)**

		£				£
Jan. 1 To Balance	b/d	40,000	Jan. 28 By Bank			45,000
,, 28 ,, Sales Control		50,000	,, 28 ,, Balance	c/d		45,000
		£90,000				£90,000
Jan. 29 To Balance	b/d	£45,000				

(A)   *Creditors Control Account*   **(A)**

		£				£
Jan. 28 To Bank		22,000	Jan. 1 By Balance	b/d		24,000
,, 28 ,, Balance	c/d	15,800	,, 28 ,, Stores Control and Material Price Variance A/c			10,000
			,, 28 ,, *Cost Control:*			
			Direct Material			200
			Indirect Material			2,000
			Selling and Distribution Materials			1,000
			Administration Material			600
		£37,800				£37,800
			Jan. 29 By Balance	b/d		£15,800

(S)   *Work-in-progress Account*   **(S)**

		£				£
Jan. 1 To Balance	b/d	12,000	Jan. 28 By Finished Goods			28,390
,, 28 ,, Cost Control		19,340	,, 28 ,, Balance	c/d		11,500
,, 28 ,, Cost Control		5,800				
,, 28 ,, Cost Control		2,750				
		£39,890				£39,890
Jan. 29 To Balance	b/d	£11,500				

NOTE.—Transfer to Finished Goods Account is "difference" on Account after entering closing Work-in-progress.

(A)   *Bank Account*   **(A)**

		£				£
Jan. 1 To Balance	b/d	18,000	Jan. 28 By *Cost Control:*			
,, 28 ,, Debtors Control		45,000	Wages			10,540
			Salaries			3,200
			Expenses			2,100
			,, 28 ,, Creditors Control			22,000
			,, 28 ,, Balance	c/d		25,160
		£63,000				£63,000
Jan. 29 To Balance	b/d	£25,160				

        Share Capital Account   **(A)**

					£
		Jan. 1 By Balance	b/d		£300,000

Dr.   *Profit and Loss Account*   (A)   Cr.

	Jan. 1 By Balance	b/d	£76,000

P.A.Y.E. Income Tax   (A)

Jan. 28 By Cost Control		£500

NOTE.—The above account could be merged with the Accruals Account.

(A)   *Cost Control Account*   (A)

	£		£
Jan. 28 To Bank:		Jan. 28 By Prepayments A/cs (Rates)	400
Wages	10,000	,, 28 ,, *Work-in-progress A/c and*	
National Ins.	540	*Variance A/cs:*	
,, 28 ,, P.A.Y.E. Income Tax	500	(a) Direct Costs	20,540
,, 28 ,, Creditors Control	200	(b) Indirect Costs	6,000
,, 28 ,, Creditors Control	2,000	(c) Administration Costs	2,750
,, 28 ,, Creditors Control	1,000	,, 28 ,, Cost of Sales (Selling and	
,, 28 ,, Creditors Control	600	Distribution)	3,150
,, 28 ,, Stores Control	11,300		
,, 28 ,, Stores Control	900		
,, 28 ,, Bank:			
Salaries	3,200		
Expenses	2,100		
,, 28 ,, Depreciation of Plant and			
Machinery	300		
,, 28 ,, Accruals (Rent)	200		
	£32,840		£32,840

NOTES

1. The above account replaces the separate Wages Control Account and Overhead Control Account used in previous examples.

2. Corresponding entries in respect of (a) and (b) on the credit side of the Account, are to be found in the following Accounts:

(a) Work-in-progress		Dr.	£19,340
Material Usage Variance		Dr.	£800
Labour Rate Variance		Dr.	£100
Labour Efficiency Variance		Dr.	£300
			£20,540

(b) Work-in-progress		Dr.	£5,800
Overhead Budget Variance		Dr.	£100
Overhead Efficiency Variance		Dr.	£150
			£6,050
Less Overhead Volume Variance (CREDIT)			£50
			£6,000

Particular notice should be taken of the treatment of the Material Price Variance. It does *not* appear in the Cost Control Account.

Dr.   (S)   *Cost of Sales Account*   (S)   Cr.

			£			£
Jan. 28 To Finished Goods			38,390	Jan. 28 By Sales Control A/c		55,000
,, 28 ,, Cost Control			3,150			
,, 28 ,, Balance	c/d		13,460			
			£55,000			£55,000
				Jan. 29 By Balance	b/d	£13,460

NOTE.—Alternatively, the balance could be taken to Profit and Loss Account.

      (S)   *Sales Control Account*   (S)

	£		£
Jan. 28 To Cost of Sales	55,000	Jan. 28 By Debtors Control	50,000
		,, 28 ,, Sales Price Variance	5,000
	£55,000		£55,000

      (A)   *Prepayments Account*

Jan. 28 To Cost Control A/c	£400

NOTE.—The amount prepaid to cover the period *after* January 28th is included in the above account.

      Accruals Account   (A)

Jan. 28 By Cost Control A/c	£200

NOTE.—The amount due for the period *to* Jan. 28th is included in the above account.

      Material Price Variance Account

Jan. 28 To Creditors Control A/c	£1300

      Material Usage Variance Account

Jan. 28 To Cost Control A/c	£800

      Labour Rate Variance Account

Jan. 28 To Cost Control A/c	£100

      Labour Efficiency Variance Account

Jan. 28 To Cost Control A/c	£300

Dr.   Cr

Overhead Budget Variance Account

Jan. 28 To Cost Control A/c	£100		

Overhead Efficiency Variance Account

Jan. 28 To Cost Control A/c	£150		

Overhead Volume Variance Account

		Jan. 28 By Cost Control A/c	£50

Sales Price Variance Account

Jan. 28 To Sales Control	£5000		

SPECIAL NOTE.—The totals shown immediately below would be obtained from analysis sheets, summaries and other forms. The background work of building up these totals will go on daily and, at the end of each accounting period, they will be used to complete the Third Entries.

Summarising of Costs (Third Entries)
Cost Sheets for January

	Production		Administra-tion	Selling and Distribution
	Direct	Indirect		
	£	£	£	£
Materials	200	2,000		
Materials	11,300	900	600	1,000
Wages	9,040	2,000	—	—
Salaries			2,000	1,200
Expenses		1,100	200	800
Depreciation		300		
Rent Accrued				200
	20,540	6,300	2,800	3,200
Less Rates Prepaid	—	300	50	50
	£20,540	£6,000	£2,750	£3,150

NOTE.—The Actual Costs are analysed, the totals then being used to complete transfers to Work-in-progress and Cost of Sales.

Trial Balance of Bradley & Co. Ltd.

January 28th, 19...

	Dr. £	Cr. £
Land and Buildings Account	200,000	
Plant and Machinery Account	60,000	
Depreciation: Plant and Machinery Account		10,300
Stores Control Account	46,500	
Finished Goods Account	20,000	
Debtors Control Account	45,000	
Creditors Control Account		15,800
Work-in-progress Account	11,500	
Bank Account	25,160	
Share Capital Account		300,000
Profit and Loss Account		76,000
P.A.Y.E. Income Tax		500
Cost of Sales Account		13,460
Prepayments Account	400	
Accruals Account		200
Material Price Variance Account	1,300	
Material Usage Variance Account	800	
Labour Rate Variance Account	100	
Labour Efficiency Variance Account	300	
Overhead Budget Variance Account	100	
Overhead Efficiency Variance Account	150	
Overhead Volume Variance Account		50
Sales Price Variance Account	5,000	
	£416,310	£416,310

EXAMINATION QUESTIONS

1. (a) What do you understand by *integral accounts*.

(b) Design a code of accounts illustrating the principles of integral accounts in a limited liability company selling a single standardised product which passes through one production department.

(I.C.W.A.)

2. From the undernoted information you are required to prepare the Ledger Accounts maintained at Factory A, at Factory B, and at head office, indicating the source of each entry made in these accounts.

	£
Invoice value of materials purchased by Factory A at 10% over Standard	31,350
Invoice value of materials purchased by Factory B	68,590
Standard cost of materials issued from stock by Factory A	29,490
Standard cost of materials issued from stock by Factory B	66,400
Favourable (or gain) price variance of materials issued from stock by Factory B	5%

	£
Sales of Factory A at 10% above standard sales	64,200
Sales of Factory B at 10% above standard sales	121,660

Materials invoices are sent by suppliers to the factories.
Suppliers' accounts are maintained at head office.

Sales invoices for goods dispatched by Factory A are prepared at head office.
The accounts of Factory A's customers are maintained at head office.

Factory B prepares its own invoices and maintains its own customers' records.

(I.C.W.A.)

3. Define:

    (a) calendar ratio;
    (b) indirect wages;
    (c) labour hour rate;
    (d) standard hour;
    (e) premium bonus;
    (f) capacity usage ratio.

(I.C.W.A.)

4. You are required to record in the accounts in the Financial Ledger, maintained at head office, the following transactions for the year ended 30th June, 1969. All factories, being at a distance from the head office, maintain their own cost accounts which are integrated with the financial accounts. You are also required to provide for depreciation at 5% (2½% on additions made during the year), and to transfer the appropriate balances to a profit and loss account.

Credit purchases made by—

	£
Factory A	146,200
Factory B	97,300
Factory C	103,900
Factory D	72,300
Head office administration	8,970
Head office selling	22,850

Cash paid by head office to or on behalf of—

	£
Factory A	97,800
Factory B	143,200
Factory C	169,500
Factory D	47,900
Head office administration	95,650
Head office selling	49,500

Stocks at 1st July, 1968, at—

	£
Factory A	23,260
Factory B	15,090
Factory C	36,000
Factory D	9,060

	£
Cash in hand at—	
Factory A	600
Factory B	500
Factory C	800
Factory D	500
Cash received from trade debtors	1,376,500
Credit sales	1,196,800
Balance at 1st July, 1968, on Fixed Assets account in financial ledger*	1,073,000
Cash paid to trade creditors	509,370
Cost of new plant, equipment, etc., invoiced to—	
Factory A	24,500
Factory B	2,600
Factory C	5,900
Factory D	17,200
Head office administration	8,300
Head office selling	8,500
Cost of alterations (capitalised) at—	
Factory B	3,800
Factory C	9,200
Stocks at 30th June, 1969 at—	
Factory A	25,900
Factory B	12,600
Factory C	42,500
Factory D	11,300

	£
* Representing Fixed Assets at—	
Factory A	280,150
Factory B	228,000
Factory C	400,450
Factory D	84,800
Head office administration	31,850
Head office selling	47,750

(I.C.W.A.)

5. From the undernoted information you are required to write up and close off the necessary accounts in the General Ledger maintained at the accounts department at Hilltop. The accounts of the factories at Endville and Middletown are integrated with the General Ledger.

Each factory maintains its own stock records and operates a bank account maintained on the imprest system. All factory purchase invoices are passed locally and sent to the accounts department for payment.

	Endville £	Middletown £	Hilltop £
Value of purchase invoices for materials passed by	302,746	186,934	875
Value of purchase invoices for "expenses" passed by	14,923	10,840	9,384
Value of purchase invoices for fixed assets passed by	27,700	16,300	—
Value of debit notes for materials issued by	5,116	—	—
Value of debit notes for "expenses" issued by	—	—	1,032
Reimbursement of payments made by	73,128	43,527	11,500
Cost of fixed assets in use at beginning of year at	111,500	60,150	4,000
"Expenses" prepaid at end of year by	—	360	—
Wages due and unpaid at end of year by	1,420	1,540	2,300
"Expenses" due and unpaid at end of year by	3,610	1,260	2,970
Stock at cost held at beginning of year by	18,500	27,900	—
Cash at bank and on hand at beginning of year at	2,400	4,600	—
Cash at bank and on hand at end of year at	2,600	4,000	—
Cost of sales invoiced to customers by	426,161	254,861	—

Cost of materials, etc., invoiced by Endville to Middletown: £14,650

Cost of materials, etc., invoiced by Middletown to Endville: £25,650

Cost of production, invoiced by Endville to Hilltop, of fixed assets erected
at: Endville £9300

Middletown £4800

Rate of depreciation for year on fixed assets chargeable to: Endville $12\frac{1}{2}\%$

Middletown 10%

Hilltop $7\frac{1}{2}\%$

(*I.C.W.A.*)

6. As at 30th November, 1969, the following balances existed in a company's integrated standard cost and financial accounts:

Balance Sheet Accounts	£'000	
Capital and reserves	300	
Creditors and accruals	88	
Fixed assets	140	
Raw materials in store and process	80	
Direct wages in process	20	(at Standard)
Factory overhead in process	10	
Finished stock	90	
Debtors	100	
Cash at bank	10	

Trading Accounts	£'000	
Budgeted sales	585	
Sales variance	12	(debit)
Standard factory cost of sales	493	
Materials variance	5	(credit)
Direct wages variance	7	(debit)
Factory overhead variance	2	(debit)
Administration and selling expense	14	

During December 1969 the following transactions took place:

	£'000
Budgeted sales	105
Actual sales	98
Cash received—from debtors	95

	£'000	
Cash paid—to creditors	63	
Cash paid—direct wages	23	
Raw materials purchased	40	(Actual cost)
Excess materials issued	1	(at Standard)
Factory expenses incurred	17	
Administration and selling expenses incurred	3	
Output finished (at standard cost)		
Materials	50	
Direct wages	26	
Factory overhead	13	
Standard factory cost of actual sales	82	

The standard cost of materials purchased is £42,000

The closing valuations of work-in-progress accounts (which are debited at Actual, and credited at Standard) are:

Direct wages (at Standard)	£15,000
Factory overhead (at Standard)	£13,000

You are required to:

    (a) write up and close off the Ledger Accounts, *and*
    (b) prepare a trial balance of the closing balances.

                                                      (*I.C.W.A.*)

CHAPTER 16

FLEXIBLE BUDGETS: MANUFACTURING OVERHEAD COSTS

THERE are two types of budget:

1. Fixed budget.   2. Flexible budget.

Both budgets under Standard Costing show, for stated conditions and volume of production, what overhead costs should be. The fixed budget portrays an inflexible, rigid plan. There is one set of conditions, one volume of output, and a simple collection of costs. According to the budget, management expect all conditions, etc., to operate without variation. However, any enlightened management is unlikely to anticipate no deviation from a stated target. In fact, for actual production and costs to coincide with budgeted output and costs, would be most unusual. Except, therefore, for projecting what the management expect and desire, the fixed budget is of limited value. If actual volume and conditions are not those expected in the budget the analysis of the overhead budget and volume variances cannot be very informative. For these reasons the flexible budget is normally essential.

With a flexible budget all possible volumes of output are covered. Costs for any volume not specifically covered may be obtained by interpolation. The important fact to remember is that the relevant Standard Costs can readily be "attached" to actual production. At all times related factors are being compared—so essential for intelligent decision-making.

To be able to prepare the budgets with some degree of accuracy it is necessary to analyse overhead costs into those which are "fixed," those which are "variable," and those which are "semi-variable." In each case the reference is, of course, to *total* cost. Fixed cost in total will be variable *per unit* of output or per hour, depending upon volume or number of hours achieved. The definitions of these different types of cost apply, therefore, to totals and not costs of individual products.

The semi-variable costs present a problem. Total fixed costs are the same irrespective of activity. Variable costs are a specific sum per unit of output or standard hour, so total variable cost is found by multiplying unit cost by units. To relate semi-variable costs to activity it will be necessary to assess the effects of increases or decreases in volume on these costs. Clearly an attempt at setting a rate to cover variability is essential. Suggested approaches are:

1. A definite rate for each unit to be produced (the variable overhead rate) and a total for the fixed overhead cost.
2. Two rates—
    (a) A variable rate per unit for *any* volume of output.
    (b) A fixed rate which will change with changes in volume of output.
3. One composite rate to cover both fixed and variable costs. When volume changes so will the composite rate.

The ambiguity of the terms may again be noticed. In 2 (a), the variable rate remains the *same* per unit, but varies in total with changes in output. The *unit* fixed cost, referred to in 2 (b), varies with activity, but, in total, remains the same.

To obtain results which are as accurate as possible a separate rate for variable costs is necessary (2 above). That is to say, the semi-variable costs have to be segregated into their fixed and variable elements. Reference to past records may provide the basis of an intelligent estimate of what the division should be, but a better approach is via:

1. Regression or Scattergraph Charts, plotting a line by inspection.
2. Least Squares with or without Regression Charts.

Flexible budgeting makes use of these techniques, any "gaps" being covered by interpolation or extrapolation.

For each type of semi-variable cost an attempt is made to show the correlation which exists between production and the incurring of expenditure. Neither charts nor least squares are perfect, for there are factors, other than volume of production, which may influence expenditure incurred. For example, in one month there may be an exceptionally long run of rejected parts, but, in another, very few. This and similar irregular occurrences can clearly negate any conclusions that may be reached from the figures determined by *any* method used for separating the fixed and variable cost elements.

PROBLEM: SEPARATION OF FIXED AND VARIABLE ELEMENTS

Past 6 months	Semi-variable cost (power)	Volume of production (units of output or standard hours)
	£	
January	2800	3000
February	2500	2800
March	3000	3200
April	2000	1800
May	2100	1900
June	3200	3500

REGRESSION CHARTS

The procedure for preparing a regression chart is enumerated below.

1. *On the horizontal axis of the chart, plot the volume of production or sales*

The figures used may be physical units or sterling values. Alternatively, activity may be expressed in terms of standard hours. Since the standard overhead rate is likely to be "so much per hour," the use of the budgeted number of the latter on the chart is likely to prove very useful.

2. *On the vertical axis plot the overhead cost*

The class intervals for both production data and costs will largely be determined by the size of the figures in the problem being solved. Thus, for example, when reasonably small sums are involved, the costs may be graduated in intervals of £50, *i.e.* £0–£50–£100, etc. When quite large figures are being dealt with, the scale may be, say, £0–£200–£400–£600, etc. The object must be to keep the chart within reasonable dimensions and, at the same time, be able to use figures, when calculating the degree of correlation, which are small enough to be of value.

3. *Prepare cost schedule and production or sales schedule*

Obtain a schedule of figures of, say, the past six or twelve months, relating to:

(*a*) Overhead cost incurred each month.

(*b*) Production or Sales for each month.

4. *Plot the first point on the chart*

Referring to the schedule in (3), take the overhead cost for the first month, say, January and find the appropriate point on the vertical axis on the chart. Similarly, take the production figure (units, sterling, or standard hours) for January and then "match" the cost and production figures on the chart, plotting a point where the two meet. An example of this is shown below (Fig. 33). On the chart the £2800 and 3000 units are taken together and the point of meeting shown.

5. *Plot subsequent points*

Each month is dealt with as in (4) until all the points have been plotted.

6. *Draw regression line*

By inspection, draw a straight line through the points plotted, or through the mean of all points, with the same number of points, of equal distance from it, on each side of the line. When drawing the regression line any abnormal costs may be disregarded.

7. Establish fixed cost

The point where the regression line intersects the vertical axis is taken to be the amount of the fixed cost, *i.e.* approximately £850 in Fig. 32.

Clearly the slightest bias exhibited in drawing the line, will make a difference of £100 in fixed cost. This fact is a serious objection to the method.

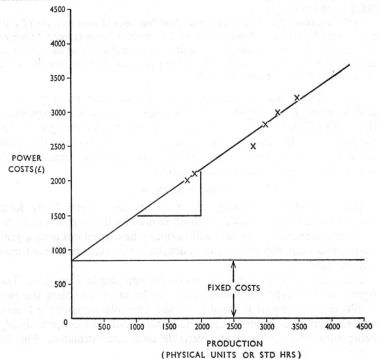

FIG. 33.—*Regression Chart.*
Separation of Fixed and Variable Elements.

USE OF CHART

The degree of correlation may now be seen. Referring to the horizontal axis, it will be possible to see the extent of an increase in variable costs which follows an increase in output. For example, on the chart an increase in output of 1000 units results in approximately £650, indicating that the variable cost per unit is £0·65 (*see* lines forming triangle).

This unit cost may be checked by noting that an increase of 4000 units will result in an increase in total variable cost of £2650, which is approximately £0·65 per unit.

No attempt has been made to obtain exactness. As indicated earlier, the variable unit cost can only be an approximation.

SOLUTION

The regression chart shown indicates that each additional unit will result in a variable cost of approximately £0·65. For any activity the cost equation FC + (U × VC) will apply. FC = Fixed Cost, U = Units of Output or Standard Hours and VC = Variable Cost per unit. For an output of 1000 units the cost structure will therefore be £850 + (1000 × £0·65) = £850 + £650 = £1500, whereas for 2000 units the cost will be £850 + (2000 × £0·65) or £2150.

In the Problem the volume of production has been shown as units of output *or* standard hours. Unless each unit of output has a standard time of one hour the two will obviously not coincide: normally one *or* the other will have to be used. In the example it has been assumed that they are the same, *i.e.* one unit takes one hour to produce.

The student should experiment by copying the chart on graph paper and by drawing, at slightly different angles, two or three regression lines. He will notice that variable cost per unit may be changed, within the range of a few shillings, simply by estimating differently the angle of the line. It is for this reason that the method of least squares, which is not affected by biased estimates, is adopted.

LEAST SQUARES

The calculations necessary for obtaining an "average" by least squares are more involved than those required when regression charts are used. However, since they will normally be carried out once a year only, and a more objective result is obtained, this extra refinement may well be justified.

Below is an outline of the procedures for applying least squares. The figures used for the regression chart will be taken and then the two results can be compared. Needless to say, an explanation of the theory of least squares is beyond the scope of this book, the concern simply being with how the fixed and variable costs are estimated. Fig. 34 summarises the necessary calculations.

(1) Power cost (y)	(2) Production (units) (x)	(3) No. of units squared (x^2)	(4) (1) × (2) (xy)
£			
2,800	3,000	9,000,000	8,400,000
2,500	2,800	7,840,000	7,000,000
3,000	3,200	10,240,000	9,600,000
2,000	1,800	3,240,000	3,600,000
2,100	1,900	3,610,000	3,990,000
3,200	3,500	12,250,000	11,200,000
15,600	16,200	46,180,000	43,790,000

FIG. 34.—*Separation of Fixed and Variable Elements: Least Squares*

The steps involved are:

1. Calculate the monthly average output or activity $\left(i.e. \dfrac{\Sigma x}{N}\right)$.

2. Obtain the monthly average cost $\left(i.e. \dfrac{\Sigma y}{N}\right)$.

3. Square the number of units of production for each month and find the monthly average $\left(i.e. \dfrac{\Sigma x^2}{N}\right)$.

4. Multiply, for each month, units by costs and find the monthly average $\left(i.e. \dfrac{\Sigma xy}{N}\right)$.

The variable element may then be found by the formula:

$$VC = \frac{(4) - ((1) \times (2))}{(3) - (1)^2}$$

The fixed element formula is:

$$FC = (2) - (VC \times (1))$$

By reference to the table and omitting noughts it will be seen that the following relate to the above steps:

Step (1) $= \dfrac{162}{6} = 27$.

Step (2) $= \dfrac{156}{6} = 26$.

Step (3) The multiplication has already been done, so the final calculation is:

$$\frac{4618}{6} = 769 \cdot 7$$

Step (4) Again referring to the table it will be seen that the final figures are:

$$\frac{4379}{6} = 729 \cdot 8$$

The variable element is found, therefore, as shown below:

$$\frac{729 \cdot 8 - (27 \times 26)}{769 \cdot 7 - 27^2}$$

$$= \frac{729 \cdot 8 - 702}{769 \cdot 7 - 729} = \frac{27 \cdot 8}{40 \cdot 7}$$

$$= £0 \cdot 683.$$

Comparison with the result obtained by means of the regression chart will indicate that there is little difference in the two answers. A variable cost of between £0·650 and £0·683 per unit is obviously a good enough estimate.

NOTE ON ACCURACY OF METHODS

The method of least squares is likely to give the most accurate separation of the fixed and variable elements in a semi-variable cost. Moreover, as already observed, the necessary objectivity is achieved.

Both the direct estimate or the use of a regression chart leaves much to be desired. When a chart is used it is important to observe that, for a reasonably accurate estimate, it is essential for (1) all the plotted points to appear *on* the regression line, and (2) the conditions which operated in the past, from which the basic data have been taken, to operate in the future.

From these observations, it follows that the greater is the degree of scatter of the points from the estimating line and the more changed are actual conditions when compared with past conditions, then the less accurate will be the estimate.

PREPARATION OF THE FLEXIBLE BUDGETS

A flexible budget has to be prepared for each cost centre. For the ultimate control plan to operate efficiently, thus keeping expenditure within the stated limits, the co-operation of managers, foremen, and supervisors, and the compiling of budgets in a way that makes them readily understood by all levels of management, are essential. Only in this way will the budget represent a workable idea and not merely a manipulation of figures.

Fig. 35 shows a flexible budget for outputs which vary between 90 and 115%. Generally, a 5% interval will be quite adequate to obtain the required accuracy. The precise lay-out and presentation will have to be determined by the Accountant concerned. Provided he makes his figures understood, he is achieving the main objective.

CHARGING OF SERVICE COSTS TO PRODUCING COST CENTRES

The aim, with each budget, is to locate responsibility for costs. So far as charging service costs to producing cost centres is concerned, the best plan appears to be that which:

1. Calculates a standard rate per hour (or other basis) for each service cost centre.
2. Charges each producing cost centre, using a service, at the appropriate standard rate for the *actual* usage.

FLEXIBLE BUDGET OF MANUFACTURING OVERHEAD COSTS
Month January   Dept. A.B.

Overhead Cost Description	Bases for calculating Total Cost		Output in Percentages					
	Fixed	Variable	90%	95%	100%	105%	110%	115%
	£	Per Std. hr.	£	£	£	£	£	£
Variable Costs:								
Spoilage		£0·05	450	475	500	525	550	575
Indirect Materials		£0·10	900	950	1,000	1,050	1,100	1,150
Semi-Variable Costs:								
Indirect Labour	500	£0·25	2,750	2,875	3,000	3,125	3,250	3,375
Power and Light	400	£0·10	1,300	1,350	1,400	1,450	1,500	1,550
Heat and Water	200	£0·10	1,100	1,150	1,200	1,250	1,300	1,350
Insurance on Stocks *	150	£0·025	375	388	400	413	425	438
Repairs and Maintenance	600	£0·25	2,850	2,975	3,100	3,225	3,350	3,475
Fixed Costs:								
Supervision	1000		1,000	1,000	1,000	1,000	1,000	1,000
Depreciation	4000		4,000	4,000	4,000	4,000	4,000	4,000
Rent Charges	1500		1,500	1,500	1,500	1,500	1,500	1,500
Other Space Charges	900		900	900	900	900	900	900
			£17,125	£17,563	£18,000	£18,438	£18,875	£19,313

Rate per Standard Hour   £1·90   £1·85   £1·80   £1·76   £1·72   £1·68

NOTE.—100% = 10,000 Standard Hours.
* Figures taken to nearest £1.

FIG. 35.—*Flexible Budget of Manufacturing Overhead Costs*

NOTES
1. The figures used are purely hypothetical.
2. Output may be stated in terms of:
   (*a*) Percentages, when it is quite usual to state what "100%" represents (*e.g.* as in example, 10,000 standard hours or, say, 10,000 units of product X).
   (*b*) Units of Output.
   (*c*) Sales Values.
   (*d*) Standard Hours.
3. The semi-variable costs will have been separated into their fixed and variable elements by one of the methods already covered earlier in the chapter.
4. Comparison with the budget shown in the section on Selling Costs may be made with advantage.
5. Costs for any output which is not an exact multiple of 5% may be found by interpolation.
6. The charge "per hour" is used for simplicity—in practice, for many costs, it would be unrealistic.

Since the standard capacity of a service cost centre will be determined by the anticipated demands on the service by producing departments, this method of absorbing the service costs will show:

(*a*) How many "units" of service are being consumed and, in view of the actual volume of output, whether or not there is a high or low degree of efficiency in utilisation. Any variance on usage can be made the subject of enquiry and efficiency improved.

(*b*) Any variance on producing and distributing a service will be shown in the accounts of the service cost centre concerned.

A budget variance and volume variance are usually calculated.

The same fixed costs have to be incurred irrespective of exact output of service and, for this reason, a method which charges out *all* fixed costs on a basis of potential usage by each producing department is often advocated. The argument advanced for this method is that the producing departments require a certain capacity to be available: this involves definite, fixed (standing) charges. If full use is *not* made of available resources, then the producing departments should still be charged according to relative, expected usage for the service *can* be used should they so desire it. Variable costs are then charged on a basis of actual usage. The importance of recovering all fixed costs through a producing department is clearly, at times, over-rated. Strictly speaking, neither a service cost centre nor a producing cost centre is responsible for fixed costs, so attempts to locate responsibility in a precise manner, do not further cost control. To be able to show the costs of operating the service cost centres in their accounts appears to be a much more profitable approach to the problem of keeping inefficiency to a minimum.

An example of how the costs of a service cost centre may be dealt with is shown below:

Repairs and Maintenance Cost Centre
Budget for January

Cost	Bases of calculation		Capacity percentages		
	Fixed	Variable per hour	90%	95%	100%
	£	£	£	£	£
Labour	600	0·25	5,100	5,350	5,600
Equipment Charges	300	0·05	1,200	1,250	1,300
Materials		0·25	4,500	4,750	5,000
Rent and Space Charges	400	0·25	4,900	5,150	5,400
Other Overhead Costs	700	0·10	2,500	2,600	2,700
	2000		18,200	19,100	20,000

$$\text{Standard Rate} = \frac{£20,000}{20,000 \text{ hours}} = £1 \text{ per hour.}$$

$$100\% = 20,000 \text{ hours}$$

Producing Cost Centre XY

Maintenance service for January:

Standard = 750 hours
Actual = 800 hours

Actual and Budgeted Costs for Repairs and Maintenance Service Cost Centre

Cost	95% Capacity	
	Standard	Actual
	£	£
Labour	5,350	5,800
Equipment Charges	1,250	1,300
Materials	4,750	4,260
Rent and Space	5,150	5,350
Other Overhead Costs	2,600	2,900
	19,100	19,610

Total Production Cost Centre Hours for Service R & M
$$= 19,000 \ (95\%)$$

Charges to Cost Centre XY.

800 hours at £1 = £800

This amount would be debited to a Factory Overhead Account XY, such amount, at the end of each month, being transferred to the Work-in-progress Account. Below is shown an account for the Service Cost Centre.

Service Cost Centre Account
Repairs and Maintenance

Actual	£	Actual at Standard	£
Jan. 28 To Journal (detailed)	19,610	Jan. 28 By Factory Overhead A/c—XY	800
		,, 28 ,, Other Producing Depts. (detailed)	18,200
		,, 28 ,, Overhead Budget Variance	510
		,, 28 ,, Overhead Volume Variance	100
	£19,610		£19,610

The account has been debited with the Actual Cost and credited with Standard Cost. Any difference on the account will represent a Budget Variance and, when capacity does not reach 100%, a Volume Variance. In the example the variances are:

1. Budget Variance £510 (unfavourable).

2. Volume Variance £100 (unfavourable).

There has been a failure to keep within the expenses allowed and also, due to the department not operating at 100% capacity, fixed costs have not been fully recovered. The calculations are as follows:

Volume Variance

	£
Budget at Actual Level of Operation	19,100
Less Actual usage × Standard rate	
(19,000 × £1)	19,000
	£ 100(unfavourable)

This may be checked by working out the Volume Variance for a fixed budget and then deducting the variable cost *saved* by not working the full number of hours at 100% capacity.

$$\text{Thus} \left(\frac{20,000}{\text{hours}} - \frac{19,000}{\text{hours}}\right) \times \frac{\text{Standard Overhead}}{\text{Rate £1}} = £1000$$

The variable cost is clearly £0·90 per hour (an increase of 1000 hours results in £900 increase in costs) so a total of £900 (1000 hours saved) is deducted from the £1000 to give a new volume Variance of £100 (unfavourable).

Budget Variance

Actual Overhead Cost	£19,610
Less Budgeted Cost Adjusted to 95%	
Capacity	£19,100
	£ 510(unfavourable)

NOTE.—Overhead Price and Utilisation Variances could be calculated for service costs. *See* "Alternative Approach to Calculations" later in this chapter.

RELATION OF SERVICE AND PRODUCING COST CENTRE BUDGETS

The example shown to illustrate the principle of calculating a standard rate for a service cost centre and then charging the user cost centre was deliberately simplified. In practice, there will clearly be a number of service and producing cost centres, many dependent upon each other. Service cost centres may require "service," and this fact may have to be shown in the accounts. As pointed out earlier, unless the usage is quite small, a transfer of part of the cost of the service cost centre will have to be transferred to *all* cost centres using the "service." The budgeted cost of the estimated usage will appear in the flexible budgets of the cost centres involved. Thus, for example, service cost centres A and B may be budgeted to cost (at 100% working), before adjustment for interrelationship, £8000 and £10,000 respectively. If

10% of A is used by B a transfer of £800 should be made to the budget for B. The £7200 and £10,800 would then be included in the flexible budget of the primary departments on the basis of expected usage.

Transfers from service cost centres to user departments may be made by taking appropriate percentages or by taking standard usage hours at the standard rate. For convenience, the rates applied in the flexible budgets shown have been *per hour*. This practice has much to recommend it, for, obviously, in a complete system of Production Planning and Control the standard hours may be adopted for many purposes. There are, however, when compiling budgets, other bases which may be more convenient and which are a more accurate measure of usage. For Power service, a rate per kilowatt hour or, for Building service, a rate per square foot, may be much more realistic. These would be shown in the flexible budgets concerned.

CALCULATION OF OVERHEAD VARIANCES WITH FLEXIBLE BUDGET

Unless the levels of activity—budget and actual—coincide, the Overhead Volume and Budget Variances * will *not* present a true indication of the state of efficiency. The more the two levels vary from each other, the less reliable become the variances. Clearly, there is no justification for comparing the budgeted costs for an activity of 10,000 hours when the actual hours are only 8000. Indeed, if the Budget Variance turned out to be anything but "favourable," there would be something sadly amiss.

Fortunately, the flexible budget allows the two sets of costs, budgeted and actual, to be compared without the cost accountant being forced to try to bring together quite unrelated species. The calculation of the variances presents no great problem, following lines similar to those already explained. An illustration is given below.

PROBLEM

MX Department
Summary Budget for January

Total Hours	4000	4200	4400
Total Cost	£8200	£8400	£8600

Product Y takes 1 hour to produce. 100% capacity is 4200 hours.

Actual Overhead = £8500.
Actual Output = 4000 units of Y.
Actual Hours = 4100.

Required: (*a*) Overhead Variances assuming a fixed budget.
(*b*) Overhead Variances with a flexible budget.

* The Budget Variance shown here is not exactly the same as the Expenditure Variance. An explanation is given later in this chapter.

SOLUTION (a)

Overhead Cost Variance

Actual Overhead Cost = £8500.

Standard Cost for Actual Output:

$$4000 \times £2 = £8000$$

£500 (unfavourable)

Overhead Budget Variance

Actual Cost = £8500
Cost per Budget = £8400

£ 100 (unfavourable)

Overhead Efficiency Variance

(AH − SH)SOR (the now familiar formula!)

$$= (4100 − 4000) \times £2$$
$$= £200 \text{ (unfavourable)}$$

Overhead Volume Variance

Budgeted Hours (100%) = 4200
Actual Hours = 4100

100

100 Hours × £2 = £200 (unfavourable)

SOLUTION (b)

Overhead Cost Variance

As for (a) above = £500 (unfavourable)

Overhead Budget Variance

The concern is with the budgeted cost for the *actual* level of activity. This is the only way of obtaining a true measure of efficiency in spending.

Budgeted Cost for 4100 hours = £8300
Actual Cost = £8500
Budgeted Cost = £8300

Budget Variance = £200 (unfavourable)

Overhead Efficiency Variance

The calculation and answer is precisely the same as for a fixed budget: *i.e.* in this solution, £200 (unfavourable).

Overhead Volume Variance

Again the concern must be with budgeted cost for the *actual* level of activity, *i.e.* £8300.

Actual hours are 4100 which, multiplied by the standard overhead rate, gives £8200 so the volume variance is £100 (unfavourable).

Because 4100 hours only were worked, it is logical that the costs should relate to these and to no others.   There is thus a £100 reduction in the Volume Variance, but Budget Variance is increased by £100.

Once again the new Volume Variance figure may be checked. For the fixed budget the Volume Variance was £200. Considering the flexible budget, it will be seen that 4100 hours have been taken as the basis of the Overhead Variances. In other words, 100 hours less than the anticipated volume have been worked. The variable cost for these is $100 \times £1$ (the variable rate) = £100. This, deducted from the fixed budget Volume Variance of £200, gives the amended Volume Variance of £100.*

SUMMARY

Fixed Budget

	£
Overhead Budget Variance	100
Overhead Efficiency Variance	200
Overhead Volume Variance	200
Overhead Cost Variance	£500 (unfavourable).

Flexible Budget

	£
Overhead Budget Variance	200
Overhead Efficiency Variance	200
Overhead Volume Variance	100
Overhead Cost Variance	£500 (unfavourable).

ALTERNATIVE APPROACH TO CALCULATIONS: MULTIPLE ANALYSIS

The variance analysis given above is the *three-way* approach defined in Chapter 6. As stressed earlier, there is no standardisation of the terms or methods used. For this reason students are advised to make themselves familiar with the alternative approaches to variance analysis.

* A formula for calculating the Overhead Volume or Capacity Variance is:

$$\left(\begin{array}{c} \text{Actual Hours} \\ \text{for period} \end{array} - \begin{array}{c} \text{Standard Hours} \\ \text{for period} \end{array} \right) \times \begin{array}{c} \text{Standard rate for} \\ \text{fixed overheads} \end{array}$$

In the example the fixed overhead rate at normal capacity is £1 per hour; *i.e.* £42 00 divided by 4200 hours. Accordingly the variance is $(4200 - 4100) \times £1 = £100$ as shown. It is a coincidence that the variable overhead rate is also £1.

Using the same problem shown above, but with slight modifications, a different approach is given. In this case, instead of the *three-way* analysis, the following variances are required:

1. Overhead Volume Variance.
2. Overhead Capacity Usage Variance.
3. Overhead Volume Efficiency Variance.
4. Overhead Expenditure Variance.
5. Overhead Efficiency Variance.

A note of explanation on the Overhead Price and Utilisation Variances is also given.

SUGGESTED SOLUTION

From the information given it will be seen that the appropriate rates are as follows:

Fixed Overheads   £1·00
Variable Overheads   £1·00

Overhead Volume Variance

This variance is a measure of the under- or over-absorption of fixed overhead costs. The first stage is as follows:

Standard hours	4200
Actual hours	4100
	100 hours lost

100 hours × £1·00 = **£100**

This represents an unfavourable variance—the amount which has not been fully absorbed into the product costs.

With the *three-way* analysis shown above, the volume variance would be £100. With the method used in this section, the effect on fixed costs of efficiency actually achieved is considered. The actual production is the equivalent 4000 hours, which means in effect that 100 hours have been "wasted": 100 × £1·00 = **£100·00** (unfavourable), which is due to inefficiency.

If the two figures are taken together, the Overhead Volume Variance is **£200** (unfavourable: 200 hours × £1·00 fixed overhead rate).

Overhead Capacity Usage Variance

A formula for calculating the Capacity Usage Variance is:

$$\left(\begin{matrix}\text{Budgeted} \\ \text{Hours}\end{matrix} - \begin{matrix}\text{Actual} \\ \text{Hours}\end{matrix}\right) \times \text{Standard Overhead Rate (Fixed)}$$

$$(4200 - 4100) \times £1·00$$

$$= 100 \times £1·00 = \underline{\underline{£100·00}} \text{ (unfavourable)}$$

In this case the total capacity available (4200 hours) has not been fully utilised.

—It will be seen that the Capacity Usage Variance under this method is the same as the Volume Variance when the *two-* or *three-way* analysis is employed.

Overhead Volume Efficiency Variance

With the Volume Efficiency Variance the concern is with the time taken to produce the actual output. This affects the utilisation of the facilities available. Again, a formula can be used:

$$\left(\frac{\text{Actual}}{\text{Hours}} - \frac{\text{Standard}}{\text{Hours}}\right) \times \text{Standard Overhead Rate (Fixed)}$$

$$(4100 - 4000) \times £1·00$$

$$= 100 \times £1·00 = \underline{£100·00} \text{ (unfavourable)}$$

Overhead Expenditure Variance

With this method of analysis the term "Expenditure" is used, but many writers prefer to use "Budget" indicated earlier. However, a possible difference in meaning is given below. The concern is with *variable* costs.

The calculations for this variance are as follows:

	£
Actual Variable Expenditure	4300
Budgeted Expenditure for Actual Activity	
4000 × £1·00 Variable Overhead Rate	4000
	£ 300 (unfavourable)

[NOTE]

	£
Total Expenditure	8500
Less Fixed Costs	4200
Total Variable Costs =	£4300

Overhead Expenditure Efficiency Variance

A formula for calculating this variance is:

$$\left(\frac{\text{Actual}}{\text{Hours}} - \frac{\text{Standard}}{\text{Hours}}\right) \times \text{Standard Overhead Rate (Variable)}$$

$$(4100 - 4000) \times £1·00$$

$$= 100 \times £1·00 = \underline{£100·00} \text{ (unfavourable)}$$

The reader will notice that with the method used earlier the variance is £200. However, £100 represents under-absorption of fixed costs when the alternative method is employed.

The remainder of the Expenditure Variance represents overspending for the hours worked. The Expenditure Efficiency Variance shows the effect of working 100 hours more than standard for the *actual* output.

This difference of £200 means that for the 4100 hours worked a higher than standard price has been paid for the services (Overhead Price Variance) or more than the standard quantity of services has been used (Overhead Utilisation Variance). This is in effect the Budget Variance shown in the *three-way* analysis given earlier.

In the absence of further details it is not possible to separate the price and utilisation variances. However, once the price and quantity (actual and standard) of a service are known, it becomes a relatively simple matter to calculate these variances along the lines indicated for material price and usage.

SUMMARY

Overhead Cost Variance (as previously)	£ 500 (unfavourable)

	£
1. Overhead Volume Variance	200
2. Overhead Expenditure Variance	300
	£500 (unfavourable)

Breakdown 1

	£
Capacity Usage Variance	100
Volume Efficiency Variance	100
Volume Variance =	£200 (unfavourable)

Breakdown 2

	£
Expenditure Efficiency Variance	100
Price/Utilisation Variance	200
	£300 (unfavourable)

CHOICE OF VOLUME FOR DETERMINING OVERHEAD RATE

The student will recall that the number of units of output, or hours, to be taken as a basis for calculating the standard overhead rate has to be determined before the Standard Costs are set. If, in the above example, 4000 standard hours had been taken as the appropriate volume, then the standard overhead rate would have been £2·05: with 4400 hours it would be £1·95. Different figures for the variances would result from the use of these alternative rates.

DEPARTMENTAL OPERATING STATEMENTS WITH A FLEXIBLE BUDGET

At the end of each accounting period the cost accountant should prepare a tabulation of overhead costs showing:

1. Budgeted Costs for actual activity.
2. Actual Costs.
3. Analysis of variances.
4. Controllable and uncontrollable elements of the variances.

DEPARTMENTAL OPERATING STATEMENT

Department AB   **Period January 19...**

Activity $\left\{\begin{array}{l}\text{Standard: 10,000 Standard Hours}\\\text{Actual: 9,500 Hours}\end{array}\right.$

Overhead Cost	Actual	Budgeted for Actual Hours	Analysis of Variances			Remarks
			Favourable	Unfavourable	Controllable	
	£	£	£	£	£	
Variable Costs:						
Spoilage	480	475		5	5	
Indirect Materials	975	950		25		Uncontrollable price increase
Semi-Variable Costs:						
Indirect Labour	3,000	2,875		125	125	Investigate
Power and Light	1,390	1,350		40	40	Investigate
Heat and Water	1,100	1,150	50		50 *	Investigate
Insurance on Stocks	390	388		2	2	
Repairs and Maintenance	2,900	2,975	75		75 *	Repairs kept to a minimum this period. Major breakdown X Dept.
Fixed Costs:						
Supervision	1,000	1,000	—	—	—	
Depreciation	4,000	4,000	—	—	—	
Rent Charges	1,500	1,500	—	—	—	
Other Space Charges	900	900	—	—	—	
	£17,635	£17,563	£125	£197	£47	

* Favourable Variance deducted to arrive at total "Controllable."

FIG. 36.—*Departmental Operating Statement*

NOTES

1. The budgeted costs refer to *actual* activity, thus making the Variance Analysis figures more realistic.

2. The Insurance on Stocks cost *may* be regarded as an uncontrollable cost, but in the illustration the variation between Standard and Actual is, in any event, too small to warrant any action being taken.

3. Whether or not any deviation from Standard warrants investigation depends upon its size in relation to the Standard Cost. In practice, the cost analyst will know, from experience, which items require attention. Some businesses fix a percentage (*e.g.* 10%); any deviations from Standard are converted to percentages, and those below the stated figure are ignored, whereas all others are investigated.

Often the uncontrollable variations from Standard are omitted from the tabulation. The foreman or other departmental manager can control certain costs only: fixed costs and costs which change through operation of economic factors such as a general price increase, resulting in a wage award, are not his responsibility. Accordingly, there is nothing to be gained so far as cost control is concerned by bringing them to his notice.

The form used to summarise these figures is known by a number of different names. It may be called a Variance Analysis Sheet, a Comparison of Budgeted and Actual Costs Sheet, or a Departmental Operating Statement. An example is given (Fig. 36) which uses the figures shown in the flexible budget at the beginning of the chapter.

Usually a Departmental Operating Statement is prepared for each department or cost centre: both producing and service departments' costs may be controlled by this method. The departmental manager is called upon to explain why variances have occurred and, quite clearly, if he, without good reason, consistently exceeds his budgeted costs he will be failing to do his work efficiently.

THE ACTIVITY RATIO

A useful measure, when comparing budgeted production and actual production, is the "activity ratio." Its inclusion on operating statements or other forms may, therefore, be considered desirable.

A formula for its calculation is:

$$\frac{\text{Standard Hours for Actual Output}}{\text{Standard Hours for Budgeted Output}} \times \frac{100}{1}$$

Thus if Product Y should take one hour to produce and the outputs are as follows:

Actual Output   10,000 units of Y
Budgeted Output 12,500 units of Y

then the Activity Ratio is:

$$\frac{10,000}{12,500} \times \frac{100}{1} = 80\%$$

Except in an indirect manner, the ratio does not measure efficiency. It shows what part of the "work-load" has actually been completed, a very important fact for the production manager.

EXAMINATION QUESTIONS

1. Design a summary operating statement for use with Standard Costing. Assume that there are two production departments, and provide also for:

(a) general works service;
(b) materials;
(c) head office expense.

Each production department has achieved less output than planned, and the level of performance is below standard.

Enter appropriate columnar figures reflecting the foregoing. Show also total variances, and analyse these in adjacent columns, one of which should be headed, "Works Controllable Variance." This last should be further analysed in a subsidiary tabulation.

Cost figures for each production and service department, and for materials, should be totals only.

(I.C.W.A.)

2. What is a departmental operating statement?

Prepare such a statement to indicate the efficiency of the use of each element of cost.

(I.C.W.A.)

3. What difficulties would you expect to find in the compilation of a flexible budget?

Give sufficient detail to justify any assumptions you make. How would such a budget be used?

(I.C.W.A.)

4. Draw up a budget of service department costs, using your own figures.

(I.C.W.A.)

5. Draw up a summary operating statement for a factory with four production departments, giving figures for activity, efficiency, Standard cost of output, Actual cost of output, and total variance. A variance analysis should be appended to the main statement, giving the composition of the total variance under the five main variance headings, of which works controllable variance is one. This last should be further analysed into the individual variances of which it is made up.

(I.C.W.A.)

6. Draft a departmental operating statement for a factory using a flexible budgeting system (figures are not required).

(I.C.W.A.)

7. The following is an extract from the flexible budget of a service department in a manufacturing company:

Flexible budget for 4-weekly period

Units of service to be performed	8,000	10,000	12,000
Costs:	£	£	£
Depreciation and insurance of equipment	220	220	220
Power	100	120	140
Supervision	140	140	170
Cleaning	20	20	30
Rent and rates	110	110	110
Consumable supplies	80	120	160
Repairs	70	90	90
Heat and light	30	30	40
Indirect wages	160	180	200
	£930	£1030	£1160

The budgeted activity for the four-weekly period No. 12 was at 10,000 units of service.

The Actual activity and expenditure during period No. 12 were:

Units of service performed   9000

Costs:	£
Depreciation and insurance of equipment	220
Power	130
Supervision	155
Cleaning	20
Rent and rates	110
Consumable supplies	90
Repairs	95
Heat and light	35
Indirect wages	180
	£1035

You are required to:

    (a) tabulate the variances from budget for each item of expenditure which is controllable by the department head;

    (b) calculate the following variances from budget for the whole department for period No. 12—

        (i) Budget Overhead Variance,
        (ii) Budget Controllable Variance.

(*I.C.W.A.*)

CHAPTER 17

STANDARD COSTS FOR SELLING AND DISTRIBUTION

INTRODUCTION: DEFINITIONS

SELLING COSTS

Selling costs are incurred in order to sell; that is, in order to change demand conditions. The principal object is to let the consumer know the actual or alleged superiority of the product over other, similar, products. Once a consumer is "converted" he must be held—advertising and other forms of sales promotion may do this.

All overhead costs incurred in furthering sales are grouped together under the one heading: typical examples with the usual subdivisions are as follows:

1. Direct Selling Costs

   (a) "External" costs relating to salesmen.

   Under this heading can be grouped salaries, bonuses, commissions, car and travelling expenses, telephones, printing, and stationery.

   (b) "Internal" costs of Sales Office.

   These include salaries, bonuses and commissions and car and travelling expenses of sales executives and similar personnel. In addition there are the establishment charges relating to the Sales Office—rent, rates, insurance, depreciation, telephones, stationery, postages.

2. Advertising and Sales Promotion Costs

   All types of advertising are included, whether in newspapers, journals, periodicals, catalogues, or on the television or cinema screen.

   The salaries and expenses of the promotional staff also belong to this category and, where there is a clear line of demarcation between Sales Office and Promotional Office, any establishment charges of the latter are normally treated as Sales Promotion Costs. The costs of demonstrations, samples, and any work carried out to promote sales, such as holding exhibitions, are other examples.

3. Credit and Collection Costs

   Under this heading can be grouped the salaries of supervisors and clerical workers, legal expenses, rent, rates, and taxes relating to the office used, and telephones, postages, and stationery costs incurred in connection with the granting of credit and the collection of debts.

Bad Debts may also be regarded as being a legitimate inclusion. Some accountants contend, however, that these are really revenues which have not materialised and should not, therefore, be treated as costs. Instead, they should be taken direct to Profit and Loss Account. Other accountants, although admitting Bad Debts as a cost, treat them as part of Administration Overhead Costs. If the selection of customers is to be a selling function—and it normally is regarded as such—then there appears to be a strong case for viewing bad debts as a selling cost.

General Observations on Selling Costs

Where the selling costs involved are a substantial part of total cost a division on functional lines will usually be essential. They will be collected and controlled within these categories.

The suggested division may, of course, be adapted to meet particular circumstances. One business may treat, say, Sales Ledger Office Costs as selling costs, whereas another may treat them as administration costs. Provided the particular method adopted is used consistently, there is, obviously, nothing lost by adopting any reasonable classification, even though standardisation of terms is very desirable. Maximum control for minimum cost should be the principal objective.

DISTRIBUTION COSTS

Once products are manufactured they must be stored and then delivered direct to the consumer or to some intermediate point, which may be a store or depot, a wholesaler, or a retailer. All overheads incurred for these purposes are known as distribution costs. Often the term is used to cover both selling costs *and* the limited definition given in this paragraph, but this appears to be too wide an application and, in the interests of clarity, is not to be recommended.

Examples of distribution costs are shown below:

1. Transportation Costs.

    Salaries of supervisors and clerks, wages of lorry-drivers, van-drivers, and garage mechanics, vehicle running and maintenance costs, and the depreciation and insurance of vehicles all come under this category.

2. Storage and Warehousing Costs

    All expenses incurred for storage and warehousing are collected under this heading. Warehouse office expenses, salaries, wages, heat, light and power, internal transport running costs, and depreciation, are typical examples.

THE IMPORTANCE OF SELLING AND DISTRIBUTION COSTS

More attention is being paid to the question of control of these expenses because in some cases they equal, or even exceed, the cost of manufacture.

The reasons for the increase in these costs in recent years are many, but worthy of specific mention are those set out in the following paragraphs:

The desire to increase turnover leads, in many cases, to the entering of markets where the potential volume is small. Large-scale production can bring about a tremendous reduction in average unit cost. The aim, therefore, is to expand sales so that minimum average unit costs can be obtained. Often unprofitable areas are worked in the hope that, eventually, the extra costs incurred will be covered by increased sales.

The need to create a demand for speciality products, such as accounting machines, washing machines, vacuum cleaners, refrigerators, and television sets. Once established, the speciality lines offer large profit margins, but a large amount of advertising and sales promotion is essential before this is achieved. Moreover, to keep abreast with competitors, continuous efforts are essential, so that at all times selling costs tend to be large.

With the growth in competition, in all types of business, there has been an increase in direct selling costs and in advertising and sales-promotion costs. In addition, there is an increased tendency to grant "services" to shopkeepers and other tradespeople. The cost of painting a shop front or a delivery van for a retailer may be met by the manufacturer, provided the retailer incorporates a particular advertisement into the painting or sells a particular line of product only. There are other similar benefits which can also be awarded.

By the provision of improved delivery services, distribution costs have also increased in some types of business.

The reasons given above have tended to increase the total amount spent on selling and distribution. On the other hand, with increased sales there has often been a reduction in unit production costs. There is no doubt that efforts should be made to predetermine standards of performance, to compare Actual performance with Standards, and to find out, by variance analysis, the reasons for any deviations from efficient performance. Unfortunately, for reasons now to be outlined, these ideals are not easy to accomplish.

COST STANDARDS FOR SELLING AND DISTRIBUTION

The setting of Standard Costs in respect of the selling and distribution functions cannot be overlooked. The task is, admittedly, difficult, but this is no excuse for neglecting the problem. In fact, in the interests of cost control, some attempt is essential. The difficulties associated with the setting of Standards are many; they may be summarised as shown below:

1. Effective supervision of salesmen, vehicle drivers, and other "external" employees is difficult to achieve.

   Compared with the manufacturing function the lack of effective supervision may be regarded as being due to:

   (a) Remoteness of control from the official responsible for the selling and distribution functions. (In the factory the employees are under constant supervision so control is possible.)

   (b) Machines do not set the pace as is often the case in manufacturing.

2. Selling and distribution methods cannot, because of diverse conditions, be subjected to a high degree of standardisation. The methods adopted must suit the particular conditions: standardisation may result in a loss of sales.

3. The degree of competition within an industry will tend to vary from period to period. There is the intensity of the efforts of competitors and, also, the changes in customers' tastes: both affect the expenditure made on selling.

4. It is extremely difficult to measure a salesman's efficiency. In the highly organised factory it is possible to measure, with reasonable accuracy, the performances of both men and machines.

5. The lack of knowledge and experience in this particular field. Accountants and engineers receive both practical and theoretical training on factory procedures and organisation, but up to now, the selling and distribution functions have been neglected.

6. The costs that are incurred "internally," such as warehousing, storage, and packing expenses, are difficult to estimate because, in practice, there is often no clear indication as to what part of a function is "consumed" by a particular line of product. This problem of apportioning joint costs is to be found with all selling and distribution costs.

IMPORTANCE OF ATTEMPTING TO SET STANDARDS

There are advantages and disadvantages associated with the setting of Standards for selling and distribution. It is possible to argue that the additional clerical expense necessary to set Standards and then to isolate and explain variances is unjustifiable. Moreover, because of the difficulties which arise in connection with setting Standards, the latter are, inevitably, very "loosely" set so that deviations from predetermined performances will be of little or no value.

Often selling and distribution costs are very large, so, accordingly, in such cases, the arguments against setting Standards can usually be dismissed. The fact that costs are being watched indicates to those responsible that careful spending is essential. Each class of expense can be examined in relation to amounts sold or delivered and can be analysed so as to show functional responsibility. These, along with remedies shown by analysis of variances by causes, should control costs, for the necessary lines of action will be clearly indicated. Managerial decisions will also tend to be simplified. Standard Costs are the "real" costs of a product and, therefore, any comparisons between alternative approaches—relative profitability of areas or products—are made much easier and more realistic. Day-to-day fluctuations such as Actual Costs show are, of course, avoided.

EXAMINATION QUESTIONS

1. Discuss the application of costing to non-manufacturing concerns. What information would you expect the cost department to provide in the following instances:

    (a) wholesale and distributing house;
    (b) retail stores;
    (c) transport company.

                                        (I.C.W.A.)

2. A brewery maintains a motor service consisting of twelve lorries delivering barrelled and bottled beer and bringing back empties.

Outline a system of cost control, covering cost of running, maintenance, and depreciation, recommending the unit of measurement to be applied.

                                        (I.C.W.A.)

3. Draft a statement of the Costs of a Sales Depot, and state how the various items of expense would be controlled.

                                        (I.C.W.A.)

4. The Actual sales exceed budgeted sales by 5% yet the Actual profit is 10% less than budgeted profit. Analysis shows this to be due to variations in sales mix of products earning different rates of profit.

Draft a report presenting an explanation.

                                        (I.C.W.A.)

CHAPTER 18

PROCEDURE FOR SETTING STANDARD COSTS FOR SELLING AND DISTRIBUTION

THERE are two main problems and these are:

1. To estimate Volume of Sales in physical units and value.
2. To estimate Costs involved in obtaining the Volume of Sales—

    (a) For selling—that is, the function of maintaining, or changing, demand conditions.

    (b) For distribution—that is, the function of getting the products to the consumers.

Often the costs involved, and especially selling costs, are only in-directly affected by volume of production. Frequently, the *present* volumes of sales and selling costs are not closely correlated: it may be that high selling costs are incurred now, but the benefits will accrue in the future. There may be high costs and low sales, or vice versa. It is possible to treat part of the present costs as being the cost of a future period and thus relate, as far as possible, costs to sales—this will cer-tainly apply where a major selling campaign is being conducted, for it would be unfair to burden one year with the costs from which benefits accrue for, say, four or five years. In practice, unless there is an extra-ordinarily large sum spent on selling and distribution in one particular year, the costs incurred in one period are charged to that period. Although this method has much to recommend it, certainly as regards simplicity, because like is not being matched with like, the value of accounting statements tends to be reduced.

BUDGET FOR SALES

A Sales Forecast in terms of physical units is the first step. This may be obtained from past records of the business concerned or from exter-nal past records, such as newspapers, trade journals, and reports and information issued by trade associations, chambers of commerce, and similar bodies. Market research will also be utilised. The object will be to show the quantity of each type of product expected to be sold in, say, the next six to twelve months: the length of forecast period depend-ing upon the nature of the industry, which in turn determines the ease or difficulty with which forecasts can be made.

In industries producing non-standard products or supplying services it will be impossible to forecast physical units, so, in that case, a Sales Budget in terms of sales expected, expressed in sterling, will be the first consideration. Again the information may be obtained from past records and market research.

With both standard and non-standard products the aim should be to show, in the Sales Budget, the revenue which can be expected under future conditions. The past is merely an approximate guide to what may occur in the future, so modification of past records to bring them into line with expected conditions is essential.

The prices used in the Sales Budget will, generally speaking, be determined by supply and demand conditions; that is, both by the cost of the product and what the consumer is willing to pay.

Reports from salesmen may be very useful in determining both the quantities that will sell and at what prices. Obviously though, any estimate from a salesman will have to be treated with reserve until someone with a good knowledge of market conditions has examined it, and made any necessary adjustments. In this way a sales quota can be fixed for each salesman and possibly used as the basis for the payment of a bonus.

In certain industries there may be "key ratios," and these may provide a fair guide to what can be expected in the future. A rise in income in a particular area may be followed by increased sales of a certain product. Thus a 5% rise in wages of workers in that area may have resulted in approximately a 2% addition to sales. These relationships, and the degree of reliability which may be placed on the correlation, may be shown by examination of past records.

Once the sales volume has been determined, any deviations can be expressed as variances, a matter which will be covered later.

STANDARD COSTS FOR THE VOLUME OF SALES

Some costs tend to vary with volume of output or sales, whereas others remain constant irrespective of volume. The separation of "fixed," "semi-variable," and "variable" costs is, therefore, essential before an estimate of costs can be made. This is especially so when the Flexible or Sliding-scale Budget is adopted, for then the fixed element in total cost will tend to be lower, *per unit*, the larger the volume achieved. The Flexible Budget is likely to be the only sensible way of projecting costs for, with a Fixed Budget (one volume of sales only), the budgeted costs lose their significance when there is a failure to achieve what is expected in terms of sales. Only when volume and costs are linked together will variances have any meaning.

Before drawing up the Costs Budget it will be necessary to consider functional responsibilities for each class of cost, unit standards for each function, and the extent of each territory or sales area. Only in this way can maximum control over costs be exercised.

EXAMPLES OF IMPORTANT FACTORS TO BE CONSIDERED

The important factors mentioned above can be illustrated or explained further as shown below:

1. Analysis into fixed and variable cost

(a) *Fixed costs—selling:*
Salaries (Sales Management).
Rent of Sales Office and Show Rooms.
Depreciation and Insurance of Sales Office.
Part of Sales Clerical and Office Costs.

(b) *Semi-variable costs—selling:*
Salesmen's Salaries and Travelling Expenses.
Part of Sales Clerical and Office Costs.

(c) *Variable costs—selling:*
Part of Clerical Costs.
Salesmen's Commission.

The distribution costs are classified in a similar manner.

2. Functional responsibilities for each type of cost

Location of responsibility is essential; this may be done as follows:

(a) Costs which are the responsibility of the Sales Manager. These include all these costs listed above in (1).

(b) Costs which are the responsibility of the Advertising Manager. All advertising costs come under this heading. Such costs may be fixed or variable or a combination of both (semi-variable).

(c) Costs which are the responsibility of the Distribution Manager. All costs relating to transport, storage, and warehousing.

3. Unit Standards for each operation

By careful classification of the operations involved in selling and distribution and the deliberate choice of a "unit" which can be applied to each operation it should be possible to fix a Standard Cost for each operation. Once done, two principal advantages emerge: the build-up of cost budgets is simplified and the control over the cost of each operation is maximised. The technique should, however, be used with caution, for some costs remain fixed irrespective of function and, moreover, there is some difficulty in obtaining the necessary standardisation both for operations and units.

Examples of possible operations and related units are shown below.

Function and operations	Unit for which Standard Cost set
1. Direct Selling:	
Travelling expenses.	The day or mile travelled.
Salesmen's salaries.	The call or the day.
Salesmen's telephones.	The call.
2. Advertising and Sales Promotion:	
Mail order publicity.	The potential customer.
General advertising.	The unit of product.
3. Credit and Collection:	
Invoicing (except pricing and calculations).	The order.
Pricing and calculation of invoices.	The invoice line.
Credit control and cash collection.	The customer.
4. Transportation:	
Delivery costs.	The hour, mile, hundredweight or package.
5. Storage and Warehousing:	
Handling.	The invoice line or hundredweight or size of order (so many units).
Storage.	Storage space—square or cubic footage.

These are, of course, only suggestions. The unit which best serves the business concerned should be the one to adopt. Obviously, it should be as realistic as possible and capable of being thought of in terms of cost. The list does not cover all operations, but is an illustration of the line to follow to arrive at a Standard Unit Cost which can be used to measure efficiency.

4. The extent of each territory or sales area

The market covered by the particular business must be divided into territories. This division may be based on geographical considerations or on the responsibilities of each salesman. Thus in the former case there may be a North-east Area, a North-west Area, and so on, or each county may represent a sales area. On salesmen's responsibilities there could be Mr. Brown's Area, Mr. Smith's Area, and Mr. Black's Area. Even when geographical areas are adopted, the second method will often be essential to obtain maximum control over costs.

Because conditions, from one area to another, may differ to a considerable extent, it will often be necessary to fix a Standard Cost for each £ of sales or unit of product sold for each area. This may be done along with the preparation of the Selling and Distribution Cost Budget or, at a later date, after that Budget has been prepared. Certainly though, the nature of the territories must be understood before any budget is compiled.

STANDARDS FOR EACH CLASS OF COST: SELLING

The guide to the Standards for selling and distribution must come, principally at any rate, from past experience. Knowledge and facts accumulated in the past must be linked with the possible volumes of sales expected in the future. Changes in circumstances or conditions may, of course, dictate a modification of past records. It is impossible to formulate rigid rules to follow in fixing typical allowances for each class of cost, but the observations made below will serve to show the principles involved.

In particular, it should be noticed that, whenever possible, each function is carefully studied before the cost, which that function incurs, is set. Just as with manufacturing Standard Costs, there should be an effort made to determine efficient operations before the allowances are set.

"Allowance Schedules" will normally be compiled in respect of each type of cost. These schedules may be regarded as the "work sheets" used in the building of the final budget. All the relevant information is listed in detail, thus allowing a total cost to be found for transfer to the budget. Thus for Sales Expenses the Allowance Schedule would show details and totals of the number of salesman days, the allowance per salesman day, and the total cost.

ALLOWANCE FOR SALESMEN'S SALARIES

The number of men required to sell the possible volumes of sales will have to be estimated. The setting of a sales quota for each salesman will do much to simplify both the setting of a sales volume and salesmen's salaries and other expenses. A "quota" is the volume that is expected to be sold by each man. It is a target which can, under stated conditions, be achieved. There is thus a definite task for each man, and any deviations from such task, provided adequate records are maintained, can be quickly and effectively dealt with. If the quota is used as a basis for an incentive payment, each salesman is encouraged to give of his best, which, naturally, makes control much simpler. By publishing results, a measure of competitiveness between salesmen can be attained—again making control more effective. It will be obvious that the quotas must be set carefully and in such a way that each salesman is given a fair assignment.

After the number of salesmen has been ascertained it will be necessary to classify each salesman according to his salary category. If only one product is sold this task may be quite simple. There may be, say, thirty salesmen all being paid a basic salary of £10 per week and commission on sales. In other cases there may be a variety of products, some requiring a more specialised knowledge than others and, in addition, a range of salaries, to reflect age and experience, may be adopted. A classification of salesmen, into groups, will thus be necessary. Each number in a group, multiplied by the appropriate salary, and then all sub-totals added together, will give an estimate of the cost for salesmen's salaries.

SALESMEN'S BONUSES AND COMMISSIONS

The basis of the calculation for both bonuses and commissions will depend upon sales policy. Whenever possible some form of incentive payment should be adopted; in fact, the selling of some products requires great effort on the part of a salesman, so material encouragement is essential. Bonus or commission may be paid on all orders taken by a salesman, or on all orders taken within a salesman's territory (even though he does not personally take them), or on sales which exceed the quota, or on new business only, or on some other basis. The precise method will be determined by the management; once settled, an amount to cover bonuses and commissions for each volume of sales can be calculated.

SALESMEN'S TRAVELLING AND RELATED EXPENSES

The policy may be to pay all reasonable expenses, each salesman's expenses sheet being "approved" each week. Alternatively, a fixed sum to cover *all* expenses may be paid, the salesman being left to manage his spending within the limits prescribed by the amount allowed. Another method is the payment of a daily rate for each major expense. A scale to cover meals, hotel expenses, train or bus fares, car and other necessary expenses can be compiled. Regulations covering expenses which will be allowed, and those which will not be allowed, are usually issued.

By reference to the particular scheme, the number of salesmen, and the volumes of sales, it should be possible to prepare the Allowances Schedule.

OTHER SELLING EXPENSES

Telephones and Telegrams, Sales Office Salaries, Lighting, Heating, Depreciation, Subscriptions, Rates and Taxes, Printing and Stationery, Bad Debts, and Rent may be estimated by reference to past records and, where applicable, present contracts.

A.B. & Co. Ltd., Flexible Budget—Selling Costs. Year Ending December 31st, 19…

Functional Cost	Fixed Variable Semi-Variable	Fixed element £	Variable element per Std. Unit	Source of information	Possible Sales Volumes (in £000s) and Related Costs					
					£600 £	£620 £	£640 £	£660 £	£680 £	£700 £
Variable and Semi-Variable Costs:										
Salesmen's Salaries	S.V.	14,000	1% on sales		20,000	20,200	20,400	20,600	20,800	21,000
Salesmen's Commissions	V.	—	2% ,,		12,000	12,400	12,800	13,200	13,600	14,000
Salesmen's Telephones	S.V.	200	½% ,,		3,200	3,300	3,400	3,500	3,600	3,700
Salesmen's Travelling	S.V.	3,500	1% ,,		9,500	9,700	9,900	10,100	10,300	10,500
Salesmen's Stationery	V.	—	¼% ,,		1,500	1,550	1,600	1,650	1,700	1,750
Salesmen's Postages	V.	—	¼% ,,		1,500	1,550	1,600	1,650	1,700	1,750
Bad Debts	V.	—	½% ,,		3,000	3,100	3,200	3,300	3,400	3,500
					50,700	51,800	52,900	54,000	55,100	56,200
Fixed Costs:										
Sales Administration Salaries	F.	8,000		No. of employees	8,000	8,000	8,000	8,000	8,000	8,000
Rent of Sales Office	F.	10,000		Contract	10,000	10,000	10,000	10,000	10,000	10,000
Rent of Show Rooms	F.	5,000		Contract	5,000	5,000	5,000	5,000	5,000	5,000
Depreciation of Equipment	F.	2,000		5% on Cap. values	2,000	2,000	2,000	2,000	2,000	2,000
Insurance	F.	1,500		Insurance Policy	1,500	1,500	1,500	1,500	1,500	1,500
Administration Costs—Sales Office	F.	1,000		Estimate Past Records	1,000	1,000	1,000	1,000	1,000	1,000
Advertising	F.	12,000		Contract Adv. Agency	12,000	12,000	12,000	12,000	12,000	12,000
					£90,200	£91,300	£92,400	£93,500	£94,600	£95,700
Standard Selling Cost per £100 of Sales					£15·03	£14·7258	£14·4375	£14·166	£13·9118	£13·671

FIG. 37—Flexible Budget—Selling Costs

FIG. 37.—NOTES

1. The figures used are not intended to show what the various classes of cost are likely to be, but to illustrate the principles involved; *i.e.* the figures are purely hypothetical.

2. By statistical analysis of past records—salesmen's reports, expense sheets, salary sheets and other records—and after making adjustments for present conditions, the variable cost percentages, in relation to Sales Volume, have been calculated.

3. The bases for calculation of the variable element may be approached in a different way. Alternative bases as follows:

Functional cost	*Alternative bases*
Salesmen's Salaries	Fixed sum per salesman or salesman day or per call
,, Commission	Units sold
,, Telephones	Per customer
,, Travelling	Rate per mile
,, Meals and Hotel	Sum per day
,, Stationery	Fixed sum per salesman
,, Postage	Fixed sum per salesman or per customer
Advertising	When regarded as Variable Cost—number of catalogues and/or percentage on sales

The division into Fixed and Variable is, of course, arbitrary. Much depends upon the basis used for computing the payment. Thus, as indicated, advertising costs may be fixed or variable. Similarly, the salaries of salesmen may be entirely fixed. Often costs are "fixed" over a certain range of physical sales and then "vary" when a certain stage is reached. Salesmen's salaries may be £20,000 for any sales volume between 450,000 and 550,000 units of product, but from 551,000 to 660,000 units the cost may be fixed at £22,000.

4. Sales Volumes are shown in monetary values. In some cases physical units would also be shown, *e.g.* when homogeneous units are sold.

5. A Flexible Budget would also be prepared to cover Distribution Costs, although these, for some concerns, would be adequately covered by inclusion in the one budget with Selling Costs.

6. For effective control the figures should be broken down further to show the costs relating to each territory, sales department, commodity, methods of sale, methods of delivery (distribution costs), sizes of orders, and salesmen. Obviously, not all enterprises will require the same detailed analysis; the nature of the business and the type of selling organisation will determine how much detail will be necessary. Generally speaking, however, the more complex the business—multiplicity of products, sales offices, showrooms, and so on—the more important is the need for analysis. Standard Unit Costs would also be used to measure the efficiency achieved. The Actual Unit Cost incurred for a particular operation, such as travelling, will be compared with the predetermined Standard Unit Cost and any significant differences investigated.

7. The costs relating to a volume of sales which fall between two of the volumes shown on the Budget may be obtained by interpolation. The fixed costs will of course remain the same irrespective of volume.

STANDARD SELLING COSTS FOR AREAS

If separate sales areas exist it will usually be necessary to compile a budget for each. Any overheads which cannot be charged directly to an area will, of course, have to be apportioned on some equitable basis. Possible bases are shown below:

Bases	Type of overhead (predetermined)
1. Population or number of radios or televisions.	Radio or television advertisements on a national basis.
2. Size of area or number of salesmen.	Salaries of executives and similar head office costs.

These are merely suggestions; they should serve as a guide for apportionment of costs to areas.

COMPILING THE FLEXIBLE BUDGET FOR SELLING COSTS

An example of a flexible budget for selling costs is shown in Fig. 37. Notes of explanation, on the way the budget is compiled, are also given.

Once all costs have been allocated or apportioned to sales areas Standards Costs may be fixed for each type of product. This involves the apportionment of the total cost to the various classes of product to be sold. Clearly, though, if a particular line is responsible for certain costs, then these may be a direct charge to that line. If only a small range of products is being sold a rate per unit may be calculated. Sometimes a percentage is added to manufacturing cost to cover the selling cost. Alternatively, an apportionment according to turnover (units or cost values) is made to each class of product and then a unit cost calculated for each class.

DETERMINATION OF STANDARD AMOUNTS FOR EACH CLASS OF COST: DISTRIBUTION

As already stated, the two main categories of costs involved in distribution are those connected with:

1. Transport.
2. Storage and Warehousing.

The setting of Standard Costs for these will now be considered.

TRANSPORT COSTS

Since many businesses have their own road-transport departments, it is the setting of Standards, for this method of distribution, that will be covered. Obviously, a company keeping its own vehicles implies that delivery by this means is the cheapest and—just as important—most convenient. For some products rail, air, or other method may be necessary; if this is so, little or no control over the charges for delivery may be possible. Control over costs will have to be exercised by carefully planning the routes and size of the despatches.

With a company's own vehicles a complete control system will be possible. Standard Costs can be set and detailed procedures can be installed so that any deviations from a determined plan are quickly located. The transport manager and his staff will maintain detailed records and statistics, thus enabling a close watch to be kept on the performance of every vehicle. Observations on setting Standards, for the principal costs, are made below.

For convenience and more effective control, costs are usually divided as follows:

1. Annual Standing Costs, divided into the costs of—

   (a) Administration of the transport function.
   (b) Vehicle Licences and Insurance.
   (c) Crew's Wages.
   (d) National and Employer's Liability Insurance.
   (e) Depreciation.

Sometimes Depreciation is regarded as a running cost; this is understandable for, strictly speaking, it is a semi-variable cost which may be regarded as a standing (fixed) charge, or as a running (variable) charge.

2. Running Costs, divided into—

   (a) Fuel.
   (b) Oil.
   (c) Tyres.
   (d) Repairs and Maintenance.

A percentage of the total Repairs and Maintenance Cost figure may be included under the Standing Costs above. Thus, for example, 25% of the total may be regarded as being of a fixed nature, the balance coming under Running Costs.

Each cost will now be considered in more detail.

Administration of the transport function

All costs relating specifically to the transport department, as well as a share of the general administration costs, will be included under this heading. Salaries of managerial and clerical staff, lighting, heating, rent, rates, telephones, and other charges are involved. Obviously, most of these costs are fixed and will be determined by contract or agreement.

Setting of Standard Costs for Administration is covered in a later chapter.

As regards individual vehicles, these may be divided into groups according to, say, carrying capacity. The costs may then be apportioned on this basis.

Vehicle Licences and Insurance

The charges for the licence and insurance of each vehicle will be definitely known, so the predetermination of the costs should not be difficult.

Crew's Wages

Rates will be fixed for drivers and drivers' mates. These may vary according to the type of vehicle driven and, accordingly, responsibility undertaken. The rate per hour, multiplied by the number of hours each man is to work, will give the standard wage.

National and Employer's Liability Insurance

National Insurance per employee is fixed by law. The employer's liability insurance is pre-paid and is therefore known.

Depreciation

The annual charge for depreciation for each vehicle will be estimated by reference to capital value, estimated residual value and serviceable life of that vehicle. This method assumes that the principal factor in determining the amount of depreciation is the passing of time (*i.e.* there is a rate per hour).

If the number of miles operated by a vehicle is taken to be the determining factor, then the depreciation may be regarded as a Running Cost. In such case the capital value will be divided by the number of miles the vehicles is expected to run, and this will give a charge per mile.

Fuel and Oil

"Ideal" fuel consumption figures may be obtained from vehicle manufacturers' figures. If Expected Standard Costs are to be used allowances will have to be made to cover the following:

1. Age of vehicle.

   Generally, the older vehicle in a particular class of vehicles will have a higher fuel consumption.

2. Conditions under which vehicles operate.

   Those vehicles operating in hilly country will tend to have a greater fuel consumption per mile than vehicles running in flat country. The weather may also affect consumption.

3. Type of work undertaken.

Vehicles on long runs with few stops should clearly obtain a greater mileage per gallon than those on local delivery work with many "stop–starts."

4. Engine condition of vehicles.

Oil consumption may also vary for similar reasons to those given above: number (4) will, however, tend to be the most important.

After making a fair assessment of the effects of (1) to (4) the Standard Costs for each vehicle, or each type of vehicle, may be set.

Tyres

The total cost of tyres and tubes for each vehicle may be determined without trouble. One of the major difficulties in setting a mileage cost is to estimate the mileage which may be obtained from the tyres before they will require replacing. Clearly, the problem is very similar to the one encountered in calculating depreciation.

Those vehicles operating on badly maintained roads or constantly having to stop, and then start, may wear out tyres at a quicker rate than vehicles running on well-constructed and maintained roads. An allowance to cover abnormal conditions should be included in a vehicle's mileage estimate.

Repairs and Maintenance

A programme of preventive maintenance can materially assist the predetermination and control of repairs and maintenance costs. By ensuring that all vehicles have regular check-ups, better performances should be obtained from them, and many major and, therefore, costly overhauls may be avoided. Because the number of "exceptions to the rule" are reduced to a minimum it should be possible to predetermine the costs more accurately.

The concern's own garage may be treated as a cost centre. The costs of space occupied, equipment used, materials used, and the wages of mechanics may all be carefully estimated. Actual Costs can be controlled by using requisitions and other necessary authorisation forms.

Standard Costs may be set for individual vehicles or for groups of similar vehicles in the same age group. Which of these approaches to follow depends chiefly upon cost. Setting Standards for individual vehicles implies that detailed records will be kept for each vehicle. Obviously, the clerical costs will tend to be higher than when costs are accumulated for groups only. There is, however, the advantage of having a much stricter control over costs.

BASES OF STANDARDS FOR TRANSPORT COSTS

The standing costs may be absorbed on an hourly basis. Each vehicle will be expected to operate a definite number of years—this number will have to be carefully determined as part of the programme of setting Standards. The number of operating hours per week will be multiplied by the number of weeks to be worked in the year and the total divided into the total Annual Standard Cost to give a rate per hour. With Ideal Standards an allowance to cover holidays only will be deducted from total possible hours. Expected Standards will also anticipate a normal loss in hours, due to breakdowns or similar occurrences.

Running costs will tend to vary with the mileage run, so obviously a rate per mile is a realistic basis for the absorption of these costs. Accordingly, Standard Costs for operating are best thought of in terms of cost per mile.

If costs are accumulated for each vehicle, variances may then be calculated. The calculation of variances is the subject of the next chapter.

Sometimes it is suggested that the ton-mile is a useful measure upon which Standard Costs may be set. This suggestion is valid only when products possess similar bulk–weight properties. A "full load" may vary a great deal in weight, depending upon the nature of the goods carried.

As regards individual products, each line sold may be given a points value which considers weight and bulk. A standard charge for each may then be found by dividing the rate per hour and the rate per mile by the total number of "points" normally contained on a full load. Exactly how this method would be applied depends upon the circumstances and, since there are so many possible variations, no further details will be given. Sufficient has been said to enable the reader to adapt the method to particular circumstances.

STORAGE AND WAREHOUSING COSTS

The setting of Standard Costs for storage and warehousing follows lines similar to those already described in connection with other overhead costs. Particular attention should be paid to handling and storage procedures before any actual attempt is made to predetermine the costs. Fork-lift trucks and other mechanical aids to handling can reduce costs considerably, so whenever the volume of work warrants them, their use is worthy of consideration.

As regards lines of product a Standard Cost may be set for a hundredweight of product handled or cubic volume—cubic foot or yard—stored. These may be useful measures of efficiency when comparing actual and expected results.

EXAMINATION QUESTIONS

1. "These budgets for tomorrow never work out just as planned. Conditions always change. So why bother to make them?"
Enumerate the points which you would make, briefly, when confronted by the argument expressed in the above quotation.

(I.C.W.A.)

2. How does budgetary control facilitate the delegation of authority and yet act as an instrument of co-ordination?

(I.C.W.A.)

3. Outline an adequate but simple system of *cost control* for a small jobbing factory employing, say, twelve people. Give your recommendations.

(I.C.W.A.)

4. The budgeted costs of a manufacturing business for a normal year are as follows:

	£	£
Direct materials		68,273
Direct wages:		
Machine shop (100,000 hours) ...	27,382	
Assembly (80,000 hours) ...	22,780	
		50,162
Works overheads:		
Machine shop	33,490	
Assembly	16,237	
		49,727
Administration overheads		12,268
Selling expenses		15,481
Distribution expenses		13,290

The absorption method of costing is in operation.
Prepare a schedule of overhead rates suitable for practical use in this business.
Complete a cost estimate for a job, the technical data for which is as follows:

Material: 20 lbs. A at £0·64 per lb.
15 lbs. B at £0·08 per lb.
Direct labour: Machine shop: 15 hours at £0·30 per hour
Assembly: 25 hours at £0·35 per hour

(I.C.W.A.)

CHAPTER 19

VARIANCES FOR SELLING AND DISTRIBUTION

THE principal variances for the selling and distribution functions will be discussed below. Those relating to selling are covered first.

SALES VARIANCES

Summarised, the principal sales variances are as follows:

1. Sales (Value) Variance.
2. Sales Margin Variances.
3. Sales Volume Variance.
4. Sales Price Variance.
5. Sales Allowance Sub-variance.*
6. Sales Mixture Sub-variance.
7. Sales Volume Sub-variance.
8. Selling Costs Variance.

Variances (2) to (8) are part of the Sales Value Variance (1). These will now be explained.

Sales (Value) Variance

This is a total variance, being obtained by deducting standard sales value from actual sales value for a favourable variance, and actual from standard for an unfavourable variance.

The formula may be stated thus:

$$\left(\begin{array}{c}\text{Actual Value} \\ \text{of Sales}\end{array}\right) \text{ minus } \left(\begin{array}{c}\text{Standard} \\ \text{Value of} \\ \text{Sales}\end{array}\right) = \begin{array}{c}\text{Favourable} \\ \text{Sales Value} \\ \text{Variance}\end{array}$$

$$\left(\begin{array}{c}\text{Standard Value} \\ \text{of Sales}\end{array}\right) \text{ minus } \left(\begin{array}{c}\text{Actual} \\ \text{Value of} \\ \text{Sales}\end{array}\right) = \begin{array}{c}\text{Unfavourable} \\ \text{Sales Value} \\ \text{Variance}\end{array}$$

The presence of the Sales (Value) Variance indicates that one or more of the following applies:

(a) Sales Volume is greater or less than expected (Sales Volume Variance).

(b) Prices received were larger or smaller than expected (Sales Price Variance).

* An explanation of the term "sub-variance" is given in Chapters 6, 7, and 8.

(c) Allowances totalled to a larger or smaller figure than anticipated (Sales Allowance Sub-variance).

(d) A variety has been sold which is different from the variety expected when Standards were set (Sales Mixture Sub-variance).

(e) Selling costs incurred are less or more than standard selling costs (Selling Costs Variance).

(f) Profit margins are not those budgeted.

Sales Margin Variance

This can be divided into a "total" variance and a number of other variances (or sub-variances). The total Sales Margin Variance can be calculated by referring to the following:

1. *Budgeted Standard Profit Margin*

$$\left(\begin{array}{c} \text{Standard Value} \\ \text{of Sales} \end{array} \right) \text{ minus } \left(\begin{array}{c} \text{Standard} \\ \text{Costs} \end{array} \right)$$

2. *Actual Standard Profit Margin*

$$\left(\begin{array}{c} \text{Actual Value} \\ \text{of Sales} \end{array} \right) \text{ minus } \left(\begin{array}{c} \text{Standard} \\ \text{Costs} \end{array} \right)$$

(1) deducted from (2) would give an unfavourable Sales Margin Variance.

If taken a stage further it will be evident that the variance will be made up of many other variances which also affect the margins obtained:

(a) Selling prices (Sales Margin Variance due to selling price).

(b) Sales allowances (Sales Margin Variance due to sales allowances).

(c) Sales mixture (Sales Margin Variance due to sales mixture).

The variance analysis should determine which of these have caused the Sales Margin Variance.

Sales Volume Variance

Possible reasons for a business not obtaining the physical volume of sales are:

1. Unexpected competition.
2. Ineffective sales promotion.
3. Ineffective advertising.
4. Customers meeting adverse business conditions, thus unable to take their usual orders.
5. Lack of proper supervision and control of salesmen.

The calculation of the variance is:

(Actual Volume − Standard Volume) × Standard Profit

This formula, abbreviated as (AV — SV)S Prt., covers a favourable variance. If a number of lines of products are sold the calculation will be made for each line.

Sales Price Variance

If actual price is less than standard price, possible reasons are:
1. Unforeseen competition.
2. Changes in the channels of distribution (*e.g.* selling through wholesalers instead of through retailers).

The price may be affected by the size of the volume sold. To sell a larger number of units it may be necessary to reduce prices. Any factor which influences volumes may also, therefore, tend to affect price.

Calculation of the Sales Price Variance should not prove difficult. The formula is:

$$(\text{Actual Price} - \text{Standard Price}) \times \text{Actual Volume}$$

or abbreviated (AP — SP)AV. This gives a favourable variance.

Again, a variance will usually be calculated for each line sold.

Sales Allowance Sub-variance

For a given volume of sales there will be a definite total for discounts, rebates, and other allowances. This total is known as the Standard Sales Allowance. If more or less than the total standard allowances for actual sales is given to customers a variance arises.

The formula for an unfavourable Sales Allowance Sub-variance is as follows:

$$\text{Actual Sales Allowance} - \text{Standard Sales Allowance}$$

Percentages may also be used to arrive at the variance.

The reasons for awarding more than the standard allowance will be similar to those stated for reducing prices. Often allowances are altered in order to avoid a change in prices.

Sales Mixture Sub-variance

When a number of different lines of products are sold a budget will be compiled to cover expected sales of each line. Thus, for example, if three different products are sold, the standard figures may be:

Product	Volume
A	10,000
B	4,000
C	6,000

If actual sales for A, B, and C are 9000, 6000, and 5000 it is evident that the standard mixture has not been achieved and a sub-variance may be calculated.

When the total number of units for actual sales is not the same as the total number for standard sales, it will be necessary to convert the standard quantity for each line to the standard quantity for the *actual sales*. That is to say, the standard proportions for actual sales have to be calculated.

If a larger than standard proportion of a more profitable line (or lines) is sold, a larger profit should result, thus giving a favourable sub-variance. When a larger proportion of a less profitable line (or lines) is sold there will be an unfavourable sub-variance. An example is given later in this chapter.

A mixture sub-variance may also be calculated when the *same* type of product is sold at different prices.

Sales Volume Sub-variance

The Sales Mixture Sub-variance and Sales Volume Sub-variance together form the Sales Volume Variance.

Failure to sell the standard number of units will allow the Sales Volume Sub-variance to be calculated. If less than the total standard sales are achieved an unfavourable sub-variance will result: if more than standard, there is a favourable sub-variance.

Calculation of the Sales Volume Sub-variance may be performed by the following formula:

(Actual Volume − Standard Volume) × Average Standard Profit

The "volumes" relate to the total number of units. Reference to the example in the next section will show how the actual calculation is carried out.

Selling Costs Variance

For the actual sales, standard selling costs may be ascertained. When the Actual Selling Costs are deducted from the Standard Costs, or vice versa, this gives the Selling Costs Variance.

RELATION OF THE SALES VARIANCES TO PROFIT

The student should notice that the above variances are closely linked with profit. Obviously, the Sales Value Variance is only of significance when thought of in terms of its relation to profit. When the variance has been adjusted, by deducting the Cost of Sales for units not sold, a profit variance is obtained. All the other variances, stated above, can then be "balanced" with the profit variance.

Armed with full knowledge of why the Standards are not being achieved, management is able to take the necessary remedial action, thus maximising profit. Such questions may arise as:

1. Can the volume of sales be increased further, enabling standard sales to be achieved?

Great care, to ensure that any extra costs do not exceed the additional revenues, will be essential.

2. Will a change in prices result in a greater or lesser volume of sales?

3. Is it possible to vary the actual sales mixture in such a way that profits will be increased?

The sales budget will consider stability as well as profitability, so the actual sales mixture should, obviously, be reasonably near to budgeted sales mixture.

These, and similar questions, will have to be answered. The answers will largely depend upon local conditions and circumstances. Sometimes volume may be changed, at other times it may be necessary to economise on costs or even to cut prices. The dynamic state of the world of business may require a number of different solutions to be found to the same problem, within the space of a very short period. As circumstances change, so must the approach to a particular problem change: one moment an increase in volume will be the answer, and the next, a reduction in cost will be the only practical solution. Clearly, any interpretation of the variances will have to be along "flexible" lines. The student should, on no account, be dogmatic. When confronted with a problem he should study its implications, list the possible solutions, and then select the solution which offers the most advantages. The reasons for the choice should be stated.

CALCULATION OF THE SALES VARIANCES

To illustrate how the Sales Variances are calculated, hypothetical figures have been taken. There is no standardised procedure for carrying out these calculations, or generally accepted definition of the terms used, so those shown below should be regarded only as possible approaches. The student may encounter variations of method and meaning in both textbooks and practice.

QUESTION

Standard Costs Data

Products

	M.	N.	O.	Total
Costs	£0·15	£0·25	£0·40	
Selling Prices	£0·30	£0·50	£0·80	
Sales (Units)	2000	2400	3600	8000

| Note: Division of Costs | £0·125 | £0·20 | £0·30 = | Manufacturing Costs (including Administration). |
| | £0·025 | £0·05 | £0·10 = | Selling Costs. |

Actual Costs Data

Products

	M.	N.	O.	Total
Costs	£0·15	£0·275	£0·40	
Selling Prices	£0·30	£0·52	£0·75	
Sales (Units)	1800	2000	3200	7000

| Note: Division of Costs | £0·125 | £0·20 | £0·30 = | Manufacturing Costs. |
| | £0·025 | £0·075 | £0·10 = | Selling Costs. |

Using the above data you are required to calculate:

1. Sales (Value) Variance.
2. Sales Margin Variance.
3. Sales Volume Variance.
4. Sales Price Variance.
5. Selling Costs Variance.

Then

6. Divide the Sales Volume Variance into—

   (a) Sales Mixture Sub-variance.
   (b) Sales Volume Sub-variance.

ANSWER (WITH NOTES)

1. SALES (VALUE) VARIANCE

Products

	M.	N.	O.	Total
	£	£	£	£
Standard Value of Standard Sales =	600	1200	2880	4680
Actual Value of Actual Sales =	540	1040	2400	3980
Sales Value Variance	£60	£160	£480	£700

Sales Value Variance = £700 (unfavourable).

This variance, by itself, means very little. Moreover, because the cost of the units *not* sold are ignored in the calculation, the figure tends to be artificial (*see below*, "Reconciliation").

2. SALES MARGIN VARIANCE

	Products			
	M.	*N.*	*O.*	*Total*
	£	£	£	£
Budgeted Standard Profit Margin =				
Standard Values	600	1200	2880	4680
Standard Costs	300	600	1440	2340
	£300	£600	£1440	£2340
Actual Standard Profit Margin =				
Actual Values	540	1040	2400	3980
Standard Costs	270	500	1280	2050
	£270	£540	£1120	£1930
Total Sales Margin Variance =				
Budgeted Standard Margin	300	600	1440	2340
Actual Standard Margin	270	540	1120	1930
	£30	£60	£320	£410

3. SALES VOLUME VARIANCE

	Products			
	M.	*N.*	*O.*	*Total*
Standard Sales (Units)	2000	2400	3600	8000
Actual Sales (Units)	1800	2000	3200	7000
	200	400	400	1000
Standard Profit per Unit	£0·15	£0·25	£0·40	
By multiplication:	£30	£100	£160	£290

Sales Volume Variance = £290 (unfavourable).

4. SALES PRICE VARIANCE

	Products			
	M.	*N.*	*O.*	*Total*
	£	£	£	£
Standard Prices per Unit	0·30	0·50	0·80	
Actual Prices per Unit	0·30	0·52	0·75	
	—	£0·02	£0·05	
Actual Volume Sold (Units)	1800	2000	3200	
	—	£40	£160	£120

NOTE.—For product N the Actual Price is more than the Standard Price, so the Variance is favourable.

Sales Price Variance = £120 (unfavourable).

5. SELLING COSTS VARIANCE

	Products		
	M.	*N.*	*O.*
	£	£	£
Actual Cost per Unit	0·025	0·075	0·10
Standard Cost per Unit	0·025	0·050	0·10
	—	0·025	—
Actual Sales (Units)	—	2000	—
	—	£50	—

Selling Costs Variance £50 (unfavourable).

Reconciliation with Sales (Value) Variance (ignoring Sales Margin Variance)

Sales Value Variance   =   £700 (unfavourable)
Less Standard Cost of Sales of Products
   not sold:

Cost	£	£
200 of M at £0·15 =	30	
400 of N at £0·25 =	100	
400 of O at £0·40 =	160	
		290 *

£410 = Profit   Variance
       provided there
       is no Costs
       Variance.

Add Unfavourable Costs Variance   50

£460 (unfavourable).

Profit Variances

NOTES.—(*a*) Because the costs of Product N are £50 above Standard, this has
   to be added back, thus increasing the Profit Variance to its true
   value.

   (*b*) The Profit Variances may also be obtained by comparing standard
   and actual profit figures as follows:

	Products			
	M.	*N.*	*O.*	*Total*
	£	£	£	£
Standard Profit	300	600	1440	2340
Less Actual Profit	270	490	1120	1880
	£30	£110	£320	£460

These are obtained by deducting Costs from the Sales Values.

* The fact that this figure is identical with the Volume Variance is a coincidence
which has no significance.

Summary of Variances

	£
Sales Profit Variance	£460
Sales Volume Variance	290
Sales Price Variance	120
	—— £410
Selling Costs Variance	£50
Total Sales Variance	£460

This reconciles the total variance and the other three variances. The reconciliation may, if required, be extended to the figures for individual products.

6. DIVISION OF VOLUME VARIANCE

(a) Sales Mixture Sub-variance

NOTE.—If the student already understands how to calculate the Material Mixture Sub-variance he should have no difficulty with the Sales Mixture Sub-variance. The principles followed are the same:

Standard Proportions for Actual Sales:

Product	Calculation	Standard proportion
M	$\frac{2000}{8000} \times \frac{7000}{1}$ =	1750 units
N	$\frac{2400}{8000} \times \frac{7000}{1}$ =	2100 units
O	$\frac{3600}{8000} \times \frac{7000}{1}$ =	3150
		7000

Actual Proportions:

M	1800
N	2000
O	3200
	7000

NOTE.—These are given in the Question, so they do not have to be calculated.

Sales Mixture Sub-variances:

$$\left(\begin{array}{c}\text{Actual} \\ \text{Proportion}\end{array} - \begin{array}{c}\text{Standard} \\ \text{Proportion}\end{array}\right) \times \begin{array}{c}\text{Standard} \\ \text{Profit}\end{array} = \begin{array}{c}\text{Favourable} \\ \text{Sub-variance}\end{array}$$

	Unfavourable £	*Favourable* £
M (1800 − 1750) £0·15 = 50 × £0·15		7·50
N (2100 − 2000) £0·25 = 100 × £0·25	25·00	
O (3200 − 3150) £0·40 = 50 × £0·40		20·00
	£25·00	£27·50

Net Sales Mixture Sub-variance = £2·50 (favourable)

(b) Sales Volume Sub-variance

Standard Volume of Sales = 8000 units
Actual Volume of Sales   = 7000 units

    Loss in Sales   = 1000 units

$$\text{Average Standard Profit for all lines} = \frac{\text{Total Profit}}{\text{Total No. of Units}}$$

$$\text{Total Profit} = \begin{pmatrix} M & 2000 \text{ units} \times £0\cdot15 \\ N & 2400 \quad,, \quad \times £0\cdot25 \\ O & 3600 \quad,, \quad \times £0\cdot40 \end{pmatrix} = £2340$$

Standard Number of Units = 8000

$$\text{Average Standard Profit} = \frac{£2340}{8000} = £0\cdot2925$$

Using the formula already explained,

(Standard Volume − Actual Volume) × Average Standard Profit

the sub-variance is (8000 − 7000) £0·2925

$$= £292\cdot5, \text{ i.e. } £292\cdot50 \text{ (unfavourable).}$$

Reconciliation with Sales Volume Variance

Sales Volume Variance ((3) above) = £290·00 (unfavourable)

Sales Volume Sub-variance   = £292·50 (unfavourable)

Less Sales Mixture Sub-variance   £2·50 (favourable)

                            £290·00 (unfavourable)

The Sales Allowance Sub-variance

Calculation of the Sales Allowance Sub-variance has not been illustrated. However, since all that is involved is deduction of total standard allowances from total actual allowances, no difficulty should be experienced.

DETAILED ANALYSIS OF SALES VARIANCES

Variances may be shown for the following:

1. Sales Areas or Territories.
2. Products.
3. Salesmen.

Possible approaches to calculating variances for (1), (2), and (3) are given below.

1. VARIANCES FOR SALES AREAS

In addition to the variances shown in the previous section—Sales Value, Volume, and Price Variances—it may also be useful to calculate a variance which considers salesmen's activities. This involves an analysis of the Selling Cost Variance according to days worked and expenses incurred. An example of this is shown below.

	Areas	
	A	B
Total Standard Cost	£1000	£2000
Standard Salesman Days	500	1000
Standard Rate per Salesman Day	£2	£2
Total Actual Cost	£1200	£2025
Actual Salesman Days	400	900
Actual Rate per Salesman Day	£3	£2·25

Variances

AREA A: Actual Cost £1200
Less Standard Cost £1000

Variance £ 200 (unfavourable).

Analysis:

Gain on Salesman Days
100 at £2 £200
Loss on Spending
£1200–£800 (*i.e.* 400 days at £2) £400

£200 (unfavourable).

AREA B: Actual Cost £2025
Less Standard Cost £2000

£ 25 (unfavourable).

Analysis:

Gain on Salesman Days
100 at £2 £200
Loss on Spending
£2025–£1800 (*i.e.* 900 days at £2) £225

£ 25 (unfavourable).

2. VARIANCES FOR PRODUCTS

When different lines of products are sold variances may be calculated for each. This may be in accordance with the ways already explained above; that is, for the Price and Volume Variances. An alternative method is as follows:

	Products	
	X	Y
Standard Cost	£1800	£1200
Standard Number of Units	7200	6000
Standard Cost per Unit	£0·25	£0·20
Actual Cost	£1950	£1260
Actual Number of Units	7500	6000
Actual Cost per Unit	£0·26	£0·21

Variances

PRODUCT X:	Actual Cost	£1950	
	Less Standard Cost	£1800	
	Variance	£ 150	(unfavourable).

Analysis:

Extra Cost for

Gain on Products Sold
300 at £0·25 .... £ 75

Loss on Spending
£1950–£1875 (*i.e.* 7500 products
at £0·25) .... £ 75

£ 150 (unfavourable).

PRODUCT Y:	Actual Cost	£1260	
	Less Standard Cost	£1200	
		£ 60	(unfavourable).

Analysis:

Loss on Spending
£1260–£1200 (*i.e.* 6000 products
at £0·20 each) .... £ 60 (unfavourable).

3. VARIANCES FOR SALESMEN

To obtain maximum control over selling costs it will be necessary to allocate responsibility for costs to each salesman. Not unnaturally, therefore, variance analysis for each salesman may prove invaluable.

Normally the following Standards will be set for each salesman:

1. Sales Quota.   2. Selling Cost.

The selling cost may be divided according to class of expense. Thus standard allowances may be set for (a) Salary, (b) Car or other Travelling Expenses, (c) Hotel and other Subsistence Expenses, (d) Stationery and Postage, (e) Telephones and Telegrams.

Variances for (1) and (2) will usually be calculated and then an analysis made according to the classes listed ((a) to (e)). If, for example, a salesman exceeds his telephone allowance of a month by £5, he will be called upon to explain the reasons for the overspending.

Each man's efficiency will, of course, be indicated by comparison of the actual and standard volume of sales and the actual and standard selling costs.

CALCULATION OF THE DISTRIBUTION VARIANCES

TRANSPORT VARIANCES

As already emphasised, transport costs are likely to be a major part of distribution costs. Control over them by calculation and analysis of variances, followed by appropriate action is, therefore, essential. For each vehicle two standard rates will be fixed; these are:

1. Standard Rate per Hour for Standing Costs.
2. Standard Rate per Mile for Running Costs.

Variations from these may occur. In addition, actual hours and mileage may be different from standard hours and mileage. The variance analysis to cover the costs of each vehicle may take the following form.

Vehicle No. 1

Standard Costs:

Standing	£100
Running	£ 75
Standard Hours	200
Standard Mileage	3000
Standard Hourly Rate	£0·500
Standard Rate per Mile	£0·025

Actual Costs:

Standing	£104
Running	£ 80
Actual Hours	220
Actual Mileage	2800
Actual Hourly Rate	£0·473
Actual Rate per Mile	£0·029

Variance: Vehicle No. 1

	Standing	Running
Actual Costs	£104	£80
Less Standard Costs	£100	£75
	£ 4 (unfavourable)	£ 5 (unfavourable).

Analysis:

(*a*) *Standing Costs*
    Gain in Hours—*Extra Cost*
        20 hours at £0·50   £10 (unfavourable).
    Gain in Spending
        £110–£104 (£110 = 220 × £0·50)   £ 6 (favourable).
                                      £ 4 (unfavourable).

(*b*) *Running Costs*
    Loss in Mileage—*Reduced Cost*
        200 at £0·025   £ 5 (favourable).
    Loss in Spending
        £80–£70 (*i.e.* 2800 miles at £0·025) £10 (unfavourable).
                                        £ 5 (unfavourable).

The reasons for these variances will be examined and appropriate action taken. So far as the spending loss is concerned it will be necessary to compare each type of cost and find out those that have exceeded the standard allowance. This is especially important for the running costs, for these are usually controllable. Excessive usage of petrol may indicate that the vehicle concerned requires attention. Consistently high repairs costs may point to a reckless driver or to the fact that the vehicle is nearing the end of its useful life. These, and other facts, may emerge from consideration of the variances.

VARIANCES FOR OTHER METHODS OF DELIVERY

Obviously, not all businesses will have their own fleet of vehicles. Even if they have, from time to time outside assistance may be sought to deal with abnormal volumes of work. Variances may also be calculated for these alternative methods of delivery. Total mileage and cost for each method may be predetermined and, each accounting period, variances calculated. Whether concerned with hired vehicles, rail, air, or water deliveries, a loss or gain in mileage, and in cost, may be ascertained.

STORAGE AND WAREHOUSING VARIANCES

The number of products stored and handled may be the basis of a volume variance. Consideration of the costs incurred would allow a spending variance to be calculated.

If a standard rate per hundredweight of product handled is calculated this may be compared with the actual rate, thus obtaining a measure of efficiency. With some types of commodity the relation of Standard and Actual Costs for each size of order may supply useful control information. Thus, for example, orders and related costs may be classified as follows:

Product X	Under 2 Gross	2 to 5 Gross	5 to 10 Gross
Standard Cost	£500	£2800	£2000
Standard Number of Orders	1000	4000	2000
Standard Unit Cost	£0·50	£0·70	£1·00
Actual Cost	£600	£3000	£1800
Actual No. of Orders	1100	4000	1900

Variance for Orders Not Exceeding 2 Gross

Actual Cost	£600
Less Standard Cost	£500
Handling Cost Variance	= £100 (unfavourable).

Analysis:

Gain in Orders—*Extra Cost*
100 at £0·50 .... £ 50 (unfavourable).

Loss in Expense
£600–£550 (*i.e.* 1100 at £0·50 per order) .... £ 50 (unfavourable).

£100 (unfavourable).

Variances for the other two classes of orders would be calculated in the same way. The student should have no difficulty in dealing with these. Clearly, this type of information is useful for analysing the reasons for any variance and, also, in determining policy. If the costs of handling orders below 2 gross become excessive, management may decide to sell to wholesalers only, with minimum orders of 2 gross.

EXAMINATION QUESTIONS

1. When Standard Costing is used it has been found that the Actual sales figures differ from the Standard sales figures.

What consequences would arise? How would you report, explaining the reasons for the variances?

(I.C.W.A.)

2. A sales budget has been formulated using Standard volumes and prices of five Standard products. Since the preparation of the budget, sales prices have increased and the sales manager has requested a monthly return which will show him to what extent each product sale has fluctuated from the budget due to volume or price.

You are required to:

(a) Calculate the respective sales variances for each product from the following information for the month of May 1968.

	Budget		Actual	
	Sales			
Product	price	Volume	Volume	Value
	£			£
A	10	1,000	1,500	16,000
B	3	700	900	5,000
C	8	800	850	7,000
D	2	300	200	500
E	5	200	100	600

(b) Design a form to meet the sales manager's request and insert the figures for May 1968.

(I.C.W.A.)

3. Give a definition of the term *Sales Mixture Variance*. In what circumstances has it significance in explaining a difference between total budget profit and actual profit?

(I.C.W.A.)

CHAPTER 20

ACCOUNTING FOR SELLING AND DISTRIBUTION COSTS

AN example of how the selling and distribution costs may be dealt with in the Ledger is given in the chapter on Integrated Accounting. The procedure followed is to debit a Control Account with the Actual Cost, the corresponding credit entry being to Creditors Control Account or Bank Account. Later a transfer is made to the Cost of Sales Account by debiting the latter with Standard Cost, debiting or crediting Sales Variance Accounts with the variances and crediting the Control Account with Actual Cost. The student who has worked through the example for Bradley & Co. Ltd. (Chapter 15) should experience no difficulty in dealing with similar problems. As will be appreciated, there will be many detailed records used to keep all facts relating to selling and distribution, but, so far as the formal Ledger is concerned, entries are kept to a minimum. Under some systems more details are given in the Ledger; the accountants concerned take the view that a more efficient control over costs is thus possible. These alternative systems are discussed below.

ACCOUNTS FOR SELLING COSTS

In addition to the Control Account for total selling costs, there will be a number of subsidiary accounts, the entries in which will be equal to the totals posted to the main control account. Separate variance accounts may serve the purpose of recording and controlling costs in sales areas or recording and controlling costs relating to each class of product or each salesman. An example to cover sales areas will now be given.

Ledger

Dr.   Cr.

(A)   **Selling Costs Control Account**   (A)
                                 (or Cost Control Account)

	£		£
To Bank	10,000	By South-East Area Control A/c and	
Creditors Control	30,000	Variance A/c	6,100
		„ South-West Area Control A/c and	
		Variance A/c	8,250
		„ Other Areas (detailed)	25,650
	£40,000		£40,000

Dr.   Cr.

South-East Area
(S)   *Selling Costs Control Account*   (S)

| To Selling Costs Control A/c | £6,000 | By Cost of Sales A/c | £6,000 |

South-West Area
(S)   *Selling Costs Control Account*   (S)

| To Selling Costs Control A/c | £8,200 | By Cost of Sales A/c | £8,200 |

North-East Area
(S)   *Selling Costs Control Account*   (S)

| To Selling Costs Control A/c | £5,500 | By Cost of Sales A/c | £5,500 |

South-West Area
(S)   *Selling Costs Control Account*   (S)

| To Selling Costs Control A/c | £6,000 | By Cost of Sales A/c | £6,000 |

London Area
(S)   *Selling Costs Control Account*   (S)

| To Selling Costs Control A/c | £6,500 | By Cost of Sales A/c | £6,500 |

Midlands Area
(S)   *Selling Costs Control Account*   (S)

| To Selling Costs Control A/c | £3,000 | By Cost of Sales A/c | £3,000 |

Scottish Area
(S)   *Selling Costs Control Account*   (S)

| To Selling Costs Control A/c | £3,800 | By Cost of Sales A/c | £3,800 |

Variance Accounts
South-East Area
Selling Costs Variance Account

| To Selling Costs Control A/c | £100 | |

South-West Area
Selling Costs Variance Account

| To Selling Costs Control A/c | £50 | |

North-East Area
Selling Costs Variance Account

| | By Selling Cost Control A/c | £100 |

Dr.   Cr.

North-West Area
Selling Costs Variance Account

| To Selling Costs Control A/c | £300 | |

South-Western Area
Selling Costs Variance Account

| To Selling Costs Control A/c | £50 | |

London Area
Selling Costs Variance Account

| To Selling Costs Control A/c | £200 | |

Midlands Area
Selling Costs Variance Account

| To Selling Costs Control A/c | £250 | |

Scottish Area
Selling Costs Variance Account

| To Selling Costs Control A/c | £150 | |

NOTES

1. The dates have been omitted and figures kept as simple as possible. The entries are self-explanatory.

2. (A) = Actual Cost ⎱ in the account so marked.
   (S) = Standard Cost ⎰

ACCOUNTS FOR DISTRIBUTION COSTS

When a number of different methods of delivery are in operation an account may be operated for each principal method. A Cost Control Account will, of course, be used, just as in the selling-costs example given above. If only one method of delivery is in force a control account may be operated for each group of similar vehicles. An illustration of the accounts that may be used to record different methods of delivery is given below.

Ledger

Dr.   Cr.

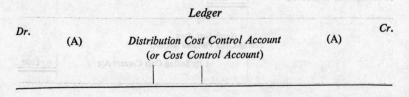

(A)   **Distribution Cost Control Account**   (A)
(or Cost Control Account)

Dr.   Cr.

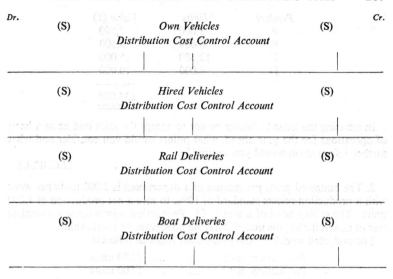

(S)   *Own Vehicles*   (S)
Distribution Cost Control Account

(S)   *Hired Vehicles*   (S)
Distribution Cost Control Account

(S)   *Rail Deliveries*   (S)
Distribution Cost Control Account

(S)   *Boat Deliveries*   (S)
Distribution Cost Control Account

NOTES

1. Variance accounts would also be opened for each method of delivery.
2. No figures have been given. The accounts are operated in exactly the same manner as shown above for Selling Costs.

EXAMINATION QUESTIONS

1. A manufacturing company produces four main lines of standard products. The following is an analysis of its trading account for the year ended 31st May, 1968:

Product	Sales (units)	Sales value	Material cost	Labour cost	Variable expenses	Margin
		£	£	£	£	£
A	4,000	3,200	800	800	600	1,000
B	5,000	5,000	1,500	1,250	1,000	1,250
C	10,000	12,500	8,400	1,600	1,300	1,200
D	3,000	7,500	1,800	2,900	2,300	500
		£28,200	£12,500	£6,550	£5,200	£3,950

Deduct: Fixed expenses   4,200

Net loss for year   £250

The Sales department have produced a sales budget for the year ending 31st May, 1969, as under:

Product	Units	Value (£)
A	3,000	2,500
B	6,000	5,500
C	12,500	15,000
D	4,000	10,000
		£33,000

In advising the Board whether or not to accept the sales budget as a basis of operations for the year ahead, what points would you consider and what further information would you require?

(*I.C.W.A.*)

2. The budgeted gross production of a department is 2,000 units per week with a production rejects standard of 10%, to give a net production of 1,800 units. The selling price of a unit is £5. Production rejects cause a complete loss of material cost, the material having no salvage or re-use value.

The budgeted weekly trading statement reads as follows:

Production, gross	2,000 units	
Production, net	1,800 units	
Sales value of output ...	£9,000	

Budgeted costs:

	£
Direct materials	3,600
Direct labour	1,200
Departmental overheads, variable	1,800
Departmental overheads, fixed	900
	7,500
Budgeted departmental contribution ...	1,500

Last week, the production and cost details were as follows:

Production, gross	1,920 units	
Production, net	1,680 units	
Direct material cost	£3,400	
Direct labour	£1,200	
Departmental overheads, variable	£1,700	
Departmental overheads, fixed	£900	

Prepare a trading statement for last week, comparing actuals with budgets, and detailing the variances which have arisen. (*I.C.W.A.*)

3. Your company employs three different types of transport vehicle in bringing into the factory heavy steel bars, and delivering to customers finished tubes and fabricated tube products. Detail the procedures necessary to instal satisfactory costing arrangements for the transport, and suggest cost control measures which might be introduced.

(*I.C.W.A.*)

CHAPTER 21

ADMINISTRATION COSTS

ALL management and administrative expenses which do not specifically relate to production, selling and distribution, or research and development, are grouped together under the heading "Administration Costs." These costs thus cover all general, secretarial, and accounting-office functions. The salaries of Production Managers and Sales Managers, and similar administrative costs, which relate to the specific functions stated above, are regarded as the costs of those functions and not administration costs. Responsibility for costs is therefore clearly shown.

Typical administration costs are shown below:

Accounting Expenses of all types.
Audit Fees.
Bank Charges.
Cleaning Costs—Office.
Depreciation of Office Buildings, Machinery and Equipment.
Directors' Fees.
Donations.
Insurance: relating to Office, Cash in Transit, etc.
Legal Costs.
Postages.
Printing and Stationery.
Rates and Taxes relating to the Office.
Rent—Office.
Salaries—Office.
Supplies—Office.
Telephones and Telegrams—Office.
Travelling Expenses—Office.

This list does not cover every type of administration cost, but should serve as a guide when determining whether or not a particular cost should be assigned to the administrative division.

SETTING STANDARD ADMINISTRATION COSTS

Modern techniques of management, linked with the complexities of present-day business operations, have tended to increase administration costs. More attention is paid to planning and determining, in advance,

283

what shall be done and then recording what has been done so that a close watch is kept on all activities. Uncertainty is reduced to a minimum, and thus, in the long run, greater stability and lower unit costs of products should result.

Changes in the volume of business will affect total administration costs, but not usually in direct relation to the increase or reduction in volume. Many costs, such as rent, rates, depreciation, and salaries, remain fixed in total, and often the variable costs may not be greatly reduced with a reduced volume of business. A clerk, whether working very hard or merely "filling in time," will need the same facilities, so a great reduction in costs may not result with a smaller output. Dismissals or transfers to other departments could, theoretically, be made, but are difficult to carry out in practice. A well-trained clerical staff is invaluable to any business, and arbitrary dismissals with a falling off in business are likely to do irreparable damage to the trust and co-operative spirit of a body of workers who rightly expect a certain security of employment. Mobility within an office may be encouraged; in fact, to cope with temporary shortages of labour due to sickness or similar causes, it is very desirable; but usually all departments are, together, either busy or slack—naturally so, since they are interrelated.

Standard Costs may be set and a budget compiled to cover, say, a year. Unless there are wide fluctuations in the volume of business a fixed budget will suffice. If necessary, a flexible budget to cover, say, two or possibly three different volumes of business may be completed. Any budget will be similar to those illustrated earlier for production and selling and distribution. To focus responsibility a budget for each department will usually be necessary; these will then go to form the administration budget for the office as a whole.

Examination of all office functions should be carried out before the Standard Costs are set. In the large or medium-size business this will usually be done by an Organisation and Methods team. All work is examined and procedures simplified and standardised. Unnecessary operations, forms, and documents are eliminated, and the best ways of performing the necessary functions are established and introduced. Once the most-efficient methods are used the setting of the Standard Costs should be much simplified. The detailed records of procedures, and standardisation, can do much towards ensuring that this is so.

Some fixed costs will be determined by existing contracts: rent, rates, insurance, and similar items will be covered in this way. Others, such as depreciation, salaries, directors' fees, and audit fees, will be covered by agreements or be part of a defined policy, so, again, no difficulty should be experienced in obtaining the total cost for budget purposes. There will, however, be difficulty in relating these costs to particular functions, such as accounting, order-writing, invoicing, and typing, although this can be done.

The variable and semi-variable costs may vary with the volume of production, the volume of sales, or some other factor. Clearly, the heating or lighting costs which will tend to be semi-variable will be affected by weather conditions and the *type* of work rather than the *amount* of work that is being performed. For example, close work, such as that involved in posting a Ledger or analysing statistics, will tend to need better lighting arrangements than general clerical work. Clerical salaries may be regarded as a fixed cost for a *specific* range of volumes of production or sales, but variable when volumes go beyond the stated point. This is usually so for office stationery—one particular form may cover a work volume of say from 70–100%, but, beyond that point, an additional form may be required. Say, for example, that the daily bookings on a particular form normally vary from twenty-eight to forty in number and a form is designed to cover forty-two entries, then one form per day will be used. If the work increases so that forty-five entries are needed, two forms per day will be required, so the stationery cost on that particular work will have doubled. Clerical salaries and stationery costs may be a considerable part of the running expenses of an office, so control over them is clearly important.

A high standard of quality in office work is essential; this will usually be obtained by an efficient system of internal checks, a senior clerk being responsible for ensuring that the necessary standards are maintained. Assuming, therefore, that the desired quality has been predetermined, the quantity of work may be estimated by using one or more of the following methods:

1. Past records and experience.

2. Use of Organisation and Methods experts.

3. Work Study.

    This can be applied only to a limited number of office tasks; there is not the same scope for standardisation of operations as in the factory.

4. Timing by the office clock or ordinary watch.

    Use of a stop-watch to time operations as under (3) is likely to be of limited value. Instead, an ordinary watch or clock may be used to provide the desired accuracy, which will not be in fractions of a minute, as is often the case for factory operations.

5. Standard work units can be developed and a cost for each determined.

Examples of standard work units are as follows:

Functions	Standard Work Unit
Addressing envelopes.	Cost per envelope.
Book-keeping.	Cost per posting or transaction.
Calculating.	Cost per 100 calculations.
Copying.	Cost per letter or statement copied.
Duplicating.	Cost per form or letter duplicated.
Filing.	Cost per item handled.
Invoicing.	Cost per invoice prepared.
Tabulation.	Cost per tabulation prepared.
Travelling.	Cost per mile or per day.

Typing:

(a) Letters from:

    (i) dictating machines.⎫
    (ii) shorthand.   ⎬ Cost per average letter.

(b) Invoices.   Cost per invoice.

Once these work units and unit costs have been determined they may be used to:

(a) Measure efficiency and, possibly, to award a bonus payment to clerical workers.
(b) Aid in amending budgets after the first, when the volume of work in a future period is expected to be reduced or increased.

When the work can be standardised these methods can be used with advantage. The "standard hour principle" can also be adopted. It will be recalled that the "standard hour" covers the quantity of work that should be performed in one hour. Thus the number of clerks required may be ascertained from the total number of standard hours. If some scheme of grading work is adopted, so that office workers are paid according to the type of work done, there will be no difficulty experienced in pre-determining salary costs. The scheme of grading suggested by the Institute of Office Management may be adapted to cover most needs.

The cost of stationery supplies, office lighting, and other items may be estimated from past records or from quantitative estimates prepared by Organisation and Methods experts.

As will be appreciated, much office work cannot be standardised. Time spent by executives in discussing and considering problems, attending meetings or conferences, and doing similar work, cannot be predetermined. Fortunately, as regards setting Standard Costs, this difficulty presents no great problem. The salaries of the executives will be a fixed cost and may appear in the budget as such.

Departmental heads should co-operate in the preparation of the budgets. They cannot be expected to follow a plan if they do not understand its objects or believe that it can be accomplished.

CONTROL OF ADMINISTRATION COSTS

Each department's costs will be shown in a departmental budget. There is, therefore, a definite allocation of responsibility for cost to the executive in charge of the department.

The Actual and Standard Costs for each type of expense may be compared and an explanation for variations obtained. Calculation of variances in terms of units of work and prices, as done for direct production costs, may be possible. When standard work units and costs have been established a useful measure of efficiency may be obtained by considering for each department or part of a department:

1. Number of standard work units expected.
2. Number of standard work units actually achieved.
3. Efficiency Variance for the work unit involved.
4. Price Variance for the work unit involved.

Thus, for example, if a particular work unit is expected to cost £0·05 and the number of units in an accounting period (*i.e.* four-weekly period) is expected to be 1800, but actual unit cost and quantity are £0·06 and 1900 respectively, then there is clearly a Price and Quantity Variance. The Price Variance is to be found by multiplying 1900 × £0·01 (£19·00—unfavourable) and the Quantity Variance by multiplying 100 × £0·05 (£5·00—favourable). These variances will not have the same significance as those obtained for production, but they could be the means of ensuring that an adequate volume of work is accomplished at a reasonable cost. The fact that the quantity of work available or cost involved may be outside the control of the department concerned should not be forgotten. Nevertheless, attempts of this kind may serve a very useful purpose.

Another possible way of checking expected and actual results is to treat each clerk as a cost centre. The floor space occupied by him is measured and costs charged directly (*e.g.* salary and stationery) or apportioned (*e.g.* depreciation, rent, rates, and taxes). A total cost for the cost centre is then established and a rate per hour or unit of work established. This is an extension of the principle of the work unit already explained. An attempt is made to carry the responsibility to individuals. Each clerk may be required to complete a time sheet showing hours worked and units completed. He may be rewarded for good work by a bonus which is over and above his basic salary. Non-standard work, if done, can also be timed, although only an arbitrary decision on whether or not it has been efficiently performed will be possible.

Some accountants may not consider that attempts at strict control over administration costs can be justified. They may argue that, since these costs are determined mainly by policy, and not by volume of production, little is to be gained by spending further money in trying to measure the effectiveness of the expenditure. Recent interest in organisation and methods work is no accident. Unless administration procedures are carefully watched and controlled they (and the costs) may grow out of all proportion to value received. For this reason alone, the establishment of Standard Costs can usually be justified. The increase in efficiency which should result from using Standard Costs will also strengthen the case for introducing a complete control system.

DISPOSITION OF ADMINISTRATION COSTS

There is no generally accepted method of absorbing administration costs. Much depends upon the views of the accountant concerned with the disposition. The principal methods, from which a choice may be made, are shown below:

1. Treat as a direct charge to products manufactured

The administration costs are charged to Work-in-progress Account, being considered a cost of production. In this way, some part of these costs is carried in the stocks of finished goods. To many accountants this fact is a failing of the method. Administration costs, it is contended, are "period costs" and should, therefore, be written off in the period in which they are incurred. To the extent that many fixed costs are incurred on a time basis, this description is quite apt. Nevertheless, the use of this method still finds favour. Certainly, if linked with an attempt to apportion the costs to products, on the basis of production costs or units produced, useful costing information is made available. If the costs are used as a guide to fixing selling prices the addition of administration (and selling and distribution) costs will clearly show what amount, on average, will have to be covered before a profit is made.

2. Apportion to work-in-progress and cost of sales

In this case the administration costs are regarded as the responsibility of both the production and selling functions. The major problem is to determine how the costs are to be apportioned. In effect, the Office is regarded as a service cost centre which serves the needs of the other two major divisions. Once the costs have been apportioned the procedure followed will be that described for production costs and selling and distribution costs; that is, the production costs are traced to individual products and the selling and distribution costs apportioned to territories, salesmen, or lines of product.

Possibly the most accurate method of apportioning the administration costs is to take each type of cost or each department's total cost and consider its relation to the Production and Selling functions. Thus, for example, assuming the Purchasing Department is part of the Administrative function, it will be necessary to consider the service rendered to the two divisions over which the apportionment is to be made. The number of purchase orders prepared for each division may serve as a suitable basis. If the Personnel Department's costs are being considered, the number of employees may be used for the apportionment.

That part of the administration cost which is treated as a selling cost will, of couse, be written off within the period concerned, whereas the remainder will be taken to production, possibly part of it being carried forward to a future period in the cost of the stock of finished goods.

3. Take to Profit and Loss Account

The fact that administration costs may be regarded as relating to the period in which they are incurred has already been stated in connection with method (1) above. Not unnaturally, therefore, they may be taken directly to Profit and Loss Account, not being apportioned over products or sales or included in the cost of stocks of finished goods. Obviously, under this method, total unit costs, on which decisions may depend, will not be known.* Some accountants regard this fact as a serious failing and advocate apportionment to products on statistical records even though a direct transfer to Profit and Loss Account is made in the double-entry books.

In favour of the method it may be said that, since any apportionment of these costs can at the best be an approximation only, direct transfer to Profit and Loss Account is a more accurate way of disposing of the cost.

CONCLUSION ON SETTING STANDARD COSTS

For similar reasons to those already discussed in connection with selling and distribution costs the setting of Standard Costs for the administrative functions is difficult. Standardisation of the operations, equipment, and office furniture can do much to simplify the task. When the repetitive procedures have been standardised it should then be possible to ascertain what the cost of performing them should be. Since the fixed costs are, in total, known and the benefits received from them are also known, so far as they are concerned the budgets for each department can be compiled without undue difficulty. The floor space occupied by a department can be used as a basis for apportioning rent and rates, depreciation of buildings, and other similar, period costs.

* This assumes that Standard Costing (i.e. using predetermined costs for each unit) is not fully developed so far as Selling and Distribution and Administration are concerned.

Depreciation of equipment and office furniture can be a direct charge based upon capital values. When all fixed costs have been dealt with the variable costs may be predetermined and included in the budget.

An alternative approach is to leave all fixed costs in an Office Fixed Costs Budget, dealing with variable costs and the variable element in semi-variable costs on a departmental basis. This has the effect of including only the controllable costs in the departmental budgets: so that the actual responsibility of any particular department for costs is more clearly defined.

For control purposes, except when dealing in terms of standard work units, it follows that a comparison of Budgeted and Actual Costs for each type of controllable cost will be the most effective method. This is an example of when Standard Costing very much takes the form of Budgetary Control. To truly extend the Standard Costing principle to the administrative function the administration costs would have to be predetermined for each unit of product manufactured or sold. Actual Costs incurred would have to be apportioned to products, and then variances for each line of product would be ascertained. In some types of business this procedure could usefully be adopted. The fact that the costs have to be apportioned on some *arbitrary* basis leaves much to be desired but, provided the basis (or bases) is (or are) carefully selected and used for both Actual and Standard Costs, quite valuable control information may be obtained. Possible methods of apportioning costs to products are as follows:

1. On Production Information.

  (*a*) Number of Units or Tonnage Produced *or*
  (*b*) Manufacturing Costs.

2. On Sales Information.

  (*a*) Sales (in £'s).
  (*b*) Selling Costs.
  (*c*) Number of units or tonnage sold.
  (*d*) Gross Profit on Sales.

Method (1) assumes that administration costs vary with production quantities or costs. The alternative method presumes that the selling function is the dominant factor in tracing responsibility for administration costs. Generally a combination of two or more of the bases under (1) and (2) will give the best results.

ACCOUNTING FOR ADMINISTRATION COSTS

A control account will be opened in the Cost or Integrated Ledger. This may be called an Administration Cost Control Account. Alternatively, when an integrated system of accounting is adopted a Cost

Control Account, in which all costs are debited, may be used, thus avoiding separate control accounts. Essentially, there is no difference between the procedures followed for an Administration Cost Control Account or a Cost Control Account.

The precise way in which the appropriate account is to be operated will very much depend upon the decision made on the disposition of the administration costs. Possible ways are as follows:

1. When costs charged to products manufactured

   (*a*) Debit: Administration Cost Control Account (or Cost Control Account)

   Credit: Bank Account (or Creditors Control Account)

in both cases, with actual expenses incurred on the administrative function. Then:

   (*b*) Debit: Work-in-progress Account (with Actual or Standard Cost depending upon Method of Accounting used)

   Credit: Administration Cost Control Account (or Cost Control Account) with Actual Cost.

To deal with any variance it will be necessary under Accounting Method I to credit the Work-in-progress Account and to debit an Administration Cost Variance Account. This procedure is, of course, for an unfavourable variance. With Accounting Method II the Work-in-progress Account will have been debited with Standard Cost, so any difference between the Actual Cost will be debited (for an unfavourable variance) or credited (for a favourable variance) to an Administration Cost Variance Account.

If one Work-in-progress Account is kept for each element of cost, then the administration cost may, for convenience, be included in the Work-in-progress Account—Factory Overhead.

An illustration of the principles involved for Accounting Method II is shown in Chapter 10.

2. When costs treated as production costs and *selling costs*

That part of total administration cost which is apportioned to production will be dealt with as already described above (1).

With that portion which goes to selling there will be the following entries:

   (*a*) Debit: Selling and Distribution Cost Control Account.
   Credit: Administration Cost Control Account.

Then

   (*b*) Debit: Cost of Sales Account (with Standard Cost).
   Credit: Selling and Distribution Cost Control Account (or Cost Control Account) (with Actual Cost).

If the Cost Control Account is used entry (*a*) will be omitted. Any variance will be isolated by debiting or crediting the Selling and Distribution Costs Variance Account. The entries shown separate the variance from selling costs; this is a matter of opinion. Some accountants will prefer to show the variance as an administrative responsibility.

3. When costs transferred to Profit and Loss Account

Summarised, the entries are:

>   Debit: Profit and Loss Account.
>   Credit: Administration Cost Control Account (or Cost Control Account).

Again, any variance may be isolated in an Administration Cost Variance Account. Whether or not this will serve a useful purpose is open to debate. Clearly, if standard administration costs are to be written off to Profit and Loss Account there is unlikely to be any suggestion of apportioning variances over work-in-progress, sales, and stocks.* Possibly, direct transfer of Actual Costs to Profit and Loss Account, with detailed analysis of any variance on statistical records only, may be a more practical solution. In this way the variance and Standard Cost are immediately written off against revenue and the Ledger will not require to show the Administration Cost Variance Account. The choice of method will have to be left to the accountant concerned with the recording—the one which suits the particular requirements will obviously be the one to take.

* See Chapter 27 on Disposition of Variances.

EXAMINATION QUESTIONS

1. How may the levels of expenditure be governed, short of fixing amounts arbitrarily, in respect of the costs of administration? Your answer should embody ideas likely to assist the various officials in controlling those costs for which they are responsible.

(I.C.W.A.)

2. What are the main difficulties likely to be encountered in the control of administration costs? Give your reasoned opinion as to the relative importance of the control of expenditure on administrative as distinct from manufacturing costs.

(I.C.W.A.)

3. Administration costs have been defined as the cost of formulating policy which is not directly related to other functions of the business.

Prepare a schedule of administration costs for a company with many departments, employing a large sales force. State on what bases you would make any appropriate apportionments.

(I.C.W.A.)

4. In many manufacturing companies, overhead is divided between:

    (*a*) production overhead;
    (*b*) administration overhead;
    (*c*) selling and distribution overhead.

Explain why such a division is made and how such costs differ. In the light of your explanation, suggest methods by which each class of overhead should be absorbed in the product cost.

(I.C.W.A.)

5. Differentiate between *research cost* and *administration cost*. Explain how you would treat each of these groups of expenditure in the cost accounts of a company and how you would ultimately charge them to the product.

(I.C.W.A.)

CHAPTER 22

CAPITAL EXPENDITURE, INCLUDING RESEARCH AND DEVELOPMENT EXPENDITURE

SIMILAR problems are encountered in attempting to control: (*a*) expenditure for capital costs, and (*b*) expenditure for research and development costs. A project is decided upon, costs are accumulated and controlled, and then the final cost has to be capitalised or written off. Accordingly, the two matters are discussed together in this chapter.

Capital expenditure covers all costs incurred on purchasing, making, and erecting assets. Research costs are incurred with the object of developing or improving products and methods. Development, and accordingly development costs, commence when the research brings about a tangible result, which is then perfected, ready for producing and selling. When formal production starts, the development stage may be regarded as being at an end, all subsequent costs being normal production costs. In practice, research and development costs are usually difficult to separate, so they are accumulated and controlled under one heading.

Research and development and capital costs are often difficult to pre-determine and control, but, with experience and practice, the accountant should not find the task impossible. In fact, provided an efficient system of pre-authorisations of, and accounting for, all costs is established, the problems are very much reduced. The procedures which may be followed are summarised:

1. Projects worthy of development are incorporated into:

   (*a*) a Capital Projects Schedule; and
   (*b*) a Research and Development Projects Schedule.

   These schedules may cover a period into the future of, say, five years.

2. Each year Budgets are prepared.

   These may cover a number of projects selected from the schedules in (1) or a specific sum of money. In both cases some form of pre-authorisation will be essential.

3. The costs of each project have to be predetermined.
4. Once each project is commenced expenditure incurred has to be recorded and controlled.

294

5. The complete body of procedures has to be fitted into the normal accounting routine, and appropriate control accounts are kept in the Ledger.

6. Costs accumulated have to be capitalised or written off to Profit and Loss Account as revenue expenditure.

These matters (1) to (6) are covered in detail below.

DETERMINATION OF LIKELY PROJECTS

Selection of future projects may be undertaken by committee and/or by the executive responsible for the field in which the work is to be undertaken. Usually executives from each functional department will be included in the committee, so as to obtain the necessary degree of co-ordination between all aspects of the business.

The policy of the business will clearly be reflected in the schedules compiled. If they cover five years they are, in effect, the policy of the management for that period. When the annual budget's projects are taken from the schedule the latter is then "made up" by adding another year's projects.

THE ANNUAL BUDGETS

All progressive concerns have to purchase or improve assets and carry out research and development projects. A limit to the costs which may be incurred will be imposed by anticipated financial resources. The management has to decide which projects are likely to give the greatest benefits and, ultimately, to achieve the target profit.* Selection by committee is a usual method, though this may also be done by responsible officials as individuals.

An allocation of total expenditure to each budget, backed by authorisations for each individual project, will give effective control over the number, type, and cost of projects. A system of authorising expenditure that has been found to be quite successful is described below:

1. An authorisation form is completed by the head of the department requiring the proposed work to be done

This form gives full details of the project, reasons for it, and expected benefits or results. In conjunction with the Purchasing and Accounts Departments, costs are budgeted and entered on the form. These costs, which may be regarded as Standard Costs for each project, may be set by reference to past records and careful estimates, linked with current, expected prices.

* This envisages normal commercial companies. Government-sponsored research may ignore the profit motive.

2. Each authorisation form is approved or rejected (with reasons) by a committee, senior manager, or Board of Directors

Often projects are divided into (*a*) Major and (*b*) Minor. The latter, say those not exceeding £500, may be authorised by a senior manager, whereas those for £500 or upwards will normally have to be sanctioned at Board level. The costs will include those to be incurred on purchasing an asset as well as the concern's direct labour, materials, and overhead costs.

3. The authorisation form, when approved, is sent to the Accounts Department, where it is given a serial number

In this department the procedure could take the following form:

(*a*) A project sheet is completed and allotted a project number. These numbers should indicate the type of expenditure, the department concerned, and the project. Thus, for example, capital expenditure in XY Department may be indicated by C 1.324; "C" denoting Capital Expenditure, "1" the code number for the department, and "324" being the project or job number.

(*b*) From invoices, material issue analysis sheets, and wages analysis sheets, details will be entered on the project sheet until the project is closed down.

(*c*) All project sheets relating to Capital and Research and Development will be kept in suitable, loose-leaf binders. When the costs of a project are written off to Profit and Loss Account the appropriate sheet will be removed from the binder concerned and an adjustment made in the ledger accounts. The total costs in each binder should, at the end of each accounting period, be equal to the total cost in the appropriate control accounts explained in the next section.

ACCOUNTING PROCEDURES

Until a final decision—on whether costs are to be treated as capital or revenue—is made, the expenditures may be "suspended" in ledger control accounts. Thus, two accounts, called (1) Quasi-Capital (Assets) Account and (2) Quasi-Capital (Research and Development) Account, can serve this purpose. These are debited, at the end of each accounting period, with the appropriate costs from the summary sheets mentioned in 3(*b*) above. Any variances may or may not be shown in the accounts —this depends upon the method of accounting for Standard Costs which is used (*see* Chapters 9 and 10 on Methods).

Any interim writing off of the cost of a project may be done by crediting the Quasi-Capital (Assets) Account and debiting production costs. Transfer of the final cost of projects to capital may be made when a project is completed or periodically, say, half-yearly or yearly.

Alternatively, transfer of all costs whether a project is complete or not may be made at the end of each year only. A Plant Register and a Research and Development Register will be maintained with corresponding accounts in the ledger. Depreciation will, of course, be written off each year.

SETTING STANDARD COSTS FOR EACH PROJECT

The procedure for compiling a budget for either capital expenditure or for research and development expenditure will follow the same lines as for other types of budget: the principal of these have already been discussed. Costs are divided according to their nature, *i.e.* whether fixed, variable, or semi-variable.

With the research and development budget many costs will be fixed. All space and building charges, salaries of research workers and technicians, and wages of skilled workers will tend to be of a fixed nature. Usage of sundry materials and supplies and the wages of unskilled labour will tend to vary from period to period. The fixed costs will be determined by the particular policy being followed, and should present no difficulty either as regards predetermination or control. Provided responsible executives are fully aware of the policy there should be no excessive spending. With variable costs, strict control will be necessary. Material requisitions, and authorisations to engage labour, must all be part of the control system.

Expenditure on assets may be classified into fixed and variable costs. Generally, a business does not make a practice of manufacturing its own assets, but, on the other hand, often does its own preparatory and installation work. Small, or comparatively simple, pieces of equipment or machinery, such as Stores bins, special furniture, and tools, may be made. In an engineering factory the tool-room may be engaged for a substantial part of its time on producing tools. When machinery is purchased from an outside supplier the purchase price may be regarded as the fixed cost. Any preparatory or installation work will involve variable costs, and it is over these that control must be exercised. Fixed costs incurred within the business, such as those involved in maintaining the Works Engineer's department, may also be charged to the particular asset concerned, but little or no control over these is possible. If complete assets are made, an estimate similar to that used for normal job production will be necessary. Production officials will predetermine what quantities of material and labour should be necessary and the best way of producing the asset. The cost accountant will then evaluate the quantities and, if necessary, add an amount for overhead costs.*

* Many accountants do not charge overhead costs to assets. There is certainly a strong case for excluding fixed overhead costs, for these relate to the period in which they are incurred and should not therefore be "deferred."

DISPOSITION OF CAPITAL AND RESEARCH AND DEVELOPMENT COSTS

The Standard Costs of the projects have either to be treated as revenue expenditure, and disposed of, or capitalised, the writing off being spread over the future years in which benefits are expected to be received from the expenditure.

Costs are normally treated as capital expenditure when an asset, patent, or other result, which helps to increase the volume or quality of products, or to reduce costs, is a consequence of capital or research and development expenditure. This is the general rule, but exceptions will be found; where border-line cases arise much depends upon the policy of the particular business concerned.

Revenue expenditure does not result in *future* benefits, so it is assumed to belong to the accounting year in which it is incurred. Often an arbitrary decision, to determine the category into which a cost falls, will be necessary. If there is doubt, the cost of a project, unless very large, is treated as revenue expenditure.

When a definite asset is produced or a patent obtained the cost of the project may be capitalised and written off over the estimated life of the asset or the known life of the patent. With many research and development projects the eventual outcome will not be so obvious, and projects may even have to be abandoned without any resultant benefits. If benefits are certain to accrue over a number of future years, then the period should be estimated and the total cost apportioned over it. Where a project does not prove to be successful the cost may be written off in the year in which it is incurred. Even in this case, however, some difficulty may be experienced in reaching a decision. If a major project involving many thousands of pounds is finally abandoned, disposal of the total cost will result in an inequitable charge in the year concerned. An alternative procedure is to transfer the cost to a deferred revenue account, which is, of course, tantamount to capitalisation.

When an entirely new product results from a research and development project then the costs may rightly be charged to the future unit costs of the product. A similar procedure may be followed when a specific line of products is improved. If methods are improved the development costs involved may be charged to the overhead concerned. With new manufacturing methods, general factory overhead costs may be increased; with an Organisation and Methods project, administration costs can be charged with the expenditure involved. Again the number of years over which the costs will be apportioned is very much a matter of policy. Generally speaking, they should be written off as quickly as possible.

In some types of business it may be possible to charge the customer with the research and development cost. For testing or analysing a product or material for a customer, a charge may be made. When research and development is necessary for a specific job or contract, then the costs involved are, legitimately, a direct charge to that job or contract. Clearly, if a charge can be made to a customer, then it should be made. Costs are recovered as quickly as possible and not carried forward to future periods. Advice or small services may, of course, result in the building of goodwill, and whether or not a charge should be made for these is a matter of policy—in the long run more profit may result by not charging for them.

STANDARD COSTS AND VARIANCES

If the Standard Costs set for each project are to be regarded as the true costs, the variances, if unfavourable, should be treated as losses due to inefficiency. They are usually taken direct to Costing Profit and Loss Account. Favourable variances may be treated in the same way. However, if these are quite large, it must be decided whether they should be credited to Profit and Loss or whether the capital item should be reduced. Showing an asset at an inflated cost, much in excess of Actual Cost, can rarely be justified. Future years will be charged with excess depreciation; the effect will be to reduce costs in one year, but to prejudice future years. Naturally, if Standard Costs are carefully set the variances, favourable or unfavourable, should not be large. With the types of cost being considered, especially those relating to research and development, no matter how much care is taken there will, from time to time, be unusual results. A flexible policy—consistent and backed by good common sense—is therefore essential.

No attempt should be made to try to keep as strict a control over expenditure incurred by research workers as over production costs. For many of the reasons discussed in connection with controlling selling and distribution costs, rigid control is extremely difficult. Nevertheless, some predetermined target is essential. Otherwise the research establishment, run by enthusiastic technologists, may very soon become a larger financial drain than the business can manage.

Variances may be ascertained for each project and for each class of expense. Separate treatment of expenditure on assets and expenditure on research and development will be essential. Close watch on expenditure incurred to ensure that each project's cost is kept within the figure authorised will be essential. The precise way this will be done depends very much upon local conditions. The problem consists of bringing deviations from Standard Cost to the notice of persons responsible for the expenditure; this has to be done in good time and, if necessary, a supplementary authorisation will have to be obtained by the official concerned.

The value received from the costs incurred does not always receive the attention it deserves. There is unlikely to be any justification for allowing assets to be made at a cost which is far in excess of the current prices of identical assets. Provided the Standard Costs are accurately set, any large unfavourable variances will probably indicate that the production of assets needed in the business is best left to outside specialists. With research and development costs the presence of a large, unfavourable variance may not be as serious as might appear. On the other hand, a major project, which shows *no* variance, may represent a serious setback. The significant factor is the outcome of the research. If there are definite results—a new or more superior product or method or reduced costs—then the costs can be justified even if the project has cost more that it should have done. Evaluation of the results may often be difficult, but an attempt should be made, for it is only in this way that a real, and not merely a nominal control over expenditure, can be exercised. Comparison of what has been achieved with what should have been achieved, if possible relating the information to profit figures, is advisable.

EXAMINATION QUESTIONS

1. Using broad headings, state what main factors would need to be estimated in order to apply budgetary control to heavy expenditure on research and development in a manufacturing organisation. Discuss briefly the application of Standards to such an outlay.

(I.C.W.A.)

2. Outline the considerations that would guide you in fixing a budget for a given period for:

    (*a*) research expenditure;
    (*b*) selling expenditure.

(I.C.W.A.)

3. Give examples of development costs in a factory and discuss their apportionment.

(I.C.W.A.)

4. The authority of the Board of Directors is being sought for the expenditure of a considerable sum of money on new plant to perform automatically work at present done by hand.

The engineering department have completed the technical details and now ask for the assistance of the cost department in putting their case forward for the Board's approval.

Draft the headings of such a capital proposal form, showing the major considerations involved.

(I.C.W.A.)

5. Owing to the exclusive nature of his product, a manufacturer is forced to undertake the manufacture of his own machinery. Discuss the problem of the application of overheads to this part of his activities and the valuation of such machinery for capital and depreciation purposes.

(I.C.W.A.)

Chapter 23

MARGINAL STANDARD COSTING

INTRODUCTION

MARGINAL STANDARD COSTING* is a fairly new technique which combines Marginal Costing and Standard Costing. It takes the desirable features of both and thereby emerges as a tool of management which can assist in solving many business problems.

Since Standard Costing has already been defined, it is only necessary to discuss Marginal Costing, remembering, of course, that Marginal Standard Costing employs Standard Costs, and not historical costs with their attendant disadvantages.

Marginal Costing is a technique of cost accounting which pays special attention to the behaviour of costs with changes in the volume of output. Like Standard Costing, it is superimposed upon a *system* of job costing or process costing.

The principal method employed for achieving its objective of showing behaviour of costs is to divide the latter into the following categories:

1. Marginal or variable costs.
2. Fixed or period costs.

These are defined on page 49, here it is important to notice that Marginal Costs are for most practical purposes the same as variable costs—those costs which tend to vary with changes in output.

The fixed costs tend to remain constant in total, irrespective of the volume of output. What is significant in this definition is that assumptions are made regarding the period covered and the range of output.

Generally the period being considered does not exceed a year. There can be no question of fixed costs being "fixed" for all time, especially in a period of rising prices. In the very long period all fixed costs will *vary*, but this fact does not invalidate the use of the definition given.

Another factor is the range of output being considered. If output is to be increased from, say, 90% of total capacity to 100%, then the same fixed costs would probably apply. However, if output is to be doubled, then there is likely to be a very different story. New factories or machinery will probably be required so that a new total for fixed costs will emerge. Again, the definition is quite logical, provided there is no substantial change in the volume of output to be produced.

* Also known as *Direct Standard Costing* or *Standard Marginal Costing*.

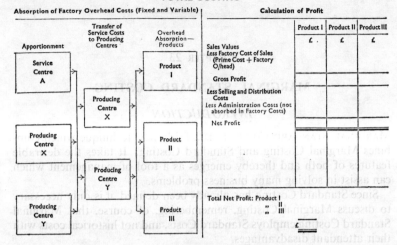

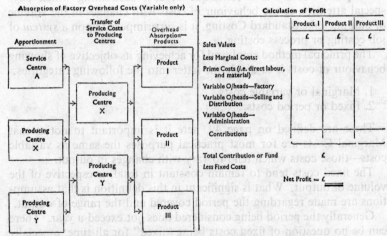

FIG. 38—*Marginal Costing and Total Costing Compared*

The significance of Marginal Costing can be appreciated better by study of the advantages and disadvantages listed below:

POSSIBLE ADVANTAGES

The advantages claimed for Marginal Costing are:

1. The cost of a product does not vary from one period to another. This assertion is based on the fact that the fixed cost *per unit* when conventional costing is employed is greater for each reduction in the volume of output.

Example:
Fixed Costs £1000
Month 1 Output   2000 units
Month 2 Output   1000 units
Fixed Cost Per Unit:
Month 1   £0·50
Month 2   £1·00

2. Because of (1), sales managers and others who are concerned with justifying prices have more confidence in the costing system. They are not faced with different costs from one period to another.
3. Marginal Costing avoids the under- or over-absorption of overhead costs. This is only partly true because variable costs also enter into any calculation of predetermined costs when job costing is employed.
4. Problems connected with a greater or smaller volume of output tend to be simplified.
5. Cost control is greatly facilitated because due recognition is given to the way costs behave. There is still a need to predetermine costs to control effectively. For this reason, Marginal Costing without Standard Costing or Budgetary Control is likely to be of limited value.
6. Due recognition is given to the fact that a profit is not earned until products are sold. When calculating profit only the relevant costs are deducted from the sales values. Fixed costs are not absorbed in the costs of individual products (see Fig. 38).

POSSIBLE DISADVANTAGES

While admitting that some of the arguments for Marginal Costing are sound, many accountants qualify the usefulness of the technique as follows:

1. In the long period a profit must be earned or the business will not survive. If prices are based on Marginal Costs, without regard to the size and nature of fixed costs, there is a danger that they will not include a profit. For this reason, reliance on Marginal Costs alone can lead to unsound decisions and unprofitable orders.
2. The separation of fixed costs is important, but this act alone does not show managers what is happening. Calculation of the appropriate variances may give much more valuable information.
3. Many costs are semi-variable and the problem of ascertaining which part is fixed and which is variable may be almost as bad as the process of apportioning these costs to products. In addition, there is the question of the accuracy being attained. Some of the methods employed for separating the fixed and variable elements may give approximations only.

Conclusion

Although there can be great justification for employing Marginal Costing the manager who is not an accountant should not jump to the conclusion that the technique cures all ailments. The other systems and methods are just as useful in appropriate circumstances.

What should be clear to the reader is that the disadvantages can to some extent be overcome by the use of Standard Costs, *i.e.* by using Marginal Standard Costing. Variance analysis will reveal what is happening in terms of cost, and especially the consequences of non-achievement of the standard volume of output.

BREAK-EVEN CHARTS

A Break-even Chart is shown in Fig. 39. This is a pictorial representation of the costs of a business, presented so as to show:

1. Fixed costs.
2. Variable costs.
3. Break-even point (where costs and revenue agree exactly).
4. The rate of earning after the break-even point has been achieved.

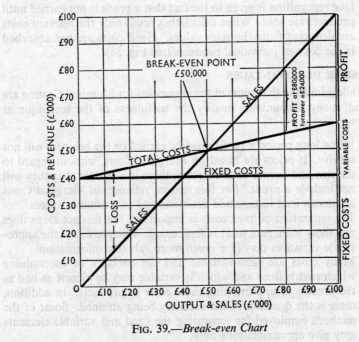

FIG. 39.—*Break-even Chart*

When based on Standard Costs a Break-even Chart represents what is expected to happen in the future. It is, in effect, the Master Budget portrayed in terms of what costs *should be* for stated conditions. Subsequently, the Standard Costs and Actual Costs can be shown on the same chart so that any total variances are revealed (Fig. 40).

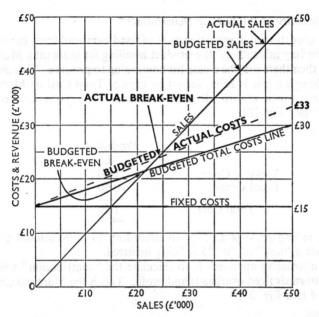

FIG. 40.—*Control Break-even Chart (comparing Budgeted and Actual Profits)*

NOTE

Profit for Budgeted Sales = £13,000	Profit for Actual Sales:	£
	Budgeted Profit	16,500
	−Actual Profit	13,800
	Profit Variance	£2,700

USES FOR MARGINAL STANDARD COSTING

Because of the separation of fixed and variable (marginal) costs, it is possible to show more clearly the effect of making a particular decision. Some of the problems which may be solved by Marginal Standard Costing are as follows:

1. *Pricing of Products*

In the short period, a company which is experiencing trading difficulties might gain business and thereby reduce losses by basing prices on Marginal Costs which are also Standard Costs. So long as Marginal Costs are covered, and some contribution is made towards fixed costs, the company will be minimising losses. However, this technique should be used with caution, because in the long run all costs have to be covered.

2. Profitability of Products or Departments *

The allocation and apportionment of fixed overhead costs can sometimes be very misleading. If a product is selling for more than Marginal Costs, then there may be a case for continuing to produce. This applies even though a loss is being shown by normal Total Costing Methods; i.e. those which absorb all fixed overhead costs in the cost of the product (see Fig. 38).

Example

	Product A £
Variable Costs	1·00
Fixed Costs	0·50
Total Cost	1·50

The selling price is £1·375, so according to conventional costing methods a "loss" of £0·125 is being incurred.

An alternative approach is to calculate the "contribution" which is made towards fixed overheads and profit. This is the Marginal Costing method (see Fig. 38).

Example

	Product A £
Marginal Costs	1·000
Selling Price	1·375
Contribution	0·375

This means that £0·375 is being earned towards fixed costs and profit. If many other products are being made, the absorption of fixed costs may be anything between a poor guess to a very good estimate. There can be no question of absolute accuracy. Accordingly, if Product A cannot be replaced with something much better (contribution-wise), then it is better to retain that product.

Examples of other uses are: make or buy decisions, closing down, expand or buy decisions and the comparison of machines and hand labour. For details of these, and practical illustrations the reader is referred to *Management Accountancy*, written by the author of this book.

* Readers are also advised to read Chapter 28, especially pages 355–358.

EXAMINATION QUESTIONS

1. "For effective management, the Manager should receive only condensed, summarised, and invariably comparative reports."

Assuming agreement with this statement, design a form and add suitable figures to present a report to management upon departmental overhead variances.

(I.C.W.A.)

2. "For planning, the manager wants information about the future; for control, about the past."

Comment on this statement, and indicate the type of information supplied by the cost accountant for these purposes.

(I.C.W.A.)

3. In a manufacturing company, where the main aim is to maximise return on investment and achieve a satisfactory growth rate, decisions are necessary from time to time whether to buy outside, or expand facilities and make, to obtain the required output.

The setting up of a make-or-buy committee is proposed. Compile a procedure, using brief numbered paragraphs, which the committee should follow and supervise from design to final recommendation. Specify desirable features of the accounting system in operation.

(I.C.W.A.)

CHAPTER 24

STATEMENTS AND REPORTS

INFORMATION is essential to all levels of management. Managers find that reports and statements are essential to be able to plan and formulate policy, to maintain and improve operating efficiency and to be able, at any time, to know the cost of products made.

All reports should serve a useful purpose. If they do not inform management in a clear and unmistakable manner of what has taken place and what action may be carried out, then they are not functioning efficiently. An unbiased presentation of facts is, obviously, the aim. Matters of opinion, to retain the essential impartiality, have to relate to the facts and not be influenced by personal feelings.

The amount of detail included in a report will vary according to the type of report and the person for whom it is intended. Reports on unusual or special occurrences will generally contain more detail than daily or weekly routine reports, and those dealing with shop-floor activities show more detail than those intended for general management. Allowing for these differences, however, conciseness is essential for all reports; relevant facts only should be presented. The action on the reports is the thing that counts, not the reading of a mass of detail—this, in itself, is useless. Accordingly, the fewer the facts, to obtain a desired degree of efficiency, the more skilled may the cost accountant be regarded, in his role as interpreter of business activity.

Scientific or technical language is probably best left out of reports. This is especially so when a supervisor or foreman is to receive the report. Simplicity of form enables him to follow, without misunderstanding, what has taken place. Often physical quantities—hours, units, feet, weight, or other measurement—will present a clearer picture than cost variances, shown in terms of sterling.

Whenever possible, the reports should show not only what has happened but also what should have happened. These objectives can be achieved by presenting, side by side, Actuals and Standards; comparisons can then be made and corrective action, to prevent recurrence of the variance, can be taken by the management concerned. Following the "principle of exceptions," allowing concentration on matters which require attention, can do much to aid management in this action-taking. Those factors which are not reported on are assumed to be operating smoothly, thus cutting down to a minimum the demands on a manager's time. The principle of exceptions can, of course, be carried too far.

A cost centre is an integral part of a complete business unit, so information on other aspects of the business may usefully be given, provided this is carefully selected. More co-operation may result, and the manager concerned will realise that other cost centres have problems. There is also the psychological aspect which is likely to arise when, say, a foreman is presented with details of *all* inefficiencies, but never any efficiencies. Praise, as well as criticism, forms part of a framework of good management principles.

Prompt presentation is imperative. One of the great advantages of Standard Costing arises from the fact that management information is gathered as a matter of ordinary routine. There is no waiting until it is obvious that something is wrong before invoices, wages sheets, clock cards, and other documents are analysed. At this stage, when the inefficiency is blatantly apparent, much damage will have already been done. With Standard Costing, deviations from efficient performances are brought to light as quickly as possible, in time to correct any adverse tendencies, before great loss has occurred. The facts emerge quickly, without undue delay, and are placed before the appropriate management.

If, even when the details have been kept to a minimum, they still tend to be excessive, it is a sound principle to summarise the main facts and conclusions. The use of a graph, chart, or other visual aid may also be worthy of consideration. Any technique which allows management to grasp, quickly and effectively, the nature of the problem has, obviously, much to recommend it.

Many of the requirements of the compiling of reports will be apparent from what has already been said. To make the description reasonably complete it should be added that the title and, if necessary, sub-titles should clearly describe the contents of the report. The units being dealt in, whether physical or £ *s. d.*, must also be shown. If abbreviations or signs are used, then footnotes or a "key" are likely to be helpful. The names of the persons to whom the report is addressed and the name of the writer should also appear on the report.

The cost of reporting should be kept to a minimum. Only essential reports will, therefore, have to be produced. Unnecessary precision with figures, or refinements in presentation of lay-out, have to be avoided, or costs will become excessive.

In the general remarks made above the word "report" has been used to mean a purely written report, with or without supporting figures, or a cost-statement type of report. Clearly, not all the observations made will apply to every type of report. A routine cost statement will probably require a title, date, and columns, with appropriate headings for comparative figures and variances. On the other hand, a written report, on a special problem, will normally comply with all the formalities discussed.

Examination questions at both intermediate and final levels, quite naturally, demand a high standard of knowledge of, and aptitude for, report writing. Once the cost man leaves the stage of merely recording cost figures and begins to design procedures and prepare reports and advise management he becomes a cost accountant and not just a cost clerk. To achieve the necessary proficiency in report writing, careful study of the correct procedures and then as much practice as possible is essential. Examples of typical reports and statements, with explanations, are given in the next two chapters. For convenience, these have been grouped into:

1. Reports to Executives and Top Management.

and

2. Reports to Foremen and Supervisors.

As already stated, Standard Costing is a complete system of accounting in itself. Strictly speaking, therefore, all kinds of reports and statements come within its framework.

EXAMINATION QUESTIONS

1. Submit a columnar ruling suitable for reporting to management upon the running hours, Standard and Actual, of machine tools. Include columns for such related cost or other data as you consider desirable. Enter specimen figures for four machines.

(I.C.W.A.)

2. The following chart is for the use of the foreman. Enumerate its faults as a method of presentation of this information.

TYPE No. 3412.   Date presented: 5th July, 1969.

PRODUCTION MADE GOOD, 994

MATERIAL LOSSES FOR MONTH ENDING 30th April, 1969

PROCESS 1 3·38%	PROCESS 2 14·56%	PROCESS 3 0·77%	PROCESS 4 6·65%

CAUSE A. 0·5%
  ,,   B. 0·4%
  ,,   C. 2·04%
  ,,   D. 0·25%
  ,,   E. 0·1%
	CAUSE A. 0·65%
	  ,, B. 1·26%
	  ,, C. 1·79%
	  ,, D. 4·78%
	  ,, E. 1·87%
	  ,, F. 2·99%
	  ,, G. 0·31%
	  ,, H. 0·37%
	  ,, I. 0·13%
		CAUSE A. 0·2%
		  ,, B. 0·32%
		  ,, C. 0·25%
			CAUSE A. 4·28%
			  ,, B. 1·45%
			  ,, C. 0·71%

(I.C.W.A.)

CHAPTER 25

REPORTS TO EXECUTIVES AND TOP MANAGEMENT

REPORTS may be classified in a variety of ways. One possibility is as follows:

1. Special Reports.

A special report is a record of facts of unusual events. Generally it will be called for when there has been a serious reduction in efficiency, when it is proposed to carry out plans which involve the consideration of a number of alternative choices, or when any other extraordinary matter arises.

2. Routine Reports which cover all normal activities.

They may be prepared and submitted—

(a) Daily.
(b) Weekly.
(c) Fortnightly.
(d) Monthly.
(e) Quarterly.
(f) Yearly.

The frequency is determined by the nature of their contents and the requirements of the particular business concerned. Routine reports may be sub-divided into:

(i) General reports.
(ii) Production reports.
(iii) Sales reports.
(iv) Distribution reports.
(v) Administration reports.

SPECIAL REPORTS

Since these cover unusual matters, a comprehensive, written coverage of all relevant details, often supported by schedules of figures, is normally essential. The precise form of the report will vary according to the specific requirements. General "pointers" can, however, be indicated. A skeleton report divided into sections is shown in Fig. 41.

SPECIAL REPORT

Names and Titles of Managers to whom   Costing Department.
Report is addressed.   Date.

Title (describing nature of report)

Section (1). The reasons for the report.

Section (2). Investigation carried out.

Section (3). Findings of investigation.

Section (4). Suggested action and conclusion.

If addressed to the board of directors or senior management the salutation "Gentlemen," "Dear Sirs," or similar form of address, ending with

Yours faithfully,

"X Y"

Cost Accountant

may be considered necessary.

Fig. 41.—*Specimen Special Report*

ROUTINE REPORTS

The routine reports to executive and top management may be divided into a number of classes. One possibility is shown below:

1. Those reports which affect all top management and especially general management (General Reports).
2. Those reports which cover production activities only and are of primary interest to production management (Production Reports).
3. Those reports which deal with the selling of the products and are the concern of the sales management (Sales Reports).
4. Those reports which cover distribution activities and are, therefore, of interest to the distribution management (Distribution Reports).
5. Those reports which show how the administrative functions of the office are being carried out and are of interest to office management (Administration Reports).

GENERAL REPORTS

To keep a watch on the overall functioning of a business it is necessary for general management to ensure:

1. That there is adequate cash available to meet commitments.
2. Sufficient orders are being received to keep the plant operating at the normal capacity.

3. The production programme is being maintained.

4. Sales, at a profitable price, are being despatched to customers.

The reports required to cover these matters will vary according to the particular needs of the business. However, some idea of their nature may be obtainable from the information given under the headings enumerated below.

1. CASH REPORT (FIG. 42)

This Report shows the trend, week by week, of cash resources; with some businesses, especially when there is a shortage of liquid resources, a daily report may be necessary. In any event a monthly report, along with budgeted figures, is also likely to prove useful.

	Jan. 2	Week ended:			
	£	£	£	£	£
Opening Balances	5,000				
Accounts Receivable	10,000				
	15,000				
Payments:					
Accounts Payable	8,000				
Loans	—				
Miscellaneous	—				
	8,000				
Closing Balances	7,000				

CASH REPORT

Date...................................

FIG. 42.—*Cash Report*

NOTES

1. The ratio of Cash and Debtors (Accounts Receivable) to Accounts Payable, is extremely important. Considering external receipts and payments only (*i.e.* ignoring wages and other internal payments) the ratio between the two totals should be at least 1 to 1. Any excess provides the *liquid* working capital.

2. The details will vary to meet the specific needs of the business. If necessary, payments for wages and petty cash items could also be listed.

3. Any occurrence which is likely to affect the liquidity position of the business should be the subject of a special report or footnote on the above report.

4. When Budgetary Control is used—and this is recommended—budgeted and actual figures will be shown.

2. DAILY ORDERS RECEIVED REPORT (FIG. 43)

This Report can show the vital statistics of a business with regard to activity—of the utmost importance if:

(a) Costs are to be kept to a minimum, particularly fixed *unit* costs.
(b) Machinery and other plant, including personnel, are kept fully employed.

An index of daily profitability may be obtained by considering:

(a) Orders received, evaluated by reference to selling prices.
(b) Standard Costs for the particular volume of work obtained.

If (b) is deducted from (a) the difference will be the profit that should be earned. The costs (b) can be obtained from the Standard Cost Card

DAILY ORDERS RECEIVED REPORT
Date: January 2nd, 19...

| | Product A | | | | Product B | | | |
| | Actual | | Budget | | Actual | | Budget | |
	Units	Price	Units	Price	Units	Price	Units	Price
Received Yesterday:								
S. East								
S. West								
N. East								
N. West								
London								
Midlands								
Scotland								
*Totals:								
*Totals to Date for January								

*Units/Value. or Units/Av. Price.	A	B
Summary: Budgeted Value of Orders		
Actual Value of Orders		
Value Variance =	£	£

FIG. 43.—*Daily Orders Received Report*

NOTE
The "Summary" may cover the daily figures or those for the month to date.

and the flexible budget. The selling prices will be determined by the policy followed. This matter is covered in Chapter 28.

3. WEEKLY PRODUCTION REPORT (FIG. 44)

This Report aids management by showing the possible and actual number of standard hours. It may immediately be seen how the work is progressing, and this is invaluable, for a backlog of work may call for overtime working or similar action.

When production follows a regular pattern the opening and closing work-in-progress figures will tend to be approximately the same. If there is a large increase in the closing work-in-progress in a particular department this *may* mean that there has been abnormal absenteeism or a large number of machine breakdowns. The student will recall from the chapter which deals with the setting of overhead costs that the "capacity" has to be selected carefully. If the number of hours actually worked varies greatly from the number anticipated the achievement of all Standards will be adversely affected. The connection between the facts on the Report and the Overhead Volume Variance will be apparent.

WEEKLY PRODUCTION REPORT

Week Ended.....................

Department:	Work Loads—Standard Hours							
	1		2		3		Total	
	Act.	Bud.	Act.	Bud.	Act.	Bud.	Act.	Bud.
Work-in-progress (Opening) *Add* Work Commenced								
Less Work Finished								
Work-in-progress (Closing)								
Backlog: In Hand:								

FIG. 44.—*Weekly Production Report*

NOTES

1. The Report may be extended to show a summary of budgeted and actual costs for the production achieved.

2. The "standard hour" is the quantity of work that should be performed in one hour.

4. DAILY SALES DESPATCHED REPORT (FIG. 45)

Despatch of an adequate volume of sales each day is essential if maximum profit is to be earned, and this Report enables the sales position to be watched.

DAILY SALES DESPATCHED REPORT

..........................Factory   Date: January 2nd, 19...

	Product A				Product B			
	Actual		Budget		Actual		Budget	
	Units	Price	Units	Price	Units	Price	Units	Price
Despatched Yesterday:								
S. East								
S. West								
N. East								
N. West								
London								
Midlands								
Scotland								
Totals:								
Totals to Date for January								

	A	B
Summary: Budgeted Value of Sales		
Actual Value of Sales		
Sales Value Variance	£	£

	A	B
Actual Value of Sales		
Less Standard Cost of Sales for Actual Sales at Volume being achieved		
Expected Profit	£	£

FIG. 45.—*Daily Sales Despatched Report*

NOTES

1. The ruling for this report is similar to that shown for the Daily Orders Received Report.

2. The profit for each day or for the month to date may be shown in summary form, as indicated.

5. COSTING PROFIT AND LOSS STATEMENT

This is a very important statement. Examples are given on pages 204 to 207. An Analysis by products is often shown on the Profit and Loss Statement: in this way the standard sales and costs for each product can readily be seen.

6. ANALYSIS OF GROSS PROFIT AND NET PROFIT STATEMENTS

GROSS PROFIT ANALYSIS STATEMENT

.............................Factory   Date.............................

	Product A		Product B		Total	
	Actual £	Budget £	Actual £	Budget £	Actual £	Budget £
Sales Value Factory Cost of Sales						
Gross Profit						
Percentage: Gross Profit to Sales						

	Products	
	A	B
Summary: Actual Gross Profit Budgeted Gross Profit		
Variance	£	£

FIG. 46.—*Gross Profit Analysis Statement*

The Gross Profit Analysis Statement (Fig. 46) and the Net Profit Analysis Statement (Fig. 47) may both be prepared at the end of each accounting period (*i.e.* monthly). They show the budgeted and actual profits for each month. Both statements will be adapted to meet particular circumstances. The addition of an analysis of profits for the year to date will serve a very useful purpose.

7. OTHER STATEMENTS AND REPORTS

The above statements and reports are given to show the type of information likely to be useful to general management. They do not pretend to meet all requirements, but, rather, aim to suggest the approach

NET PROFIT ANALYSIS STATEMENT

..............................Factory   Date..............................

	Product A		Product B		Total	
	Actual £	Budget £	Actual £	Budget £	Actual £	Budget £
Sales Value						
Factory Cost of Sales						
Gross Profit						
Administration Costs						
Selling and Distribution Costs						
Net Profit						
Percentage: Net Profit to Sales						

	Products	
	A	B
Summary: Actual Profit		
Budgeted Profit		
Variance	£	£

FIG. 47.—*Net Profit Analysis Statement*

to presenting information. Many of the reports shown below for production, selling and distribution, and administration will also be of interest to general management.

PRODUCTION REPORTS

Production management is interested in all aspects of manufacturing efficiency. Important matters to be covered are:

1. The volume of production.
2. The quality of production.
3. Efficient utilisation of all facilities.
4. The costs of the volume of production achieved.

A guide to the types of report that are likely to be required is shown below.

Needless to say, the examples will not cover all circumstances or requirements. Conditions vary so much that it would take far too much space here to cover every type of report.

1. VOLUME OF PRODUCTION REPORTS

(a) *Weekly Production Report in terms of standard hours*

An example is given above under General Reports (Fig. 44). Clearly this type of report will be a good guide to overall efficiency in each department. There should, quite obviously, be an efficient system of production planning and control; indeed, this is essential if a Standard Costing system is to be fully employed. Any lag in production will be detected quite early and the necessary corrective action can be taken before a serious problem arises.

(b) *Weekly Production Report in terms of units produced* (*Fig. 48*)

WEEKLY PRODUCTION REPORT					
.........................Factory			Date............................		
	This Month		Year to Date		Variances	
	Actual	Budget	Actual	Budget	This Month	To Date
Number of Units						
Cost per Unit:-						
Direct Labour Cost:						
(a) Total	£	£	£	£	£	£
(b) Per Unit						
Direct Material Cost:						
(a) Total	£	£	£	£	£	£
(b) Per Unit						
Factory Overhead:						
(a) Total	£	£	£	£	£	£
(b) Per Unit						

FIG. 48.—*Weekly Production Report*

This Report may be used when a simple product, or a limited range of products, is being produced. It may be prepared for each department, as well as for the factory as a whole.

2. QUALITY OF PRODUCTS REPORTS (FIG. 49)

Unless the specified quality of products manufactured is consistently maintained, profit will be lost. Correction of defective products means extra costs. Alternatively, they may be sold as seconds at a much lower price. If defective products reach the customer serious damage may be caused to the goodwill of the business. In all these cases there is lower profit, so naturally a high standard must be the aim.

QUALITY REPORT

.............................Factory   Date...............................

	Product A		Product B	
	Units	% to Total	Units	% to Total
Firsts				
Seconds				
Rejects				
Total				

FIG. 49.—*Quality Report*

NOTES

1. Daily rejection reports would be prepared showing full details of products inspected and rejections, if any, with reasons. These would be examined, any abnormal figures investigated, and necessary action taken to prevent recurrence.

2. The above Report is a summary of a number of rejection reports. This may be prepared weekly. The cost of the rejects may also be shown.

MACHINE UTILISATION REPORT

.............................Factory   Week Ended...............................

	Dept. 1	Dept. 2	Total
Total Hours (Normal Activity)			
Total Hours (Actual)			
Loss in Hours	xxx	xxx	xxx
Summary of Losses			
Machine Nos.	xxx		xxx
Machine Nos.		xxx	xxx
Other Machines	xx	xx	xxx
	xxx	xxx	xxx

FIG. 50.—*Machine Utilisation Report*

NOTES

1. The total loss figures may be analysed as shown (the Summary). Details of machines losing an abnormal amount of time can be given, the balance of lost time simply being grouped under "Other Machines."

2. Reasons for the lost time may also be stated, along with the cost of idle time. The latter may be calculated by multiplying idle time by the machine hour rate.

3. The Normal Activity Hours represent the number of hours expected, after allowing for normal delays. They are, therefore, Standards, which should be achieved if work proceeds according to plan.

3. MACHINE UTILISATION REPORT (FIG. 50)

This is a summary report. *Detailed* reports will be prepared for each department: an example of this type of report is shown in the next chapter.

4. DIRECT LABOUR REPORT (FIG. 51)

This Report will indicate the efficiency of the labour force. Each day any deviations from standard times will be reported upon on a *daily* report (*see* Chapter 14). These daily reports may be summarised on the Direct Labour Report (Fig. 51). Variations between standard and actual rates of pay will normally be reported upon once a week.

DIRECT LABOUR REPORT			
..........................Factory		Week Ended...........................	
	Dept. I	Dept. 2	Total
Actual Wages	£	£	£
Standard Wages	£	£	£
Labour Cost Variance	£	£	£
Actual No. of Hours			
Standard No. of Hours			
Loss/Gain in Hours			
	s. d.	s. d.	s. d.
Average Actual Rate			
Average Standard Rate			
Loss/Gain in Rate	£		
Labour Efficiency Variance	£		
Labour Rate Variance	£		
		I £	2 £
Reasons for Controllable Variances:			
Waiting for Materials: Hours lost at .... (rate per hour)			
Machine Breakdowns: Hours lost at .... (rate per hour)			

FIG. 51.—*Direct Labour Report*

NOTE

The reasons for the controllable variances may be further analysed on a schedule attached to the report.

5. UNIT COST STATEMENT (FIG. 52)

The purposes of the Unit Cost Statement should be clear from its contents. It shows the total cost, and breakdown of such cost, for each unit produced. There is then a further analysis by departments. The reader will appreciate that the unit cost for each product is an average figure.

UNIT COST STATEMENT

....................................Factory   Month Ended............................

Cost	Product A Actual	Std.	Product B Actual	Std.	Product C Actual	Std.
	s. d.	s. d.	s. d.	s. d.	s. d.	s. d.
Direct Materials Direct Labour Factory Overhead						
£						

Analysis by Departments:

	Dept. 1 Actual	Std.	Dept. 2 Actual	Std.	Dept. 3 Actual	Std.

Product A:
  Direct Material
  Direct Labour
  Factory Overhead						

£						

Product B:
  Direct Material
  Direct Labour
  Factory Overhead						

£						

Product C:
  Direct Material
  Direct Labour
  Factory Overhead						

£						

Remarks:

FIG. 52.—*Unit Cost Statement*

6. OTHER REPORTS ON MATERIALS, LABOUR AND OVERHEAD COSTS

Some idea of alternative types of forms which will also be invaluable to all production managers may be obtained from the next chapter, which gives reports for foremen and other departmental heads. These cover utilisation of facilities and comparisons of Standard and Actual Costs.

SALES REPORTS

Sales management will be concerned with the volume of sales, the prices obtained and the selling costs involved. Reports should, therefore, aim at showing the vital facts relating to volume, prices and costs. Examples of the types of reports which are likely to provide the necessary control information are given below.

1. SALES VOLUME REPORT (BY AREAS) (FIG. 53)

This Report compares the actual and budgeted volumes of sales in terms of units of each product. Any falling off in sales will call for

WEEKLY SALES VOLUME REPORT

..............................Factory   Week Ended...........................

Sales Area	Product A		Product B		Product C	
	Actual	Budget	Actual	Budget	Actual	Budget
	Units	Units	Units	Units	Units	Units
S. East						
S. West						
N. East						
N. West						
London						
Midlands						
Scotland						

FIG. 53.—*Weekly Sales Volume Report*

prompt action. An alternative method of presenting the information is to show the value of the sales of each product for each area.

2. SALES VOLUME REPORT (BY SALESMEN) (FIG. 54)

This Report shows, in detail, the business being obtained by each man. Again, the value of the sales may be shown as an alternative to the number of units. Clearly, values will be preferred when a wide range of products is sold. One area has been covered, but the Report could be extended to cover all areas.

	Product A		Product B		Product C	
	Actual	Budget	Actual	Budget	Actual	Budget
Salesmen	Units	Units	Units	Units	Units	Units
Ayre, J.						
Barnes, K.						
Cole, L.						
Croome, M.						
Teak, S.						
Trotter, A.						
Welsh, W.						
Wright, F.						

WEEKLY SALES VOLUME REPORT

.........................Sales Area Week Ended.........................

Fig. 54.—*Sales Volume Report*

3. SELLING PRICE REPORT

Usually prices will be predetermined and, except by special permission, the salesmen will not be permitted to exercise any discretion. However, if the nature of the business requires that prices should be allowed to vary, a useful report will be one which shows the average price obtained in each area. This information could be shown on the Sales Volume Report above. Comparison of actual and standard prices would enable the sales manager to gauge the degree of success being accomplished. Obviously, to earn profit, reasonable prices have to be obtained.

4. SELLING COSTS REPORTS

These may take a number of forms. Costs may be analysed according to:

 (a) Geographical Areas (Fig. 55).
 (b) Products (Fig. 56).
 (c) Methods of Sale.
 (d) Sizes of Orders.
 (e) Salesmen.

Actual and Standard Costs may be compared in these analyses. If the gross profit is also analysed, deduction of selling costs will show which is the most profitable area, product, method of sale, size of order,

AREA SELLING COSTS REPORT Month Ended.............................								
	S. East Area		S. West Area		N. East Area		N. West Area	
	Act.	Bud.	Act.	Bud.	Act.	Bud.	Act.	Bud.
Gross Profit *Less* Selling Costs (detailed below) £								
Salesmen's Salaries Salesmen's Commission Salesmen's Telephones Salesmen's Travelling Salesmen's Stationery Salesmen's Postage Bad Debts								
Sales Admin. Salaries Rent of Sales Office Rent of Showrooms Depreciation: Equipment Insurance Administration Costs—⎱ Sales Office ⎰ Advertising								
£								
Selling Costs per £100 of Sales =								

FIG. 55.—*Area Selling Costs Report*

NOTES

1. The report will show the profitability of each area. If the cost of selling £100 worth of sales in any particular area becomes excessive the sales management will have to consider whether to reduce the sales force, increase advertising—thus increasing demand—or take some other, appropriate action.

2. Clearly though, since some fixed costs will have to be apportioned according to floor space occupied, sales values obtained, or population in each area, the totals shown will not be 100% accurate. Accordingly, any action taken will not have to be decided hastily. Even if costs appear excessive now, the sales potential may be such that they can be justified.

PRODUCTS SELLING COSTS REPORT

Month Ended...............................

		Product A		Product B		Product C	
		Actual	Budget	Actual	Budget	Actual	Budget
Gross Profit							
Less Selling Costs							
	£						

Variance Analysis (by Products)

		Unfav.	Fav.	Unfav.	Fav.	Unfav.	Fav.
Sales Volume Variance	£						
Sales Price Variance	£						
Selling Costs Variance (detailed below)	£						

Details of Selling Costs Variance

Excessive Spending:							
Salesmen's Salaries							
Salesmen's Telephones							
Salesmen's Travelling							
Saving in Spending:							
Salesmen's Postage							
Selling Costs Variance (as above)							

Fig. 56.—*Products Selling Costs Report*

or salesman. All are very important questions which, from time to time, will have to be answered if profit is to be maximised.

Specimen reports covering geographical areas and products are shown in Figs. 55 and 56 respectively; costs for the methods of sales, sizes of orders, and salesmen may be shown on reports compiled along similar lines.

5. PERFORMANCE REPORTS

Efficiency may be measured and illustrated by compiling Performance Reports. A typical example is given in Fig. 57. On that Report are shown Work Units, Total Costs, Unit Costs and Variances. The figures are purely hypothetical, the object being to illustrate cost control possibilities.

SALES PERFORMANCE REPORT

Month Ended............................

Cost/ Function	Work Unit	No. of Work Units		Total Costs		Costs Variance		Reasons	
		Act.	Bud.	Act.	Bud.	Unfav.	Fav.	Price	Vol.
Salesmen's Salaries Salesmen's Travelling etc. etc.	No. of Calls Miles etc. etc.	2100	2000	£220	£200	£20			

FIG. 57.—*Sales Performance Report*

NOTES

1. The concept of the "work unit" has already been explained. Its meaning should be evident from the report.
2. Any large variance will call for investigation and, possibly, action.
3. The figures shown are to illustrate the principles involved in presenting the facts.

VOLUME AND COSTS REPORT—SALESMEN

Month Ended............................

Salesmen	Sales		Sales Value Variance	Selling Costs		Selling Costs Variance	Unit Costs per £100 of Sales	
	Act.	Bud.		Act.	Bud.		Act.	Std.
	£	£	£	£	£	£	£	£

FIG. 58.—*Volume and Costs Report*

NOTES

1. The effectiveness of the sales force is shown by the Report. If necessary, a more detailed analysis of the variances may be shown.
2. Bonuses may be paid on the basis of the results. If a similar report is circulated among the salesmen, a competitive spirit may be introduced.

SPECIAL NOTE.—No difficulty should be experienced in compiling suitable reports for salesmen. They will cover all matters for which the individual salesman concerned is responsible. As far as possible, the aim should be to assist the salesman by indicating where efficiency can be improved. A report which may be useful to both sales management and salesmen—although it may have to be adapted for the latter—is shown in Fig. 58.

DISTRIBUTION REPORTS

1. TRANSPORT REPORTS

The distribution of products has to be carried out as cheaply as possible, and there is also a duty to ensure that customers obtain their

VEHICLE COSTS REPORT Month Ended..............................						
	Vehicle 1		Vehicle 2		Vehicle 3	
	Act.	Std.	Act.	Std.	Act.	Std.

Standing Costs:
  Administration Costs
  Licences and Insurance
  Crew's Wages
  National Insurance
  Employer's Liab. Insurance
  Depreciation						

Running Hours						
Rate per Hour						

Running Costs:
  Fuel
  Oil
  Tyres
  Repairs and Maintenance						

Miles						
Rate per Mile						
Standing Costs Variance Running Costs Variance						

FIG. 59.—*Vehicle Costs Report*

requirements within a reasonable time and without any deterioration in the condition of the products. Obviously, the nature of the latter will play a large part in determining the appropriate method of distribution —rail, road, water, or air transport. Space will not allow coverage of typical reports for all methods of transport. The report shown (Fig. 59) is for use in a business having its own delivery vehicles.

2. STORAGE AND WAREHOUSING REPORTS

These will have to meet the needs of the particular circumstances. The departmental operating statement type of report may be used to show a comparison of actual and budgeted costs. An example, applied to manufacturing overhead costs, is included in the chapter on Flexible Budgets. A Performance Report, similar to the one shown above for the selling functions, will indicate the degree of efficiency achieved for each work unit. This is illustrated below (Fig. 60).

WAREHOUSING PERFORMANCE REPORT

Month Ended.............................

Cost/Function	Work Unit	No. of Work Units		Total Costs		Cost Variance		Reasons	
		Act.	Bud.	Act.	Bud.	Unfav.	Fav.	Price	Vol.
Fork-Lift Trucks Wages	cwt ,,								
				£					

FIG. 60.—*Warehousing Performance Report*

NOTE
All costs/functions are listed and actual and budgeted units and costs compared.

ADMINISTRATION REPORTS

Total costs may be shown on a cost statement similar to the one given overleaf (Fig. 61).

In common with other overhead costs, administration costs have to be compared and controlled on a monthly basis.

ADMINISTRATION COSTS REPORT

Month Ended.... ....

Department	Actual Cost	Budgeted Cost	Variation in Cost
	£	£	
Accounts			
Buying			
Cashiers			
Costing			
Pricing			
Sales Ledgers			

FIG. 61.—*Administration Costs Report*

NOTES

1. This Report compares actual and budgeted costs for each department.
2. A further analysis for each department will be necessary. This will show all classes of costs and variations from Standard for each.

OTHER REPORTS

The administrative function will deal, in one way or another, with most reports. Profit and Loss Accounts, Balance Sheets, budgets for all functions, as well as departmental reports intended to improve internal office efficiency, will all be the concern of the office. Examples of reports which attempt to control the clerical functions may be found in any modern textbook on Office Management.

EXAMINATION QUESTIONS

1. As cost accountant to a manufacturing company, what information relating to materials and material costs would you supply to different levels of management?

(I.C.W.A.)

2. What are the usual causes of delay in the presentation of cost figures? In citing such causes, state briefly the action you would take to speed up the routine.

(I.C.W.A.)

3. A sales budget has been formulated using Standard volumes and prices of five Standard products. Since the preparation of the budget, sales prices have increased and the sales manager has requested a monthly return which will show him to what extent each product sale has fluctuated from the budget due to volume or price.

(I.C.W.A.)

4. Draw up a monthly cost statement for three service departments of a manufacturing concern so that management may see budget comparisons.

(*I.C.W.A.*)

5. The management of a factory producing goods for which there is a seasonal demand, put forward the following argument:

"We are at present making a profit of 5% on turnover in spite of the fact that our factory is slack for six months of the year. Since our overheads are absorbed by current normal production, it will pay us to take on any business during the slack season which will show a surplus above prime cost expenditure."

Write a report to the management on the subject, using any figures you think suitable.

(*I.C.W.A.*)

6. A manufacturer instructs you to report to him on the cost of storing and handling materials in his factory. Discuss the matters which would receive your attention.

(*I.C.W.A.*)

7. As cost accountant to a large manufacturing company you are instructed to supply periodical cost information to the:

    (*a*) general manager;
    (*b*) works manager;
    (*c*) sales manager;
    (*d*) maintenance manager.

Outline the main points of information on which emphasis should be placed in each case and prepare a draft of any one of these statements to illustrate the points you have made.

(*I.C.W.A.*)

8. Outline how you would prepare a Cost Statement to show the Profit and Loss on trading in various salesmen's areas.

(*I.C.W.A.*)

9. The Board of Directors require a monthly statement detailing the factors which contribute to the net profit or loss for each month.

Give a pro-forma of the statement you would present.

(*I.C.W.A.*)

10. In a manufacturing organisation, short runs are almost invariably more costly than long runs.

Using appropriate figures, prepare a report to management illustrating this fact, first indicating the nature of the industry and the size of the business.

(*I.C.W.A.*)

11. In a business in which information is regularly given to the Works Manager, draft a *special* report on *one* of the following:

    (*a*) scrap;
    (*b*) lost time;
    (*c*) machine utilisation;
    (*d*) controllable overtime.

(*I.C.W.A.*)

CHAPTER 26

REPORTS TO FOREMEN AND SUPERVISORS

REPORTS to departmental heads can do much to control costs. Of particular importance are those for foremen and similar supervisory staff. To pay attention at the point where the expenditure is incurred is

DEPARTMENTAL OPERATING STATEMENT

Week Ending 28/I......

Dept. X   **Foreman:** Mr. M. James

Controllable Costs	Budget 100%	Actual 100%	Variance	Remarks
	£	£	£	
Supervision	15·000	15·000	—	
Indirect Wages	74·400	79·225	4·825	
Repairs	10·000	8·100	1·900 *	
Supplies	9·250	9·500	0·250	
Fuel	12·000	12·500	0·500	
Depreciation	10·000	10·000	—	
Power	20·500	22·000	1·500	
	£151·150	£156·325	£5·175	

Activity

100% = 200 units

Budgeted Unit Costs = £0·755
Actual Unit Cost   = £0·782

* Favourable, others unfavourable.

FIG. 62.—*Departmental Operating Statement*

NOTES

1. The Actual Costs are taken from Overhead Analysis Sheets or from the departmental overhead accounts.

2. The student should compare this statement with the one shown at the end of the chapter on Flexible Budgets.

the only certain way of controlling and reducing expenditure. The precise form the report will take largely depends upon the type of business and the existing local conditions. However, it is possible to indicate the kinds of reports that are likely to be useful: these are shown below.

OVERHEAD COSTS REPORTS

1. DEPARTMENTAL OPERATING STATEMENT (FIG. 62)

In this Report controllable costs only are shown, thus pointing out, to the foreman, the extent of his responsibilities for costs. Depreciation is a controllable cost in that careless handling of machinery will affect the life of that machinery. Often, however, for all practical purposes, it may be regarded as uncontrollable. Its inclusion is therefore debatable.

2. DEPARTMENTAL FLEXIBLE BUDGET (FIG. 63)

The Departmental Flexible Budget will be compiled along lines similar to those covered in earlier chapters. The variability of the costs will be reflected in the change in cost with increase in activity. In the example given the figures are purely fictitious.

DEPARTMENTAL FLEXIBLE BUDGET

Week Ended 28/1/......

Dept. X   Foreman: Mr. M. James

Cost	Activity						
	70%	80%	90%	100%	110%	120%	130%
	£	£	£	£	£	£	£
Supervision	15	15	15	15	15	20	20
Indirect Wages	65	65	70	74	74	78	80
Repairs	8	8	10	10	12	12	14
Supplies	8	8	9	9	10	10	11
Fuel	11	11	12	12	14	14	16
Depreciation	10	10	10	10	12	12	15
Power	19	19	21	21	22	22	23
	£136	£136	£147	£151	£159	£168	£179

Activity 100% = 200 units of Product Y.

FIG. 63.—*Departmental Flexible Budget*

NOTES

1. The Budget may be compiled on a weekly basis as shown or on a monthly basis.
2. It will show the foreman how costs and output are related. He will see that until 110% is reached he should not employ any extra supervisory labour.

3. DEPARTMENTAL OVERHEAD COST VARIANCE REPORT (FIG. 64)

The object of this Report is to present the overhead variances in such a way that they are understood by supervisors and foremen. Obviously, the latter will be given advice and instructions on the interpretation of variances.

OVERHEAD COST VARIANCE REPORT

Department............................ Month............................

Production: Actual................... Budgeted Hours............

Standard...................

Actual Cost ....

Standard Cost..

Overhead Cost Variance £ _____ (Unfavourable)

Divided into:

	Unfavourable	Favourable
Budget Variance (excess spending)	£	£

Efficiency Variance:
Hours Saved/Exceeded for ⎫
Production Achieved ⎬ £   £

Overhead Volume Variance:
Idle time/overtime on budgeted hours £   £

Efficiency Ratio:

Activity Ratio:

FIG. 64.—*Overhead Cost Variance Report*

NOTE

Explanatory statements or notes may be used to give detailed information on particular variances, especially if they are quite large.

MATERIAL UTILISATION REPORTS

1. MATERIAL USAGE REPORT

Daily reporting on direct material usage will enable material costs to be kept to a minimum. Excess Material Requisitions may be listed and shown on a Material Usage Report (Fig. 65). From this the foreman will be able to see the efficiency achieved in the usage of materials. If he signs the Excess Material Requisitions, the extra cost arising from them is brought to his notice.

This Report, or a similar one, can do much to ensure that material costs are controlled. Obviously, no foreman or worker will wish to receive an adverse report—a copy of which goes to the production manager.

MATERIAL USAGE REPORT

........................Dept.   Date..........................

Actual Material Quantity
Standard Material Quantity

Excess Usage
X Standard Price

Material Usage Variance = £

Excess Material Requisitions Analysis

Production Order No.	Requisition No.	Excess Quantity	Standard Price	Total £

Less Material Return Notes (Total Material Savings Only)

£

FIG. 65.—*Material Usage Report*

NOTE

The reasons for the savings or excess usages may also be shown on the report.

2. OTHER REPORTS ON MATERIAL COSTS

For some industries a useful report will be one which shows a variance analysis for each type of product. In process industries this will be so. The Material Usage Variance may be analysed to show that part which is due to using a different mixture of materials from that specified and that part due to obtaining a smaller than standard yield from the material input. Reports on price variations may also serve a useful purpose, especially if these cover price changes brought about by the action of the foreman, *e.g.* when he authorises the use of a substitute material which is more expensive than the standard material.

LABOUR UTILISATION REPORTS

At all times the aim should be effective control of labour within a department. Examples of typical statements are shown below.

1. DIRECT LABOUR OPERATION TIMES STATEMENT (FIG. 66)

The daily control of times can do much to maintain labour efficiency. A simple statement of this kind allows prompt action to be taken. The foreman concerned can investigate the reasons for the excess times, noting these on the top copy of the statement, which is returned to the Costing Department.

DIRECT LABOUR OPERATION TIMES STATEMENT							
Department A Monday, January 6th, 19... Foreman: Mr. L. Todd							
Part No.	No. Off.	P.O. No.	Operator and Operation		Std. Time	Actual Time	Variance	Remarks
102–6	200	22N	Smith, 101	Drills	10 hrs.	14 hrs. 15 mins.	4 hrs. 15 mins.	
Statement in Duplicate: Top copy to Costing after Action.							

FIG. 66.—*Direct Labour Operation Times Statement*

NOTES

1. The daily statements, with reasons, can be summarised weekly and monthly. Workers who have a regular tendency to fall below Standard can receive assistance with personal difficulties, if any, or be transferred to work which is more suitable to their capabilities.

2. If Excess Time Tickets are used to authorise extra times a modification of the statement will be necessary.

2. DIRECT LABOUR VARIANCE REPORT (FIG. 67)

This Report allows each man's performance constantly to be observed. Output is measured in terms of standard hours, then the

DIRECT LABOUR VARIANCE REPORT ....Dept.									
Employees	Clock No.	Output (Std. Hrs.)		D.L. Cost		Variance		Analysis of Variance	
		Act.	Std.	Act.	Std.	Unfav.	Fav.	Eff'y	Rate
Abbott, O.	1								
Burke, N.	2								
Briggs, H.	3								
Franks, M.	4								
Gough, G.	6								
Rank, S.	8								

FIG. 67.—*Direct Labour Variance Report*

actual and budgeted hours are compared and the Labour Cost Variance is analysed.

3. LABOUR COSTS AND TURNOVER REPORT (FIG. 68)

The Labour Costs and Turnover Report will indicate to the foremen and other managers the overall efficiency of the departmental labour force and the effectiveness of the policy followed.

Any significant variation between Actual and Budgeted figures will call for prompt attention. For the particular business "ideal ratios" may be established: these may cover the relation between direct and indirect wages and between the numbers of direct and indirect employees. Labour turnover has also to be watched: if employees leave and have to be replaced costs are involved. There are expenses of recruitment and training; there are increases in costs connected with the reduced volume of *good* production and, brought about by the increase in the number of untrained workers, with the more rapid deterioration of tools, equipment and machinery. These additional costs clearly have to be kept to a minimum. In fact, if profit is to be maximised, both the quality and quantity of products have to be maintained at a high level.

MISCELLANEOUS STATEMENTS AND REPORTS

Other reports which are likely to be prepared will cover such matters as maintenance costs, spoilage, quality control, utilisation of machinery and equipment, work-in-progress, and any other matters which affect operating efficiency.

LABOUR COSTS AND TURNOVER REPORT				
..........................Dept.		Week Ended...........................		

	This Week	Budget	Variation	
			Loss	Gain
Men Employed (beginning of week) Add New Employees				
Less Employees leaving				
Men Employed (end of week)				
Total Wages Paid	£	£		
Direct Wages Paid	£	£		
Indirect Wages Paid % Indirect to Direct	£	£		
No. of Employees: Direct Indirect % Indirect to Direct				
Average Wage Earned: Direct Indirect	£ £	£ £		
Hours Worked: Direct Indirect				
Average Hourly Rate: Direct Indirect				
Labour Turnover				

FIG. 68.—*Labour Costs and Turnover Report*

A typical report to cover utilisation of machinery is shown opposite (Fig. 69). Only when the machines are kept fully operating will maximum profits be earned. This Report is therefore a vital source of information.

GENERAL REMARKS ON REPORTS SHOWN

The reports shown should give the student an insight into the type of report that is likely to aid efficiency in any particular set of circumstances. It has been impossible to give examples of all forms. Those given are intended to illustrate the principles of reporting, not to show

M/c No.	Type	Actual Operating Hours	Budgeted Operating Hours	Variation		% Act. to Budget	Remarks
				Loss	Gain		

FIG. 69.—*Machinery Utilisation Report*

NOTE

A very useful addition to the report will be the cost of the idle time.

specific forms which *should* be compiled and presented to management. The needs of the particular business will dictate the types of reports that will be used.

EXAMINATION QUESTIONS

1. Design a return of analysis of the pay-roll for the use of the shop superintendents. The form should be for presentation weekly and should be designed so that changes from week to week can be interpreted as trends which may call for action.

(*I.C.W.A.*)

2. What factors should be borne in mind when presenting labour cost reports to foremen? Illustrate with a specimen form and show how you would distinguish between:

(*a*) the Actual labour efficiency of the section, and
(*b*) the way in which the labour force has been planned, utilised, and supervised.

(*I.C.W.A.*)

3. Prepare an idle machine report for use in an engineering factory. Provision should be made for all the details you consider necessary, including causes, and such percentages as may be usefully informative.

(*I.C.W.A.*)

4. Design a return analysis of the pay-roll for the use of the shop super-intendents. The form should be for presentation weekly and should be designed so that changes from week to week can be interpreted as trends which may call for action.

(I.C.W.A.)

5. To what extent and with what object would you give statistical information as to Overheads to Works Managers and Foremen?

(I.C.W.A.)

6. State briefly the information the cost accountant should provide for the following:

(*a*) chargehand;
(*b*) foreman;
(*c*) service department manager;
(*d*) works manager;
(*e*) managing director.

(I.C.W.A.)

CHAPTER 27

THE DISPOSITION OF VARIANCES AND STOCK VALUATION

GENERAL PRINCIPLES OF STOCK VALUATION

THE normal rule for stock valuation has been for many years "cost or market value whichever is lower." This generally means that, in a period of rising prices, stocks would be shown at cost less any deductions for obsolete or unusable stocks.

Recommendation N. 22 issued by the Institute of Chartered Accountants in England and Wales recognises that the term "cost or market value" covers a multitude of possible meanings without being definite on any particular one. A number of alternative descriptions are given and these are summarised below:

NORMAL BASES

1. "At cost."
2. "At the lower of cost and net realisable value."
3. "At the lowest of cost, net realisable value and replacement price."
4. "At cost less provision to reduce to net realisable value" (or "to the lower of net realisable value and replacement price").

SPECIAL BASES

5. At selling prices; *i.e.* prices realised subsequent to the balance sheet date less only selling costs. This is a basis customary in some tea, rubber, and mining companies.
6. Long-term contracts including a reasonable proportion of earned profit (provided this is certain).
7. Base stock valuation.
8. Last in, first out (LIFO).

The appropriate description should be used in the final accounts produced annually. If the word "cost" is used to describe the valuation it is recommended that a clear explanation of what is included in the term should be shown; *i.e.* whether: prime cost only, prime cost plus variable overheads *or* prime cost plus production and administration overhead costs.

In most businesses the Recommendation suggests that descriptions

(2) and (3) would be appropriate. In connection with "cost" and these two descriptions the Recommendation contains the following explanations:

The following are the meanings attributed to "cost," "net realisable value," and "replacement price" in this Recommendation:

(*a*) "Cost" means all expenditure incurred directly in the purchase or manufacture of the stock and the bringing of it to its existing condition and location, together with such part, if any, of the overhead expenditure as is appropriately carried forward in the circumstances of the business instead of being charged against the revenue of the period in which it was incurred.

(*b*) "Net realisable value" means the amount which it is estimated, as on the Balance Sheet date, will be realised from disposal of the stock in the ordinary course of business, either in its existing condition or as incorporated in the product normally sold, after allowing for all expenditure to be incurred on or before disposal.

(*c*) "Replacement price" means an estimate of the amount for which in the ordinary course of business the stock could have been acquired or produced either at the Balance Sheet date or in the latest period up to and including that date. In a manufacturing business this estimate would be based on the replacement price of the raw material content plus other costs of the undertaking which are relevant to the condition of the stock on the Balance Sheet date.

The comparison between cost and net realisable value or replacement price may be made by considering each article separately, or by grouping articles in categories having regard to their similarity or interchangeability, or by considering the aggregate cost of the total stock in relation to its aggregate net realisable value or, as the case may be, aggregate replacement price. The aggregate method involves setting foreseeable losses against unrealised profits on stock and may not be suitable for businesses which carry stocks which are large in relation to turnover.

The Institute recommend that the most appropriate method once selected, should be employed consistently. Stock should not be omitted* or included at a false figure. There should be no anticipation of profit unless justified by a special basis; in all cases there should be provision made for losses. The method selected should be such that the accounts show a true and fair view of the trading results and the financial position. Finally, if a change in the basis or method of valuing stocks is necessary

---

* This does not apply to stocks which are of no value due to obsolescence or other reasons.

because of changed circumstances, then, if material, the fact that a change has been made should be shown by way of note in the Profit and Loss Account.

STANDARD COSTING AND STOCK VALUATION

The question of stock valuation at the end of an accounting period, especially for the preparation of Final Accounts—Profit and Loss and Balance Sheet—is extremely important. Under Accounting Method I, for Current Standard Costs, work-in-progress and finished goods are valued at Standard Cost. Method II goes further and, in addition, values raw material at Standard Cost. Because any action taken regarding stock valuation must affect the disposition of the variances, the two matters are closely related. In fact, any controversy on how variances should be dealt with usually centres round the problem of stock valuation.

There are three principal approaches to the treatment of variances and, its corollary, the valuation of stocks: they may be summarised as:

1. Keep Stocks at Standard Cost.
2. Adjust Stocks to Actual Cost.
3. Adopt a Compromise.

These will be explained below.

Before any step is taken to dispose of variances there should be a clear understanding of their nature. Whether the variances merely represent deviations from poorly set Standards (not true variances at all), or are due to *actual* inefficiencies, should be the first question. True costs of products can, legitimately, be charged to production. Inefficiencies such as an abnormal loss of time or extravagance cannot, it is often argued, be regarded as the true costs of products. Moreover, these costs are not, under normal conditions, price determinants. The price prevailing, under competitive conditions, and provided there is no shortage or excess supply of the particular commodity, although determined by supply and demand, will be a reflection of the costs of one or more businesses in an industry. To cover costs and obtain a reasonable margin of profit will be the aim. To sell all its products the *efficient* business will consider true costs only—the others will be non-existent. Therefore, the other members of the industry should exclude the costs of inefficiencies from the costs of the products.

The general rule for valuation—cost or market value or other description—can still be followed. "Cost" is "Standard Cost" when Standards are used for valuation. If market value is lower than Standard Cost, some accountants would advocate adjustments to bring stock valuations down to market value. The economic environment may thus influence a decision on disposition of variances. When prices are rising there will, normally, be debit price variances and market value will be greater than Standard Cost. Accordingly, the latter can be used. If prices are falling the credit variances should, to adhere to conservative accounting practice, be used to reduce stocks to market value.

These are general observations, more specific reference to the three approaches can now be made.

1. KEEP STOCKS AT STANDARD COST

The variances are written off to Costing Profit and Loss Account each period.* In Journal entry form the action necessary is as follows:

	Dr.	Cr.
Profit and Loss Account	Dr. £xxx	
To Material Price Variance		£xx
„ Material Usage Variance		£xx
„ Labour Rate Variance		£xx
„ Labour Efficiency Variance		£xx
„ Factory Overhead Budget Variance		£xx
„ Factory Overhead Efficiency Variance		£xx
„ Factory Overhead Volume Variance		£xx

Being disposition of Variances for month ended January 28th, 19...

NOTES

1. All variances are unfavourable.
2. No Selling and Distribution Overheads Variances.
3. No Administration Overhead Variances.
4. If (2) and (3) had been present they could have been dealt with in the same manner.

The advantages claimed for this method are as follows:

1. Only true costs of products are represented in the values placed on stocks. Any inefficiencies, it is argued, are really losses not product costs and, therefore, should be written off to Profit and Loss Account. To show inflated stock figures is to carry forward losses to another period.

2. A major advantage of Standard Costing is the saving in clerical costs. This is obtained to its fullest extent when stocks are kept at Standard.

3. The adoption of this method recognises the principle of writing off unusual or abnormal costs or losses to Profit and Loss Account. Thus the cost of idle facilities, due to a trade recession, is generally taken to Profit and Loss.

* Some variances, particularly overhead variances, may be dealt with better once a year (see pages 205 and 347).

There is no difference, except of degree, it is contended, between the cost of idle facilities and variances due to inefficiencies.

Undoubtedly, if Standard Costs are to be used as a basis for stock valuation they should represent attainable conditions: if not, large variances, which may not mean much, when thought of as measures of efficiency, may arise. Another point is that the Standard Costs should be based on *present* conditions, *i.e.* be Current Standards not requiring revision. The presence of large unfavourable variances due to unattainable Standards means that the period in question will be charged with more than its share of costs (including variances), whereas stocks will be undervalued. Standards which are too easy to attain will result in losses being hidden and, therefore, carried in stock valuations. In other words, only when a certain degree of inefficiency has been reached will variances emerge, the loose Standards hiding the true position.

2. ADJUST STOCKS TO ACTUAL COST

The arguments used to support this method may be summarised as shown below:

1. Any credit variances taken to Profit and Loss Account will represent an anticipation of profit which is contrary to sound accounting principles. Stocks should therefore be valued at Actual Cost or market value, whichever is lower.
2. The profit figure, shown by accounts using Standard Costs for Stock valuation, may have to be adjusted so as to arrive at an amount which would be acceptable to the Commissioners of Inland Revenue for taxation purposes. This argument does not now carry great weight because Standard Costs are acceptable, provided they are reasonably accurate and are up-to-date. (*See* "Stock Valuation—The Revenue's View," by H. G. Thomas; *The Accountant*, February 17th, 1962.)
3. There is no generally accepted definition of the conditions to "adopt" for setting Standards. Accordingly, profit and stock valuation will vary with changes in definition. One business may set Standards in anticipation of ideal conditions, whereas another may assume actual conditions, *i.e.* those expected with existing plant.

The procedure necessary to carry out the conversion to Actual Cost needs to be explained. This can best be done by taking hypothetical figures and illustrating the necessary calculations by reference to such figures.

Data (hypothetical figures)

A process costing system is in operation, and the relevant data for January are as follows:

Jan. 1st.   Balance: Finished Goods.   20 units.

Jan. 28th. Production for Month:

        100 Units completed Material.

        20 Half-completed Labour and Factory Overhead.

        Sales for Month: 60 units.

        Variances at end of Month:

Material Price Variance	£8·00
Material Usage Variance	£12·00
Labour Rate Variance	£8·00
Labour Efficiency Variance	£10·00
Overhead Variances	£40·00

        All variances are unfavourable.

There is a debit balance of £8·00 in the Actual Cost Adjustment (Finished Goods) Account (brought down from previous month).

All variances have to be apportioned to appropriate accounts, thus bringing the values of Finished Goods and Work-in-progress to Actual Cost.

The Raw Material Account is kept at "Actual," so no adjustment is necessary for raw materials.

There is no opening balance of work-in-progress.

SUGGESTED SOLUTION (USING PHYSICAL UNITS FOR APPORTIONMENT)

The steps to take may be summarised as follows:

1. Ascertain the "equivalent production" (physical units) for work-in-progress

    This is: 20 units Material (*i.e.* 20 complete).

          10   „   Labour (*i.e.* 20 only half complete).

          10   „   Overhead (*i.e.* 20 only half complete).

2. Apportion the variances between work-in-progress and finished goods

    This may be done on the following bases:

    (*a*) Material Variances.

$$\left.\begin{array}{l} \frac{80}{100} \text{ Finished Goods} \\[2mm] \frac{20}{100} \text{ Work-in-progress} \end{array}\right\} \textit{i.e. according to physical units.}$$

    (*b*) Labour Variances.

$$\left.\begin{array}{l} \frac{80}{90} \text{ Finished Goods} \\[2mm] \frac{10}{90} \text{ Work-in-progress} \end{array}\right\} \textit{i.e. according to physical units.}$$

    (*c*) Overhead Variances.

        (*i*) Total to Finished Goods; or

        (*ii*) Apportion between Finished Goods and Work-in-progress.

The one to use is a matter of opinion, much depending upon the nature of the variances. Many accountants argue that overhead costs, particularly fixed costs, should not be shown in stock valuations. Here (*i*) is adopted.

3. Show by Journal entry the apportionment

For this purpose "Adjustment Accounts" can be used, thus enabling the actual stock accounts to be retained at Standard Cost. Any adjustments to stocks can be made on financial or cost statements.

Journal Entry

		Dr.	Cr.
Jan. 28	Actual Cost Adjustment (Finished Goods) Account	Dr. £72	
28	Actual Cost Adjustment (Work-in-progress) Account	Dr. £6	
	To Material Price Variance		£8
	„ Material Usage Variance		£12
	„ Labour Rate Variance		£8
	„ Labour Efficiency Variance		£10
	„ Overhead Variances		£40

Being apportionment of variances between finished goods and work-in-progress as follows:

Finished Goods

$$\text{Material:} \quad \frac{80}{100} \times \frac{£20}{1} = £16$$

$$\text{Labour:} \quad \frac{80}{90} \times \frac{£18}{1} = £16$$

$$\text{Overhead:} \quad \text{Total} \quad £40$$

$$\overline{£72}$$

Work-in-progress

$$\text{Material:} \quad \frac{20}{100} \times \frac{£20}{1} = £4$$

$$\text{Labour:} \quad \frac{10}{90} \times \frac{£18}{1} = £2$$

$$\text{Overhead:} \quad —$$

$$\overline{£6}$$

4. Adjust the Actual Cost Adjustment (Finished Goods) Account to allow for the transfer of goods sold to Cost of Sales Account

If all goods have been sold the full amount will, of course, be taken to Cost of Sales.

In the example the total to be apportioned is £80 (£72 + £8 debit balance on Adjustment Account). The units *available* for sales are 100 (80 finished January and 20 on hand January 1st), whereas actual sales are 60 units. The necessary Journal entry is, therefore:

Journal Entry

	Dr.	Cr.
Cost of Sales Account $\left(\dfrac{60}{100} \times \dfrac{£80}{1}\right)$ Dr.	£48	
To Actual Cost Adjustment (Finished Goods) A/c		£48

Being transfer of variances relating to goods sold.

In the interests of clarity the figures, in the example, have been kept as simple as possible. The principles can be applied to the more difficult problems found in practice. The number of physical units is not the only basis for apportioning the variances. Total costs, labour hours, machine hours, or other suitable bases may serve equally well.

3. ADOPT A COMPROMISE

Many accountants do not agree whole-heartedly with either extreme —Standard Cost or Actual Cost—but, instead, are willing to admit that there are favourable arguments for both, provided they are used with discrimination. Accordingly, the recommended procedure is to adopt a compromise.

Clearly, when a compromise is adopted the method should not be changed from one year to another, giving at one time great emphasis to Actual Cost and then, later, to Standard Cost and, once more, back to Actual Cost. The variances which are to be included in stock valuation should be clearly defined and the definition consistently applied; otherwise, little or no reliance can be placed upon stock and profit figures.

The fundamental question to answer, when adopting a compromise, is whether the variance is the result of:

(*a*) A normal occurrence which is controllable.
(*b*) A normal occurrence which is uncontrollable.
(*c*) An abnormal or unusual occurrence.

With (*b*) and (*c*) the variance is a loss and not a true cost. Accordingly, the amount should, it is argued, be written off to Profit and Loss Account.

When a variance arises from normal factors which are controllable, then it can be apportioned, on some equitable basis, to Work-in-progress, Finished Goods, and Cost of Sales. The procedure to follow has already been discussed.

In determining the category into which a variance falls it is necessary to consider the reason, or reasons, for its existence. Once the underlying influences are known, the tracing of responsibility and the classifying into (*a*), (*b*), or (*c*) becomes relatively simple. Some idea of the principles to follow may be obtained from the following:

Name of Variance	Possible reason	Classification
Material Price Variance	Changes in basic prices	N. (U.C.)
	Purchasing Dept. not obtaining from cheapest supplier	N. (C.)
Material Usage Variance	Defective material	N. (U.C.)
	Careless usage	N. (C.)
Overhead Budget Variance	Price changes	N. (U.C.)
	Excess spending	N. (C.)
Overhead Volume Variance	Idle facilities due to trade depression	AB.
	Idle time due to large number of machine breakdowns	N. (C.)
	Lost time due to fire, flood, or similar, unavoidable, circumstance	AB.
Overhead Efficiency Variance	Workers taking excessive times on operations	N. (C).

NOTES

N. (C.)   = Normal Variance which is Controllable.
N. (U.C.) = Normal Variance which is Uncontrollable.
AB.   = Abnormal Variance.

This list is not intended to provide a complete guide on how to deal with variances. Moreover, the divisions into the three classes is arbitrary. A more suitable classification may be possible; this is a matter for the individual accountant concerned.*

The difference in approach, from when Standard Costs only are used, is the division of Normal Variances into "controllable" and "uncontrollable." When overhead variances, from month to month, have been anticipated, no action may be necessary. Thus, for example, if extra spending occurs in one month it may be balanced by under-spending the following month. Similar considerations apply to seasonal variations. However, generally, all variances should be dealt with, in some way, at the end of each year. In this way each financial year is standing on its own gains or losses. Many accountants take this view, although an exception is sometimes made in the case of large, favourable variances. Instead of writing these off, they are shown on the Balance Sheet as a special reserve, later to be used to cancel out unfavourable variances. An account, such as a Credit Variance Suspense Account, can be opened for this purpose.

* A strong argument can be advanced for apportioning a Normal Variance which is Uncontrollable, especially the Material Price Variance (see example overleaf).

Ratios can be used to convert stocks from Standard Cost to Actual Cost or to include a particular variance in a stock valuation. Thus, if it is felt that the Material Price Variance should be the basis of an adjustment of the stock of raw materials, the ratio between Actual and Standard Cost is used. An example will illustrate this point:

Stock of Raw Material December 31st = £20,000
Ratio between Actual and Standard
    Cost (Average for Year)   = 101% Actual being greater than Standard.

NOTE.—Put another way, Actual Costs have exceeded Standard Costs by 1%. This percentage will, of course, show the relation of the Material Price Variance to Standard Cost. To arrive at the percentage when both Material Usage and Material Price Variances are present, it will probably be easier to consider a particular variance only, in relation to total Standard Cost of materials purchased. However, neither way should present great difficulties.

An example of the calculation involved, using the figures shown above, is given below.

The Actual Cost is found as follows:

$$\frac{\text{Standard Cost of Stock} \times \text{Ratio (\%)}}{100} = \frac{£20,000 \times 101}{100}$$

$$= £20,200$$

The balance left in the Material Price Variance Account, after deducting the £200, will apply to Work-in-progress, Finished Goods, and Cost of Sales. Whether these would be adjusted also depends upon the views of the accountant concerned. If it is felt that no useful purpose can be served by carrying out the adjustments, the remaining amount can be written off to Profit and Loss Account.

CONCLUSION

The method adopted for dealing with variances must, of course, in the absence of definite rules or conventions, be left to the opinion of the accountant concerned. Provided the one chosen is consistently used, there appear to be advantages on the side of each. The method which gives the greatest advantages, in the business concerned, will tend therefore to be the one adopted.

However, there is much to be gained by adopting Standard Costs for stock valuation. If a Standard Costing system is to be used, then let it be used fully! In this way *all* the advantages may be obtained, and management, by clearly distinguishing losses and costs, is following a logical procedure. Inefficiencies are not lost in inventory valuations, but, instead, their cumulative effect can be seen in the total variances carried to Profit and Loss.

EXAMINATION QUESTIONS

1. In valuing inventories should Standard cost be used instead of Actual cost, or market price, if the Standard cost be lower than either of these? State your reasons.

(I.C.W.A.)

2. Write brief notes on stock valuation, dealing in particular with the inclusion or exclusion of certain items and different types of overhead.

(I.C.W.A.)

3. A company manufacturing one product has a quarterly production capacity of 20,000 units which are sold at £5 each. Its forecasts for the next three quarters are:

Quarters	1st	2nd	3rd
Volume of sales (% of capacity) ...	80%	70%	55%
Production overhead (per quarter)	£11,000	£10,500	£9,750
Selling and administration overhead (per quarter)	£7,200	£6,800	£6,200

Fixed overhead per quarter included in the above figures is £7000 for production and £4000 for selling and administration. Opening and closing stocks are expected to be equal. Direct wages cost is £1 per unit for all quarters. Direct material cost is £2·50 per unit for quarters 1 and 2 and £2 per unit for quarter 3 due to an abnormally favourable purchase in that quarter.

You are required to present a statement to highlight the effect on net profit of the declining volume of sales over the next three quarters.

(I.C.W.A.)

CHAPTER 28

POLICY DECISIONS AND PRICING

BECAUSE Standard Costs are the true costs of producing and selling they are much more reliable than Actual Costs as a guide to managerial decisions. There is no question of making "adjustments" to allow for possible inefficiencies—they are removed via the variance accounts. These remarks apply equally to long- and short-term planning. Variations in day-to-day costs, due to changes in volume of output, are avoided. Instead, the predetermined costs are established for a period.

Policy making and planning often involve the comparison of two or more possible courses of action. There is usually, in this, consideration of the cost *now* with the expected cost in the future. If Actual Costs are used for this purpose, misleading results will tend to emerge. The *present* cost will include losses that could, with proper controls, be avoided. An estimate of *future* cost will usually be based on present costs, so, again, avoidable losses will tend to be included. Most likely, to bring the future cost to a "realistic" figure adjustments will be made. These, needless to say, will be influenced by the character of the person carrying out the adjustments: his optimism or other state of mind will be reflected in the final cost selected. The setting of Standard Costs involves a study of all factors which influence costs and, to predetermine what costs should be, the use of methods which eliminate as far as possible any estimating which may be biased and subjective. At times the achievement of complete objectivity, especially with overhead costs, will be very difficult, but with practice and by making the best use of available knowledge, even with these costs, the officials setting Standards should be able to arrive at figures which represent efficient performances. Once the Standard Costs are set, for the two or more alternatives, any differences in cost that will arise from adopting one or other proposal will be readily apparent.

A decision on whether to make a component by hand or by the use of a machine will involve, among other things, consideration of the relative costs of the two methods of production. Deciding whether to manufacture a part or to purchase it ready made will also involve a comparison—the price quoted by an outside supplier will be compared with the cost of production. There may be factors other than cost to be considered; a part may be purchased from an outside supplier simply because the necessary production facilities are not possessed by the business concerned. However, in the absence of such special factors, the alternative which is expected to maximise profit (*i.e.* has the lowest cost) will be the one to take. For the reasons stated, only a comparison of the Standard Costs of the two or more proposals will truly show which one should maximise profit.

PRICING PRODUCTS

An extremely important policy decision is connected with fixing selling prices. In the long run a business will attempt to cover all its costs and earn a profit. How this will be done depends upon the type of business and product involved. There can be no question of stating that a certain policy should be followed in all circumstances. For success, flexibility will be essential. Another fact to remember is that although at times the charging of prices which would give a very high margin of profit may be possible, from a long-term view this may not be desirable. Satisfaction of the customer and the building up of goodwill should not be overlooked. Below are some general observations on costs and pricing; they are intended to show the student that Standard Costs can be employed as an aid to pricing.

Manufacturers engaged on producing non-standard products to customers' specifications may not be able to utilise a Standard Costing system fully. Instead, job costing may be used and estimates prepared to show expected, actual costs, profit, and price. However, if some of the components are common to many jobs it should be possible to set Standard Costs to cover those, thus obtaining a higher degree of accuracy and control for at least a portion of the necessary activities.

When a standard product is being manufactured full use of Standard Costs will be possible. For stated conditions and level of operations, a manufacturer will know the true cost of his product. If the apportionment of fixed overhead costs to products causes some anxiety, then the contribution theory, which uses the marginal-costing technique, may be applied to the problem of pricing. Even in this case though, the costs used should be the Standard Costs, the only difference being in the way they are employed to meet the particular circumstances.

For pricing purposes, two distinct types of business may be distinguished. There is first the business which cannot influence price because its sales are but a small part of the total sales. Secondly, there is the business which, due to its size or favourable position in the industry concerned, is able, within certain limits, to say what the price shall be.

When the price has to be accepted as an indisputable fact the enterprise concerned will carefully have to control and, if possible, reduce costs to be able to maximise profit. Standard Costing, being a complete control system, is obviously ideal for controlling costs. The reduction of costs may be brought about by improvement of methods of producing and selling, thus allowing the Standard Costs to be reduced. A criticism sometimes levelled against Standard Costs is that, once the Standards have been determined, there is a danger of stagnation. Employees become complacent because Standards are being achieved, and there is, therefore, no further progress made. Undoubtedly, there may be some truth in this objection in some circumstances. However, the modern progressive business will constantly be on the alert for developing new ideas; in this way the Standards will be challenged and improved.

For the same class of business, another approach to earning maximum profit will be for the business to anticipate demand conditions for products coming within its scope, then estimate what the prices of the products are likely to be, and concentrate production on the most profitable variety. The use of Standard Costs should enable management to see what the costs will be, before products are actually made, thus simplifying the decision on which is likely to be the most profitable variety in the future. Instead of both costs and prices being "unknowns," the price only will remain.

If a business is able to influence the price of a product the costs will be of great importance. At all times the aim will be to cover costs and obtain a reasonable margin of profit. If sales are low a business may be content to cover all its variable costs and, if possible, some of its fixed costs. To be able to arrive at a correct decision, irrespective of circumstances, it should be clear that Standard Costs will be invaluable. For the particular volume of output the true costs will be known facts. Any prices quoted will, therefore, be made with a complete understanding of the results of the quotations. There will be no fear of the business pricing itself into liquidation. If lower-than-cost prices are accepted, they will be part of a stated policy and not merely a "hope for the best" gesture to obtain more business.

At this stage the importance of carefully fixing the "capacity" for setting Standards for overhead costs should be noticed. By apportioning the overhead costs over the production volume anticipated in the long run it is possible to fix a price that will cover all costs. For a discussion of the various meanings given to production capacity the student should turn to the chapter on the Setting of Standard Overhead Costs. What is important to remember is that overhead standard rates may be fixed for:

1. Normal Capacity to Manufacture.
2. Normal Capacity to Manufacture and Sell.
3. Short-period Capacity to Sell.

If necessary, all three may be shown in statistical records and used as a background against which managerial decisions can be made. As already noticed, the unit costs obtained when (1) is adopted will tend to be more realistic than when (2) is taken. In the short period the aim should be to charge a price which will cover all costs, including overhead costs, shown by the Normal Capacity to Manufacture basis. If necessary, however, to obtain sales, a business may, again in the short period, have to accept a price which does not fully cover the unit cost. In the long run, of course, the price will have to cover the unit costs, containing the overhead rate determined by the Normal Capacity to Manufacture and Sell, and, in addition, a reasonable margin of profit. The costs of any idle facilities are then covered by the prices charged.

With Standard Costs there will be no month-to-month variations in unit costs brought about by changes in volume. The costs shown, for Current Standard Costs, will be in force for at least a year: with Basic Standard Costs a much longer period will be involved. If, within a particular year, there are changes in the prices of material or the wage-rates it will be a simple matter to adjust the Standard Costs on statistical records, leaving the figures at their original values for accounting purposes. Prices can be amended on the basis of the statistical records.

The use of "average" costs (*i.e.* those that contain fixed costs) of products, under a Standard Costing system, provides a guide to the minimum price which can safely be accepted to cover *all* costs. If necessary, as already suggested, the contribution theory can be adopted to provide a pricing mechanism. This may be used in conjunction with the Unit Standard Costs. Briefly the operation of the theory involves the following:

1. Variable costs are separated from fixed costs. The variable costs include direct labour and material costs and variable overhead costs. Any semi-variable costs are divided into their fixed and variable elements.
2. The variable cost per unit is assumed to remain the same. This assumption is normally justified.
3. The fixed costs are not apportioned over the units of production. There is no really satisfactory basis for tracing responsibility for fixed costs to individual products and, therefore, the treatment of these as a period cost may be felt desirable.
4. By estimating the volume of business which can be expected, a selling price, which will bring adequate revenue to cover fixed costs and a desired profit figure, may be fixed.

Clearly, if nothing is produced there will be a loss equal to total fixed costs. The larger the number of units produced and sold at a stated price (above variable costs), the larger will be the contribution made towards fixed costs and profit.

Let us take an example. If 10,000 units of a certain product are expected to be produced and the variable costs are £0·60, then the price in all circumstances—whether boom or slump conditions—should not be allowed to fall below £0·60. To earn a profit, if fixed costs total £2000, a price exceeding £0·80 per unit should be charged. If £1 per unit is the selling price a profit of £2000 will be earned. Put another way, at a price of £1 the contribution towards fixed costs and profit will be £4000.

The information supplied by the application of the contribution theory will, obviously, be invaluable to a business which is not able to operate at full capacity due to adverse trade conditions. A flexible policy, which will enable losses to be kept to a minimum, will be possible. It should be noticed that, if variances are taken to the Profit and Loss Account, a slight amendment of the theory will be necessary. The contribution will clearly have to cover both fixed costs and variances, the latter being losses and not costs.

The variable element contained in total costs may, of course, be obtained from a flexible budget. If, for example, a difference in output of 100 units causes an increase in total budgeted costs of £100, then it will be apparent that the variable cost is £1 per unit.

Getting away from the contribution theory an interesting point to note, in connection with producing a lower volume brought about by a trade recession, is the effect on variable and fixed costs per unit of production. With a fall in prices generally, the costs of producing—the variable costs—will tend to fall. On the other hand, if fixed costs remain the same in total a reduced volume of production will mean that the rate per unit will be larger. Remember that, although fixed costs are regarded as being "fixed" for all conditions, this is not strictly correct. If there is a change in policy fixed costs may change. Administration costs may be reduced, premises may be sub-let, or similar actions may be taken in an effort to reduce the burden of fixed costs. Nevertheless, even if they are reduced in total, the unit cost will usually be increased.

The state of business confidence will tend to influence the control of costs. When times are good and high profits are being earned management may relax controls, with the result that expenditure rises. Because higher profits can be earned, the competition for labour and materials will tend to increase, which, in turn, will raise their value. The overall effect will be increased costs. If trade slackens, the opposite effects may result. Again, irrespective of the economic conditions, the consistent adoption of Standard Costing principles can do much to reduce trade hazards. In boom periods, by using Standard Costs, maximum control over costs is exercised, and any "relaxing" is quickly brought to light through the variance analysis. If there is a trade recession, the effective control given by Standard Costs will enable management to minimise losses and reduce the danger of "panic measures" being adopted to try to overcome the difficulties.

From what has been said, some idea of the role of costs in pricing should have been obtained. Many people point out that, when it comes to selling, the price that rules is the best that can be obtained; in other words, the amount that will be paid by the customer. As will be shown in a moment, there is often much truth in this view. However, two very important facts should not be forgotten. The first is that, under normal conditions, the prices in an industry will tend to be based on the costs of the efficient concerns. Only by keeping costs low, and thus keeping its prices within reasonable dimensions, can a business hope to meet direct competition and competition from substitutes. The other important fact is connected with the possibility of external direction or control from government action. Public feeling against excessive prices or a routine probe by a government-sponsored commission of enquiry may indicate that prices are too high. The only way for a business to defend itself logically is to show that its prices and costs are related and that the former are not abnormally in excess of the latter. Some businesses do actually work on a small percentage added to cost; they depend on a very large volume of business to enable them to earn adequate profits. Clearly, any enquiry into the reasonableness of a price cannot ignore the cost.

Some difficulties of accepting cost as the sole basis for price fixing will now be enumerated:

1. Anticipated demand conditions may not be realised. If demand is under-estimated prices will tend to rise; if it is over-estimated, prices may not cover costs. In such circumstances, the Standard Costs will indicate the size of the profit earned or loss incurred by each line of product. The full consequences of the miscalculation, as affecting that particular business, will thus be fully appreciated.

2. Costs may be incurred on producing a commodity which turns out to be of no value and therefore cannot be sold except for scrap. This reason is linked with (1) above.

3. Many costs are determined by an estimate of the price that can be expected for a certain quality product.

The market is carefully studied and the price at which profits should be maximised is determined. Working backwards from the price, the quality of product which will give the desired volume of sales is estimated and then the product is made. In this way, so the argument runs, costs are determined by price. Thus, for example, if it was felt that a cheap family car would have a ready demand, a suitable price would be determined and then the cost would be worked out within the boundaries laid down by the price minus expected profit. A similar procedure may be followed in clothing and footwear industries.

Clearly, this reversal of the apparent normal order of things cannot be denied, and it is not as unusual as some people seem to believe. The very act of entering into the business of manufacturing and selling of commodities implies that, consciously or otherwise, the manufacturer decides he should be able to earn a profit. This assumption is based on expected cost and price, so although perhaps the selection of price as a first step may not be so obvious, the selection is, nevertheless, still present.

4. When products are produced jointly with each other the cost of each cannot be determined accurately.

Sometimes an apportionment of cost is made on the basis of sales values. There is thus a reliance on price, to determine how much cost a product will stand. Such a procedure cannot be regarded as sound costing practice; it is often done merely to arrive at a satisfactory cost–price relationship. If Standard Costing is adopted, with its use of modern, management techniques, the selection of an equitable basis for tracing responsibility for costs should not be impossible. Certainly there is no need to rely on sales values as a means of apportioning costs.

CONCLUSION

There is no doubt that the greater accuracy obtained from Standard Costing will inspire management to look more and more to costs as a guide to fixing selling prices. Provided the full facts, relating to volume and any abnormal conditions, are made known to management there can be no safer policy for them than to consider product costs fully before fixing prices. Any decisions can then be made with full knowledge of the possible effects of proposed actions on profits.

EXAMINATION QUESTIONS

1. Explain clearly what you understand by contribution in a cost accounting sense. How is it related to profit?

List three benefits that management can obtain from knowing the contribution from its units.

(*I.C.W.A.*)

2. What considerations govern management in the fixing of selling prices when business is difficult to obtain and competition is keen? Discuss the statistics and graphs which you would prepare for the guidance of management at such a time.

(*I.C.W.A.*)

3. The sales manager contends that costs should be based on maximum output as otherwise he cannot compete with more efficient competitors, while the works manager contends that they should be based on average output in past periods.

Give your views on these contentions, dealing particularly with:

(*a*) selling prices,

(*b*) significance of quantity variations as an indication of factory efficiency.

(*I.C.W.A.*)

4. Many companies apportion their selling costs to products as a percentage on realised price. It is argued that this means that a product with low material cost, a wide margin of profit, and an easy sales market is charged with, say, 10% on £1, whereas a product with very expensive materials, a very narrow profit margin, and a restricted and strongly competitive market is charged with, say, 10% on £5.

This is considered inequitable. What suggestions would you make?

(I.C.W.A.)

5. Assuming adequate facilities are available in either case, what considerations would guide you in deciding whether certain work should be done in your own factory or placed with outside contractors?

(I.C.W.A.)

6. "The three factors of price, cost and volume are fundamental to virtually every business activity, every business decision." Discuss this statement, explaining the inter-relation of the factors named.

(I.C.W.A.)

7. A business manufacturing a variety of products finds that there is an export market for some of these products at lower prices than are at present being charged in home markets. As cost accountant, report on the important problems to be considered, and recommend how they be dealt with.

(I.C.W.A.)

8. A price containing a very slender profit margin has been submitted for a tender, which it now appears is not competitive enough, and your company has been asked to re-quote. It is also apparent that owing to lack of orders your company may shortly revert to a four-day working week for a few months. Give the main points of a price advisory report to the general manager.

(I.C.W.A.)

9. It is contended that competition governs prices and that where production efficiency is good there is no need for a proper system of costing. What arguments would you advance to educate this opinion?

(I.C.W.A.)

10. It has been stated that for price-fixing purposes, total costing cannot be compared for efficiency with the accuracy and clarity afforded by the marginal costing technique. Discuss the significance of this statement from the Cost Accountant's point of view.

(I.C.W.A.)

INDEX